THE

CONSTITUTIONAL HISTORY

OF THE

PRESBYTERIAN CHURCH

IN THE UNITED STATES OF AMERICA.

BY

CHARLES HODGE, D.D.,

PROFESSOR IN THE THEOLOGICAL SEMINARY, PRINCETON, NEW JERSEY

PART II.

1741 TO 1788.

PHILADELPHIA:
PRESBYTERIAN BOARD OF PUBLICATION,
No. 265 CHESTNUT STREET.

PREFACE.

THE design of this history is to exhibit the character and constitution of the Presbyterian Church in the United States. To accomplish this object, it was necessary to bring to view, not only the declarations, but the acts of its highest judicatory. The work has thus become rather a history of the Synod, than of the whole church, and does not pretend to enter into those details which would be necessary in a more comprehensive work. Those controversies, however, which affected the action of the Synod, come legitimately within the scope of this history. Hence an account of the great revival which occurred towards the middle of the last century, was necessary, in order to render intelligible the history of the dissensions which agitated and ultimately divided the Synod. To that revival, therefore, the introductory chapter of the present volume is devoted. The principal sources of information on this subject, to which the writer has had access, are the following: Prince's Christian History, in two volumes, a contemporaneous work, originally published in numbers, containing accounts of the revival in this country and in Scotland, written, in general, by the pastors of the churches in which the revival occurred; Gillies' Collections, which, as far as it relates to this country, is principally a reprint of the former work; Whitefield's Life and Journals; Edwards's Life, Correspondence, and Sermons; Chauncey's Seasonable Thoughts, another contemporaneous work, containing the dark side of the picture; Fisk's nine sermons, preached in Stonington after the revival, and containing many valuable historical details; Trumbull's History of Connecticut; President Dickinson's Works; Works of the Rev. Samuel Blair. Besides these, there are a great many smaller works, principally pamphlets, for and against the men and measures of those days, quoted and referred to in the following pages, which need not be particularly mentioned here.

The authorities relied upon for the account given of the schism, besides the official records of the Synod, which themselves contain much of the history, are the contemporaneous works of the leading men of the two parties. As the controversy ostensibly arose out of the disregard, on the part of the Presbytery of New Brunswick, of two acts of the Synod, the Apology of that Presbytery presented in 1739, for their conduct, stands first in order. The only copy of that work, of which the writer has any knowledge, is in the library of the Massachusetts Historical Society at Worcester; for the use of which he is indebted to the kind intervention of the Rev. Dr. Anderson of Boston. The greater part of the Apology, however, is reprinted in Mr. Thompson's Government of the Church of Christ, published in 1741, where, according to the good old method of controversy, it is quoted in order to its being refuted. Mr. Thompson's strictures on the Apology were answered by the Rev. Samuel Blair, in his vindication of the New Brunswick brethren, contained in the printed volume of his works. In 1740, Mr. Gilbert Tennent and Mr. Samuel Blair presented to the Synod two memorials containing various complaints against their brethren. These memorials are given at length in Mr. Thompson's work above-mentioned. This latter work, therefore, is itself one of the most important books relating to this period of our history, embracing as it does the views of both parties as to most of the points in controversy. It was before the schism also that Mr. Tennent preached at Nottingham, his sermon on the Dangers of an Unconverted Ministry, which is contained in volume 143, of the valuable collection of pamphlets extending to near a thousand volumes, presented by the Rev. Dr. Sprague of

Albany, to the library of the Theological Seminary in this place. In 1741, Mr. John Thompson published his sermon on the Doctrine of Conviction, which was answered by the Rev. Samuel Finley in 1743.

The Protest presented to the Synod in 1741, which was the immediate cause of the schism, was printed with a historical preface and appendix, and is preserved in the Philadelphia Library. Mr. Tennent immediately published Remarks upon that Protest, which are included in the collection of his works in the library at Worcester. Those Remarks were answered in a work entitled, Refutation of Mr. Tennent's Remarks, &c., by some of the members of the Synod, Philadelphia, 1742. The brethren, who had been excluded from the Synod, published a Declaration of their sentiments on the subjects of doctrine and church government. This tract the writer has not been able to find. It is, however, largely quoted in the Detector Detected, by the Rev. Robert Smith, contained in vol. 561, of Dr. Sprague's collection.

The year after the schism, Mr. G. Tennent printed his sermons against the Moravians. Those sermons an anonymous writer in Boston contrasted with Mr. Tennent's Nottingham discourse, in a book called the Examiner, or Gilbert versus Tennent. This was answered by Mr. Tennent, in the Examiner Examined, printed in 1743. Both of these works are generally accessible. Mr. Tennent's Irenicum, or Plea for the Peace of Jerusalem, published in 1749, with the design to heal the divisions in the church, is another of the most important works relating to these controversies.

The writer has faithfully given the results of a careful examination of these contemporaneous publications. The conclusions to which he has arrived, as to the merits of the controversy, differ in some measure from his own previous impressions; and may differ still more from the accounts preserved by tradition in various parts of the church. It is believed, however, that the reader will find no conclusion in the following pages materially different from those to which Mr. Tennent had arrived in 1749.

With regard to the two other chapters contained in this volume, there is less to be said. They are little more than a digest of the minutes. In the one a history is given of the synods of Philadelphia and New York, during the seventeen years the separation lasted, by classifying their acts under certain heads. The same method is pursued in reference to the united Synod, which was formed in 1758, and dissolved in 1788, after having formed itself into four synods, and prepared the constitution under which we have acted for fifty years; a period crowded with manifestations of the mercy and faithfulness of God to our church.

PRINCETON, May 6, 1840.

CONTENTS.

CHAPTER IV.

THE GREAT REVIVAL OF RELIGION, 1740–1745.

CHAPTER V.

THE SCHISM, 1741.

CHAPTER VI.

HISTORY OF THE CHURCH DURING THE SCHISM, 1741–1758.

CHAPTER VII.

SYNOD OF NEW YORK AND PHILADELPHIA,

1758–1788.

PRESBYTERIAN CHURCH.

PART II.

CHAPTER IV.

THE GREAT REVIVAL OF RELIGION, 1740–45.

Introductory Remarks.— State of Religion before the Revival in the Presbyterian Church; in New England, in Scotland, in England.— History of the Revival in the Presbyterian Church; in New Jersey, at Freehold, at Lawrenceville, Pennington, Amwell, Newark, and Elizabethtown; in Pennsylvania, at Philadelphia, New Londonderry, Neshaminy, Nottingham, &c.; in Virginia; in New England.— Proofs of the genuineness of the Revival; from the judgment of contemporary witnesses; from the doctrines preached; from the experience of its subject; from its effects.— State of Religion after the Revival.—Evils attending the Revival; spurious religious feelings, bodily agitations, enthusiasm, censoriousness, disorderly itinerating, and lay-preaching.— Conclusion.

THE great revival, which about a hundred years ago visited so extensively the American Churches, is so much implicated with the ecclesiastical history of our own denomination, that the latter cannot be understood without some knowledge of the former. The controversies connected with the revival are identical with the disputes which resulted in the schism which divided the Presbyterian Church in 1741. Before entering, therefore, upon the history of that event, it will be necessary to present the reader with a general survey of that great religious excitement, which arrayed in conflicting parties the friends of religion in every part of the country. This division of sentiment could hardly have occurred, had the revival been one of unmingled purity. Such a revival, however, the church has never seen. Every luminous body is sure to cause shadows in every direction and of every form. Where the Son of man sows wheat, the evil one is sure to sow tares. It must be so. For it needs be that offences come, though woe to those by whom they come.

The men who, either from their character or circumstances, are led to take the most prominent part, during such seasons of excitement, are themselves often carried to extremes, or are so connected with the extravagant, that they are sometimes the last to perceive and the slowest to oppose the evils which so frequently mar the work of God, and burn over the fields which he had just watered with his grace. Opposition to these evils commonly comes from a different quarter; from wise and good men who have been kept out of the focus of the excitement. And it is well that there are such opposers, else the church would soon be over-run with fanaticism.

The term 'revival' is commonly used in a very comprehensive sense. It includes all the phenomena attending a general religious excitement; as well those which spring from God, as those which owe their origin to the infirmities of men. Hence those who favour the work, for what there is divine in it, are often injuriously regarded as the patrons of its concomitant irregularities, and those who oppose what is unreasonable about it, are as improperly denounced as the enemies of religion. It is, therefore, only one expression of that fanaticism which haunts the spirit of revivals, to make such a work a touchstone of character; to regard all as good who favour it, and all as bad who oppose it. That this should be done during the continuance of the excitement, is an evil to be expected and pardoned; but to commit the same error in the historical review of such a period, would admit of no excuse. Hard as it was then either to see or to believe, we can now easily perceive and readily credit that some of the best and some of the worst men in the church, were to be found on either side, in the controversy respecting the great revival of the last century. The mere geographical position of a man, in many cases, determined the part he took in that controversy. A sober and sincere Christian, within the sphere of Davenport's operations, might well be an opposer, who, had he lived in the neighbourhood of Edwards, might have approved and promoted the revival. Yet Edwards and Davenport were then regarded as leaders in the same great work.

That there had been a lamentable declension in religion both in Great Britain and in this country, is universally acknowledged by the writers of this period. The Rev. Samuel Blair, speaking of the state of religion in Pennsylvania at that time, says: "I doubt not but there were some sincerely religious persons up and down; and there were, I believe, a considerable number in several congregations pretty exact, according to their education, in the observance of the external forms of religion, not only as to attendance upon public ordinances on the Sabbath, but also as to the practice of family worship, and perhaps secret prayer too; but with those things, the most part seemed, to all appearance, to rest contented, and to satisfy their conscience with a dead formality in religion. A very lamentable ignorance of the essentials of true practical religion, and of the doctrines relating thereto, very generally prevailed. The nature and necessity of the new-birth were little known or thought of; the necessity of a conviction of sin and misery, by the Holy Spirit opening and applying the law to the conscience, in order to a saving closure with Christ, was hardly known at all to most. The necessity of being first in Christ by a vital union and in a justified state, before our religious services can be well pleasing or acceptable to God, was very little understood or thought of; but the common notion seemed to be, that if people were aiming to be in the way of duty as well as they could, as they imagined, there was no reason to be much afraid." In consequence of this ignorance of the nature of practical religion, there were, he adds, great carelessness and indifference about the things of eternity; great coldness and unconcern in public worship; a disregard of the Sabbath, and prevalence of worldly amusements and follies.*

In 1734, the Synod of Philadelphia found it necessary to issue

* Narrative of the late remarkable revival of religion in the congregation of New Londonderry, and in other parts of Pennsylvania. By Rev. Samuel Blair, printed in his works, p. 336; and in Gillies' Collections, vol. ii. p. 150.

a serious admonition to the presbyteries to examine candidates for the ministry and for admission to the Lord's supper, "as to their experience of a work of sanctifying grace in their hearts; and to inquire regularly into the life, conversation, and ministerial diligence of their members, especially as to whether they preached in an evangelical and fervent manner?"* This admonition shows that there was a defect as to all these points, on the part of at least some of the members of the Synod.

In 1740, Messrs. Gilbert Tennent and Samuel Blair presented two representations, complaining of "many defects in our ministry," that are, say the Synod, "matter of the greatest lamentation, if chargeable upon our members. The Synod do therefore solemnly admonish all the ministers within our bounds, seriously to consider the weight of their charge, and, as they will answer it at the great day of Christ, to take care to approve themselves to God, in the instances complained of. And the Synod do recommend it to the several presbyteries to take care of their several members in these particulars."†

In these papers, which will be noticed more at length in the following chapter, complaint is made of the want of fidelity and zeal in preaching the gospel, and in the discharge of other ministerial duties; and the strong conviction is expressed that many of the members of the Synod were in an unconverted state. It is true indeed that such general complaints might be uttered now, or at almost any period of the church, and that of themselves they give us but little definite information of the character of the clergy. When or where might it not be said, that many of the preachers of the Gospel were too worldly in their conversation, too little urgent, discriminating, and faithful in their preaching? That these faults, however, prevailed at the period under consideration, to a greater extent than usual, there is little reason to doubt. Mr. Thompson, in his answer to these charges, says, with respect to the complaint, "concerning the low state of religion and experimental godliness, and the influence which the negligence and remissness of ministers in the duties of their office have upon the same, I acknowledge that

* See Part I. of this History, p. 240. † Minutes of Synod, vol. ii. p. 72.

I believe there is too much ground for it, and that it is just matter of mourning and lamentation to all who have the welfare of Zion and the prosperity of souls at heart; yea, I am firmly persuaded that our barrenness and fruitlessness under the means of grace, the decay of vital godliness in both ministers and people, our too great contentedness with a lifeless lukewarm orthodoxy of profession, is one principal evil whereby our God hath been provoked against us, to suffer us to fall into such divisions and confusions as we are visibly involved in."* He makes the same acknowledgment with regard to some of the more specific charges. In reference to that respecting their talking to the people more about secular matters than about religion, he says: "I may charge myself in particular with being guilty of misimproving many a precious opportunity that might have been improved to much better purpose for edification of myself and others. Yet I hope the generality of us are not degenerate to that desperate degree in this matter as to prove us altogether graceless; or to give our hearers just ground to believe that we do not desire them to be deeply and heartily concerned about their eternal estate." As to the more serious charge of "endeavouring to prejudice people against the work of God's power and grace in the conviction and conversion of sinners," he pronounces it to be, as far as he knows, "a downright calumny." "It is true," he adds, "there are some things in our brethren's conduct which we cannot but condemn, and have condemned and spoken against both in public and private; and some things also which are the frequent effects of their preaching on many of their hearers which we cannot esteem so highly of, as both they and their admirers do." He then refers to their censoriousness, to their endeavours to prejudice their people against them as unconverted, their intruding into other men's congregations against their will, and the extravagances which they allowed and encouraged in public worship. He also denies the charge, that they insisted on external duties to the "neglect of vital religion and the necessity of regeneration;" and the assertion that they "seldom or never preached on the nature and necessity of conversion," he declares to be another slander taken up from prejudiced persons.

* Church of Christ, p. 29.

It is worthy of remark that neither Mr. Tennent nor Mr. Blair, when professedly bringing forward grounds of complaint against their brethren, mentions either the denial of any of the leading doctrines of the Bible, or open immorality. It is not to be doubted, that had error or immoral conduct prevailed, or been tolerated among the clergy, it would have been prominently presented.* We know, however, from other sources, that there was no prevalent defection from the truth among the ministers of our church. The complaint against the old-side was, that they adhered too rigidly to the Westminster Confession; and the theology of every leading man on the new-side, is known from his writings, to have been thoroughly Calvinistic. There is not a single minister of that age in connection with our church, whose name has come down to us under the suspicion of Arminianism. False doctrine, therefore, was not the evil under which the church then suffered. It was rather a coldness and sluggishness with regard to religion. There was, undoubtedly, before the revival, a general indifference and lukewarmness among the clergy and people; and there is too much reason to fear, that in some cases the ministers, though orthodox, knew nothing of experimental religion. These cases were indeed not so numerous as the representations of Tennent would lead us to expect, as he himself afterwards freely acknowledged.

As far, then, as the Presbyterian Church is concerned, the state of religion was very low before the commencement of the great

* The charge which Mr. Tennent makes against the Synod, of error in doctrine, respecting the foundation of moral obligation, is so evidently unjust, that it may be safely disregarded. It will be remembered that he and Mr. Cowell had a long dispute upon this subject, which was brought before the Synod, and that President Dickinson and others, as a committee, brought in a report condemning the opinions against which Mr. Tennent contended, in such terms that he himself voted for the adoption of the report. He has certainly, therefore, no right to charge the adoption of that report as a proof of unsound doctrine. As to the other point, which he specifies, viz.: that there is a certainty of salvation annexed to the efforts of unrenewed men, we know nothing, except that Mr. Thompson says, "If there be any of the members of the Synod of this judgment, it is more than I know, and I am persuaded there are very few; for my own part, I know not one whom I so much as suspect, in this particular." See on this subject, ch. iii. p. 197 of this work.

revival. As that work extended over the whole country, and was perhaps more general and powerful in New England than any where else, in order to have any just idea of its character, our attention must be directed to the congregational churches, as well as to those of our own denomination. After the first generation of Puritans had passed away, religion seems to have declined very rapidly, so that the writings of those who had seen what the churches in New England were at the beginning, are filled with lamentations over their subsequent condition, and with gloomy prognostications as to the future. As early as 1678, Dr. Increase Mather says, "The body of the rising generation is a poor, perishing, unconverted, and (unless the Lord pour down his Spirit) an undone generation. Many are profane, drunkards, swearers, lascivious, scoffers at the power of godliness, despisers of those that are good, disobedient. Others are only civil and outwardly conformed to good order by reason of their education, but never knew what the new birth means."* In 1721, he writes thus: "I am now in the eighty-third year of my age; and having had an opportunity to converse with the first planters of this country, and having been for sixty-five years a preacher of the Gospel, I cannot but be in the disposition of those ancient men, who had seen the foundation of the first house, and wept to see the change the work of the temple had upon it. I wish it were no other than the weakness of Horace's old man, the *laudator temporis acti*, when I complain there is a grievous decay of piety in the land, and a leaving of her first love; and that the beauties of holiness are not to be seen as once they were; a fruitful Christian grown too rare a spectacle; yea, too many are given to change, and leave that order of the Gospel to set up and uphold which, was the very design of these colonies; and the very interest of New England seems to be changed from a religious to a worldly one."† We must, however, be on our guard against drawing false conclusions from such statements. We should

* Prince's Christian History, vol. i. p. 98.

† Prince, vol. i. p. 103. This writer, in Nos. 12, 13, and 14, has collected many other testimonies "to the great and lamentable decay of religion" in the generations following the first settlement of New England.

remember how high was the standard of piety which such writers had in view, and how peculiarly flourishing was the original condition of those churches whose declension is here spoken of. There may have been, and doubtless was much even in that age, over which we, in these less religious days, would heartily rejoice. What was decay to them, would be revival to us. The declension, however, did not stop at this stage. The generation which succeeded that over which Increase Mather mourned, departed still further from the doctrines and spirit of their pious ancestors. "The third and fourth generations," says Trumbull, "became still more generally inattentive to their spiritual concerns, and manifested a greater declension from the purity and zeal of their ancestors. Though the preaching of the Gospel was not altogether without success, and though there were tolerable peace and order in the churches; yet there was too generally a great decay as to the life and power of godliness. There was a general ease and security in sin. Abundant were the lamentations of pious ministers and good people poured out before God, on this account."* As a single example of such lamentations, we may quote the account of the state of religion in Taunton, in 1740, as given by the Rev. Mr. Crocker. "The church was but small, considering the number of inhabitants; and deadness, dulness, formality, and security prevailed among them. Any who were wise virgins (and I trust there were a few such) appeared to be slumbering and sleeping with the foolish; and sinners appeared to be at ease in Zion. In a word, it is to be feared there was but little of the life or power of godliness among them, and irreligion and immorality of one kind or another seemed awfully to increase."†

The defection from sound doctrine was also very extensive at this period; an evil which the revival but partially arrested, and that only for a few years. Edwards speaks of Arminianism as making a great noise in the land in 1734,‡ and his biographer says, there was a prevailing tendency to that system, at that time, not

* History of Connecticut, vol. ii. p. 135.

† See Prince, No. 93, and also Nos. 30 and 50, for similar accounts.

‡ Dwight's Life of Edwards, p. 140.

only in the county of Hampshire, but throughout the province.* This tendency was not confined to Massachusetts; it was as great, if not greater, in Connecticut. President Clapp, though himself a Calvinist, was elected to the presidency of Yale College in 1739, "by a board of trustees exclusively Arminian, and all his associates in office held the same tenets."† We know not on what authority this specific statement rests, but it is rendered credible by other facts; such, for example, as the ordination of Mr. Whittlesey at Milford, notwithstanding the strenuous opposition of a large majority of people, founded on the belief "that he was not sound in the faith, but had imbibed the opinions of Arminius;"‡ in which matter the ordaining council were fully sustained by the Association of New Haven.

In Scotland there had been a general decay in the power of religion from the revolution in 1688 to the time of which we are now speaking. In 1712 Halyburton complained, upon his death-bed, of the indifference to the peculiarities of the gospel and to the power of godliness which prevailed among a great portion of the clergy. There had indeed been no general defection from the truth; though the lenity with which the Assembly treated the errors of Professor Simson of Glasgow, and Professor Campbell of Aberdeen, is appealed to by the Seceders, in their Act and Testimony of 1736, with too much reason, in proof of a criminal indifference to the doctrines of the church. Though there had been extensive revivals in the West of Scotland in 1725, and a most remarkable effusion of the Spirit at the kirk of Shotts in 1730, as well as in other parts of the kingdom, the general state of religion was low, and upon the decline.

In England the case was far worse. From the accession of Charles II. in 1660 and the exclusion of the non-conformists, true religion seems to have declined rapidly in the established church. Bishop Butler says, in his Introduction to his Analogy, that in his day Christianity itself seemed to be regarded as a fable "among all persons of discernment;" and in his first charge to the clergy

* Dwight's Life of Edwards, p. 434.

† Ibid. p. 211.

‡ Trumbull, vol. ii. p. 335.

of the diocess of Durham he laments over "the general decay of religion in the nation," the influence of which, he says, seems to be wearing out the minds of men.* Before the rise of the Methodists, says John Newton, "the doctrines of grace were seldom heard from the pulpit, and the life and power of religion were little known."

Such in few words was the state of religion in England, Scotland and America, when it pleased God, contemporaneously in these several countries, remarkably to revive his work. The earliest manifestation of the presence of the Holy Spirit, in our portion of the church, during this period, was at Freehold, N. J., under the ministry of the Rev. John Tennent, who was called to that congregation in 1730, and died in 1732. "The settling of that place," says his brother, the Rev. Wm. Tennent, "with a gospel ministry, was owing under God, to the agency of some Scotch people, that came to it; among whom there was none so pains-taking in this blessed work as one Walter Ker, who, in 1685, for his faithful and conscientious adherence to God and his truth as professed by the church of Scotland, was there apprehended and sent to this country, under a sentence of perpetual banishment. By which it appears that the devil and his instruments lost their aim in sending him from home, where it is unlikely he could ever have been so serviceable to Christ's kingdom as he has been here. He is yet (1744) alive; and, blessed be God, flourishing in his old age, being in his 88th year."

The state of religion for a time in this congregation was very low. The labours of Mr. J. Tennent, however, were, greatly blessed. The place of public worship was generally crowded with people, who seemed to hear as for their lives. Religion became the general subject of discourse; though all did not approve of the power of it. The Holy Scriptures were searched by people on both sides of the question; and knowledge surprisingly increased. The terror of God fell generally on the inhabitants of the place, so that wickedness, as ashamed, in a great measure hid its head.

* Butler's Works, vol. ii. p. 238.

Mr. William Tennent, who succeeded his brother in 1733 as pastor of that church, says the effects of the labours of his predecessor were more discernible a few months after his death, than during his life. The religious excitement thus commenced continued, with various alternations, until 1744, the date of this account. As to the number of converts, Mr. T. says, "I cannot tell; my comfort is, that the Lord will reckon them, for he knows who are his." Those who were brought to the Saviour, "were all prepared for it by a sharp law-work of conviction, in discovering to them, in a heart-affecting manner, their sinfulness both by nature and practice, as well as their liableness to damnation for their original and actual transgressions. Neither could they see any way in themselves by which they could escape the divine vengeance. For their whole past lives were not only a continued act of rebellion against God, but their present endeavours to better their state, such as prayers and the like, were so imperfect, that they could not endure them, and much less, they concluded, would a holy God. They all confessed the justice of God in their eternal perdition; and thus were shut up to the blessed necessity of seeking relief by faith in Christ alone."

The sorrows of the convinced were not alike in all, either in degree or continuance. Some did not think it possible for them to be saved, but these thoughts did not continue long. Others thought it possible, but not very probable on account of their vileness. The greatest degree of hope which any had under a conviction which issued well, was a may-be: Peradventure, said the sinner, God will have mercy on me.

The conviction of some was instantaneous, by the Holy Spirit applying the law and revealing all the deceit of their hearts, very speedily. But that of others was more progressive. They had discovered to them one abomination after another, in their lives, and hence were led to discover the fountain of all corruption in the heart, and thus were constrained to despair of life by the law, and consequently to flee to Jesus Christ as the only refuge, and to rest entirely in his merits.

After such sorrowful exercises such as were reconciled to God were blessed with the spirit of adoption, enabling them to cry, "Abba, Father." Some had greater degrees of consolation than others in proportion to the clearness of the evidences of their sonship. The way in which they received consolation, was either by the application of some particular promise of Scripture; or by a soul-affecting view of the method of salvation by Christ, as free, without money and without price. With this way of salvation their souls were well pleased, and thereupon they ventured their case into his hands, expecting help from him only.

As to the effects of this work on the subjects of it, Mr. Tennent says, they were not only made to know but heartily to approve of the great doctrines of the Gospel, which they were before either ignorant of, or averse to (at least some of them;) so that they sweetly agreed in exalting free, special, sovereign grace, through the Redeemer; being willing to glory only in the Lord, who loved them and gave himself for them. They approved of the law of God after the inward man, as holy, just, and good, and prized it above gold. They judged it their duty as well as privilege to wait on God in all his ordinances. A reverence for his commanding authority and gratitude for his love conspired to incite them to a willing, unfeigned, universal, unfainting obedience to his laws; yet they felt that in every thing they came sadly short, and bitterly bewailed their defects. They loved all such as they had reason to think, from their principles, experience and practice, were truly godly, though they differed from them in sentiment as to smaller matters; and looked upon them as the excellent of the earth. They preferred others to themselves, in love; except when under temptation; and their failures they were ready to confess and bewail, generally accounting themselves that they were the meanest of the family of God.

Through God's mercy, adds Mr. Tennent, we have been quite free from enthusiasm. Our people have followed the holy law of God, the sure word of prophecy, and not the impulses of their own minds. There have not been among us, that I know of, any visions, except such as are by faith; namely, clear and affecting views of the new and living way to the Father through his dear Son Jesus

Christ; nor any revelations but what have been long since written in the sacred volume.*

The leading characteristics of this work were a deep conviction of sin, arising from clear apprehensions of the extent and spirituality of the divine law. This conviction consisted in an humbling sense both of guilt and corruption. It led to the acknowledgment of the justice of God in their condemnation, and of their entire helplessness in themselves. Secondly, clear apprehensions of the mercy of God in Christ Jesus, producing a cordial acquiescence in the plan of salvation presented in the Gospel, and a believing acceptance of the offers of mercy. The soul thus returned to God through Jesus Christ, depending on his merits for the divine favour. Thirdly, this faith produced joy and peace; a sincere approbation of the doctrines of the Gospel; delight in the law of God; a constant endeavour to obey his will; love to the brethren, and a habitually low estimate of themselves and their attainments. This surely is a description of true religion. Here are faith, hope, charity, obedience, and humility, and where these are, there is the Spirit of God, for these are his fruits.

The revival in Lawrence, Hopewell, and Amwell, three contiguous towns in New Jersey, commenced under the ministry of Rev. John Rowland, of the Presbytery of New Brunswick. As the churches in two of these towns belonged to the Presbytery of Philadelphia, and as a large portion of the people did not unite in the call to Mr. Rowland, he at first preached in barns. In 1744, however, a new congregation was formed under the care of the Presbytery of New Brunswick.† According to the account of Mr. Row-

* Letter to Rev. Mr. Prince, of Boston, by William Tennent, dated Oct. 9, 1744; published in the Christian History, Nos. 90, 91, and reprinted in Gillies' Collections, vol. ii. p. 28. In the preceding account the language of the original narrator is almost uniformly retained, though his statements are very much abridged and condensed. The usual indication of quotation, therefore, has not been given. We shall pursue the same plan in giving an account of the revival in other places.

† In a letter from Mr. William Tennent to Mr. Prince, dated October 11, 1744, he says, "About four weeks since, at the invitation of the people, and desire of our Presbytery, I gathered a church, and celebrated the Lord's

land, the revival in these towns was at first slow in its progress, one or two persons only being seriously affected under each sermon. In the spring of 1739, the number increased; and the power of the Spirit evidently attended the word on several occasions, until May, 1740, when the work became more extensive. On one occasion the people cried out so awfully that the preacher was constrained to conclude. After the sermon he inquired of those whose feelings had thus overcome them, what was the real cause of their crying out in such a manner. Some answered, "They saw hell opening before them and themselves ready to fall into it." Others said, "They were struck with such a sense of their sinfulness that they were afraid the Lord would never have mercy upon them." During the summer of 1740, the people, on several occasions, were deeply affected, and at times their convictions were attended with great horror, trembling, and loud weeping. Many continued crying in the most doleful manner, along the road, on their way home, and it was not in the power of man to restrain them, for the word of the Lord remained like fire upon their hearts. Of those who were thus affected by a sense of their guilt and danger, many became to all appearance, true Christians; many went back, and became stiff-necked. The number in the latter class was small, Mr. Rowland says, in comparison to what he had seen in most other places of his acquaintance. Those who were regarded as real converts gave a very distinct account of sin both original and actual. Their views of the corruption of their own hearts, and of their distance from God, were very clear and affecting. Their hardness, unbelief, ignorance, and blindness, pressed very heavily upon them. Their apprehension of their need of Christ, and of his Spirit, was such that they could find rest or contentment in nothing, until they had obtained an interest in Jesus Christ, and had received his Spirit to sanctify their hearts. Those under conviction were very watchful over themselves, lest they should receive false comfort, and thus rest in unfounded hopes. Their views of the Lord Jesus, as to his person, nature, and offices, and of the actings of their own faith and

supper at a newly-erected congregation in the towns of Maidenhead (Lawrence) and Hopewell."— *Christian History*, No. 91.

love towards him, were clear and satisfactory. They continued, until the date of this account, careful to maintain a holy communion with God, in the general course of their lives, were zealous for his truth, and walked steadily in his ways.*

Here, as in the case of Freehold, are to be recognized the essential features of a genuine revival, conviction of sin, faith in Christ, joy and peace in believing, and a holy life. There was, however, apparently, a greater admixture of mere animal feeling in this than in the preceding case.

In Newark and Elizabethtown, according to President Dickinson, religion was in a very low state until 1739. In August of that year a remarkable revival, especially among the young, commenced in Newark, which continued and increased during the months of November, December, and January following. There was a general reformation among the young people, who forsook the taverns and other places of amusement. All occasions for public worship were embraced with gladness. Great solemnity and devout attention were manifested in their assemblies. In March the whole town was brought under an uncommon concern about eternal things; which, during the summer, sensibly abated, though it did not entirely die away. Nothing remarkable occurred until February, 1741, when they were again visited with the special effusion of the Spirit of God. A plain, familiar sermon then preached, without any peculiar terror, fervour, or affectionate manner of address, was set home with power. Many were brought to see and feel that till then they had no more than a name to live; and professors in general were put upon solemn inquiry into the foundation of their hope. During the following summer, this religious concern sensibly decayed; and, though the sincere converts held fast their profession without wavering, too many of those who had been under conviction grew careless and secure. What seemed greatly to contribute to this growing security, was the pride, false and rash zeal, and censoriousness among some who made high pretences to religion. This opened the mouths of many against the whole work,

* Letter of Rev. Mr. Rowland to Mr. Foxcroft, of Boston, printed at Philadelphia, in 1745, and reprinted in Gillies' Collections, vol. ii. p. 132.

and raised that opposition which was not before heard of. Almost every body seemed to acknowledge the finger of God in those wonderful appearances, until this handle was given to their opposition; and the dreadful scandals of the Rev. Mr. C., which came to light about this time, proved a means to still further harden many in their declension and apostasy. That unhappy gentleman having made such high pretensions to extraordinary piety and zeal, his scandals gave the deeper wound to vital and experimental godliness.

Thus far regarding Newark. In the fall of 1739, the Rev. Mr. Whitefield preached in Elizabethtown to a numerous and attentive audience, but without any marked result. There was no apparent success attending the labours of Mr. Dickinson during that winter; which severely tried his faith and patience, as the neighbouring town was then so remarkably visited. In June, 1740, he invited the young people to hear a discourse designed particularly for their benefit. A large congregation assembled, and he preached a plain, practical sermon, without any special liveliness or vigour, as he was himself in a remarkably dull frame, until enlivened by a sudden and deep impression which visibly appeared on the whole congregation. There was no crying out, or falling down, (as elsewhere happened,) but the distress of the audience discovered itself by tears and by audible sobbing and sighing in almost all parts of the house. From this time the usual amusements of the young were laid aside, and private meetings for religious exercises were instituted by them in different parts of the town. Public worship was constantly attended in a very solemn manner by the people generally. More persons applied, in a single day, during this period, to their pastor for spiritual direction, than in half a year before. In another letter, dated September 4, 1740, Mr. Dickinson says: "I have had more young people address me for direction in their spiritual concerns within these three months than within thirty years before." Though there were so many brought under conviction at the same time, there was little appearance of those irregular heats of which so much complaint was made in other parts of the land. Only two or three occurrences of that nature took place, and they were easily and speedily regulated. This work was substantially the same in all the subjects of it. Some indeed suffered more than others, yet all were brought under a deep sense of sin, guilt and danger, and none obtained satisfactory discoveries of their safety in Christ, till they were brought to despair of all help for themselves, and to feel that they lay at the mercy of God. There were no instances of such sudden conversions, nor of those ecstatic raptures spoken of in other places. Some who at one time were deeply affected, soon wore off their impressions, but Mr. Dickinson says he did not know of any two persons who gave reasonable evidence of conversion, who had disappointed his hopes. About sixty persons in Elizabethtown, and a number in the adjoining parish, were regarded as having experienced a change of heart during this revival.*

In New Brunswick and its neighbourhood, Mr. Gilbert Tennent informs us, the labours of the Rev. Mr. Frelinghuysen, of the Dutch Reformed Church, had been much blessed, especially about the time of his first settlement over that people in the year 1720. When Mr. Tennent took charge of the Presbyterian Church in New Brunswick, about 1727, he had the pleasure of seeing many proofs of the usefulness of his worthy fellow-labourer in the cause of Christ. Mr. Tennent was much distressed at his own apparent want of success; for eighteen months after his settlement, he saw no evidence that any one had been savingly benefited by his labours. He then commenced a serious examination of the members of his church, as to the grounds of their hope, which he found, in many cases, to be but sand. Such he solemnly warned and urged to seek converting grace. By this method many were awakened, and not a few, to all appearance, converted. As the effect of his labours increased, adversaries were multiplied; and his character was unjustly aspersed, which, however, did not discourage him. He preached much, at this time, upon original sin, repentance, the nature and necessity of conversion; and endeavoured to alarm the secure by the terrors of the Lord, as well as to affect them by other topics of persuasion. These efforts were followed by the conviction and conversion of a considerable number of persons at va-

* President Dickinson's Letter to Rev. Mr. Foxcroft, dated August 23, 1743, in the Christian History, No. 32.

rious places, and at different times. During his residence at New Brunswick there was no great ingathering of souls, at any one time, though there were frequent gleanings of a few here and there. During the revival of 1740, New Brunswick, he says, felt some drops of the spreading rain, but no general shower.*

In his Journal, under the date of November 20, 1739, Whitefield has the following entry, relating to New Brunswick: "Preached about noon near two hours, in worthy Mr. Tennent's meeting-house, to a large assembly gathered from all parts. About 3 P. M. I preached again, and at 7 I baptized two children and preached a third time with greater freedom than at either of the former opportunities. It is impossible to tell with what pleasure the people of God heard those truths confirmed by a minister of the Church of England, which, for many years, had been preached by their own pastor."

With regard to the revival at Baskinridge, about twenty miles to the north of New Brunswick, we know little, beyond what is stated in Mr. Whitefield's Journal, under the date just quoted. He there speaks of what he had heard of the wonderful effusions of the Spirit in that congregation, of the frequent sudden conversions which had there occurred, &c. &c. These are all, however, second-hand reports, on which little reliance can be placed, especially as the pastor of that church, though making the highest pretensions to zeal and piety, was left to bring a sad disgrace upon the ministry and upon the revival of which he was one of the most prominent advocates.

Whitefield visited Philadelphia in November, 1739. He found the Episcopal churches, for a time, freely opened to him. On one occasion, he says, "After I had done preaching, a young gentleman, once a minister of the Church of England, but now secretary to Mr. Penn, stood up, and with a loud voice warned the people against the doctrine which I had been delivering; urging that there was no such term as imputed righteousness in Holy Scripture, and that such a doctrine put a stop to all goodness. When he had

* Letter to Rev. Mr. Prince, dated Philadelphia, August 24, 1744.—*Christian History*, Nos. 88, 89, 90.

ended, I denied his first proposition, and brought a text to prove that imputed righteousness was a scriptural expression; but thinking the church an improper place for disputation, I said no more at that time. The portion of Scripture appointed to be read, was Jeremiah xxiii., wherein are the words, 'The Lord our righteousness.' Upon them I discoursed in the afternoon, and showed how the Lord Jesus was to be our whole righteousness; proved how the contrary doctrine overthrew divine revelation; answered the objections that were made against the doctrine of an imputed righteousness; produced the Articles of our Church to illustrate it; and concluded with an exhortation to all, to submit to Jesus Christ, who is the end of the law for righteousness to every one that believeth. The word came with power. The church was thronged within and without; all wonderfully attentive, and many, as I was informed, convinced that the Lord Jesus Christ was our righteousness."

Whitefield's sentiments, manner of preaching, and clerical habits were so little in accordance with those of the majority of his Episcopal brethren, that this harmonious intercourse did not long continue. Their pulpits were soon closed against him, and he commenced preaching in the open air. One of his favourite stations was the balcony of the old court-house in Market street. Here he would take his stand, while his audience arranged themselves on the declivity of the hill on which the court-house stood.* The effects produced in Philadelphia by his preaching, "were truly astonishing. Numbers of all denominations, and many who had no connection with any denomination, were brought to inquire, with the utmost earnestness, what they must do to be saved. Such was the eagerness of the multitude for spiritual instruction, that there was public worship regularly twice a day for a year; and on the Lord's day it was celebrated thrice, and frequently four times."†

* It is said that his voice was so distinct, that every word he uttered, while preaching from the court-house, could be heard by persons in a vessel at Market street wharf, a distance of more than four hundred feet. It is even stated that his voice was heard on the Jersey shore, a distance of at least a mile.—*Gillies' Life of Whitefield*, p. 39.

† Memoirs of Mrs. Hannah Hodge, Philadelphia, 1806.

During the winter of 1739–40, Whitefield visited the South, and returned to Philadelphia by sea the following spring. His friends now erected a stage for him on what was called Society Hill, where he preached for some time to large and deeply affected audiences. When he left the city, he urged his followers to attend the ministry of the Tennents and their associates. These gentlemen, accordingly, continued to labour among the people, and thus cherished and extended the impressions produced by Whitefield's preaching. In the course of this year, he collected funds for the erection of a permanent building for the use of itinerant ministers. This house afterwards became the seat of the college, and subsequently, university of Pennsylvania. Here Whitefield preached whenever he visited the city, and here his associates, especially the Tennents, and Messrs. Rowland, Blair, and Finley, ministered during his absence.

In 1743, the people who had been accustomed to attend upon the occasional ministrations of the above-named gentlemen, determined to form themselves into a church, and to call a stated pastor. They accordingly presented a call to the Rev. Gilbert Tennent, who accepted their invitation, and was installed over them by the Presbytery of New Brunswick. In the letter already quoted, Mr. Tennent, after speaking of the low state of religion in Philadelphia, before the visits of Mr. Whitefield, and of the immediate effects of his preaching, says, that though some who were then awakened had lost their seriousness, and others fallen into erroneous doctrines, yet many gave every rational evidence of being true Christians. That some should have been led astray by the fair speeches and cunning craftiness of those that lie in wait to deceive, he thought was not to be wondered at, considering that the greater portion of them had not had the benefit of a strict religious education. He says he knew of none, who had been well acquainted with the doctrines of religion, in their connection, and established in them, who had been thus turned aside.

In May, 1744, he administered the Lord's supper to his people, for the first time, as a distinct church. The number of communicants was above one hundred and forty, almost all of whom were the fruits of the recent revival. Besides these, many others connected with other churches were regarded as Mr. Whitefield's converts. Mr. Tennent concludes his account by stating, that though there was a considerable falling off in the liveliness of the religious feeling of the people, yet they were growing more humble and merciful, and that their whole conversation made it evident that the bent of their hearts was towards God.*

The Rev. Samuel Blair gives substantially the following account of the revival in New Londonderry, (Fagg's Manor,) in Pennsylvania. The congregation was formed in that place about the year 1725, and consisted, as did all the Presbyterian churches in Pennsylvania, with two or three exceptions, of emigrants from Ireland. Mr. Blair, who was the first pastor of the church at Londonderry, was installed there, November, 1739. During that winter, some four or five persons were brought under deep convictions; and in the following March, during a temporary absence of the pastor, while a neighbouring minister was preaching in his place, such a powerful impression was made upon the people, that some of them broke out into audible crying; a thing previously unknown in that part of the country. A similar effect was produced by the first sermon preached by Mr. Blair, after his return. The number of the awakened now increased very fast, and the Sabbath assemblies were exceedingly large, people coming from all quarters to a place where there was an appearance of the divine presence and power. There was scarcely a sermon preached during that summer, without manifest evidence of a deep impression being made upon the hearers. Often this impression was very great and general; some would be overcome to fainting; others deeply sobbing; others crying aloud; while others would be weeping in silence. In some few cases, the exercises were attended by strange convulsive agitations of the body. It was found that the greater portion of those thus seriously affected were influenced by a fixed and rational conviction of their dangerous condition.

The general behaviour of the people was soon very manifestly altered. Those who were concerned, spent much time in reading

* Letter to Mr. Prince, No. 89.

the Bible and other good books, and it was a great satisfaction to the people to find how exactly the doctrines which they daily heard preached to them, agreed with those taught by godly men in other places and in former times. Mr. Blair insisted much in his preaching upon the miserable state of man by nature, on the way of recovery through Jesus Christ, on the nature and necessity of faith, warning his hearers not to depend upon their repentance, prayers, or reformation; nor to seek peace in extraordinary ways, by visions, dreams, or immediate inspirations, but by an understanding view and believing persuasion of the way of life, as revealed in the gospel, through the suretyship—obedience and sufferings of Jesus Christ. His righteousness they were urged to accept as the only means of justification and life.

Many of those who were convinced, soon gave satisfactory evidence that God had brought them to a saving faith in Christ. In most cases, the Holy Spirit seemed to use for this purpose some particular passage of the Scriptures, some promise or some declaration of the way of salvation through Jesus Christ. In others, there was no such prominence in the mind of the inquirer, given to any one particular passage. Those who experienced such remarkable relief could not only give a rational account of the change in their feelings, but also exhibited the usual fruits of a genuine faith; particularly humility, love, and affectionate regard to the will and honour of God. Much of their exercises was in self-abasing and self-loathing, and admiring the astonishing condescension and grace of God towards those who were so unworthy. They freely and sweetly chose the way of his commands, and were desirous to live according to his will and to the glory of his name. There were others who had no such lively exercises, and yet gave evidence of faith in Christ, though it was not attended with such a degree of liberty and joy. Such persons, however, generally long continued to be suspicious of their own case.

As to the permanent results of this work, it is stated that those who had merely some slight impressions of a religious character, soon lost them; and some who were for a time greatly distressed, seemed to have found peace in some other way than through faith in Christ. There were, however, a considerable number who gave scriptural evidenco of having been savingly renewed. Their walk was habitually tender and conscientious; their carriage towards their neighbours was just and kind, and they had a peculiar love to all who bore the image of God. They endeavoured to live for God, and were much grieved on account of their imperfections, and the plague of their hearts. Entire harmony prevailed in the congregation. Indeed there was scarcely any open opposition to the work from the beginning, though some few of the people withdrew, and joined the ministers who unhappily opposed the revival.

During the summer of 1740, the shower of divine influence spread extensively through Pennsylvania, and beyond the borders of that province. Certain ministers distinguished for their zeal were earnestly sought for in all directions; vacant congregations solicited their services; and even some of the clergy who were not disposed heartily to co-operate in the work, yielded to the importunity of their people, and invited those ministers to visit their congregations. Great assemblies would ordinarily meet to hear them, upon any day of the week, and frequently a surprising power attended their preaching. Great numbers were thus convinced of their perishing condition, and there is every reason to believe that many were savingly converted to God.*

Among the places in Pennsylvania particularly favoured during this season, were New Providence, Nottingham, White Clay Creek, and Neshaminy. With regard to the first of these places, Mr. Rowland, who after leaving New Jersey laboured much among those churches, says that it was while he was travelling among them that God chose as the time of their ingathering to Christ, and that since he laboured statedly among those people he was as much engaged in endeavouring to build up those who had been called into fellowship with God, as to awaken and convince the careless. "As to their conviction, and conversion unto God," he adds, "they are able to give a scriptural account of them. I forbear to speak of many extraordinary appearances, such as scores crying out at one instant,

* Letter of Mr. Blair to Mr. Prince, dated August, 6, 1744, Christian History, No. 83; published also in Mr. Blair's Works, p. 336.

falling, and fainting. These people are still increasing, blessed be the Lord, and are labouring to walk in communion with God and one another."*

Whitefield mentions his having preached at Neshaminy on the 23d of April, 1740, to more than five thousand persons; "upwards of fifty," he adds, "I hear, have lately been brought under conviction of sin in this place." With regard to Nottingham he gives the following account. "There a good work had begun some time ago, by the ministry of Mr. Blair, Messrs. Tennent, and Mr. Cross; the last of whom was denied the use of the pulpit, and was obliged to preach in the woods, where the Lord manifested his glory, and caused many to cry out, What shall we do to be saved? It surprised me to see such a multitude gathered together at so short a notice, in such a desert place. I believe there were near twelve thousand hearers. I had not spoken long, when I perceived numbers melting. And as I preached, the power increased, till at last, both in the morning and afternoon, thousands cried out, so that they almost drowned my voice. Never before did I see a more glorious sight. O what strong crying and tears were shed and poured forth after the dear Lord Jesus! Some fainted; and when they had got a little strength, would hear and faint again. Others cried out in a manner almost as if they were in the sharpest agonies of death. I think I was never myself filled with greater power. After I had finished my last discourse, I was so pierced, as it were, and overpowered with God's love, that some thought, I believe, that I was about to give up the ghost." The next day he preached at Fagg's Manor, where the congregation was nearly as large as it had been at Nottingham, and "the commotion in the hearts of the people" as great, if not greater.

It is evident there must have been an extraordinary influence on the minds of the people to produce such vast assemblies, and such striking effects from the preaching of the gospel. There is no reason to doubt that there was much that was rational and scriptural in the experience of the persons thus violently agitated; yet there can be as little doubt that much of the outward effect above de-

* Gillies, vol. ii. p. 324.

scribed was the result of mere natural excitement, produced by powerful impressions made upon excited imaginations by the fervid eloquence of the preacher, and propagated through the crowd by the mysterious influence of sympathy.

Mr. Whitefield preached in New York repeatedly, during his second and third visits to this country, and was kindly received by the Rev. Mr. Pemberton, pastor of the Presbyterian church in that city, but no very remarkable results seem to have there attended his ministry.

In no part of our country was the revival more interesting, and in very few was it so pure as in Virginia. The state of religion in that province was deplorable. There was "a surprising negligence in attending public worship, and an equally surprising levity and unconcernedness in those that did attend. Family religion a rarity, and a solemn concern about eternal things a greater. Vices of various kinds triumphant, and even a form of godliness not common."* "Much the larger portion of the clergy were, at this time, deficient in the great duty of placing distinctly before the people the fundamental truths of the gospel."† Various circumstances had conspired to supply the established church of Virginia with ministers unfitted for their stations; and under the influence of men unqualified to be either the teachers or examples of their flocks, religion had been reduced to a very low state. There were indeed some faithful ministers, and some who were sincerely seeking the Lord in the communion of the Church of England.‡ Still all accounts agree as to the general prevalence of irreligion among both the clergy and the laity.

It seems that even before the year 1740, some persons had been led, partly by their own reflections, and partly by the perusal of some of the writings of Flavel and others, to feel a deep interest in the concerns of religion. This was the case particularly with Mr. Samuel Morris, who having obtained relief to his own mind, became anxious for the salvation of his neighbours. He accord-

* Davies's Letter to Mr. Bellamy, *Gillies' Collection*, vol. ii. p. 330.

† Hawks's Contributions to the Ecclesiastical History of the United States, vol. i. p. 115.

‡ Davies's Narrative.

ingly began to read to them the works which he had found so useful to himself, especially Luther on the Galatians. In the year 1740, Mr. Whitefield preached at Williamsburg. Though the little company, of which Mr. Morris was the centre, did not enjoy the advantage of hearing Mr. Whitefield preach, his visit awakened interest in the man, and prepared them to receive his writings with favour. Accordingly, when in 1743, a volume of his sermons was brought into the neighbourhood, Mr. Morris invited his friends to meet and hear them read. A considerable number of persons attended for this purpose every Sabbath, and frequently on other days. Mr. Morris' dwelling being too small to accommodate his audience, a meeting-house was soon erected, merely for the purpose of reading; not being accustomed to extempore prayer, no one of the company had courage to attempt to lead in that exercise. The attention thus excited gradually diffused itself, so that Mr. Morris was frequently invited to distant places to read his sermons to the people. These meetings soon attracted the attention of the magistrates, and those who frequented them were called upon to account for their non-attendance on the services of the established church, and to state to what denomination of Christians they belonged. This latter demand puzzled them not a little. The only dissenters of whom they knew any thing were Quakers, and as they were not Quakers, they could not tell what they were. At length recollecting that Luther was a great reformer, and that his writings had been particularly serviceable to them, they determined to call themselves Lutherans. About this time, the Rev. William Robinson, on a mission from the Presbytery of New Brunswick, visited that part of Virginia. He founded a church in Lunenburg, now Charlotte, and preached with much success. Also in Hanover, Mr. Morris and his friends begged him to preach in their reading-house, an invitation which he gladly accepted. "The congregation," says Mr. Morris, "was large the first day, and vastly increased the three ensuing ones. It is hard for the liveliest imagination to form an image of the condition of the assembly on those glorious days of the Son of man. Such of us as had been hungering for the word before, were lost in agreeable astonishment, and could not refrain from publicly declaring our transport. We were overwhelmed with the thoughts of the unexpected goodness of God, in allowing us to hear the gospel preached in a manner which surpassed our hopes. Many that came from curiosity were pricked in the heart, and but few in the numerous assemblies appeared unaffected." Soon after Mr. Robinson's departure, the Rev. John Blair visited them, when former impressions were revived and new ones made in many hearts. He was succeeded by the Rev. Mr. Roan, who was sent by the Presbytery of New Castle, and continued with them longer than either of the others. The good effects of this gentleman's labours were very apparent. He was instrumental in beginning and promoting a religious concern, in many places where there was little appearance of it before. "This, together with his speaking pretty freely of the degeneracy of the clergy in this colony," says Mr. Morris, "gave a general alarm, and some measures were concerted to suppress us. To increase the indignation of the government the more, a perfidious wretch deposed that he heard Mr. Roan utter blasphemous expressions in his sermon. An indictment was accordingly drawn up against Mr. R., though he had by that time departed the colony, and some who had invited him to preach at their houses were cited to appear before the general court, and two of them were fined." The indictment, however, against Mr. Roan was dropped, the witnesses cited against him testifying in his favour, and his accuser fled the province. Still as the opposition of those in authority continued, and "all circumstances seeming to threaten the extirpation of religion among the dissenters," they determined to apply to the Synod of New York for advice and assistance. This application was made in 1745, when that body drew up an address to the governor, Sir William Gooch, and sent it by Messrs. William Tennent and Samuel Finley. These gentlemen having been kindly received by the governor, were allowed to preach, and remained about a week. After their departure, the meetings for reading and prayer were continued, though Mr. Morris was repeatedly fined for absenting himself from church and keeping up unlawful assemblies. In 1747, the opposition of the government became more serious, and a proclamation was affixed to the door of the meeting-house, calling on the magistrates to prevent all itinerant preaching. This prevented the usual services for one Sabbath, but before the succeeding Lord's day the Rev. Mr. Davies arrived in the neighbourhood, having been sent by the Presbytery of New Castle, and legally qualified to preach according to the act of toleration. He petitioned the general court for permission to officiate in four meeting-houses in and about Hanover, and his request, after some delay, was granted. Ill health prevented Mr. Davies from commencing his labours among this people as their pastor, until the spring of 1748. In October, 1748, three additional places of worship were licensed. The people under his charge were sufficiently numerous, if compactly situated, to form three distinct congregations. In 1751, the date of Mr. Davies's narrative, there were three hundred communicants in these infant churches. There were at this period two other Presbyterian congregations, one in Albemarle, and the other in Augusta, which were supplied with ministers in connection with the Synod of Philadelphia. The Presbyterians in Virginia, in connection with the Synod of New York, though much more numerous than those belonging to the other Synod, were, except the churches in Hanover, destitute of pastors. President Davies says they were numerous enough to form at least five congregations; three in Augusta, one in Frederick, and one in Amelia and Lunenburg. "Were you a bigot," says Mr. Davies to Dr. Bellamy, "you would no doubt rejoice to hear that there are hundreds of dissenters in a place where a few years ago there were not ten;* but I assure myself of your congratulations on a nobler account, because a considerable number of perishing sinners are gained to the blessed Redeemer, with whom, though you never see them here, you may spend a blissful eternity. After all, poor Virginia demands your compassion; religion at present is but like the cloud which Elijah's servant saw." †

* This remark of course relates to Hanover, where President Davies was settled. The Presbyterians in the other counties were principally Scotch and Irish emigrants from Pennsylvania.

† Letter of Mr. Davies to Mr. Bellamy, dated June 28, 1751.—*Gillies' Collections*, vol. ii. p. 330.

My venerated father in Christ, Dr. Alexander, remarked on part of the above narrative in relation to the establishment of Presbyterian congregations

While the revival was thus extending itself through almost all parts of the Presbyterian Church, it was perhaps still more general and remarkable throughout New England. In Northampton, where President Edwards had been settled since 1726, there had been a revival in 1734–35, which extended more or less through Hampshire county, and to many adjoining places in Connecticut.* In

in Virginia, that it would not be very intelligible to Virginians. "The counties of Amelia and Lunenburg are mentioned as the seat of flourishing congregations; now those counties as at present bounded have scarcely ever had more than a sprinkling of Presbyterian families. When Mr. Morris's letter was written, Cumberland and Prince Edward counties formed part of Amelia, and Charlotte of Lunenburg, and these were the counties in which Presbyterian congregations were planted, and where they flourish to this day. So also, Augusta at that time comprehended all the great valley from Frederick south-westward; since then, Rockbridge on the south-west, and Rockingham on the north-east, have been taken off and formed into new counties. The Presbyterians of what is now Augusta, were mostly of the old-side, but those of Rockbridge were of the new-side."

Dr. Alexander further remarked, "That very little is said in the above narrative, concerning the labours of Mr. Davies. He, in his modesty, speaks as if Mr. Robinson had converted more souls in a few days, than he in eight years. But I can bear witness that, half a century after Mr. Davies's departure, I met with numerous Christians of eminent piety, who acknowledged him as the instrument of their awakening. Every spring and fall he was accustomed to take an extensive tour for preaching. He generally preached in the woods to numerous congregations, and multitudes were benefited savingly by him, of whom he never knew any thing. He was also very attentive to the blacks, and had many of them taught to read; and by the assistance of the society in London for propagating Christianity, he supplied them with Bibles and Watts's Hymns. I knew three old men, born in Africa, brought over when boys, who were members of his church, and could all read and were eminent for piety. There is no where in print any just account of Mr. Davies's evangelical labours in Virginia. While he preached faithfully, he conducted himself with so much dignity, affability, and prudence, that he gained the high respect of all the distinguished laymen in that part of the State. "The melancholy decline of the Hanover congregation after his removal, was owing to a variety of causes, chiefly to the emigration of the members. Many of the congregations in the newer parts of the State were commenced by members of his congregation."

* Edwards's Narrative, &c., Works, vol. iv. p. 25.

the spring of 1740, before the visit of Mr. Whitefield, there was a growing seriousness through the town, especially among the young people. When that gentleman came to the place in October, he preached four or five sermons with his usual force and influence. In about a month there was a great alteration in the town, both in the increased fervour and activity of professors of religion, and in the awakened attention of sinners. In May, 1741, a sermon was preached at a private house, when one or two persons were so affected by the greatness and glory of divine things, that they were not able to conceal it, the affection of their minds overcoming their strength, and having an effect on their bodies. After the exercises, the young people removed to another room to inquire of those thus exercised, what impressions they had experienced. The affection was quickly propagated round the room; many of the young people and children appeared to be overcome with the sense of divine things, and others with distress about their sinfulness and danger, so that "the room was full of nothing but outcries, faintings, and such like." Others soon came to look on; many of whom were overpowered in like manner. The months of August and September of this year were most remarkable for the number of convictions and conversions, for the revival of professors, and for the external effects of this state of excitement. It was no uncommon thing to see a house, as Edwards expresses it, full of outcries, faintings, convulsions, and the like, both from distress, and also from admiration and joy. The work continued much in the same state until February, 1742, when Mr. Buel came and laboured among the people during a temporary absence of the pastor. The effect of his preaching was very extraordinary. The people were greatly moved, great numbers crying out during public worship, and many remaining in the house for hours after the services were concluded. The whole town was in a great and continual commotion night and day. Mr. Buel remained a fortnight after Mr. Edwards's return, and the same effects continued to attend his preaching. There were instances of persons lying twenty-four hours in a trance, apparently senseless, though under strong imaginations, as though they went to heaven and had there visions of glorious objects. When the people were raised to this height, Satan took the advantage, and his interpositions, in many instances, soon became apparent, and a great deal of pains was necessary to keep the people from running wild.

President Edwards states, that he considered this revival much more pure than that of 1734–5, at least during the years 1740, 1741, and the early part of 1742. Towards the close of the last-mentioned year, an unfavourable influence was exerted upon the congregation from abroad. This remark shows that he did not consider the scenes which he describes as attending Mr. Buel's preaching, as affording any reason to doubt the purity of the revival. What he disapproved of occurred at a later period, and had a different origin. When his people saw that there were greater commotions in other places, and when they heard of greater professions of zeal and rapture than were common among themselves, they thought others had made higher attainments in religion, and were thus led away by them. These things plainly show, says Mr. Edwards, that the degree of grace is not to be judged by the degree of zeal or joy; that it is not the strength, but the nature of religious affections which is to be regarded. Some, who had the highest raptures, and the greatest bodily exercises, showed the least of a Christian temper. Though there were few cases of scandalous sin among professors, the temper and behaviour of some, he adds, led him to fear that a considerable number were awfully deceived. On the other hand, there were many whose temper was truly Christian; and the work, notwithstanding its corrupt admixtures, produced blessed fruit in particular persons, and some good effects in the town in general.*

If such scenes as those just referred to occurred in Northampton, under the eye of President Edwards, we may readily imagine what was likely to occur in other places under men far his inferiors in judgment, knowledge, and piety. Though Edwards never regarded these outcries and bodily affections as any evidence of true religious affections, he was at this time much less sensible of the dan-

* Letter of Mr. Edwards to Mr. Prince, dated December 12, 1743. Christian History, No. 46, and Dwight's Life of Edwards, p. 160.

ger of encouraging such manifestations of excitement, than he afterwards became. Nor does he seem to have been sufficiently aware of the nature and effects of nervous disorders, which in times of excitement are as infectious as any form of disease to which the human system is liable. When he speaks of certain persons being seized with a strange bodily affection, which quickly propagated itself round the room, especially among the young; and of spectators, after a while, being similarly affected, he gives as plain an example of the sympathetic propagation of a nervous disorder, as is to be found in the medical records of disease. There may have been, and no doubt there was, much genuine religious feeling in that meeting, but these bodily affections were neither the evidence, nor, properly speaking, the result of it.

In September, 1740, Mr. Whitefield first visited Boston, when multitudes were greatly affected by his ministry. Though he preached every day, the houses continued to be crowded until his departure. The December following, Mr. G. Tennent arrived, whose preaching was followed by still greater effects. Many hundreds, says Mr. Prince, were brought by his searching ministry to be deeply convinced of sin; to have clear views of the divine sovereignty, holiness, justice, and power; of the spirituality and strictness of the divine law, and of the dreadful corruption of their own hearts, and "its utter impotence either rightly to repent or believe in Christ, or change itself;" of their utter unworthiness in the sight of a righteous God, of their being "without the least degree of strength to help themselves out of this condition." On Monday, March 2, 1741, Mr. Tennent preached his farewell sermon, to an extremely crowded and deeply affected audience. "And now was a time such as we never knew. Mr. Cooper was wont to say, that more came to him in one week, in deep concern about their souls, than in the whole twenty-four years of his previous ministry." In three months, he had six hundred such calls, and Mr. Webb above a thousand. The very face of the town was strangely altered. There were some thousands under such religious impressions as they never knew before; and the fruits of the work, says Mr. Cooper, in 1741, as far as time had been allowed to test them, promised to be abiding. The revival in Boston seems to have been much more pure than in most other places, and it thus continued until the arrival of Mr. Davenport in June, 1742. Mr. Prince says he met with only one or two persons who talked of their impulses; that he knew of no minister who encouraged reliance on such enthusiastic impressions. "The doctrinal principles," he adds, "of those who continue in our congregations, and have been the subjects of the late revival, are the same as they all along have been instructed in, from the Westminster Shorter Catechism, which has generally been received and taught in the churches of New England, from its first publication, for one hundred years to the present day; and which is therefore the system of doctrine most generally and clearly declarative of the faith of the New England churches." There seems also to have been far less extravagance in Boston than attended the excitement in most other places. "We have neither had," says Dr. Colman, "those outcries and faintings in our assemblies, which have disturbed the worship in many places, nor yet those manifestations of joy inexpressible which now fill some of our eastern parts."*

When Mr. Whitefield left Boston in October, 1740, he went to Northampton, preaching at most of the intervening towns. After spending a few days with President Edwards, as already mentioned, he proceeded to New Haven, and thence to New York. Everywhere, during this journey, the churches and houses were freely opened to him, and everywhere, to a greater or less degree, his discourses were attended by the same remarkable effects as elsewhere followed his preaching. Mr. Tennent also, after leaving Boston, made an extended tour through New England, and was very instrumental in awakening the attention of the people. His stature was large, and his whole appearance commanding. He wore his hair undressed, and his usual costume in the pulpit, at least during this journey, was a loose great coat with a leathern girdle about his loins.† As a preacher he had few equals. His reasoning powers

* See for an account of the revival in Boston, Prince's Christian History, No. 100, &c.; or Gillies, vol. ii. p. 162.

† Assembly's Magazine.

were strong; his expressions nervous and often sublime; his style diffusive; his manner warm and pathetic, such as must convince his audience that he was in earnest; and his voice clear and commanding.* "When I heard Mr. Tennent," says the celebrated Dr. Hopkins, then a student in Yale College, "I thought he was the greatest and best man, and the best preacher that I had ever seen or heard."† Mr. Prince of Boston, says, "He did not at first come up to my expectations, but afterwards far exceeded them. He seemed to have as deep an acquaintance with experimental religion as any I have ever conversed with; and his preaching was as searching and rousing as any I ever heard."‡ Such appears to have been the general style of his preaching during this tour; for the Rev. W. Fish, in giving an account of the origin of the revival, says, "When the ears of the people were thus opened to hear, and their hearts awake to receive instruction, there came a son of thunder, Rev. Gilbert Tennent, through these parts, by whose enlightening and alarming discourses, people were more effectually roused up, and put upon a more earnest inquiry after the great salvation."§ Mr. Tennent, in a letter to Mr. Whitefield, dated April, 1741, says that, on his return homeward from Boston, he preached daily, ordinarily three times a day, and sometimes oftener, (a few days only excepted;) and that his success had far exceeded his expectations. He enumerates at least twenty-three towns in which he had thus laboured, and adds that, on a moderate calculation, "divers thousands had been awakened."||

The transient impressions, however, made by a passing preacher would, in all probability, have been of little avail, had they not been followed by the laborious and continued efforts of the settled pastors. Such efforts were in most cases made, and the revival soon became general through almost the whole of Massachusetts and Connecticut, and a considerable part of Rhode Island. In Connecticut, the work was probably more extensive than in any other

* Funeral Discourse by President Finley.

† Life of Edwards by Dwight, p. 156.

‡ Christian History, No. 100.

§ Fish's Nine Sermons, p. 114.

|| Gillies, vol. ii. p. 132.

of the colonies, and was greatly promoted by the labours of Messrs. Pomeroy, Mills, Wheelock, and Bellamy. "Dr. Pomeroy was a man of real genius; grave, solemn, and weighty in his discourses, which were generally well composed, and delivered with a great degree of animation and affection. His language was good, and he might be reckoned among the best preachers of his day."* Dr. Wheelock, says the same authority, "was a gentleman of a comely figure, of a mild and winning aspect. His voice smooth and harmonious, the best by far that I ever heard. His preaching and addresses were close and pungent, and yet winning almost beyond all comparison, so that his audience would be melted even to tears before they were aware of it." Dr. Bellamy "was a large man and well built, of a commanding appearance. He had a smooth strong voice, and could fill the largest house without any unnatural effort. He possessed a truly great mind; generally preached without notes; had some great point of doctrine commonly to establish, and would keep close to his subject until he had sufficiently illustrated it, and then in an ingenious, close, and pungent manner, would make the application."† Such were the more prominent promoters of this great revival. As this work was more extensive in Connecticut than elsewhere, so it was there attended with greater disorders, and was more violently opposed, and in many cases led to disastrous separations and lasting conflicts. Severe penal laws were enacted against itinerant preaching; several ministers were transported out of the colony; others were deprived of their salaries or fined. The act for the indulgence of sober consciences was repealed in 1743, so that there "was no relief for any persons dissenting from the established mode of worship in Connecticut, but upon application to the assembly, who were growing more rigid in enforcing the constitution."‡ The General Association, on the occasion of Whitefield's second visit in 1745, declared him to be the promoter, or at least the faulty occasion of the errors and disorders which there prevailed; and voted that it was not advisable for the

* Trumbull's Connecticut, vol. ii. p. 157. † Ibid. vol. ii. p. 159.

‡ Ibid. vol. ii. p. 173.

ministers to admit him into their pulpits, or for the people to attend his ministrations.*

Notwithstanding all the disorders and other evils attendant on this revival, there can be no doubt that it was a wonderful display, both of the power and grace of God. This might be confidently inferred from the judgment of those who, as eye-witnesses of its progress, were the best qualified to form an opinion of its character. The deliberate judgment of such men as Edwards, Cooper, Colman, and Bellamy, in New England; and of the Tennents, Blair, Dickinson, and Davies, in the Presbyterian Church, must be received as of authority on such a subject. These men were not errorists or enthusiasts. They were devout and sober-minded men, well versed in the Scriptures and in the history of religion. They had their faults, and fell into mistakes; some of them very grievous; but if they are not to be regarded as competent witnesses as to the nature of any religious excitement, it will be hard to know where such witnesses are to be found. Besides the testimony of these distinguished individuals, we have that of a convention of about ninety ministers met at Boston, July 7, 1743. Similar attestations were published by several associations in Connecticut and elsewhere.† The Presbyteries of New Brunswick and New Castle, and the whole Synod of New York, repeatedly and earnestly bore their testimony to the genuineness and value of this revival.‡

We have, however, ourselves sufficient ground on which to form a judgment on this subject. We can compare the doctrines then taught, the exercises experienced, and the effects produced, with the word of God, and thus learn how far the work was in accordance with that infallible standard. The first of these points is a matter of primary importance. It would be in vain for any set of men to expect the confidence of the Christian public in the genuineness of any religious excitement, unless it could be shown that the truth of God was instrumental in its production. There have been great excitements where Pagan, Mohammedan, and Popish doctrines were

* Trumbull's Connecticut, vol. ii. p. 190.

† Prince's History, No. 20, 21.

‡ Gillies, vol. ii. p. 318, 319.

preached, but no one regards such excitements with approbation, who does not regard those doctrines as true. Any revival, therefore, which claims the confidence of the people of God, must show that it is the child of the truth of God. If it cannot do this, it may safely be pronounced spurious. How will the revival under consideration abide this test? Is there any doubt as to the doctrines taught by Whitefield, the Tennents, Blair, Dickinson, and the other prominent preachers of that day? They were the doctrines of the Reformation, and of the standards of the Presbyterian Church. Indeed, these men often went to a length in their statements of the peculiarities of those doctrines, that would shock the delicacy of modern ears.* These great truths were not kept under a bushel during this period. They were prominently presented, and gave to the work, as far as it was genuine, its distinctive character. "The doctrines preached," says Trumbull, "by those famous men, who were owned as the principal instruments of this remarkable revival of God's work, were the doctrines of the reformers; the doctrine of original sin, of regeneration by the supernatural influences of the divine Spirit, and of the absolute necessity of it, that any man might bear good fruit, or ever be admitted into the kingdom of God; effectual calling; justification by faith, wholly on account of the imputed righteousness of Christ; repentance towards God and faith towards our Lord Jesus Christ; the perseverance of saints; the indwelling of the Holy Spirit in them, and its divine consolations and joys."†

The contemporary accounts of the doctrines inculcated by the zealous preachers of that day, fully sustain the statement just quoted. Edwards mentions that his sermon on justification by faith, though it gave offence to many, was greatly blessed, and that it was on the doctrine therein taught, the revival was founded in its begin-

* See Tennent's Sermons, especially those on original sin, regeneration, and the nature and necessity of conversion: Blair's Works, his Dissertation on Predestination and Reprobation: President Dickinson's Familiar Letters; his Dialogues, his Five Points, &c. &c. Whitefield's Theology at least was such as to satisfy even Toplady, who pronounced him a sound divine.

† History, vol. ii. p. 158.

ning and during its whole progress.* In the account of the revival at Plymouth, we are told that the doctrines principally insisted upon, were "the sin and apostasy of mankind in Adam; the blindness of the natural man in things of God; the enmity of the carnal mind; the evil of sin, and the ill desert of it; the utter inability of fallen man to relieve himself; the sovereignty of God, his righteousness, holiness, truth, power, eternity, and also his grace and mercy in Christ Jesus; the way of redemption by Christ; justification through his imputed righteousness received by faith, this faith being a gift of God, and a living principle that worketh by love; legal and evangelical repentance; the nature and necessity of regeneration, &c."†

The Rev. Mr. Crocker, in his history of the revival at Taunton, enumerates the doctrines which had been chiefly "blessed by God to the awakening, convincing, and converting of sinners," or to

* In that sermon he teaches that a person is said "to be justified when he is approved of God as free from the guilt of sin and its deserved punishment, and as having that righteousness belonging to him that entitles him to the reward of life." Works, vol. v. p. 354. He argues at length against the opinion that justification is nothing more than pardon. He shows that the righteousness by which we are justified is not faith, nor any thing in us, but the righteousness of Christ; that in order to our receiving that righteousness we must be united to him, and that this union is at once legal and vital. Without union, he says, "our sins could not be imputed to him," nor his righteousness to us: p. 366. This imputation he extends to the obedience of Christ, as well as the merit of his sufferings. "The opposers of this doctrine," he says, "suppose there is an absurdity in supposing that God imputes Christ's obedience to us; it is to suppose that God is mistaken, and thinks that we performed that obedience which Christ performed. But why cannot that righteousness be reckoned to our account, and accepted for us, without any such absurdity? Why is there any more absurdity in it than in a merchant's transferring a debt or credit from one man's account to another, so that it shall be accepted as if that other had paid it? Why is there any more absurdity in supposing that Christ's obedience is imputed to us, than that his satisfaction is imputed? If Christ has suffered the penalty of the law in our stead, then it will follow that his suffering that penalty is imputed to us; that is, accepted for us, and in our stead, and is reckoned to our account, as though we had suffered it. But why may not his obeying the law be as rationally reckoned to our account as his suffering the penalty of the law?" p. 395.

† Prince's Christian History, No. 92.

the edification of believers. His list contains all the distinguishing doctrines of the gospel; as original sin, that all men by nature are dead in trespasses and sins, legally and spiritually dead; the natural impotence and enmity of men; their natural blindness in spiritual things; the covenant of works and of grace; God's sovereignty in dispensing grace to whomsoever he will; justification by the imputed righteousness of Christ; the necessity of regeneration; the necessity of the special and supernatural influences of the Holy Spirit; the necessity of a holy life, &c. &c.*

The Rev. Mr. M'Gregore, pastor of the Presbyterian church at Londonderry, New Hampshire, preached a sermon on the trial of the spirits, which was subsequently published, with a preface by certain of the ministers of Boston. In that preface it is said: "As the Assembly's Shorter Catechism has been all along agreeable to the known principles of the New England churches, and has been generally received and taught in them as a system of Christian doctrine agreeable to the Holy Scriptures, wherein they happily unite; it is a great pleasure to us that our Presbyterian brethren who came from Ireland, are generally with us in these important points, as also in the particular doctrines of experimental piety arising from them, and the wondrous work of God agreeable to them, at this day making its triumphant progress through the land." The writers say that they rejoice to add their testimony to that of the author of the sermon, to the same doctrines of grace, and to the wondrous works of God.† "The doctrines which the promoters of this work teach," says the author, and by which he insists they ought to be tried, to know whether they are of God, "are the doctrines of the gospel, of the Apostles' Creed, of the Thirty-nine Articles of the Church of England, and of the Westminster Confession of Faith. More particularly these men are careful to teach and inculcate the great doctrine of original sin, in opposition to Pelagius, Arminius, and their respective followers:

* Christian History, vol. ii. p. 351.

† Sermon on 1 John iv. 1, preached in Boston, Nov. 3, 1741, by Rev. David M'Gregore. The preface above quoted is signed by Messrs. Prince, Webb, and Cooper.

that this sin has actually descended from Adam, the natural and federal head, to all his posterity proceeding from him by ordinary generation; that hereby the understanding is darkened, the will depraved, and the affections under the influence of a wrong bias, to that degree that they are utterly indisposed to any thing that is spiritually good; that man, as a sad consequence of the fall, has lost all power in things spiritual. They teach likewise, with due care, the doctrine of the imputation of the righteousness of the second Adam, Jesus Christ; that this righteousness is apprehended and applied by faith alone, without the deeds of the law; that the faith which justifies the soul is living and operative. They teach that this faith is the gift of God; that a man cannot believe by any inherent power of his own. As to regeneration, they hold it to be absolutely necessary; that the tree must be made good before the fruit be so; that unless a man undergo a supernatural change by the operation of the Holy Ghost upon his soul, or be born of water and of spirit, he cannot enter into the kingdom of God." * Such were the doctrines of the promoters of this revival, by which they wished to be tried themselves, and to have their work tested. Those who believe these doctrines will of course be disposed to have confidence in these men, and in the revival which attended their preaching. Whereas those who reject these doctrines may be expected to pronounce the men nothing-doers, passivity-preachers, destroyers of souls, and the like, and their work a mere delusion; unless, indeed, an exaggerated deference for public opinion, or the amiable prejudice of education should lead them still to laud the men and the revival, while they condemn the sentiments which gave both it and them their distinctive character.

The second criterion of the genuineness of any revival is the nature of the experience professed by its subjects. However varied as to degree or circumstances, the experience of all true Christians is substantially the same. There is and must be a conviction of sin, a sense of ill-desert and unholiness in the sight of God, a desire of deliverance from the dominion as well as penalty of sin;

* See pp. 13, 14, of the sermon for a full statement of these doctrines, which we have weakened by abridging them.

an apprehension of the mercy of God in Jesus Christ; a cordial acquiescence in the plan of redemption; a sincere return of the soul to God through Christ, depending on his merits for acceptance. These acts of faith will ever be attended with more or less of joy and peace, and with a fixed desire and purpose to live in obedience to the will of God. The distinctness and strength of these exercises, the rapidity of their succession, their modifications and combinations, admit of endless diversity, yet they are all to be found in every case of genuine conversion. It is here as in the human face; all men have the same features, yet no two men are exactly alike. This uniformity of religious experience, as to all essential points, is one of the strongest collateral proofs of the truth of experimental religion. That which men of every grade of cultivation, of every period, and in every portion of the world, testify they have known and felt, cannot be a delusion. When we come to ask what was the experience of the subjects of this revival, we find, amidst much that is doubtful or objectionable, the essential characteristics of genuine conversion. This is plain from the accounts already given, which need not be here repeated. In a great multitude of cases, the same feelings were professed which we find the saints, whose spiritual life is recorded in the Bible, experienced, and which the children of God in all ages have avowed; the same sense of sin, the same apprehension of the mercy of God, the same faith in Christ, the same joy and peace in believing, the same desire for communion with God, and the same endeavour after new obedience.

Such however is the ambiguity of human language, such the deceitfulness of the human heart, and such the devices of Satan, that no mere detail of feeling, and especially no description which one man may give of the feelings of others, can afford conclusive evidence of the nature of those feelings in the sight of God. Two persons may, with equal sincerity, profess sorrow for sin, and yet their emotions be essentially different. Both may with truth declare that they believe in Christ, and yet the states of mind thereby expressed be very dissimilar. Both may have peace, joy, and love, yet the one be a self-deceiver, and the other a true Christian.

We must, therefore, look further than mere professions or detail of experiences, for evidence of the real character of this work. We must look to its effects. The only satisfactory proof of the nature of any religious excitement, in an individual or a community, is its permanent results. What then were the fruits of this revival? Mr. William Tennent says that the subjects of this work, who had come under his observation, were brought to approve of the doctrines of the gospel, to delight in the law of God, to endeavour to do his will, to love those who bore the divine image; that the formal had become spiritual; the proud, humble; the wanton and vile, sober and temperate; the worldly, heavenly-minded; the extortioner, just; and the self-seeker, desirous to promote the glory of God.* This account was written in 1744.

The convention of ministers that met in Boston in 1743, state, that those who were regarded as converts confirmed the genuineness of the change which they professed to have experienced, "by the external fruits of holiness in their lives, so that they appeared to those who had the nearest access to them, as so many epistles of Jesus Christ, written not with ink, but by the Spirit of the living God."† President Edwards, in his Thoughts on the Revival, written in 1743, says, there is a strange alteration almost all over New England among the young. Many, both old and young, have become serious, mortified and humble in their conversation; their thoughts and affections are now about the favour of God, an interest in Christ, and spiritual blessedness. The Bible is in much greater esteem and use than formerly. The Lord's day is more religiously observed. There has been more acknowledgment of faults and restitution within two years, than in thirty years before. The leading truths of the gospel are more generally and firmly held; and many have exhibited calmness, resignation, and joy, in the midst of the severest trials.‡ It is true his estimate of this work, a few years later, was far less favourable, but he never ceased to regard it as a great revival of genuine religion.

* Gillies, vol. ii. p. 34.

† Gillies, vol. ii. p. 252. See similar testimonies in the Christian History, pp. 252, 286, *et passim.*

‡ Edwards's Works, vol. iv. p. 105.

Trumbull, a later witness, says, "the effects on great numbers were abiding and most happy. They were the most uniform exemplary Christians with whom I was ever acquainted. I was born and had my education in that part of the town of Hebron in which the work was most prevalent and powerful. Many, who at that time imagined that they were born of God, made a profession of their faith in Christ, and were admitted to full communion, and appeared to walk with God." They were, he adds, constant and serious in their attendance on public worship, prayerful, righteous, and charitable, strict in the government of their families, and not one of them, as far as he knew, was ever guilty of scandal. Eight or ten years after the religious excitement, there was not a drunkard in the whole parish. "It was the most glorious and extensive revival of religion and reformation of manners which this country has ever known. It is estimated that, in the term of two or three years, thirty or forty thousand souls were born into the family of heaven in New England, besides great numbers in New York, New Jersey, and the more southern provinces."* It is to be feared, indeed, that Trumbull was led from the favourable specimens which fell under his own observation, and from his friendship for some of the leading promoters of the revival, to form a more favourable opinion of its general results than the facts in the case would warrant. His testimony, however, is important, belonging as he did to the next generation of ministers, and familiarly acquainted as he was with some of the most zealous preachers of the preceding period.

The rise of the Methodists in England, the extensive revival of religion in Scotland, were contemporaneous with the progress of the revival in this country. This simultaneous excitement in the different parts of the British empire, was marked every where, in a great measure, with the same peculiar features. It would be interesting to trace its history abroad, in connection with what occurred on our side of the Atlantic. This, however, the nature of the

* History of Connecticut, vol. ii. p. 263. The same estimate, as to the number of converts, is given in a Historical Narrative and Declaration of the rise and progress of the strict Congregational Churches, (i. e. of the separated,) in Connecticut. Providence, 1781.

present work forbids. It is enough for our purpose to know that the revival was not confined to this country. It was essentially the same work here, in Scotland and in England, modified by the peculiar circumstances of those several countries.

If the evidence was not perfectly satisfactory, that this remarkable and extended revival was indeed the work of the Spirit of God, it would lose almost all its interest for the Christian church. It is precisely because it was in the main a work of God, that it is of so much importance to ascertain what were the human or evil elements mixed with it, which so greatly marred its beauty and curtailed its usefulness. That there were such evils cannot be a matter of doubt. The single consideration, that immediately after this excitement the state of religion rapidly declined, that errors of all kinds became more prevalent than ever, and that a lethargy gradually settled on the churches, which was not broken for near half a century, is proof enough that there was a dreadful amount of evil connected with the revival. Was such, however, actually the case? Did religion thus rapidly decline? If this question must be answered in the affirmative, what were the causes of this decline, or what were the errors which rendered this revival, considered as a whole, productive of such evils? These are questions of the greatest interest to the American churches, and ought to be very seriously considered and answered.

That the state of religion did rapidly decline after the revival, we have abundant and melancholy evidence. Even as early as 1744, President Edwards says, "the present state of things in New England is, on many accounts, very melancholy. There is a vast alteration within two years." God, he adds, was provoked at the spiritual pride and self-confidence of the people, and withdrew from them, and "the enemy has come in like a flood in various respects, until the deluge has overwhelmed the whole land. There had been from the beginning a great mixture, especially in some places, of false experiences and false religion with true; but from this time the mixture became much greater, and many were led away into sad delusions."* In another letter, dated May 23, 1749, he says,

* Letter to Mr. McCulloch, of Scotland, dated March 5, 1744. Life of Edwards, p. 212.

"as to the state of religion in these parts of the world, it is, in general, very dark and melancholy."* In the preceding October, when writing to Mr. Erskine of Edinburgh, he communicates to him an extract from a letter to himself, from Governor Belcher of New Jersey, who says, "The accounts which I receive from time to time, give me too much reason to fear that Arminianism, Arianism, and even Socinianism, in destruction to the doctrines of grace, are daily propagated in the New England colleges."† In 1750, he writes to Mr. McCulloch in the following melancholy strain: "It is indeed now a sorrowful time on this side of the ocean. Iniquity abounds, and the love of many waxes cold. Multitudes of fair and high professors, in one place or another, have sadly backslidden, sinners are desperately hardened; experimental religion is more than ever out of credit with far the greater part; and the doctrines of grace and those principles in religion which do chiefly concern the power of godliness, are far more than ever discarded. Arminianism and Pelagianism have made a strange progress within a few years. The Church of England in New England, is, I suppose, treble what it was seven years ago. Many professors are gone off to great lengths in enthusiasm and extravagance in their notions and practices. Great contentions, separations, and confusions in our religious state prevail in many parts of the land."‡ In 1752, in a letter to Mr. Gillespie, relating to his difficulties with his congregation, he says, "It is to be considered that these things have happened when God is greatly withdrawn, and religion was very low, not only in Northampton, but all over New England."§ The church in Stonington, Connecticut, was torn to pieces by fanaticism, and a separate congregation erected. The excellent pastor of that place, the Rev. Mr. Fish, a warm friend of the revival, exerted himself in vain to stem the torrent; "and other ministers," he says, "that came to our help carried on the same design of correcting the false notions which new converts had embraced about religion; particularly the late judicious and excellent Mr. David

* Letter to Mr. Robe, of Kilsyth. Life, p. 279.

† Life of Edwards, p. 268. ‡ Ibid. p. 413. § Ibid. p. 467.

Brainerd, who, in this desk, exposed and remonstrated against the same errors, and told me that such false religion as prevailed among my people, had spread almost all the land over."*

That false doctrines increasingly prevailed after the revival, is strongly asserted in the letter of Edwards already quoted. Other

* Fish's Nine Sermons, p. 137. In order to show "what food the separatists turned their backs upon, and what doctrines they could not bear," Mr. Fish gives, in a note, an outline of a sermon which he preached during the revival, and which was the immediate cause of many of his people leaving him. The text of the sermon was, Eph. v. 1. "Be ye followers of God as dear children." The design of the discourse was to show, 1. What it is to follow God. 2. That the distinguishing character of God's children lies in their being followers of him. To follow God implies, 1. Our yielding up ourselves wholly to be governed by his laws and commands. 2. Imitating his moral perfections; that is, being conformed to them in heart and life; particularly in purity of heart, truth, faithfulness, justice, uprightness, &c. The second head he passes over, and gives the application of the sermon, viz.:

1. Hence, see the only rule by which we may try and know God's children. So far as heart and life appear to be conformed to God, they show themselves to be his children.

2. Hence, see a safe rule of conduct. Set the Lord always before your eyes, as he is revealed in his word.

3. Learn wherein true religion consists, viz.: in following God, imitating his moral perfections; resembling him in spirit, temper, and carriage, habitually, in a steady course of life. It is therefore a mistake to place religion in ecstasies and raptures of joy, loud expressions of distress for souls in public meetings; in powerful impressions to do things of a religious nature; in visions or lively imaginations of a bleeding Saviour; an outward Christ with open and inviting arms, a local hell or heaven, and such like. (Which things, adds the author, at that day, were in high repute, treated with the greatest reverence, called *the power*, &c.) God's children, indeed, may have these things, but these are no evidences that they are his children, as they are no parts of true religion, nor do they belong to the character of the followers of God.

This sermon, says Mr. Fish, gave an amazing shock to the assembly, and proved extremely offensive. The house was filled with outcries against the preacher, or loud expressions of concern for him. He was upon this declared an opposer of the work of God, making the hearts of his children sad, and strengthening the hands of the wicked. And now matters ripened fast for a separation. The kind of religion of which this extract gives us a glimpse, had, at that early period, according to David Brainerd, spread almost all the land over.

proofs of the fact might easily be adduced. The Rev. John Graham, in a sermon preached in 1745, complains that many had gone forth who preached not the gospel of our Lord Jesus Christ, who denied the doctrines of personal election, of original sin, of justification by the perfect righteousness of Christ, imputed by an act of sovereign grace; instantaneous regeneration by the divine energy of special irresistible grace; and of the final perseverance of the saints. "The Pelagian and Arminian errors," he adds, "cannot but be exceedingly pleasing to the devil; and such as preach them most successfully, are the greatest instruments of supporting his kingdom in the world, and his dominion in the hearts of men. What necessity is then laid upon ministers of the gospel, who see what danger precious souls are in by the spread and prevalence of such pernicious errors, which are like a fog or smoke, sent from the bottomless pit on purpose to prevent the shining of the gospel sun into the hearts of men, to be very close and strict in searching into the principles of such as are candidates for the sacred ministry." *

Somewhat later, President Clap found it necessary, on account of the increasing prevalence of error, to write a formal defence of the doctrines of the New England churches. The leading features of the new divinity, of which he complained, were, 1. That the happiness of the creature is the great end of creation. 2. That self-love is the ultimate foundation of all moral obligation. 3. That God cannot control the acts of free agents. 4. That he cannot certainly foreknow, much less decree such acts. 5. That all sin consists in the voluntary transgression of known law; that Adam was not created in a state of holiness, but only had a power to act virtuously; and every man is now born into the world in as perfect a state of rectitude as that in which Adam was created. 6. The actions of moral agents are not free, and consequently have no moral character, unless such agents have plenary ability and full power to the contrary. Hence it is absurd to suppose that God should implant grace or holiness in any man, or keep him

* Sermon preached at the ordination of Nathan Strong, Oct. 9, 1745, by John Graham, of Southbury.

from sin. 7. Christ did not die to make satisfaction for sin, and hence there is no need to suppose him to be essentially God, but only a perfect and glorious creature. No great weight ought to be laid upon men's believing Christ's divinity, or any of those speculative points which have been generally received as the peculiar and fundamental doctrines of the gospel; but we ought to have charity for all men, let their speculative principles be what they may, provided they lead moral lives.* These doctrines were a great advance on the Arminian or even Pelagian errors over which President Edwards lamented, and show what might indeed be expected, that the churches had gone from bad to worse.

This is certainly a gloomy picture of the state of religion so soon after a revival, regarded as the most extensive the country had ever known. It is drawn not by the enemies, but in a great measure by the best and wisest friends of religion. The preceding account, it is true, relates principally to New England. In the Presbyterian Church the same rapid decline of religion does not appear to have taken place. In 1752, President Edwards, in a letter to Mr. McCulloch, says, "As to the state of religion in America, I have little to write that is comfortable, but there seem to be better appearances in some of the other colonies than in New England."† He specifies particularly New Jersey and Virginia. And we know from other sources that, while the cause of truth and piety was declining in the Eastern States, the Presbyterian Church, especially that portion of it in connection with the Synod of New York, was increasing and flourishing. With regard to orthodoxy, at least, there was little cause of complaint. The only instance on record, during this whole period, of the avowal of Arminian sentiments by a Presbyterian minister, was that of the Rev. Mr. Harker, of the Presbytery of New Brunswick; and he was suspended from the ministry as soon as convicted.‡

* Brief History and Vindication of the Doctrines of the Churches of New England, with a specimen of the new scheme of religion beginning to prevail. By Thomas Clap, President of Yale College. New Haven, 1755.

† Life of Edwards, p. 518.

‡ That there has never been any open and avowed departure from Calvinistic doctrines in the Presbyterian Church, while repeated and extended defec-

This low state of religion, and extensive departure from the truth, in that part of the country where the revival had been most extensive, is certainly *prima facie* proof that there must have been something very wrong in the revival itself. It may, however, be

tions have occurred in New England, is a fact worthy of special consideration. The causes of this remarkable difference in the history of these two portions of the church, may be sought by different persons in different circumstances. Presbyterians may be excused if they regard their form of government as one of the most important of those causes. New England has enjoyed greater religious advantages than any other portion of our country. It was settled by educated and devoted men. Its population was homogeneous and compact. The people were almost all of the same religious persuasion. The Presbyterian Church, on the contrary, has laboured under great disadvantages. Its members were scattered here and there, in the midst of other denominations. Its congregations were widely separated, and, owing to the scattered residences of the people, often very feeble; and, moreover, not unfrequently composed of discordant materials, Irish, Scotch, German, French, and English. Yet doctrinal purity has been preserved to a far greater extent in the latter denomination than in the former. What is the reason? Is it not to be sought in the conservative influence of Presbyterianism? The distinguished advantages possessed by New England, have produced their legitimate effects. It would be not less strange than lamentable, had the institutions, instructions, and example of the pious founders of New England been of no benefit to their descendants. It is to these sources that portion of our country is indebted for its general superiority. The obvious decline in the religious character of the people, and the extensive prevalence, at different periods, of fanaticism and Antinomianism, Arminianism, and Pelagianism, is, as we believe, to be mainly attributed to an unhappy and unscriptural ecclesiastical organization. Had New England, with her compact and homogeneous population, and all her other advantages, enjoyed the benefit of a regular Presbyterian government in the church, it would, in all human probability, have been the noblest ecclesiastical community in the world.

It is well known that a great majority of all the distinguished ministers whom New England has produced, have entertained the opinion here expressed, on the subject. President Edwards, for example, in a letter to Mr. Erskine, said, "I have long been out of conceit of our unsettled, independent, confused way of church government; and the Presbyterian way has ever appeared to me most agreeable to the word of God, and the reason and nature of things." Life, p. 412. Where the preservation of the purity of the church is committed to the mass of the people, who, as a general rule, are incompetent to judge in doctrinal matters, and who, in many cases, are little under the influence of true religion, we need not wonder that corruption should from

said, that the decay of religion through the land generally, is perfectly consistent with the purity of the revival and the flourishing state of those particular churches which had experienced its influence. The facts of the case, unfortunately, do not allow us the benefit of this assumption. It is no doubt true, that in some congregations, as in that of Hebron, mentioned by Trumbull, religion was in a very desirable state, in the midst of the general decline; but it is no less certain, that in many instances, in the very places where the revival was the most remarkable, the declension was the most serious. Northampton itself may be taken as an illustration. "That church was pre-eminently a city set upon a hill. Mr. Stoddard, during a remarkably successful ministry, had drawn the attention of American Christians for fifty-seven years. He had also been advantageously known in the mother country. Mr. Edwards had been their minister for twenty-three years. In the respect paid to him as a profound theological writer, he had no competitor from the first establishment of the colonies, and even then, could scarcely find one in England or Scotland. He had also as high a reputation for elevated and fervent piety as for superiority of talents. During the preceding eighty years, that church had been favoured with more numerous and powerful revivals than any church in Christendom."* This account, though given in the characteristically large style of Edwards's biographer, is no doubt in the main correct. Here then, if any where, we might look for the most favourable results of the revival. During the religious excitement in the years 1734 and 1735, within six months, more than three hundred persons, whom Edwards regarded as true converts, were received into the church.† In 1736, the whole number of communicants was six hundred and twenty, including almost the whole adult population of the town.‡ The revival of 1740–2, was considered still more pure and wonderful. What was the state of

time to time prevail. As Christ has appointed presbyters to rule in the church according to his word, on them devolve the duty and responsibility of maintaining the truth. This charge is safest in the hands of those to whom Christ has assigned it.

* Dwight's Life of Edwards, p. 446. † Edwards's Works, vol. iv. p. 28.

‡ Ibid. p. 27.

religion in this highly favoured place, soon after all these revivals? In the judgment of Edwards himself it was deplorably low, both as to Christian temper and adherence to sound doctrine. In 1744, when an attempt was made to administer discipline somewhat injudiciously, it is true, as to the manner of doing it, it was strenuously resisted. The whole town was thrown into a blaze. Some of the accused "refused to appear; others, who did appear, behaved with a great degree of insolence, and contempt for the authority of the church, and little or nothing could be done further in the affair." * From 1744 to 1748, not a single application was made for admission to the church.† In 1749, when it became known that Edwards had adopted the opinion that none ought to be admitted to the Lord's Supper but such as gave satisfactory evidence of conversion, "the town was put into a great ferment; and before he was heard in his own defence, or it was known by many what his principles were, the general cry was to have him dismissed." ‡ That diversity of opinion between a pastor and his people on such a practical point, should lead to a desire for a separation, might not be very discreditable to either party. But when it is known that on this occasion the church treated such a man as Edwards, who not only was an object of veneration to the Christian public, but who behaved in the most Christian manner through the whole controversy, with the greatest injustice and malignity, it must be regarded as proof positive of the low state of religion among them. They refused to allow him to preach on the subject in dispute; they pertinaciously resisted the calling of a fair council to decide the matter; they insisted on his dismission without making any provision for his expensive family; and when his dismission had taken place, they shut their pulpit against him, even when they had no one else to occupy it. On the unfounded suspicion that he intended to form a new church in the town, they presented a remonstrance containing direct, grievous, and criminal charges against him, which were really gross slanders.§ This was

* Life of Edwards, p. 300. † Ibid. p. 438. ‡ Ibid. p. 306.

§ Ibid. p. 421. See the whole details of this extraordinary history, pp. 288–404.

not the offence of a few individuals. Almost the whole church took part against Edwards.* Such treatment of such a man certainly proves a lamentable state of religion, as far as Christian temper is concerned. With regard to orthodoxy the case was not much better. Edwards in a letter to Erskine, in 1750, says, there seemed to be the utmost danger that the younger generation in Northampton would be carried away with Arminianism as with a flood; that it was not likely that the church would choose a Calvinist as his successor, and that the older people were never so indifferent to things of this nature.†

The explanation which has been proposed of these extraordinary facts, is altogether unsatisfactory. It is said that the custom which had long prevailed in Northampton, of admitting those to the Lord's Supper who gave no sufficient evidence of conversion, sufficiently accounts for all this ill conduct on the part of the church. But where were the three hundred members whom Edwards regarded as "savingly brought home to Christ," ‡ within six months, during the revival of 1734–5? Where were all the fruits of the still more powerful revival of 1740–42? The vast majority of the members of the church had been brought in by Edwards himself, and of their conversion he considered himself as having sufficient evidence. The habit of free admission to the Lord's table, therefore, by no means accounts for the painful facts above referred to. After all that had been published to the world of the power of religion in Northampton, the Christian public were entitled to expect to see the people established in the truth, and an example in holiness to other churches. Instead of this, we find them resisting the administration of discipline in less than eighteen months after the revival; alienated from their pastor; indifferent to the truth, and soon driving from among them the first minister of his age, with every aggravating circumstance of ingratitude and injustice. It is all in vain to talk of the religion of such a people. This fact

* In one place it is said, about twenty heads adhered to their pastor, (Life, p. 464;) in another, that only twenty-three, out of two hundred and thirty male members of the church, voted against his dismission. p. 410.

† Ibid. p. 411. Compare his Farewell Sermon. ‡ Works, vol. iv. p. 28.

demonstrates that there must have been something wrong in these revivals, even under the eye and guidance of Edwards, from the beginning. There must have been many spurious conversions, and much false religion which at the time were regarded as genuine. This assumption is nothing more than the facts demand, nor more than Edwards himself frequently acknowledged. There is the most marked difference between those of his writings which were published during the revival, and those which appeared after the excitement had subsided. In the account which he wrote in 1736, of the revival of the two preceding years, there is scarcely an intimation of any dissatisfaction with its character. Yet, in 1743, he speaks of it as having been very far from pure;* and in 1751, he lamented his not having had boldness to testify against some glaring false appearances, and counterfeits of religion, which became a dreadful source of spiritual pride, and of other things exceedingly contrary to true Christianity.† In like manner, in the contemporaneous account of the revival of 1740–42, he complains of nothing but of some disorders introduced towards the close of the year 1742, from other congregations; whereas, in his letters written a few years later, he acknowledges that many things were wrong from the first. This is, indeed, very natural. While in the midst of the excitement, seeing and feeling much that he could not but regard as the result of divine influence, he was led to encourage many things which soon brought forth the bitter fruits of disorder and corruption. His correspondence affords abundant evidence how fully sensible he became of the extent to which this revival was corrupted with false religion. When his Scottish friends had informed him of the religious excitement then prevailing in some parts of Holland, he wrote to Mr. Erskine, June 28, 1751, expressing his anxiety that the people might be led to "distinguish between true and false religion; between those experiences which are from the saving influence of the Spirit of God, and those which are from Satan transformed into an angel of light." He wished that they had the experience of the church of God in America, on this subject, as they would need all the warning that

* Life, p. 168. † Ibid. p. 465.

could be given them. "The temptation," he adds, "to religious people in such a state to countenance the glaring, shining counterfeits of religion, without distinguishing them from the reality," is so strong that they can hardly be restrained from committing the mistake. In reference to the wish of the Dutch ministers to have attestations of the permanently good effects of the revivals in Scotland and America, he says, "I think it fit they should know the very truth in the case, and that things should be represented neither better nor worse than they are. If they should be represented worse, it would give encouragement to unreasonable opposers; if better, it might prevent a most necessary caution among the true friends of the awakening. There are, undoubtedly, very many instances in New England, in the whole, of the perseverance of such as were thought to have received the saving benefit of the late revivals of religion, and of their continuing to walk in newness of life as becometh saints; instances which are incontestable. But I believe the proportion here is not so great as in Scotland. I cannot say that the greater portion of the supposed converts give reason to suppose, by their conversation, that they are true converts. The proportion may, perhaps, be more truly represented by the proportion of the blossoms on a tree which abide and come to mature fruit, to the whole number of blossoms in the spring."* In another letter, dated Nov. 23, 1752, he expresses his conviction that there was a greater mixture of evil with good in the revival in Holland, than the ministers there supposed; that the consequences of not distinguishing between true and false religion would prove worse than they had any conception of. He then refers to the history of the revival here, and adds that it is not to be expected that "the divines of Europe would lay very much weight on the admonitions which they received from such an obscure part of the world. Other parts of the church of God must be taught as we have been, and when they see and feel, then they will believe. Not that I apprehend there is in any measure so much enthusiasm and disorder mixed with the work in Holland, as was in many parts of America, in the time of the last revival of religion here."†

* Life, p. 459.

† Ibid. p. 508.

These passages give a melancholy account of the results of the great religious excitement now under consideration. In the preceding estimate, Edwards does not speak of those who were merely awakened, or who were for a time the subjects of serious impressions, but of those who were regarded as converts. It is of these, he says, that only a small portion proved to be genuine. If this be so, it certainly proves that, apart from the errors and disorders universally reprobated by the judicious friends of the revival, there were serious mistakes committed by those friends themselves. If it was difficult then, it must be much more so now, to detect the causes of the spurious excitement which then so extensively prevailed. Two of these causes, however, are so obvious that they can hardly fail to attract attention. These were laying too much stress on feelings excited through the imagination, and allowing, and indeed encouraging the free and loud manifestation of feeling during public or social worship.

It is one office of the imagination to recall and reconstruct conceptions of any object which affects the senses. It is by this faculty that we form mental images, or lively conceptions of the objects of sense. It is to this power that graphic descriptions of absent or imaginary scenes are addressed; and it is by the agency of this faculty that oratory, for the most part, exerts its power over the feelings. That a very large portion of the emotions so strongly felt, and so openly expressed during this revival, arose not from spiritual apprehensions of divine truth, but from mere imaginations or mental images, is evident from two sources; first, from the descriptions given of the exercises themselves; and, secondly, from the avowal of the propriety of this method of exciting feeling in connection with religious subjects. Had we no definite information as to this point, the general account of the effects of the preaching of Whitefield and others would satisfy us that, to a very great extent, the results were to be attributed to no supernatural influence, but to the natural powers of oratory. There is no subject so universally interesting as religion, and therefore there is none which can be made the cause of such general and powerful excitement; yet it cannot be doubted that had Whitefield selected any worthy object of benevolence or patriotism, he would have produced a great commotion in the public mind. When therefore he came to address men on a subject of infinite importance, of the deepest personal concern, we need not be surprised at the effects which he produced. The man who could thaw the icy propriety of Bolingbroke; who could extort gold from Franklin, though armed with a determination to give only copper; or set Hopkinson, for the time being, beside himself; might be expected to control at will the passions of the young, the ignorant, and the excitable. It is far from being denied or questioned that his preaching was, to an extraordinary degree, attended by a divine influence. That influence is needed to account for the repentance, faith, and holiness, which were in a multitude of cases the result of his ministrations. It is not needed, however, to account for the loud outcries, faintings, and bodily agitations which attended his course. These are sufficiently explained by his vivid descriptions of hell, of heaven, of Christ, and a future judgment, addressed to congregated thousands of excited and sympathizing hearers, accompanied by the most stirring appeals to the passions, and all delivered with consummate skill of voice and manner. It was under such preaching, the people, as he tells us, soon began to melt, to weep, to cry out, and to faint. That a large part of these results was to be attributed to natural causes, can hardly be doubted; yet who could discriminate between what was the work of the orator, and what was the work of the Spirit of God? Who could tell whether the sorrow, the joy, and the love expressed and felt, were the result of lively imaginations, or of spiritual apprehensions of the truth? The two classes of exercises were confounded; both passed for genuine, until bitter experience disclosed the mistake. It is evident that Whitefield had no opportunity of making any such discrimination; and that for the time at least, he regarded all meltings, all sorrowing, and all joy following his fervid preaching, as evidence of the divine presence. It is not, however, these general accounts so much as the more particular detail of the exercises of the subjects of this revival, which shows how much of the feeling then prevalent was due to the imagination. Thus Edwards speaks of those who had a lively picture in their minds of hell as a dreadful furnace, of Christ as one of glorious majesty, and of a sweet and gracious aspect, or as of one hanging on the cross, and blood running from his wounds.* Great stress was often laid upon these views of "an outward Christ," and upon the feeling resulting from such conceptions. Though Edwards was from the beginning fully aware that there was no true religion in such exercises;† and though in his work on the Affections, written in 1746, he enters largely on the danger of delusion from this source, it is very evident that at this period he was not properly impressed with a sense of guarding against this evil. Just after stating how commonly such mental pictures were cherished by the people, he adds, "surely such things will not be wondered at by those who have observed, how any strong affections about temporal matters will excite lively ideas and pictures of different things in the mind."‡ In his sermon on the distinguishing marks of a work of the Spirit of God, he goes much further. He there says, "Such is our nature, that we cannot think of things invisible without some degree of imagination. I dare appeal to any man of the greatest powers of mind, whether he is able to fix his thoughts on God, or Christ, or the things of another world without imaginary ideas attending his meditation."§ By imaginary ideas, he means mental images, or pictures.|| In the same connection, he adds, "the more engaged the mind is, and the more intense the contemplation and affection, still the more lively and strong will the imaginary idea ordinarily be." Hence, he insists, "that it is no argument that a work is not a work of the Spirit of God, that some who are the subjects of it, have been in

* Works, vol. iv. p. 55.

† See his account of the revival in 1734–5, written in 1736.

‡ Works, vol. iv. p. 55.

§ Ibid. vol. iii. p. 567.

|| This is plain from his own account of them. In his work on the Affections, he says, "All such things as we perceive by our five senses, seeing, hearing, smelling, tasting, and feeling, are external things; and where a person has an idea or image of any of these sorts of things, when they are not there, and when he really does not see, hear, smell, taste, or feel them, that is to have an imagination of them, and these ideas are imaginary ideas." P. 236 of the Elizabethtown edition.

a kind of ecstacy, wherein they have been carried beyond themselves, and have had their minds transported in a train of strong and pleasing imaginations, and a kind of visions, as though they were rapt up even to heaven, and there saw glorious sights."*

It is not to be denied that there is a legitimate use of the imagination in religion. The Bible often addresses itself to this faculty. The descriptions which it gives of the future glory of the church, and of heaven itself, are little else than a series of images; not that we should conceive of the millennium as of a time when the lion and lamb shall feed together, or of heaven as a golden city, but that we may have a more lively impression of the absence of all destructive passions, when Christ shall reign on earth, and that we may learn to think of heaven as a state of surpassing glory. In all such cases, it is the thought which the figure is meant to convey, and not the figure itself, that the mind rests upon in all truly religious exercises. When, on the other hand, the mind fixes on the image, and not upon the thought, and inflames itself with these imaginations, the result is mere curious excitement. So far then as the imagination is used to render the thoughts which the understanding forms of spiritual things distinct and vivid, so far may it minister to our religious improvement. But when it is made a mere chamber of imagery, in which the soul alarms or delights itself with spectres, it becomes the source of all manner of delusions.

It may still further be admitted, that images borrowed from sensible objects often mix with and disturb the truly spiritual contemplations of the Christian, but this is very different from teaching that we cannot think of God, or Christ, or spiritual subjects, without some pictorial representations of them. If such is the constitution of our nature that we must have such imaginary ideas of God himself, then we ought to have and to cherish them. But by the definition, these ideas are nothing but the reproduction and varied combinations of past impressions on the senses. To say, therefore, that we must have such ideas of God, is to say that we must conceive of him and worship him under some corporeal form,

* Works, vol. iii. p. 568.

which is nothing but refined idolatry, and is as much forbidden as the worship of stocks or stones. It certainly needs no argument to show that we cannot form any pictorial representation of a spirit, and least of all, of God; or that such representations of Christ or heaven cannot be the source of any truly religious affections. What have such mental images to do with the apprehension of the evil of sin, of the beauty of holiness, of the mercy of God, of the merits of Christ, or with any of those truths on which the mind acts when under the influence of the Spirit of God?

From the accounts of this revival already quoted, from the detail given of the experience of many of its subjects, and especially from the arguments and apologies just referred to, it is evident that one great source of the false religion, which, it is admitted, then prevailed, was the countenance given to these impressions on the imagination and to the feelings thus excited. It was in vain to tell the people they must distinguish between what was imaginary and what was spiritual; that there was no religion in these lively mental images, when they were at the same time told that it was necessary they should have them, and that the more intense the religious affection, the more vivid would these pictures be. Under such instruction they would strive to form such imaginations; they would doat on them, inflame themselves with them, and consider the vividness of the image, and the violence of the consequent emotion, as the measure of their religious attainment. How deeply sensible Edwards became of the evil which actually arose from this source, may be learned from his work on the Affections. When an "affection arises from the imagination, and is built upon it, as its foundation, instead of a spiritual illumination or discovery, then is the affection, however elevated, worthless and vain."* And in another place he says, "When the Spirit of God is poured out, to begin a glorious work, then the old Serpent, as fast as possible, and by all means, introduces this bastard religion, and mingles it with the true; which has from time to time, brought all things into confusion. The pernicious consequence of it is not easily imagined or conceived of, until we see and are amazed with the awful effects of it, and the

* Religious Affections, p. 320.

dismal desolation it has made. If the revival of true religion be very great in its beginning, yet if this bastard comes in, there is danger of its doing as Gideon's bastard, Abimelech, did, who never left until he had slain all his threescore and ten true-born sons, excepting one, that was forced to flee. The imagination or phantasy seems to be that wherein are formed all those delusions of Satan, which those are carried away with, who are under the influence of false religion, and counterfeit graces and affections. Here is the devil's grand lurking-place, the very nest of foul and delusive spirits."*

If Edwards, who was *facile princeps* among the friends of this revival, could, during its early stages, fall into the error of countenancing the delusions which he afterwards so severely condemned, what could be expected of Whitefield and others, who at this time, (dates must not be neglected, a few years made a great difference both in persons and things,) passed rapidly from place to place, neither making nor being able to make, the least distinction between the effects of an excited imagination, and the exercises of genuine religion? That they would test the experience of their converts by its fruits, is not denied; but that they considered all the commotions which attended their ministrations, as proofs of the Spirit's presence, is evident from their indiscriminate rejoicing over all such manifestations of feeling. These violent agitations produced through the medium of the imagination, though sufficiently prevalent, during the revival in this country, were perhaps still more frequent in England, under the ministrations of Wesley, and, combined with certain peculiarities of his system, have given to the religion of the Methodists its peculiar, and, so far as it is peculiar, its undesirable characteristic.

Another serious evil was the encouragement given to loud outcries, faintings, and bodily agitations during the time of public worship. It is remarkable that these effects of the excitement prevailed generally, not only in this country, but also in Scotland and England. The fanatical portion of the friends of the revival not only encouraged these exhibitions, but regarded them as proofs

* Religious Affections, p. 316.

of the presence and power of the Spirit of God.* The more judicious never went to this extreme, though most of them regarded them with favour. This was the case with Whitefield, Edwards, and Blair.

The manner in which Whitefield describes the scenes at Nottingham and Fagg's Manor, and others of a similar character, shows that he did not disapprove of these agitations. He says he never saw a more glorious sight, than when the people were fainting all round him, and crying out in such a manner as to drown his own voice. Edwards took them decidedly under his protection. He not only mentions, without the slightest indication of disapprobation, that his church was often filled with outcries, faintings, and convulsions, but takes great pains to vindicate the revival from all objection on that account. Though such effects were not, in his view, any decisive evidence of the kind of influence by which they were produced, he contended that it was easy to account for their being produced by a "right influence and a proper sense of things." † He says, ministers are not to be blamed for speaking of these things "as probable tokens of God's presence, and arguments of the success of preaching, because I think they are so indeed. I confess that when I see a great outcry in a congregation, I rejoice in it much more than merely in an appearance of solemn attention, and a show of affection by weeping. To rejoice that the work of God is carried on calmly and without much ado, is in effect to rejoice that it is carried on with less power, or that there is not so much of the influence of God's Spirit." ‡ In the same connection he says, that when these outcries, faintings, and other bodily effects attended the preaching of the truth, he did not "scruple to speak of them, to rejoice in them, and bless God for them," as probable tokens of his presence.

The Boston ministers, on the other hand, appear to have disapproved of these things entirely, as they mention their satisfaction that there had been little or nothing of such "blemishes of the work" among their churches.§ The same view was taken of them

* Fish's Sermons. Trumbull's History, vol. ii. p. 161. Chauncey's Seasonable Thoughts, p. 78, 93.

† Works, vol. iii. p. 563.

‡ Ibid. vol. iv. p. 169.

§ Christian History, vol. ii. p. 386.

by President Dickinson, William Tennent, of Freehold, and many others.

That the fanatics, who regarded these bodily agitations and outcries as evidences of conversion, committed a great and dangerous mistake, need not be argued; and that Edwards and others, who rejoiced over and encouraged them, as probable tokens of the favour of God, fell into an error scarcely less injurious to religion, will, at the present day, hardly be questioned. That such effects frequently attend religious excitements is no proof that they proceed from a good source. They may owe their origin to the corrupt, or at least merely natural feelings, which always mingle, to a greater or less degree, with strong religious exercises. It is a matter of great practical importance to learn what is the true cause of these effects; to ascertain whether they proceed from those feelings which are produced by the Spirit of God, or from those which arise from other sources. If the former, we ought to rejoice over them; if the latter, they ought to be repressed and discountenanced.

That such bodily agitations owe their origin not to any divine influence, but to natural causes, may be inferred from the fact that these latter are adequate to their production. They are not confined to those persons whose subsequent conduct proves them to be the subjects of the grace of God; but, to say the least, are quite as frequently experienced by those who know nothing of true religion. Instead, therefore, of being referred to those feelings which are peculiar to the people of God, they may safely be referred to those which are common to them and to unrenewed men. Besides, such effects are not peculiar to what we call revivals of religion; they have prevailed, in seasons of general excitement, in all ages and in all parts of the world, among pagans, papists, and every sect of fanatics which has ever disgraced the Christian church. We are, therefore, not called upon to regard such things with much favour, or to look upon them as probable tokens of the presence of God. That the bodily agitations attendant on revivals of religion are of the same nature, and attributable to the same cause, as the convulsions of enthusiasts, is in the highest degree probable, because they arise under the same circumstances, are propagated by the same means, and cured by the same treatment. They arise in seasons of great, and especially of general excitement; they, in a great majority of cases, affect the ignorant rather than the enlightened, those in whom the imagination predominates over the reason, and especially those who are of a nervous temperament, rather than those of an opposite character. These affections all propagate themselves by a kind of infection. This circumstance is characteristic of this whole class of nervous diseases. Physicians enumerate among the causes of epilepsy "seeing a person in convulsions." This fact was so well known, that the Romans made a law, that if any one should be seized with epilepsy during the meeting of the comitia, the assembly should be immediately dissolved. This disease occurred so frequently in those exciting meetings, and was propagated so rapidly, that it was called the *morbus comitialis*. Among the enthusiasts who frequented the tomb of the Abbé Paris, in the early part of the last century, convulsions were of frequent occurrence, and never failed to prove infectious. During a religious celebration in the church of Saint Roch, at Paris, a young lady was seized with convulsions, and within half an hour between fifty and sixty were similarly affected.* A multitude of facts of the same kind might be adduced. Sometimes such affections become epidemic, spreading over whole provinces. In the fifteenth century, a violent nervous disease, attended with convulsions, and other analogous symptoms, extended over a great part of Germany, especially affecting the inmates of the convents. In the next century something of the same kind prevailed extensively in the south of France. These affections were then regarded as the result of demoniacal possessions, and in some instances, multitudes of poor creatures were put to death as demoniacs.†

* Dictionaire des Sciences Médicales, Article Convulsionnaire. In this same article it is stated, that a young woman affected with a spasmodic and continued hiccup, producing a noise very similar to the barking of a dog, was placed in a hospital in the same room with four other female patients, and in a few days they were all seized with the same nervous disease.

† Marshal Villars says in his Memoires, "Qu'il a vu dans les Cevennes une ville entière dont toutes les femmes et les filles, sans exception, paraissaient

The bodily agitations attending the revival, were in like manner propagated by infection. On their first appearance in Northampton, a few persons were seized at an evening meeting, and while others looked on they soon became similarly affected; even those who appear to have come merely out of curiosity did not escape. The same thing was observable at Nottingham, Fagg's Manor, and other places, under the preaching of Whitefield. It was no less obvious in Scotland. It was exceedingly rare for any one to be thus affected in private; but in the public meetings, when one person was seized, others soon caught the infection. In England, where these affections were regarded at least at first, by Wesley, as coming from God, and proofs of his favour, they were very violent, and spread with great rapidity, seizing, at times, upon opposers as well as friends. Thus on one occasion, it is stated, that a Quaker who was present at one meeting, and inveighed against what he called the dissimulation of these creatures, caught the contagious emotion himself, and even while he was biting his lips and knitting his brows, dropt down as if he had been struck by lightning. "The agony he was in," says Wesley, "was even terrible to behold; we besought God not to lay folly to his charge, and he soon lifted up his head and cried aloud, 'Now I know thou art a prophet of the Lord."* On another occasion, under the preaching of the Rev. Mr. Berridge, a man who had been mocking and mimicking others in their convulsions, was himself seized. "He was," says the narrator, "the most horrible human figure I ever saw. His large wig and hair were coal-black, his face distorted beyond all description. He roared incessantly, throwing and clapping his hands together with his whole force. Some of his brother scoffers were calling for horsewhips, till they saw him extended on his back at full length; they then said he was dead; and indeed the only sign of life was the working of his breast, and the distortions of his face, while the veins of his neck were swelled as if ready to burst. His agonies lasted some hours; then his body

possédées du diable; elles tremblaient et prophétisaient publiquement dans les rues," &c.

* Southey's Life of Wesley, vol. i. p. 221.

and soul were eased."* "At another meeting," he says, "a stranger who stood facing me, fell backward to the wall, then forward on his knees, wringing his hands and roaring like a bull. His face at first turned quite red, then almost black. He rose and ran against the wall, till Mr. Keeling and another held him. He screamed out, 'Oh! what shall I do! what shall I do! oh, for one drop of the blood of Christ!' As he spoke, God set his soul at liberty; he knew his sins were blotted out; and the rapture he was in seemed too great for human nature to bear." "One woman tore up the ground with her hands, filling them with dust and with the hard trodden grass, on which I saw her lie as one dead. Some continued long, as if they were dead, but with a calm sweetness in their looks. I saw one who lay two or three hours in the open air, and being then carried into the house, continued insensible another hour, as if actually dead. The first sign of life she showed, was a rapture of praise intermixed with a small joyous laughter."† These accounts, however, must be read in detail, in order to have any adequate conception of the nature and extent of these dreadful nervous affections. Wesley at one time regarded them as direct intimations of the approbation of God. Preaching at Newgate, he says, he was led insensibly, and without any previous design, to declare strongly and explicitly, that God willed all men to be saved, and to pray that, if this was not the truth of God, he would not suffer the blind to go out of the way; but if it was, he would bear witness to his word. "Immediately one and another sunk to the earth; they dropt on every side as thunderstruck." "In the evening I was again pressed in spirit to declare that Christ gave himself a ransom for all. And almost before we called upon him to set to his seal, he answered. One was so wounded by the sword of the Spirit, that you would have imagined she could not live a moment. But immediately his abundant kindness was shown, and she loudly sang of his righteousness."‡

* Southey's Life of Wesley, vol. ii. p. 238. † Ibid. vol. ii. p. 237.

‡ Southey's Life of Wesley, vol. i. p. 219.—How Wesley viewed this subject at a somewhat later period, may be learned from the following extract: "The danger *was*," says he, "to regard extraordinary circumstances too

The various bodily exercises which attended the Western revivals in our own country, in the early part of the present century, were of the same nature, and obeyed precisely the same laws. They began with what was called the falling exercise; that is, the person

much; such as outcries, convulsions, visions, trances, as if they were essential to the inward work, so that it could not go on without them. Perhaps the danger *is*, to regard them too little; to condemn them altogether; to imagine they had nothing of God in them, and were a hinderance to his work; whereas the truth is, 1. God suddenly and strongly convinced many that they were lost sinners; the natural consequences whereof were sudden outcries, and strong bodily convulsions. 2. To strengthen and encourage them that believed, and to make his work more apparent, he favoured several of them with divine dreams; others with trances and visions. 3. In some of these instances, after a time, nature mixed with grace. 4. Satan likewise mimicked this work of God, in order to discredit the whole work; and yet it is not wise to give up this part any more than to give up the whole. At first it was, doubtless, wholly from God; it is partly so at this day; and he will enable us to discern how far, in every case, the work is pure, and when it mixes and degenerates. Let us even suppose that, in some few cases, there was a mixture of dissimulation; that persons pretended to see and feel what they did not, and imitated the cries and convulsive motions of those who were really overpowered by the Spirit of God; yet even this should not make us either undervalue or deny the real work of the Spirit. The shadow is no disparagement of the substance, nor the counterfeit of the real diamond." Quoted by Southey, vol. ii. p. 242. Wesley seems to have felt himself obliged to regard these agitations as springing from dissimulation, from Satan's influence, or from the Spirit of God. The far more natural solution, that they were a nervous disease, common in all ages, during seasons of excitement, he overlooks.

The Rev. Richard Watson, in his Life of Wesley, says very little on this subject. He evidently took much the same view of the matter as that presented in the above extract. "Of the extraordinary circumstances," says he, "which have usually accompanied such visitations, it may be said, that if some should be resolved into purely natural causes, some into real enthusiasm, and (under favour of our philosophers) others in satanic imitation, a sufficient number will remain, which can only be explained by considering them as results of a strong impression made upon the consciences and affections of men, by an influence ascertained to be divine by its unquestionable effects upon the heart and life. Nor is it either irrational or unscriptural to suppose, that times of great national darkness and depravity, the case certainly of this country at the outset of Wesley and his colleagues in their glorious career, should require a strong remedy; and that the attention of a sleeping people should

affected would fall on the ground helpless as an infant. This was soon succeeded, in many places, by a species of convulsions called the jerks. Sometimes it would affect the whole body, jerking it violently from place to place, regardless of all obstacles; at others, a single limb would be thus agitated. When the neck was attacked, the head would be thrown backwards and forwards with the most fearful rapidity. There were various other forms in which this disease manifested itself, such as whirling, rolling, running, and jumping. These exercises were evidently involuntary. They were highly infectious, and spread rapidly from place to place; often seizing on mere spectators, and even upon those who abhorred and dreaded them.*

Another characteristic of these affections, whether occurring among pagans, papists, or protestants, and which goes to prove their identity, is, that they all yield to the same treatment. As they arise from impressions on the nervous system through the imagination, the remedy is addressed to the imagination. It consists in removing the exciting causes, that is, withdrawing the patient from the scenes and contemplations which produced the disease; or in making a strong counter-impression, either through fear, shame, or sense of duty. The possessions, as they were called, in the south of France, were put a stop to by the wisdom and firmness of certain bishops, who insisted on the separation

be roused by circumstances which could not fail to be noticed by the most unthinking."—Life of Wesley, by Richard Watson, p. 28.

* Biblical Repertory, 1834, p. 351.—An intelligent physician, who had many opportunities of personal observation, gives the following account of these singular exercises: "Different persons are variously affected. Some rise to their feet and spin round like a top; while others dance till they fall down exhausted. Some throw back their heads with convulsive laughter, while others, drowned in tears, break forth in sighs and lamentations. Some fall from their seats in a state of insensibility, and lie for hours without consciousness; while others are affected with violent convulsions resembling epilepsy. During the convulsive paroxysm, recollection and sensation are but little impaired; a slight stupor generally supervenes. The animal functions are not much interrupted; the pulse is natural; the temperature is that of health throughout the paroxysm. After it has subsided, there is a soreness of the muscles, and a slight pain in the head, which soon pass away."

and seclusion of all the affected. On another occasion, a strange nervous agitation, which had for some time, to the great scandal of religion, seized periodically on all the members of a convent, was arrested by the magistrates bringing up a company of soldiers, and threatening with severe punishment the first who should manifest the least symptom of the affection.* The same method has often been successfully resorted to.† In like manner the convulsions attending revivals have been prevented or arrested, by producing the conviction that they were wrong or disgraceful. They hardly ever appeared, or at least continued, where they were not approved and encouraged. In Northampton, where Edwards rejoiced over them, they were abundant; in Boston, where they were regarded as "blemishes," they had nothing of them. In Sutton, Massachusetts, they were "cautiously guarded against," and consequently never appeared, except among strangers from other congregations.‡ Only two or three cases occurred in Elizabethtown, under President Dickinson, who considered them as "irregular heats," and those few were speedily regulated. There was nothing of the kind at Freehold, where William Tennent set his face against all such manifestations of enthusiasm. On the other hand, they followed Davenport and other fanatical preachers, almost wherever they went. In Scotland, they were less encouraged than they were here, and consequently prevailed less. In England, where Wesley regarded them as certainly from God, they were fearful both as to frequency and violence. The same thing was observed with regard to the agitations attending the Western revivals. The physician already quoted, says: "Restraint often prevents a paroxysm. For

* Dictionnaire des Sciences Médicales. Article Convulsionnaire.

† It was by an appeal to the principle of shame, that the frequent suicides among the young women of Miletus were prevented. Under the influence of an epidemic alienation, according to Plutarch, the young females hung themselves in great numbers; but when the magistrates threatened the disgraceful exposure of the body of the next *felo de se*, the epidemic was arrested. A similar alienation, which had seized the women in a portion of the department of Simplon, was cured by a strong appeal to their moral sense and religious feelings.

‡ Christian History, vol. ii. p. 168.

example, persons always attacked by this affection in churches where it is encouraged, will be perfectly calm in churches where it is discouraged, however affecting may be the service, and however great the mental excitement."* It is also worthy of consideration that these bodily affections are of frequent occurrence at the present day, among those who continue to desire and encourage them.

It appears, then, that these nervous agitations are of frequent occurrence in all times of strong excitement. It matters little whether the excitement arise from superstition, fanaticism, or from the preaching of the truth. If the imagination be strongly affected, the nervous system is very apt to be deranged, and outcries, faintings, convulsions, and other hysterical symptoms, are the consequence. That these effects are of the same nature, whatever may be the remote cause, is plain, because the phenomena are the same; the apparent circumstances of their origin the same; they all have the same infectious nature, and are all cured by the same means. They are, therefore, but different forms of the same disease; and, whether they occur in a convent or a camp-meeting, they are no more a token of the divine favour than hysteria or epilepsy.

It may still be said, that, although they do sometimes arise from other causes, they may be produced by genuine religious feeling. This, however, never can be proved. The fact that undoubted Christians experience these effects, is no proof that they flow from a good source; because there is always a corrupt mixture in the exercises of the most spiritual men. These affections *may*, therefore, flow from the concomitants of genuine religious feelings, and

* The characteristic now under consideration did not escape the accurate observation of Edwards, though it failed to disclose to him the true nature of these nervous agitations. "It is evident," he says, "from experience, that custom has a strange influence in these things. If some person conducts them, that much countenances and encourages such manifestations of great affections, they naturally and insensibly prevail, and grow by degrees unavoidable; but afterwards, when they come under another kind of conduct, the manner of external appearances will strongly alter. It is manifest that example and custom have some way or other a secret and unsearchable influence upon those actions which are involuntary, in different places, and in the same place at different times."—Thoughts on the Revival. Works, vol. iv. p. 232.

not from those feelings themselves. And that they do in fact flow from that source, may be assumed, because in other cases they certainly have that origin; and because all the known effects of true religious feelings are of a different character. Those apprehensions of truth which arise from divine illumination, do not affect the imagination, but the moral emotions, which are very different in their nature and effects from the feelings produced by a heated fancy. This view of the subject is greatly confirmed by the consideration, that there is nothing in the Bible to lead us to regard these bodily affections as the legitimate effects of religious feeling. No such results followed the preaching of Christ, or his apostles. We hear of no general outcries, faintings, convulsions, or ravings in the assemblies which they addressed. The scriptural examples cited by the apologists of these exhibitions are so entirely inapplicable, as to be of themselves sufficient to show how little countenance is to be derived from the Bible for such irregularities. Reference is made, for example, to the case of the jailer at Philippi, who fell down at the apostles' feet; to Acts ii. 37, ("Now when they heard this, they were pricked in their heart, and said, Men and brethren, what shall we do?") and to the conversion of Paul. It is, however, too obvious to need remark, that in no one of these cases was either the effect produced, or the circumstances attending its production, analogous to the hysterical convulsions and outcries now under consideration.

The testimony of the Scriptures is not merely negative on this subject. Their authority is directly opposed to all such disorders. They direct that all things should be done decently and in order. They teach us that God is not the God of confusion, but of peace, in all the churches of the saints. These passages have particular reference to the manner of conducting public worship. They forbid every thing which is inconsistent with order, solemnity, and devout attention. It is evident that loud outcries and convulsions are inconsistent with these things, and therefore ought to be discouraged. They cannot come from God, for he is not the author of confusion. The apology made in Corinth for the disorders which Paul condemned, was precisely the same as that urged in defence of these bodily agitations. We ought not to resist the Spirit of God, said the Corinthians; and so said all those who encouraged these convulsions. Paul's answer was, that no influence which comes from God destroys our self-control. "The spirits of the prophets are subject to the prophets." Even in the case of direct inspiration and revelation, the mode of communication was in harmony with our rational nature, and left our powers under the control of reason and the will. The man, therefore, who felt the divine afflatus had no right to give way to it, under circumstances which would produce noise and confusion. The prophets of God were not like the raving Pythoness of the heathen temples; nor are the saints of God converted into whirling dervishes by any influence of which he is the author. There can be little doubt that Paul would have severely reprobated such scenes as frequently occurred during the revival of which we are speaking. He would have said to the people substantially, what he said to the Corinthians. If any unbeliever or ignorant man come to your assemblies, and hear one shouting in ecstacy, another howling in anguish; if he see some falling, some jumping, some lying in convulsions, others in trances, will he not say, Ye are mad? But if your exercises are free from confusion, and your discourses addressed to the reason, so as to convince and reprove, he will confess that God is among you of a truth.

Experience, no less than Scripture, has set the seal of reprobation upon these bodily agitations. If they are of the nature of an infectious nervous disease, it is as much an act of infatuation to encourage them, as to endeavour to spread epilepsy over the land. It is easy to excite such things, but when excited, it is very difficult to suppress them, or to arrest their progress; and they have never prevailed without the most serious mischief. They bring discredit upon religion, they give great advantage to infidels and gainsayers, and they facilitate the progress of fanaticism. When sanctioned, the people delight in them, as they do in all strong excitement. The multitude of spurious conversions, the prevalence of false religion, the rapid progress of fanaticism, and the consequent permanent declension of religion immediately after the great revival, are probably to be attributed to the favour shown to these bodily agitations, as much as to any one cause.

Besides the errors above specified, which were sanctioned by many of the best friends of the revival, there were others which, though reprobated by the more judicious, became, through the patronage of the more ardent, prolific sources of evil. There was from the first a strong leaven of enthusiasm, manifesting itself in the regard paid to impulses, inspirations, visions, and the pretended power of discerning spirits. This was decidedly opposed by Edwards,* by the Boston clergy, by Tennent, and many others. Whitefield, on the contrary, was, especially in the early part of his career, deeply infected with this leaven. When he visited Northampton, in 1740, Edwards endeavoured to convince him of the dangerous tendency of this enthusiastic spirit, but without much success.† He had such an idea of what the Scriptures mean by the guidance of the Spirit, as to suppose that by suggestions, impressions, or sudden recollection of texts of the Bible, the Christian's duty was divinely revealed, even as to the minutest circumstance, and that at times even future events were thus made known. On the strength of such an impression he did not hesitate publicly to declare that his unborn child would prove to be a son.‡ "An unaccountable but very strong impression," that he should preach the gospel, was regarded as a revelation of the purpose of God respecting him.§ The question whether he should return to England was settled to his satisfaction, by the occurrence to his mind of the passage, When Jesus was returned, the people gladly received him.‖ These few examples are enough to illustrate the point in hand.

In Whitefield there was much to counteract the operation of this spirit, which in others produced its legitimate effects. When Davenport was asked by the Boston ministers the reason of any of his acts, his common reply was, God commanded me. When asked

* Thoughts on the Revival, Works, vol. iv. p. 180.

† Life of Edwards, p. 147.

‡ Gillies' Life of Whitefield, p. 63.

§ Whitefield's account of his own Life, p. 11.

‖ Journal from Savannah to England, p. 28.

whether he was inspired, he answered, they might call it inspiration, or what they pleased. The man who attended him he called his armour-bearer, because he was led to take him as a follower, by opening on the story of Jonathan and his armour-bearer. He considered it also as revealed, that he should convert as many persons at a certain place, as Jonathan and his armour-bearer slew of the Philistines.*

This was the only one of the forms in which this spirit manifested itself. Those under its influence pretended to a power of discerning spirits, of deciding at once who was and who was not converted; they professed a perfect assurance of the favour of God, founded not upon scriptural evidence, but inward suggestion. It is plain that when men thus give themselves up to the guidance of secret impressions, and attribute divine authority to suggestions, impulses, and casual occurrences, there is no extreme of error or folly to which they may not be led. They are beyond the control of reason or the word of God. They have a more direct and authoritative communication of the divine will than can be made by any external and general revelation. They of course act as if inspired and infallible. They are commonly filled with spiritual pride, and with a bitter denunciatory spirit. All these results were soon manifested to a lamentable extent during this revival. If an honest man doubted his conversion, he was declared unconverted. If any one was filled with great joy, he was pronounced a child of God. These enthusiasts paid great regard to visions and trances, and would pretend in them to have seen heaven or hell, and particular persons in the one or the other. They paid more attention to inward impressions than to the word of God. They laid great stress on views of an outward Christ, as on a throne, or upon the cross. If they did not feel a minister's preaching, they maintained he was unconverted, or legal. They made light of all meetings in which there was no external commotion. They had a remarkable haughtiness and self-sufficiency, and a fierce and bitter spirit of zeal and censoriousness.†

* Chauncy's Seasonable Thoughts, p. 196–198.

† Trumbull's History, vol. ii. p. 169; whose account is here abridged.

The origin and progress of this fanatical spirit is one of the most instructive portions of the history of this period. In 1726, a religious excitement commenced in New Milford, Connecticut, which was at first of a promising character, but was soon perverted. Its subjects opened a communication with the enthusiasts of Rhode Island, and began to speak slightly of the Bible, especially of the Psalms of David, and to condemn the ministers of the gospel and civil magistrates. They organized themselves into a separate society, and appointed officers not only to conduct their meetings, but to regulate their dress. They made assurance essential to faith; they undervalued human learning, and despised the ordinances of baptism and the Lord's supper. They laid claim to sinless perfection, and claimed that the standing ministers were unfit to preach, and that the people ought to leave them.* One of the leaders of this company was a man named Ferris, who entered Yale College in 1729. A contemporary writer says of this gentleman, He told me he was certain not one in ten of the communicants in the church in New Haven could be saved; that he should have a higher seat in heaven than Moses; that he knew the will of God in all things, and had not committed any sin for six years. He had a proud and haughty spirit, and appeared greatly desirous of applause. He obtained a great ascendency over certain of the students, especially Davenport, Wheelock, and Pomeroy, who lived with him most familiarly. He remained in college until 1732, and then returned to New Milford. He ultimately became a Quaker preacher.†

Such was the origin of that enthusiastical and fanatical spirit, which swept over the New England churches. Messrs. Wheelock and Pomeroy seem soon to have escaped from its influence; but Davenport remained long under its power, and was the cause of incalculable mischief. He was settled as pastor of the church in Southhold, Long Island. In March, 1740, he became satisfied that God had revealed to him that his kingdom was coming with

* Letter of the Rev. D. Boardman, pastor of the church at New Milford, dated, 1742, and printed in Chauncy's Seasonable Thoughts, p. 202.

† Chauncy, p. 212–15.

great power, and that he had an extraordinary call to labour for its advancement. He assembled his people on one occasion, and addressed them, continuously, for nearly twenty-four hours; until he became quite wild.* After continuing for some time his exciting labours in his own neighbourhood, he passed over into Connecticut. The best and most favourable account of his erratic course, is given by the Rev. Mr. Fish,† who knew him intimately. The substance of this account, given nearly in the language of its author, is as follows. The good things about him, says this writer, were, that he was a fast friend of the doctrines of grace; fully declaring the total depravity, the deplorable wretchedness and danger, and utter inability of men by the fall. He preached with great earnestness the doctrines of man's dependence on the sovereign mercy of God; of regeneration; of justification by faith, &c. The things that were evidently and dreadfully wrong about him were, that he not only gave full liberty to noise and outcries, but promoted them with all his power. When these things prevailed among the people, accompanied with bodily agitations, the good man pronounced them tokens of the presence of God. Those who passed immediately from great distress to great joy, he declared, after asking them a few questions, to be converts; though numbers of such converts, in a short time, returned to their old way of living, and were as carnal, wicked, and void of experience, as ever they were. He was a great favourer of visions, trances, imaginations, and powerful impressions in others, and made such inward feelings the rule of his own conduct in many respects. He greatly encouraged lay exhorters, who were soon, in many cases, preferred by the people to the letter-learned rabbies, scribes, pharisees, and unconverted ministers, phrases which the good man would frequently use with such peculiar marks not only of odium, but of indication, as served to destroy the confidence of the people in their ministers. The worst thing, however, was his bold and daring enterprise of going through the country to examine all the ministers in private, and then publicly declaring his judgment of their spiritual state. This he did wherever he could be admitted to ex-

* Chauncy, p. 189.

† Sermons, p. 116.

amine them. Some that he examined, (though for aught that ap peared as godly as himself,) were pronounced in his public prayer, immediately after the examination, to be unconverted. Those who refused to be examined, were sure to suffer the same fate. By this tremendous step many people, relying on his judgment, were assured they had unconverted ministers; others became jealous of their pastors; and all were told by this wild man, that they had as good eat ratsbane as hear an unconverted minister. In his zeal to destroy idolatry, that is, pride in dress, he prevailed upon a number of his followers in New London, to cast into a fire, prepared for the purpose, each his idol. Whereupon some article of dress, or some ornament, was by each stripped off and committed to the flames. In like zeal to root out heresy, a number of religious books, some of them of real excellence, were cast into the fire.*

When he visited Saybrook in August, 1741, he requested Mr. Hart to grant him the use of his pulpit. Mr. Hart replied, that he wished to know, before he could decide on his application, whether he had denounced many of his fathers and brethren in the ministry as unconverted. He said he had, and that his object was the purification of the church, and that he freely urged the people not to attend the ministry of those whom he had thus judged. The pulpit was of course refused him. He then rose and calling to his adherents, said, Come, let us go forth without the camp, after the Lord Jesus, bearing his reproach. Oh this is pleasant to suffer reproach for the blessed Jesus, sweet Jesus!† How true to nature this is! The man who was going about the country de-

* Among the books thus consumed were Beveridge's Thoughts on Religion; part of Flavel's works; one piece of Dr. Increase Mather's, one of Dr. Colman's, &c. &c. Another contemporary gives us an illustration of his manner in the following account. On one occasion, having made a fervent address, "he called all the distressed into the foremost seats. He then came out of the pulpit and stripped off his upper garments, got up on the seats, and leapt up and down for some time, and clapt his hands, and cried out in these words: The war goes on; the fight goes on; the devil goes down, the devil goes down. And he took himself to stamping and screaming most dreadfully." Chauncy, p. 99.

† Chauncy, p. 154, where the account of this interview, signed by Mr. Hart and four other persons, is given at length.

nouncing ministers, and overturning congregations, complains of persecution, because a pastor shuts his pulpit against him.

Mr. Davenport went to Boston in June, 1742. He attended the morning service upon the Sabbath, but in the afternoon absented himself "from an apprehension of the minister's being unconverted, which," says Mr. Prince, "greatly alarmed us." The following day the ministers had a friendly conference with him, which led to their publishing a declaration testifying against his depending on impulses, his condemning ministers, his going through the streets singing, and his encouraging lay exhorters. This declaration was signed by fourteen ministers of Boston and Charlestown. Mr. Davenport denounced the pastors, naming some as unconverted, and representing the rest as Jehoshaphat in Ahab's army, and exhorting the people to separate from them. This, adds Mr. Prince, put an effectual stop to the revival.*

The same year he was arrested and taken before the legislature of Connecticut, on the charge of disorderly conduct. The Assembly judged that although his conduct had a tendency to disturb the peace, yet as "the said Davenport was under the influence of enthusiastical impressions and impulses, and thereby disordered in the rational faculties of his mind, he is rather to be pitied and compassionated, than to be treated as otherwise he might be." They therefore ordered that he should be transported out of the colony, and handed over to his friends. The solution here given of Davenport's conduct, is certainly the most charitable. That any young man should go about the country to examine grey-headed ministers on their experience, denouncing such as would not submit to his inquisition; declaring some of the best men in the church to be unconverted; exhorting the people to desert their ministry; making religion to consist in noisy excitement, and trampling on order and decency in the house of God, can only be accounted for on the assumption of insanity or wickedness. Davenport's subsequent retractions, his altered conduct, and the judgment of his contemporaries, are all in favour of the former solution.

After having pursued his disorderly and destructive course for

* Christian History, vol. ii. p. 407–8.

a number of years, he was convinced of his errors, and published a confession, in which he acknowledged that he had been influenced by a false spirit in judging ministers; in exhorting their people to forsake their ministry; in making impulses a rule of conduct; in encouraging lay exhorters; and in disorderly singing in the streets. He speaks of the burning the books and clothes at New London, as matter for deep and lasting humiliation, and prays that God would guard him from such errors in future, and stop the progress of those who had been corrupted by his word and example.* This latter petition was not granted. He found it easy to kindle the flame of fanaticism, but impossible to quench it. "When he came," says Mr. Fish, "to Stonington, after his recantation, it was with such a mild, pleasant, meek, and humble spirit, broken and contrite, as I scarce ever saw exceeded or equalled. He not only owned his fault in private, and in a most Christian manner asked forgiveness of some ministers whom he had before treated amiss, but in a large assembly made a public recantation of his errors and mistakes."† This same writer informs us, however, that those who were ready to adore him in the time of his false zeal, now denounced him as dead, as having joined with the world and carnal ministers. The work of disorder and division, therefore, went on, little hindered by Mr. Davenport's repentance; and the evils continue to this day. Davenport afterwards removed to New Jersey, and settled at Pennington, within the bounds of the Presbytery of New Brunswick. His remains lie in a grave-yard attached to a small church, long since in ruins.

The censorious spirit, which so extensively prevailed at this period, was another of those fountains of bitter waters, which destroyed the health and vigour of the church. That it should characterize such acknowledged fanatics as Davenport and his associates, is what might be expected. It was, however, the reproach and sin of far better men. Edwards stigmatizes it, as the worst disease which attended the revival, "the most contrary to the spirit and rules of Christianity, and of the worst consequences."‡ The

* Christian History, No. 82, 83. Gillies, vol. ii. p. 180.

† Sermons quoted above. ‡ Works, vol. iv. p. 238.

evil in question consists in regarding and treating, on insufficient grounds, those who profess to be Christians, as though they were hypocrites. The only adequate ground for publicly discrediting such profession, is the denial of those doctrines which the Bible teaches us are essential to true religion, or a course of conduct incompatible with the Christian character. There are, indeed, cases where there is no want of orthodoxy, and no irregularity of conduct, in which we cannot avoid painful misgivings. But such misgivings are no sufficient ground on which to found either public declarations, or public treatment of those who may be the object of them. Does any one dare, on any such ground, to declare a man of reputable character a thief, or a drunkard, or to surmise away the honour of a virtuous woman? Such conduct is not only a sin against God, but a penal offence against society. Yet in no such case is the pain inflicted, or the mischief occasioned, comparable to what arises from taking from a minister his character for piety, and teaching the people to regard him as a hypocrite. This is often done, however, with heartless unconcern. It was by the dreadful prevalence of this habit of censorious judging during the revival, that the confidence of the people in their pastors was destroyed, their usefulness arrested, their congregations divided, and the fire-brands of jealousy and malice cast into every society, and almost into every household. It was this, more than any thing else, that produced that conflagration in which the graces, the peace, and union of the church were consumed. Though this censorious spirit prevailed most among those who had the least reason to think themselves better than others, it was to a lamentable degree the failing of really good men.

It is impossible to open the journals of Whitefield without being painfully struck, on the one hand with the familiar confidence with which he speaks of his own religious experience, and on the other with the carelessness with which he pronounces others to be godly or graceless, on the slightest acquaintance or report. Had these journals been the private record of his feelings and opinions, this conduct would be hard to excuse; but as they were intended for the public, and actually given to the world almost as soon as written, it constitutes a far more serious offence. Thus he tells us, he called on a clergyman, (giving the initials of his name, which, under the circumstances completely identified him,) and was kindly received, but found "he had no experimental knowledge of the new birth." Such intimations are slipped off, as though they were matters of indifference. On equally slight grounds he passed judgment on whole classes of men. After his rapid journey through New England, he published to the world his apprehension "lest many, nay most that preach do not experimentally know Christ."* After being six days in Boston, he recorded his opinion, derived from what he heard, that the state of Cambridge college for piety and true godliness, was not better than that of the English universities,† which he elsewhere says, "were sunk into mere seminaries of paganism, Christ or Christianity being scarce so much as named among them." Of Yale he pronounces the same judgment, saying of it and Harvard, "their light is now become darkness, darkness that may be felt." A vindication of Harvard was written by the Rev. Edward Wigglesworth, a man "so conspicuous for his talents, and so exemplary for every Christian virtue," that he was unanimously appointed the first Hollis professor of divinity in the college. The President of Yale, at that time, was the Rev. Dr. Clap, an orthodox and learned man, "exemplary for piety," and zealous for the truth.‡ Whitefield was much in the habit of speaking of ministers as being unconverted; so that the consequence was, that in a country where "the preaching and conversation of far the bigger part of the ministers were undeniably as became the gospel, such a spirit of jealousy and evil surmising was raised by the influence and example of a young foreigner, that perhaps there was not a single town," either in Massachusetts or Connecticut, in which many of the people were not so prejudiced against their pastors, as to be rendered very unlikely to be benefited by them.§ This is the testimony of men who had received Mr. Whitefield, on his

* New England Journal, p. 95.

† Ibid. p. 12.

‡ Allen's American Biographical Dictionary.

§ Letter to the Rev. George Whitefield, by Edward Wigglesworth, in the name of the faculty of Harvard College, 1745.

first visit with open arms. They add, that the effect of his preaching, and of that of Mr. Tennent, was, that before he left New England, ministers were commonly spoken of as pharisees and unconverted.* The fact is, Whitefield had, in England, got into the habit of taking it for granted, that every minister was unconverted, unless he had special evidence to the contrary. This is not to be wondered at, since, according to all contemporaneous accounts, the great majority of the episcopal clergy of that day did not profess to hold the doctrines of grace, nor to believe in what Whitefield considered experimental religion. There was, therefore, no great harm in taking for granted that men had not, what they did not profess to have. When, however, he came to New England, where the great majority of the ministers still continued to profess the faith of their fathers, and laid claim to the character of experimental Christians in Whitefield's own sense of the term, it was a great injustice to proceed on the assumption that these claims were false, and take it for granted that all were graceless who had not to him exhibited evidence to the contrary.

The same excuse cannot be made for Mr. Tennent; and as his character was more impetuous, so his censures were more sweeping and his denunciations more terrible than those of Whitefield. It has been already mentioned, that in 1740 he read a paper before the Synod of Philadelphia, to prove that many of his brethren were "rotten-hearted hypocrites;" assigning reasons for that belief, which would not have justified the exclusion of any private member from the communion of the church. About the same time he published his famous sermon on an unconverted ministry, which is one of the most terrible pieces of denunciation in the English language. The picture there drawn, he afterwards very clearly intimated, (what was indeed never doubted,) was intended for a large portion of his own ministerial brethren. As, however, this conduct was one of the main causes of the schism in the Presbyterian Church, which occurred in 1741, it will more properly come under consideration in the following chapter.

* Letter to the Rev. George Whitefield, by Edward Wigglesworth, in the name of the faculty of Harvard College, 1745, p. 60.

The great sinfulness of this censorious spirit, and his own offences in this respect, Mr. Tennent afterwards very penitently acknowledged. In a letter to President Dickinson, dated February 12, 1742, he says, "I have had many afflicting thoughts about the debates which have subsisted for some time in our Synod. I would to God the breach were healed, were it the will of the Almighty. As for my own part, wherein I have mismanaged in doing what I did, I do look upon it to be my duty, and should be willing to acknowledge it in the openest manner. I cannot justify the excessive heat of temper which has sometime appeared in my conduct. I have been of late, (since I returned from New England,) visited with much spiritual desertion and distresses of various kinds, coming in a thick and almost continual succession, which have given me a greater discovery of myself, than I think I ever had before. These things, with the trial of the Moravians, have given me a clear view of the danger of every thing which tends to enthusiasm and division in the visible church. I think that while the enthusiastical Moravians, and Long-Beards, or Pietists, are uniting their bodies, (no doubt to increase their strength, and render themselves more considerable,) it is a shame that the ministers, who are in the main of sound principles of religion, should be divided and quarrelling. Alas, for it, my soul is sick for these things! I wish that some scriptural healing methods could be fallen upon to put an end to these confusions. Some time since I felt a disposition to fall upon my knees, if I had opportunity, to entreat them to be at peace. I add no more at present, but humble and hearty salutations; and remain, with all due honour and respect, your poor worthless brother in the gospel ministry.

"P. S. I break open the letter myself, to add my thoughts about some extraordinary things in Mr. Davenport's conduct. As to his making his judgment about the internal state of persons, or their experience, a term of church fellowship, I believe it is unscriptural, and of awful tendency to rend and tear the church. It is bottomed upon a false base, viz.: That a certain and infallible knowledge of the good estate of men is attainable in this life from their experience. The practice is schismatical, inasmuch as it sets up a new term of communion which Christ has not fixed.

"The late method of setting up separate meetings upon the supposed unregeneracy of pastors of places, is enthusiastical, proud, and schismatical. All that fear God ought to oppose it, as a most dangerous engine to bring the churches into the most damnable errors and confusions. The practice is built upon a two-fold false hypothesis, viz.: Infallibility of knowledge, and that unconverted ministers will be used as instruments of no good to the church.

"The practice of openly exposing ministers who are supposed to be unconverted, in public discourse, by particular application of such times and places, serves only to provoke them, instead of doing them any good, and to declare our own arrogance. It is an unprecedented, divisial, and pernicious practice. It is lording it over our brethren to a degree superior to what any prelate has pretended since the coming of Christ, so far as I know, the pope only excepted; though I really do not remember to have read that the pope went on at this rate.

"The sending out of unlearned men to teach others, upon the supposition of their piety, in ordinary cases, seems to bring the ministry into contempt; to cherish enthusiasm, and bring all into confusion. Whatever fair face it may have, it is a most perverse practice. The practice of singing in the streets is a piece of weakness and enthusiastical ostentation.

"I wish you success, dear sir, in your journey; my soul is grieved for such enthusiastical fooleries. They portend much mischief to the poor church of God, if they be not seasonably checked. May your labours be blest for that end. I must also express my abhorrence of all pretence to immediate inspiration, or following immediate impulses, as an enthusiastical perilous ignis fatuus."*

A few years later, when the evils arising from the rash denunciation of professing Christians and ministers had become more apparent, Mr. Tennent protested against it in the strongest terms. "It is cruel and censorious judging," he says, "to condemn the state of those we know not, and to condemn positively and openly the spiritual state of such as are sound in fundamental doctrines,

* The above letter was printed in the Pennsylvania Gazette, August 12, 1742; and transcribed into Mr. Hazard's MSS.

and regular in life. The way to obtain quickening grace is the path of duty, and not the scandalous practice of that God-provoking, church-rending iniquity, rash judging. This may quicken indeed, but not to any thing good, but to backbiting, slandering, wrath, and malignity, and all manner of mischief. Oh that a gracious God would open the eyes of the children of men, to see the inexpressible baseness and horrors of this detestable impiety, which is pregnant with innumerable evils."* He even denies the right of any man to judge of the spiritual state of others on the ground of their inward experience, or to make such judgment the ground of his public conduct towards them. "The terms of Christian fellowship," he says, "which God has fixed, are soundness in the main doctrines of religion, and a regular life. I know of no passage of the Bible that proves converting grace, or the church's judgment of it, to be a term of Christian communion, of divine appointment."† And in another place, he says, "I desire to know where Almighty God has given any of the children of men the right to inspect into the spiritual experiences of others, so as to make our judgment of them, abstract from their doctrine and life, the ground of our opinion concerning the state of their souls, and of our public conduct towards them. For my part, I know of no place in Scripture which gives such a power to any of the sons of men, and much less to every man."‡ Yet this good man allowed himself publicly to denounce as graceless, multitudes of his brethren, whom he admitted to be sound in the faith and orderly in their lives, and thus greatly aided in producing that state of con-

* Irenicum, or Plea for the Peace of Jerusalem, by Gilbert Tennent. Philadelphia, 1749, p. 90.

† Ibid. p. 79.

‡ Ibid. p. 55.—On page 79, he has the following note: "I cannot find that the Christians of the first three centuries after Christ, made gracious experiences, or the church's judgment about them, terms of communion. They made no inquiries about them as to baptism, and all that were baptized, and of adult age and free from church censure, were admitted to the sacrament." A few years before, he charged some of his brethren with acting on this principle (though they denied it), and made it one of his most prominent reasons for believing them to be unconverted. See the paper which was read before the Synod in 1740.

fusion and strife which he afterwards so strenuously laboured to correct.

The extent to which the sin of censoriousness prevailed during this revival, may be inferred, not only from the complaints of those who were unrighteously condemned, but from the frequency with which it was testified against by the best friends of religion, and the confessions of those who had most grievously offended in this respect. One great evil of this spirit is, that it is contagious, and in a sense, hereditary. That is, there always will be men disposed to rake up the sins and errors of these pious denouncers; and on the score of these deformities, to proclaim themselves the Tennents and Whitefields of their own generation. If the fruit of the Spirit of God is love, joy, peace, long-suffering, gentleness, goodness, faith, meekness, then may we be sure that a proud, arrogant, denunciatory, self-confident, and self-righteous spirit is not of God; and that any work which claims to be a revival of religion, and is characterized by such a spirit, is so far spurious and fanatical. All attempts to account for, or excuse such a temper on the ground of uncommon manifestations, or uncommon hatred of sin, or extraordinary zeal for holiness and the salvation of souls, are but apologies for sin. The clearer our apprehensions of God, the greater will be our reverence and humility; the more distinct our views of eternal things, the greater will be our solemnity and carefulness; the more we know of sin, of our own hearts, and of Jesus Christ, the more shall we be forbearing, forgiving, and lamb-like, in our disposition and conduct. "Gracious affections do not tend to make men bold, noisy, and boisterous, but rather to speak trembling. When Ephraim spake trembling, he exalted himself in Israel."* The evidence from Scripture is full and abundant, "that those who are truly gracious are under the government of the lamb-like, dove-like Spirit of Jesus Christ, and this is essentially and eminently the nature of the saving grace of the gospel, and the proper spirit of true Christianity. We may therefore undoubtedly determine that all truly Christian affections are attended with this spirit, that this is the natural tendency of the fear

* Edwards on the Affections, p. 393.

and hope, the sorrow and joy, the confidence and zeal of true Christians."*

Another of the evils of this period of excitement, was the disregard shown to the common rules of ecclesiastical order, especially in the course pursued by itinerant preachers and lay exhorters. With respect to the former, no one complained of regularly ordained ministers acting the part of evangelists; that is, of their going to destitute places, and preaching the gospel to those who would not otherwise have an opportunity of hearing it. The thing complained of was, that these itinerants came into parishes of settled ministers, and without their knowledge, or against their wishes, insisted on preaching to the people. This was a thing of very frequent, almost daily occurrence, and was a fruitful source of heart-burnings and divisions.

It is the plain doctrine of the Scriptures and the common understanding of the Christian church, that the pastoral relation is of divine appointment. Ministers are commanded to take heed to the flocks over which the Holy Ghost has made them overseers. If the Holy Ghost has made one man an overseer of a flock, what right has another man to interfere with his charge? This relation not only imposes duties, but it also confers rights. It imposes the duties of teaching and governing; of watching for souls as those who must give an account. It confers the right to claim obedience as spiritual instructers and governors. Hence the people are commanded to obey them that have the rule over them, and to submit themselves. They have indeed the right to select their pastor, but having selected him, they are bound by the authority of God, to submit to him as such. They have moreover, in extreme cases, the right to desert or discard him; as a wife has in extreme cases, the right to leave her husband, or a child to renounce the authority of a parent. But this cannot be done for slight reasons, without offending God. In like manner, as a stranger has a right, in extreme cases, to take a child from the control and instruction of a father, or withdraw a wife from the authority and custody of her husband, so also there are cases, in which he may interfere between

* Edwards on the Affections, p. 387.

a pastor and his people. Interference in any one of these cases, is a violation of divinely recognized rights; and to be innocent, must, in every instance, have an adequate justification.

Mr. Tennent admitted these principles to their fullest extent; he justified his conduct and that of his associates, on the ground that the ordinary rules of ecclesiastical order cease to be obligatory in times of general declension.* When the majority of ministers are unconverted men, and contentedly unsuccessful in their work, it was, he maintained, the right of any one who could, to preach the gospel to their people, and the duty of the people to forsake the ministrations of their pastors. Admitting the correctness of this principle, when can it be properly applied? When may it be lawfully taken for granted, that a minister is unconverted and unfit for his office? According to Tennent's own sober and deliberate judgment, this could be rightfully done only when he either rejected some fundamental doctrine, or was immoral in his conduct. And even when this was the case, the obviously correct course would be, to endeavour to have him removed from office by a competent authority. Not until this had been proved to be impossible, would any man be justified in trampling upon the rights of a brother minister. The conduct of Mr. Tennent and that of his associates, cannot stand the test of his own principles. They not only made no effort to have those ministers removed from office, whom they regarded as unregenerate or unfaithful, but they chose to assume them to be unconverted, and on the ground of that assumption, to enter their congregations, and to exhort the people to forsake their ministry, though they admitted them to be sound in all the main articles of religion, and regular in their lives. This disorderly course was, in many cases, productive of shameful

* Speaking of such rules, which he had enforced with great earnestness in his discourse against the Moravians, he says, in vindication of his consistency, "On the supposition that a number of ministers are either unsound in doctrine, or unfaithful and contentedly unsuccessful in their work, then is it not lawful to suspend the aforesaid rules for a season?" — Remarks on the Protest, by which the members of the New Brunswick Presbytery were excluded from Synod.

conflicts, and was in general one of the most crying evils of the times.

Whitefield far out-did Mr. Tennent, as to this point. He admitted none of the principles which Mr. Tennent believed, in ordinary times, ought to be held sacred. He assumed the right, in virtue of his ordination, to preach the gospel wherever he had an opportunity, "even though it should be in a place where officers were already settled, and the gospel was fully and faithfully preached. This, I humbly apprehend," he adds, "is every gospel minister's indisputable privilege." * It mattered not whether the pastors who thus fully and faithfully preached the gospel, were willing to consent to the intrusion of the itinerant evangelist or not. "If pulpits should be shut," he says, "blessed be God, the fields are open, and I can go without the camp, bearing the Redeemer's reproach. This I glory in; believing if I suffer for it, I suffer for righteousness' sake." † If Whitefield had the right here claimed, then of course Davenport had it, and so every fanatic and errorist has it. This doctrine is entirely inconsistent with what the Bible teaches of the nature of the pastoral relation, and with every form of ecclesiastical government, episcopal, presbyterian, or congregational. Whatever plausible pretences may be urged in its favour, it has never been acted upon without producing the greatest practical evils.

As soon as this habit of itinerant preaching within the bounds of settled congregations, began to prevail, it excited a lively opposition. The Synod of Philadelphia twice unanimously resolved that no minister should preach in any congregation without the consent of the presbytery to which the congregation belonged.‡ As soon, however, as the revival fairly commenced, Mr. Tennent and his associates refused to be bound by the rule; and, for the sake of peace, it was given up. The legislature of Connecticut made it penal for any minister to preach within the bounds of the parish of another minister, unless duly invited by the pastor and people.§

* Whitefield's letter to the president, professors, &c. of Harvard College. Boston, 1745: p. 17.

† Ibid. p. 22.

‡ See Part First of this History, p. 206.

§ Trumbull's Connecticut, vol. ii. p. 162.

The General Association of Connecticut, in 1742, after giving thanks for the revival, bear their testimony against "ministers disorderly intruding into other ministers' parishes." * The convention of ministers of Massachusetts, in 1743, declared this kind of itinerant preaching, "without the knowledge, or against the leave of settled pastors," to be "a breach of order, and contrary to the Scriptures, and the sentiments of our fathers, expressed in their Platform of Church Discipline." † And the assembly of pastors held at Boston, July, 1743, in their testimony in behalf of the revival, express it as their judgment "that ministers do not invade the province of others, and, in ordinary cases, preach in another's parish, without his knowledge and consent." ‡ Notwithstanding this general concurrence among the friends of religion, in condemning this disorderly practice, it prevailed to a great extent, and resulted in dividing congregations, unsettling ministers, and introducing endless contentions and confusion.

As to lay preaching, though of frequent occurrence, it found little favour with any but the openly fanatical. Tennent in a letter to Edwards, written probably in the autumn of 1741, says, "As to the subject you mentioned, of laymen being sent out to exhort and teach, supposing them to be real converts, I cannot but think, if it be encouraged and continued, it will be of dreadful consequence to the church's peace and soundness in the faith. It is base presumption, whatever zeal be pretended to, notwithstanding, for any persons to take this honour to themselves, unless they be called of God, as was Aaron. I know most young zealots are apt, through ignorance, inconsideration, and pride of heart, to undertake what they have no proper qualifications for; and through their impru-

* Trumbull's Connecticut, vol. ii. p. 173.

† Testimony of the pastors of churches in the province of Massachusetts Bay, at their annual convention in Boston, May 25, 1743, pages 6, 7.

‡ Some of the ministers present on that occasion signed this testimony and advice as to the substance merely, which Mr. Prince informs us was owing principally to the clause above cited. Some of the pastors thought that it was not explicit enough against the practice which it condemned, while others thought it might "be perverted to the great infringement of Christian and human liberty." — Christian History, vol. i. p. 198.

dence and enthusiasm the church of God suffers. I think all that fear God should rise and crush the enthusiastic creature in the egg. Dear brother, the times are dangerous. The churches in America and elsewhere are in great danger of enthusiasm; we need to think of the maxim *principiis obsta*."* This irregularity was freely condemned also by the association of Connecticut, the convention of Massachusetts, and the assembly of pastors in Boston, in the documents already referred to. Yet it was through the influence of these lay exhorters, encouraged by a few such ministers as Davenport, and Mr. Park, of Westerly, Rhode Island,† that fanaticism and false religion were most effectually promoted among the churches.

This is a formidable array of evils. Yet as the friends of the revival testify to their existence, no conscientious historian dare either conceal or extenuate them. There was too little discrimination between true and false religious feeling. There was too much encouragement given to outcries, faintings, and bodily agitations, as probable evidence of the presence and power of God. There was, in many, too much reliance on impulses, visions, and the pretended power of discerning spirits. There was a great deal of censoriousness, and of a sinful disregard of ecclesiastical order. The disastrous effects of these evils, the rapid spread of false religion, the dishonour and decline of true piety, the prevalence of erroneous doctrines, the division of congregations, the alienation of Christians, and the long period of subsequent deadness in the church, stand up as a solemn warning to Christians, and especially to Christian ministers in all times to come. It was thus, in the strong language of Edwards, the devil prevailed against the revival. "It is by this means that the daughter of Zion in this land, now lies in such piteous circumstances, with her garments rent, her face disfigured, her nakedness exposed, her limbs broken, and weltering in the blood of her own wounds, and in nowise able to rise, and this so soon after her late great joys and hopes."‡

Though this, being true, should be known and well considered,

* Life of Edwards, p. 153. † See Gillies, vol. ii. p. 292.

‡ Preface to his Treatise on the Affections, written in 1746.

that the guilt and danger of propagating false religion and spurious excitement may be understood, yet we are not to forget or undervalue the great good which was then accomplished. In many places there was little of these evils, especially in New Jersey and Virginia. Dickinson and Davies successfully resisted their inroads within the sphere of their influence. And in many other places the soundness of the doctrines taught, the experience detailed, and the permanent effects produced, abundantly attest the genuineness of the revival. To the Presbyterian Church, particularly, it was the commencement of a new life, the vigour of which is still felt in all her veins.

CHAPTER V.

THE SCHISM, 1741.

The act of Synod relating to itinerant preaching, passed in 1737. — The act relating to the examination of candidates, passed in 1738. — These acts disobeyed by the Presbytery of New Brunswick. — That Presbytery censured by the Synod. — They present their apology in 1739. — Analysis of that apology. — The Presbytery continue to disobey the Synod. — The propriety of their conduct considered. — The effects of this controversy upon the congregations and other presbyteries. — The efforts made in 1740 to compromise the difficulty. — Failure of these efforts. — Mr. G. Tennent and Mr. Blair read before the Synod two papers containing complaints against their brethren. — Mr. Tennent preaches his sermon on the dangers of an unconverted ministry. —Analysis of that sermon. — The complaints against Mr. Tennent and his friends for rash-judging, and for intruding into settled congregations, and promoting divisions. — These complaints brought before the presbyteries.—The cases of Mr. Alexander Creaghead and of Mr. David Alexander before the Presbytery of Donegal. — The Synod meets in 1741 in the midst of these controversies.—The case of Mr. Creaghead taken up, and leads to a serious contention.—Mr. Robert Cross reads a protest against the New Brunswick brethren being allowed to sit as members of Synod, which is signed by twelve ministers and eight elders. — This protest throws the Synod into confusion, and leads to the irregular exclusion of nine ministers. — The proceedings of the Presbytery of New Brunswick and their correspondents immediately after the schism. — The efforts made by the members of the Presbytery of New York in 1742 to heal the schism; similar efforts made in 1743 and in 1745.—These efforts having failed, the Synod of New York formed in September, 1745. — The points of difference between the two parties considered.—The nature and extent of the opposition to the revival examined. — How far the parties differed as to the importance of learning, as to points of doctrine, and principles of church government considered.—The true cause of the schism stated.

In order properly to understand the origin and causes of the schism which in 1741 divided the Presbyterian Church, it will be necessary briefly to recapitulate some of the facts recorded in the third chapter of this history. It may be remembered, that in 1737 an act was passed by the Synod, which prohibited the members of one presbytery preaching to the congregations under the care of another presbytery, without a regular invitation. In the following year this rule was somewhat modified, and unanimously re-enacted.* It was not the design of this rule to prohibit itinerant preaching; a service which its advocates every year commissioned men to perform. It was intended to prevent the irregular intrusion of one minister or presbytery upon the acknowledged bounds of another. Under ordinary circumstances, such a rule would have excited no opposition. It is not surprising, therefore, that it was twice unanimously adopted. When, however, the revival had fairly begun, and a number of ministers had devoted themselves to preaching from place to place, they were unwilling to be trammelled by such rules, or to abstain from preaching in a particular congregation because "a graceless minister" or lukewarm presbytery might take offence. They urged that, under extraordinary circumstances, such rules should be laid aside.

A more serious difficulty arose from the passage of another act. In 1738, the Synod resolved that, in order to prevent the admission of uneducated men into the ministry, every candidate for the sacred office, before he was taken on trial, should be furnished with a diploma of graduation from some European or New England college, or with a certificate of competent scholarship from a committee of the Synod. The same year the Presbytery of New Brunswick was formed. It met for the first time August 8, 1738, and on the same day application was made by Mr. John Rowland to be taken "on trial, in order to his being licensed to preach the gospel." "The presbytery thereon entered on a serious consideration of the act of last Synod, appointing that young men should be first examined by a commission of Synod, and obtain a testimony of their approbation, before they are to be taken on trials by any presbytery belonging to the same; and, after much reasoning on the case, the Presbytery came to this unanimous conclusion, viz.: That they were not, in point of conscience, restrained by said act from using the liberty and power which presbyteries have all along

* Part First of this History, Chapter III. p. 207.

hitherto enjoyed; but that it was their duty to take the said Mr. Rowland upon trial, for which conclusion they conceive they have several weighty and sufficient reasons."* The Presbytery, accordingly, entered upon his examination, and assigned him the usual exercises to present at their next meeting. On the 7th of the following September, the Presbytery having sustained his examination, and heard him profess "the Westminster Confession of Faith, to be the confession of his faith," granted him "free license and liberty to preach the gospel of Christ."†

The following year, 1739, when the records of the Presbytery of New Brunswick came to be reviewed by the Synod, that body declared the licensing of Mr. Rowland "to be very disorderly, and admonished the said Presbytery to avoid such divisive courses for the future; and determined not to admit the said Mr. Rowland to be a preacher of the gospel within our bounds, nor to encourage any of our people to accept him, until he submit to such examinations as were appointed by this Synod for those that have had a private education. This overture," it is added, "was carried in the affirmative by a great majority."‡

The Presbytery seem to have anticipated this result, as they came prepared with their "Apology for dissenting from two acts or new religious laws passed at the last session of the Synod."§ This was a long argumentative paper, containing not merely the specific objections of its authors against the two acts in question, but a formal statement of their principles as to church government. They premise, therefore, 1. That there is a parity or equality of power among gospel ministers. 2. That a presbytery, or the smallest association of ministers, has power from Christ to ordain. 3. That consequently they have authority to judge of the qualifications of candidates for ordination. In the further exposition of their sentiments, they state, 1. That presbyteries are bound to inquire into the fitness of candidates for the sacred office, and

* Minutes of the Presbytery of New Brunswick, pp. 1 and 2.

† Ibid. p. 3.

‡ Minutes of Synod, vol. ii. p. 68.

§ This apology was presented to the Synod, May 23, 1739, signed by Gilbert Tennent, Eleazar Wales, William Tennent, Jun., and Samuel Blair.

admit or refuse them according to their best judgment. 2. That they have power to deny church communion to such as by plain scriptural directions are unqualified for it. 3. In cases of conscience, or in cases regularly brought before them from particular congregations, they ought to give their deliberate judgment, with their best counsel and advice. 4. They have liberty to agree among themselves upon such things as appear to have a good tendency to advance religion, and to engage themselves voluntarily to the observance of these things, provided they do not encroach upon the liberties of the people, nor pretend to bind their dissenting members to observe their agreements, who may have a different view and apprehension of them. 5. That it is reasonable and useful that synods consisting of several presbyteries meet together, when matters may be brought by appeal or reference from particular presbyteries, in order to obtain the judgment and sentiments of a greater number upon them. And accordingly, it is no doubt their duty to take such cases under their consideration, and to give their best advice on them; but we think that they should not proceed with any further authority, except in such cases wherein God has given particular obvious directions in his word, which are to be exactly followed; and even then they do no more than show from Scripture, what are the mind and direction of God in such cases, and declare their own resolution to act according thereto, as far as they are concerned.*

The rule relating to itinerants, as it then stood, forbade any minister belonging to one presbytery to preach to a congregation belonging to another, if warned by a member of the latter presbytery that his preaching would be likely to cause division. This prohibition was to operate only until the presbytery to which the congregation belonged, could consider the case and give the itinerant liberty to preach or not, as they saw fit. To this rule the authors of this apology objected, that it had no foundation in Scripture; that it was at variance with the command which required ministers to be instant in season and out of season; that it deprived ministers and people of privileges which Christ had given

* Apology, pp. 28, 29.

them; that the exercise of the ministerial office might be suspended for a time by one man, and that not for any fault; that any minister by the aforesaid act is invested with a power to lord it over his brethren, and to inflict upon him the most grievous church censures, and that upon mere conjecture; and finally that it was inconsistent with the right which belonged to ruling elders to invite a regular member of another presbytery to preach among them one Sabbath on his travels. This remonstrance led to a modification of the rule, which was so altered as to direct that complaint should be made to the presbytery, in case any one thought the preaching of the stranger productive of evil, and that it should be left to the presbytery to decide whether he should continue to preach. In this form it passed unanimously. These brethren, however, were no better satisfied than before, and the next year the rule was repealed.*

To the rule relating to the examination of candidates, they objected, 1. That it was unscriptural; there being no direction in the Scriptures, that a candidate should be examined by a committee of synod, before being examined by a presbytery. 2. That it was uncharitable, inasmuch as it supposed insufficiency or unfaithfulness in the presbyteries. 3. That it was anti-scriptural, as it hindered or impaired the exercise of the power of presbyteries in the examination of students, a duty enjoined upon them in the Scriptures. 4. That it was unjust, as it impaired a power given by Christ, against the will and conscience of its possessors. 5. That it was unnecessary; presbyteries having tried young men ever since the synod was formed. 6. That it was anti-presbyterial, and by taking from presbyteries their proper business, tended to make them useless.

Not satisfied with these specific objections, they attacked the general principle on which, as they supposed, these rules were founded. They say, "We humbly conceive that the aforesaid acts, in their present form, are founded upon a false hypothesis namely, that a majority of synods or other church judicatories have a power committed to them from Christ to make new rules, acts, or

* Chapter III. p. 207.

canons about religious matters, on this ground, viz.: That they judge them to be either not against or agreeable to the general directions of the word, and serviceable to religion, which shall be binding on those who conscientiously dissent therefrom, on certain penalties, which are to be inflicted upon those who judge the acts they enforce to be contrary to the mind of Christ, and prejudicial to the interest of his kingdom. This is, in brief, a legislative, or law-making power in religious matters, and this we do utterly disclaim and renounce."

Against any such power as that here described, they argued, 1. That Christ has not given such authority to church judicatories, or required his people to submit to it. 2. It is an invasion of Christ's kingly office. 3. It involves a reflection on the perfection of the Scriptures, as though they did not contain a sufficient rule of duty. 4. It is inconsistent with Christian liberty. 5. It is incompatible with the rights of conscience and of private judgment. 6. This power supposes either that the church is infallible, or that she can make what is wrong in itself, right by commanding it. 7. If such a power belongs to the church, then the reformation and dissent from the Church of England must be condemned. 8. Such religious laws are superstitious and uncharitable. 9. The power complained of would open a door for an intolerable bondage, and expose men to be persecuted for conscience' sake.*

It will appear in the sequel, that as to this latter point, viz.: the power to make laws to bind the conscience, there was no dispute between the two parties. Such a power was never claimed by any presbyterian. Still this apology greatly widened the opening breach. It made the difficulty, to all appearance, one of principle instead of detail. It was no longer a question, whether a particular rule was just, but whether a church judicatory had, on any occasion, the right to bind its dissenting members. This paper

* Each of these arguments is expanded to a considerable length in the Apology, which is printed in full as an Appendix to Remarks on the Protestation, presented to the Synod of Philadelphia, June 1, 1741, by Gilbert Tennent. Mr. Thompson, in his work on the Government of the Church of Christ, has extracted the greater part of the Apology.

seemed to allow, even in cases of appeal, nothing beyond advisory power either to synods or presbyteries. It was therefore regarded as a formal renunciation on the part of its authors, of the fundamental principles of presbyterianism. It is true, they did not so intend it, yet it was so understood, and that according to its most obvious meaning. The unfortunate character of this apology was no doubt due to Mr. Gilbert Tennent, whose impress it very distinctly bears. As a controversialist he had two prominent characteristics. The one was the habit, on all occasions, of recurring to first principles. He was not contented to object to the thing in debate, but was sure to attack the hypothesis, as he termed it, on which it was founded. This habit often got him into difficulty; for his mind, though vigorous and on many subjects well furnished, was neither discriminating nor logical. Hence, in the statement of his principles, he rarely attended to those qualifications which he himself soon found to be necessary. His controversial writings, therefore, are full of inconsistencies and contradictions, so that his authority may be fairly quoted on either side of almost every question in the discussion of which he was engaged. Another of his characteristics was a fondness for exaggeration. Every thing was stated in extremes. This was remarked by his opponents, who complained that he could not say a thing was uncharitable, but he must needs call it "a bloody, murderous charity." Thus in the present case, he could not deny that church judicatories could bind him to what he considered unscriptural and sinful, without appearing to deny that they could bind him to any thing.

The opposition of the New Brunswick brethren led to a modification of the rule respecting the examination of candidates. Instead of this examination being conducted by a committee, it was determined that it should be performed by the Synod itself or its commission. As thus modified it was adopted by a great majority. The dissentients among the ministers, were William Tennent, Sen'r, Gilbert Tennent, William Tennent, Jun'r, Charles Tennent, Samuel Blair, and Eleazar Wales.* As Mr. G. Tennent declared that he believed the rule was designed to operate against his fa-

* See chap. iii. p. 210.

ther's schools, his opponents retorted that the opposition to it was a mere family concern. Of the six dissenting or protesting brethren, as they were commonly called, four were Tennents, the fifth a pupil and friend, and the sixth a co-presbytery and neighbour. Whatever unworthy motive may, on either side, have mingled with better feelings, there is no doubt that the majority, which included almost the whole Synod, were influenced in the adoption of the rule in question, by a sincere desire to secure an adequately educated ministry, and the minority by an equally conscientious belief, that the operation of the rule would be inimical to the progress of religion in the church.

The New Brunswick Presbytery having taken its stand, continued to disregard the above-mentioned rule. In the course of the year 1739, they ordained Mr. Rowland *sine titulo*,* which was then a very uncommon thing; and licensed Mr. McCrea.† In 1740 they licensed Mr. William Robinson‡ and Mr. Samuel Finley;§ and in no one of these cases did they comply with the requisition of Synod.

In order to a proper understanding of this period of our history, it is obviously important to have a clear idea of the merits of the controversy between the New Brunswick Presbytery and the other members of the Synod. Was that Presbytery justifiable in disregarding the rule respecting the examination of candidates? It will be seen that all their objections to the rule in question, as presented in their apology, resolve themselves into one, viz.: That since Christ has given to presbyteries the power of ordination, the rule was an unwarrantable interference with their privileges. To call this interference, under so many distinct heads, anti-scriptural, uncharitable, unjust, and anti-presbyterial, does not make so many separate arguments. The single question is, was there any unwarrantable interference, on the part of the Synod, with the rights of the presbyteries? Mr. Tennent disposes of this question in a very summary manner. He thought the case was settled by say-

* Minutes of Presbytery of New Brunswick, p. 12. † Ibid. p. 13.

‡ Ibid. p. 16. § Ibid. p. 20.

ing that, as the presbyteries had the right to ordain, this involved of necessity the right to judge for themselves of the qualifications of the candidate. He seems, however, to have overlooked the obvious consideration, that the powers of a presbytery acting by itself, are necessarily and justly limited, when it comes to form one body with other presbyteries. The question was not, what a presbytery considered in itself might do, but what a presbytery making a constituent part of a whole church might properly do. Among Episcopalians the right of ordination is held to belong to bishops, and that by divine right. Yet no bishop can spurn the canons of his church, which prescribe the qualifications of priests or deacons, as anti-scriptural, uncharitable, and unjust, because they interfere with the free exercise of his power to ordain. If he chooses to act with other bishops, and form a part of an extended church, he must exercise his power in submission to general agreements, and all complaints of limiting his authority are unreasonable. If he wishes to be untrammelled, he must act by himself. The case is much stronger with regard to presbyteries; because when a man is ordained in our church, he becomes not merely a member of presbytery, but of the synod also. He is authorized to exercise jurisdiction over his brethren; he is one of those to whom they promise subjection in the Lord; he is entitled to sit in judgment on their character, orthodoxy, and conduct. Every member of the synod, therefore, has a right to know that he is properly qualified for such an office. If to secure this object, the synod agreed that all who are admitted to this sacred trust should have certain qualifications; all the members are bound to submit or to leave the body. It would be a strange usurpation to allow a small minority to force into membership and authority, men whom two-thirds or four-fifths of the body were unwilling to receive. Yet this was precisely what Mr. Tennent and his associates insisted upon. They claimed the right of making men members of the Synod, and thus judges of their brethren, to whom they were unwilling to be subject. The Synod had agreed that none but graduates of colleges, or those who had an equivalent education, should be allowed to sit as members. They believed such an education requisite in order to the proper discharge of the duties of the ministry and of synodical membership. Those who thought differently, had a right to oppose the adoption of the rule; and if they were unable with a good conscience to submit to it, they had a right to withdraw and to act on their own plan; but they assuredly had no right to insist that their brethren should admit to membership, and submit to their authority, men whom they did not think qualified, or who refused to give the stipulated evidence of their competency. This would be to make the minority rule the majority. It was in this light the matter presented itself to Mr. Tennent's opponents. They therefore accused him of a determination to domineer over his brethren, and to have his own way in matters which concerned the whole Synod as much as the Presbytery of New Brunswick. The unreasonableness of this course was so obvious, that the Tennents stood almost alone in their opposition. This is not merely inferred from the fact that the rule respecting candidates was adopted three times by "a great majority;" but it is distinctly stated that the New York Presbytery, and especially Messrs. Dickinson, Pierson, and Pemberton, sided with the majority on all these questions.*

It must be borne in mind that, at this period, the synod was not only the highest judicatory of the church, but it included all the presbyteries. Its determinations or acts, therefore, were of the same nature with our constitutional rules when adopted by a majority of the presbyteries. They were the expression of the will of the whole church. In the particular case under consideration, all the presbyteries, without an exception, sanctioned the rule in question, because it was adopted before the organization of the Presbytery of New Brunswick. And when that presbytery objected, there were four presbyteries for the rule and one against it. The conduct of the New Brunswick Presbytery, therefore, was precisely analogous to that of the Cumberland Presbytery, at a later period of our history, who refused to comply with the con-

* This is stated in the Refutation of Mr. Tennent's Remarks on the Protest, p. 13. And in the Minutes of the Synod of Philadelphia, vol. iii. p. 16. It is also distinctly referred to by Mr. Tennent himself in the Examiner Examined, p. 105.

stitutional provisions as to the qualifications of candidates; or to that of any presbytery who should insist on licensing and ordaining men destitute of a knowledge of Latin, Greek, or Hebrew, or such as refused to adopt the Westminster Confession. This may indeed often happen, but when it does occur it is an obvious breach of faith; it is a violation of the compact which the presbyteries have bound themselves to observe. And when any presbytery ordains any man who has not the constitutional qualifications as to learning, orthodoxy, or experimental religion, a positive and grievous wrong is inflicted on all the other presbyteries.

It will hardly be denied that any number of presbyteries have a right to meet together and fix their terms of communion; to agree upon the rules to be observed in admitting men to the ministry, and thus investing them with a joint authority over all the members of the body. This is a right exercised by every church in the world. The Episcopalians have their canons; the Methodists their book of discipline; and even the Congregationalists their Cambridge and Saybrook Platforms. It was, therefore, no unusual or unreasonable proceeding on the part of the Synod, embracing all the presbyteries in connection with the church, to agree on the terms on which men should be admitted to the ministry. They had exercised this power before, and they continued to exercise it afterwards. Neither Mr. Tennent nor any of his associates objected to the act of 1729, requiring the presbyteries to make the adoption of the Westminster Confession a preliminary to ordination. Yet the presbyteries had as much reason to complain of that act, as encroaching on their prerogative to judge of the orthodoxy of their candidates, as they had to complain of the act of 1738, as interfering with the right to judge of their literary qualifications. It is a decisive proof that there was nothing in the latter rule which transcended the acknowledged power of the Synod, that when the Synod of New York was formed in 1745, it was made one of their fundamental articles of agreement, that all determinations of the Synod should be obeyed, whenever the body thought fit to insist upon them as necessary to the well-being of the church; and that those who could not conscientiously submit, should peaceably withdraw. A similar provision was unanimously adopted by the two Synods at the time of their union in 1758. What is still more to the point, in th eway of acknowledgment, is that, at the first conference between the commissions of the two Synods with a view to the union, held in 1749, this very contested rule was proposed for adoption as one of the conditions, and assented to by every commissioner from the Synod of New York; Mr. Gilbert Tennent alone objecting to synodical examination of candidates, though he assented to their being required to produce a college diploma.* With this the Synod of Philadelphia were perfectly satisfied.

There was, therefore, no more interference with the rights of presbyteries in this case, than must ever take place, when several presbyteries unite and agree on what terms they will constitute one body. There was no greater interference than had been exercised by the Synod on previous occasions, or than takes place under our present constitution, which in so many ways limits the presbyteries in the exercise of their prerogatives.

This rule, however, has been objected to on another ground. It has been said that it was founded on the unwarrantable assumption on the part of the Synod of the right to exercise presbyterial powers. To this two answers may be given. In the first place, the right of the Synod to exercise such powers was then universally recognized. The Synod was regarded as a larger presbytery, and possessed of presbyterial prerogatives. There was scarcely one of the functions of a presbytery which it did not exercise, whenever occasion called for it. It received, installed, and ordained men without the slightest objection from any quarter. This was done by the old Synod before the schism, by each of the two Synods during the separation, and by the united Synod after the union. However inconsistent this may be with our present views and habits, it is evident that the objection just stated could not have been consistently urged at that time by any party in the church. In the second place, this examination of candidates was not considered a presbyterial act. It was not performed by the Synod in its character of a presbytery, but as the substitute of the officers

* Minutes of Synod of Philadelphia, vol. iii. p. 53.

of a college. After this synodical examination, the candidate was examined by his presbytery, just as he was after his reception of a college diploma. He might be as freely rejected, if in the judgment of the presbytery incompetent, his synodical certificate notwithstanding, as he could be notwithstanding his diploma. The Synod did not propose to take the examination of candidates out of the hands of the presbyteries, but simply to provide something which should have the same general significance and value for the whole church, that the evidence of graduation in a regular college possessed. Hence the defenders of the rule said, "The debate is neither in whole nor in part, who are intrusted with the power of ordination; but whether the right of choosing professors for colleges, or tutors for academies, belongs to the higher or lower church judicatures; and in case there be no professors, to take the regular examination of scholars privately educated, whether the right of choosing examiners to supply the room, or want of professors in examining scholars in the useful parts of academical learning, should be entrusted to synods or presbyteries."*

We cannot but think, therefore, that the New Brunswick Presbytery, at least at this stage of the controversy, were in the wrong. The Synod laid claim to no power either unreasonable in itself, or inconsistent with the uniform practice and acknowledged constitution of the church, as it then existed. The claim to inordinate power was all on the other side. It was a claim of a right to act in direct opposition to the will of a society regularly expressed, and yet to continue a member of it. It was in short a claim of the minority to govern the majority.

The controversy on this subject was not confined to the floor of the Synod; it soon produced difficulties in the congregations and presbyteries. In March, 1738, a portion of the people of Maidenhead and Hopewell, dissatisfied with the preaching of Mr. Guild, who was not at that time settled as their pastor, applied to the Presbytery of Philadelphia for liberty to hear some other candidate. This permission was readily granted.† In the fall of the

* Refutation of Mr. Tennent's Remarks, p. 59.

† Minutes of Presbytery of Philadelphia, p. 52.

same year they applied to the newly-erected presbytery of New Brunswick, "informing them they had liberty granted them by their presbytery to invite and receive any regular candidate from any other parts to preach among them, which also appeared by a writing from Mr. Andrews, which they adduced, and supplicating that Mr. Rowland might come among them;" and the Presbytery "granted him liberty of so doing."* As soon as this fact came to the knowledge of the Philadelphia Presbytery, they entered on their records the following minute: "The Presbytery being informed that Mr. Rowland has not complied with the order of the last Synod, relating to the examination of students by a committee of Synod appointed for that end; that he was hastily passed over in his trials by the Presbytery of New Brunswick, in direct opposition to the said order of Synod; and that Mr. Rowland had information from Mr. Cowell of the irregularity of his licensing, advising him not to preach at Hopewell at the said time; and he not attending Presbytery, although he knew of this time of its meeting; upon which consideration, the Presbytery unanimously concluded they cannot accept of Mr. Rowland as an orderly licensed preacher, nor approve of his preaching any more among the said people of Maidenhead or Hopewell, or in any other of the vacancies within our bounds, until his way be cleared by complying with the order of Synod aforesaid."† This prohibition had no effect upon the dissatisfied portion of the people, nor upon Mr. Rowland, who continued to preach with the full consent of his own Presbytery, as though it had not been made.

In order to free themselves from restraint on this subject, the people applied to the Presbytery of Philadelphia to be formed into a distinct congregation. This the Presbytery agreed to do upon condition that, in case they could not agree with the other portion of the congregation as to the site of the new place of worship, that matter should be referred to the decision of the Presby-

* Minutes of New Brunswick Presbytery, p. 3.

† Minutes of the Presbytery of Philadelphia, p. 57. There were present at this meeting of the Presbytery, Messrs. Robert Cross, Richard Treat, Hugh Carlisle, David Cowell, and Jedediah Andrews.

tery. To this the people assented, declaring "that they acknowledged the authority of the Presbytery, and would submit to its determination." They were accordingly constituted a church by themselves, whereupon they immediately requested to be allowed to join the Presbytery of New Brunswick. To this the Presbytery of course replied, that they must first fulfil the engagements into which they had just entered.* Of this decision the people complained to the Synod in 1739, who "judged that the people had behaved with great indecency towards their Presbytery, by their unmannerly reflections and unjust aspersions, both upon the Synod and Presbytery, and that they had acted very disorderly in approving Mr. Rowland as a preacher among them, when they were advised by the Presbytery that he was not to be esteemed and approved as an orderly candidate of the ministry. And the Synod," it is added, "do wholly disallow the said complainants being erected into a new congregation until they do first submit to the determination of the place for erecting a new meeting-house to their Presbytery, as was formerly agreed upon as a condition of their being a separate congregation. This overture was approved by a great majority. And it is further ordered by the Synod, that when the Presbytery of Philadelphia meet at Maidenhead and Hopewell, to fix the place of a new meeting-house, they shall call the following correspondents: Messrs. John Pierson, John Nutman, Samuel Blair, Nathaniel Hubbell, and Eleazar Wales."† There is evidence in this decision of a desire on the part of the Synod to have full justice done the complainants; as all these correspondents were members of the Presbyteries of New Brunswick and New York. A further proof that there was no disposition to thwart the reasonable wishes of the people as to their ecclesiastical connections, is found in the fact that, in the following year, the request of the two congregations of Newtown and Tinicum, to be set off from the Presbytery of Philadelphia to that of New Brunswick, was "readily granted."‡ The decision of the Synod respecting the congregation of Hopewell produced no effect. The people, Mr. Rowland,

* Minutes of the Presbytery of Philadelphia, pp. 65 and 66.

† Minutes of Synod, vol. ii. p. 68.

‡ Ibid. vol. ii. p. 72.

and the Presbytery of New Brunswick, all disregarded it. Here, again, it must be acknowledged that the Brunswick brethren were in the wrong. The congregation of Hopewell was not within their bounds; the Presbytery to which the people belonged, and whose authority they formally acknowledged, disapproved of their employing Mr. Rowland; the highest judicatory to which they appealed confirmed this decision; and yet the Brunswick Presbytery went on as though no such decision had been made, and as though the congregation was regularly under their care. It was not that these brethren denied the authority of the Presbytery or Synod, for they uniformly acknowledged and exercised this authority; but it was that, in extraordinary cases, ecclesiastical order may be safely disregarded; or, in other words, as the Presbytery of Philadelphia was indifferent to the spiritual interests of their people, the Presbytery of New Brunswick was authorized to take the charge off their hands.* In thus assuming the incompetency or unfaithfulness of their brethren, and acting as though they had forfeited their usual rights as ministers or judicatories, they unavoidably occasioned alienation and contention.

The Presbytery of Philadelphia had another difficulty about Mr. Rowland. When met at Neshaminy, September, 1739, a complaint was brought before them by some members of that congregation against their pastor, the Rev. William Tennent, senior, for having invited Mr. Rowland to preach for him. "Upon which Mr. Tennent was desired to say what he thought proper with relation to his conduct therein, which he accordingly did, and acknowledged that he did invite Mr. Rowland, as before mentioned, and withal justified the action, and disclaiming the authority of the Presbytery to take cognisance of the matter, he contemptuously withdrew. After which the Presbytery had much discourse with the people who had joined with Mr. Tennent in the aforementioned action, admonishing them of the irregularity of the said conduct, and

* Mr. Tennent says that Mr. Rowland went to the people of Hopewell, "not out of contempt (for the Presbytery or Synod) but conscience towards God, in order to relieve a pious, opposed, and oppressed people." — Examiner Examined, p. 127.

exhorting them not to encourage or consent to any like conduct for the future. They came then to consider what to do with regard to Mr. Tennent in this affair, and concluded they could not do less than condemn said conduct of Mr. Tennent, in inviting Mr. Rowland to preach as aforesaid, as irregular and disorderly, and especially when aggravated by justifying the said action, and indecently withdrawing from the Presbytery."*

The opposition of the New Brunswick Presbytery to the two acts of Synod, relating, the one to itinerant preaching, and the other to the examination of candidates, had produced so much uneasiness in the church, that when the Synod met in 1740, a general anxiety was felt to have the difficulty arranged. The former of these two acts was therefore repealed; and various efforts were made to effect such a modification of the second, as should meet the views of the New Brunswick brethren. Mr. Dickinson, as mentioned in a former chapter,† proposed that the matter in dispute should be referred to some ecclesiastical body in Scotland, Ireland, or England, or to the ministers of Boston. To this Mr. Tennent objected, principally because it would be difficult to draw up a statement of the case in which both parties would agree; because he and his friends had the smiles of God on the course which they were pursuing; and because of the low state of piety among those to whom the reference was to be made. After speaking of the Presbyterians in Scotland, Ireland, and England, as having little of the life of religion among them, he added, "By the best information we can get, a dead formality prevails too much in Boston, and many other places in New England. Indeed, we are of opinion that the majority of church judicatories almost every where, are dead formalists, if they have got even that length; and, therefore, we incline to make no more application to men in the affair aforesaid."‡

* Minutes of Philadelphia Presbytery, p. 77. Present at this meeting, besides Mr. Tennent, Messrs. J. Andrews, Robert Cross, and Richard Treat.

† Chapter iii. p. 211.

‡ Refutation of Remarks on the Protest, pp. 11, 12. The above quoted declaration respecting the ministers of Boston, illustrates Mr. Tennent's hasty

It was proposed by a member of the New Brunswick Presbytery "that the Synod might appoint two of their number to be present at the examination of candidates for the ministry; who, if they found them, (the Presbyteries,) guilty of malconduct, might accuse them to the Synod." When it was asked, whether, in the case these delegates objected to the competency of the candidate, his licensure would be put off and the question referred to the Synod, the Brunswick brethren declined. So that overture came to nothing.*

Mr. Gillespie proposed "that every Presbytery should keep a full record of the trials of candidates in the several parts of necessary learning, and exhibit the same to the Synod for their satisfaction, at the time of their admission into membership in the Synod. Now this, at the first reading, was like to take, for it seemed to cut off all colour of plea about infringing the rights of Presbyteries, and promised to the Synod, at first view, the right of judging the qualifications of their own members. But in order to come to a right understanding in the matter, Mr. Dickinson proposed, whether, in case the account given of the trials of candidates should give just ground to the Synod to judge that said candidates were really deficient in some material parts of useful learning; or in case the candidates should somehow be found out to be deficient, or upon rational grounds suspected to be so, would Mr. Tennent and his party submit such candidates to the trial or censure of Synod, to receive or reject them, as they, upon a fair trial, should form a judgment of their fitness or unfitness? To this Mr. Tennent replied, that he should be willing that the Presbytery should be subject to the Synod's censures, in case of maladministration in the matter, but would not consent that the young men should be produced, or be subject to the Synod's censures, when, or if found to be defective. On which the Synod dropped the overture, as insufficient to secure the end aimed at in our act; for it

manner of judging of the religious character of his brethren. There were at that time in Boston, Mr. Cooper, Mr. Webb, Mr. Foxcroft, the two Messrs. Prince, father and son, and several other eminently pious ministers, who, in the autumn of this very year, 1740, received Mr. Tennent with open arms.

* Refutation of Remarks on the Protest, pp. 21, 22.

now appeared that nothing would content Mr. Tennent, unless the Synod would give up the right of judging of the qualifications of their own members." *

After all these unsuccessful attempts to effect a compromise, the question was put, whether the controverted rule should be repealed, or continued until some other expedient could be found, and it was decided that the rule should be continued in force. Against this decision the six ministerial brethren who had protested the year before against the adoption of the rule, renewed their protest, and were joined by Mr. Alexander Creaghead, of the Presbytery of Donegal, and Mr. John Cross, of that of New Brunswick. Messrs. Gillespie and Hucheson, of the Presbytery of New Castle, recorded their dissent from the decision, though they did not unite in the protest.†

The unhappy state of feeling in which the failure of all efforts at accommodation had left the Synod, was greatly aggravated by a new proceeding on the part of Mr. Gilbert Tennent and Mr. Blair. They produced formal papers of complaint against their brethren, which were read not only before the Synod, but a promiscuous audience. For this latter circumstance, however, Mr. Blair states that neither Mr. Tennent nor himself was responsible, as he proposed that the Synod should be alone when the papers were read.‡ The Synod, however, said they were willing that all should hear what those brethren had to produce. Mr. Tennent then rose and read as follows:§

"Moderator and reverend brethren, I think I am obliged in duty to God and you, to present the following paper to your consideration, which contains my reasons for suspecting that a number of the members of this Synod are in a carnal state.

"First, their unsoundness in some principal doctrines of Chris-

* Refutation, &c. pp. 15, 16. † See above, chap. iii. p. 211.

‡ Vindication of the New Brunswick Presbytery, p. 225, of Blair's Works.

§ One paragraph of Mr. Tennent's paper was quoted above, chap. iii. p. 199. It is here given again for the sake of the connection. The whole is copied from Mr. Thompson's book on the Government of the Church of Christ, p. 9, et seq.

tianity, that relate to experience and practice, as particularly in the following points. 1. That there is no difference between the glory of God and our happiness; that self-love is the foundation of all obedience. These doctrines do, in my opinion, entirely overset, if true, all supernatural religion, render regeneration a vain and needless thing; involve a crimson blasphemy against the blessed God, by putting ourselves on a level with him. 2. That there is a certainty of salvation connected to the labours of natural men. This doctrine supposes the greatest falsehood, viz. that there is a free will in man naturally to acceptable good; and is attended with the most dangerous consequences, viz. fixing men upon their own righteousness, and utterly overthrowing the covenant of grace. For if there is a certainty annexed to the endeavours of natural men, it must be by promise; but a promise is a debt. As these opinions are contrary to the express testimony of the Scriptures, our Confession of Faith, and Christian experience, they give me reason to suspect at least that those who hold them are rotten-hearted hypocrites, utter strangers to the saving knowledge of God and of their own hearts.

"Secondly, there be these things in the preaching of some of our members which induces me to suspect the state of their souls, namely, 1. Their preaching seems to be powerless and unsavoury. Christ preached with authority, and not as the scribes. If any object and say, How can they be known? I answer, Christ's sheep hear his voice. Living men have sense and savour. 2. Too general, not searching sinners' hearts so narrowly as they ought, nor giving them their different portions, according to the apostle's directions to Timothy. 3. Soft and flattering. Some seem to be afraid to cry aloud and not spare; afraid to use the terrors of the Lord to persuade men. This seems too like men-pleasing and fear of the cross, whatever plausible pretences are offered to palliate it, by cowardly, covetous souls, notwithstanding. 4. Legal; many are for crying up duties, duties, and urging natural men to them almost constantly, as if outward things were the whole of religion. Is not this like the foolish builders, to pretend to build a fabric without a foundation? It is true, the externals of religion are to be pressed in their place; but their insufficiency, without inward good principles, should be shown. He, sure, that would build high, must dig deep, and lay the foundation low; but I doubt there are not many among us that open the nature, and urge the necessity of our dangerous state by nature. 5. Unsuccessful, with the appearance of contentedness under it. Aaron's rod blossomed, and brought forth almonds, while the rest of the rods were dry and barren; and by this the divine call of the tribe was manifested, while bare pretenders were blasted. God will not send ministers for nothing; no, sure, whom he sends, and who stand in his counsel, shall profit the people.

"These things following respecting their practice, incline me to suspect their state. 1. Great stiffness in opinion, generally in smaller matters wherein good men may differ; continual pertness and confidence, as if they were infallible; which shows that the pride of their understanding was never broken, and that they feel not their need of Christ as a prophet. 2. Opposition to God's servants and work; insisting much upon the real or supposed imprudences of God's servants, but passing over in silence their valuable qualifications and worthy actions. This looks pharisee-and-devil like, notwithstanding all the colourings of crafty men. 3. That there is no knowing of people's states. Though there is no infallible knowledge of the estates of some attainable, yet there is a satisfactory knowledge to be attained. Ministers crying out against this, is an evidence of their unfaithfulness in neglecting to use the properest means to convince sinners of their damnable state. It shows also their ignorance of divine things; or manifests their consciousness of their own hypocrisy and fear of discovery. 4. Letting men out into the ministry without so much as examining them about their Christian experience, notwithstanding a late canon of this Synod enjoining the same. How contrary is this practice to the Scriptures, and to our Directory, and of how dangerous a tendency to the church of God! Is it probable that truly gracious persons would thus slight the precious souls of men? 5. More zeal for outward order than for the main points of practical religion. Witness the committee's slighting and shuffling the late debate about the glory of God,* and their present contention about the committee-act. This is too much like the zeal of the old pharisees in tithing mint, anise, and cummin, while they neglected the weightier matters of the law.

"These things, my brethren, I mention in the fear and love of God, without personal prejudice against any. That God who knows my heart is witness, that I heartily desire the conviction of those ministers whom I suspect, and that they may be as burning and shining lights in the church of God. But I am obliged in faithfulness to God and the souls of men, to make mention of these things, which are distressing to my heart, as some of the reasons why I protest against all restraints in preaching the everlasting gospel in this degenerate state of the church. Rules which are serviceable in ordinary cases, when the church is stocked with a faithful ministry, are notoriously prejudicial when the church is oppressed with a carnal ministry. Besides the remarkable success that God has given of late to Mr. Whitefield's travelling labours, and several others in this country, makes me abhor the slavish schemes of bigots, as to confinement in preaching the blessed gospel of Christ. I am, reverend gentlemen, your well-wisher and humble servant, Gilbert Tennent."

The paper read by Mr. Blair contained the same general complaints. Though milder in its language, it probably gave quite as much offence, as he was at that time comparatively a young man, and addressed himself to men, some of whom were in the ministry before he was born, and who had hitherto enjoyed the confidence of the church, and led lives of great labour and self-denial in her service.

The whole proceeding, though doubtless well intended, was in every point of view exceptionable. The charges were in general so vague, that they could neither be proved or disproved; they rested on hearsay evidence, for it is not to be supposed that Mr.

* This refers to the report brought in by Messrs. Dickinson, Pierson, Pemberton, Thompson, Anderson, Boyd, and Treat, on the dispute between Mr. Tennent and Mr. Cowell. See above, chapter iii. p. 197. Very few Synods in our day could furnish a committee of seven better men.

Tennent or Mr. Blair had many opportunities of hearing how a.l their brethren preached; and worst of all they were addressed indiscriminately against the body in general; thus the innocent and guilty were made to suffer alike. The Synod and the large audience which crowded the house,* were made to know that Mr. Tennent thought that many or most of his brethren were in "a carnal state;" but who were intended no one could tell. Some of his charges referred specifically to many of the best men in the Synod; others might be applied to any or every one, just as the hearers pleased. The other members of the Synod of course expostulated with these brethren on the impropriety of this course, and "earnestly pressed and entreated them to spare no man in the Synod whom they could prove to be unsound in doctrine or immoral in practice, but prayed them only to take Christ's methods with all such, and not to condemn the innocent with the guilty."† To this Mr. Tennent replies, "we did then offer to prove the matters of charge against particular members, if the Synod required it, but this was waived."‡ This is not a very fair statement. The Synod very properly waived taking up Mr. Tennent's vague charges, and themselves instituting process on the ground of them. They urged him, however, to proceed properly, "by tabling charges in a regular way, against particular persons, and not to blacken all."§ Mr. Tennent and Mr. Blair "frankly owned," that they had not "spoken with the persons intended in the said libels," and that they had not "made any regular inquiries into the truth of said reports." The Synod then declined proceeding with the matter until the persons aimed at had been apprized of the charges, and until they "had been regularly tried in their respective presbyteries."|| And this trial these brethren were urged to institute at once. This course was urged upon them on another occasion not long afterwards. For it is stated, that "Messrs. Gilbert Tennent, Samuel Blair, and

* Mr. Thompson speaks several times of the congregation present when the above-mentioned papers were read, as very large; and it is elsewhere stated, that the house was filled with "a tumultuous crowd."—Refutation, &c. p. 32.

† Preface to the Protest.

‡ Remarks on the Protest.

§ Refutation, &c. p. 33.

|| Ibid. p. 33.

Charles Tennent, were most earnestly pressed by the Presbytery of New Castle to spare none of their number, but to table their complaints against them, if they could convict any of them of any thing unbecoming a minister of the gospel. Nay, Mr. Gillespie entreated them in open Presbytery, for the Lord's sake to do so; but all to no purpose."* Mr. Tennent's answer to this was, "That the said proposal was matter of surprise to him; that he had no thought about any such thing before it was mentioned in the face of the judicatory; that his meeting with the Presbytery was merely accidental; and that his entering on a judicial process was inconsistent with his design and appointments of itinerary preaching."† He certainly then ought not to have made the charges, unless he could stop to prove them. Besides, the Presbytery told him they would wait his leisure; or he might "leave them an account of the matter in writing, if he could not attend their meeting; and that they would take it any way."‡

The conduct of Mr. Tennent and his friends in thus condemning his brethren unheard, seems to have produced a deep and general feeling of disapprobation. Before the New York brethren would consent to join with these New Brunswick brethren, in the formation of a new Synod, it was expressly stipulated that, "if any member of their body supposes that he hath any thing to object against any of his brethren, with respect to error in doctrine, immorality in life, or negligence in his ministry, he shall on no account propagate the scandal, until the person objected against is dealt with according to the rules of the gospel, and the known methods of their discipline."§ And it has already been mentioned that Mr. Tennent himself, as soon as the excitement of the revival had subsided, condemned with unsparing severity the "God-provoking sin" of rashly judging men to be graceless who were sound in essential doctrines, and regular in their lives.|| At this time, however, as he says himself, he abhorred all confinement in preaching the gos-

* Preface to the Protest. † Remarks on the Protest.

‡ Refutation, &c. p. 34. § Minutes of the Synod of New York, p. 3.

|| See the passages quoted in his Irenicum in the preceding chapter.

pel, and would keep no terms with any man who did not come up to the standard of his own ardent zeal.

It was in this year he preached his famous Nottingham sermon on the danger of an unconverted ministry. As this sermon may be regarded as one of the principal causes of the schism, it demands particular attention. His text was Mark vi. 34: "Jesus, when he came out, saw much people, and was moved with compassion towards them, because they were as sheep not having a shepherd;" from which he deduces the following proposition: "The case of such is much to be pitied who have no other but pharisee-shepherds or unconverted teachers." Under the first head of his sermon, he describes the character of the ancient pharisees, which he unfolds under the heads of pride, policy, malice, ignorance, covetousness, and bigotry to human inventions in religious matters. "Although," he says, "some of the old pharisee-shepherds had a very fair and strict outside, yet were they ignorant of the new birth. Witness Rabbi Nicodemus, who talked like a fool about it. Hear how our Lord cursed those plastered hypocrites. Matthew xxiii. 27, 28. Ay, if they had but a little of the learning then in fashion, and a fair outside, they were presently put into the priest's office, though they had no experience of the new birth. O sad! The old pharisees, for all their prayers and other pious pretences, had their eyes with Judas fixed on the bag. Why, they came into the priest's office for a piece of bread; they took it up as a trade, and therefore endeavoured to make the best market of it they could. O shame!"

Under his second head, he shows why those who have no other than pharisee teachers are to be pitied. His reasons are, 1. Because natural men have no call of God to the ministry, under the gospel dispensation. 2. Because the ministry of natural men is uncomfortable to gracious souls. 3. The ministry of natural men is for the most part unprofitable. "What if some instances could be shown of unconverted ministers being instrumental of convincing sinners of their lost state? The thing is very rare and extraordinary. And for what I know, as many instances may be given of Satan's convincing persons by his temptations. Indeed, it is a kind of chance-medley, both in respect of the father and his children, when any such event happens. And is not this the reason why a work of conviction and conversion has been so rarely heard of for a long time in the churches till of late, viz.: That the bulk of her spiritual guides are stone blind and stone dead?" 4. The ministry of natural men is dangerous, both in respect to the doctrines and practice of piety. "The doctrines of original sin, justification by faith alone, and the other points of Calvinism, are very cross to the grain of unrenewed nature. And though men, by the influence of a good education, and hopes of preferment, may have the edge of their natural enmity against them blunted, yet it is far from being broken or removed. It is only the saving grace of God that can give us a true relish for those nature-humbling doctrines, and so effectually secure us from being infected by the contrary."

In answer to the objection to what he had said about the ministry of natural men, that Judas was sent by Christ, he answers, 1. That the ministry of Judas was partly legal. 2. That it was extraordinarily necessary, in order to fulfil some ancient prophecies concerning him. "I fear that the abuse of this instance has brought many Judases into the ministry, whose chief desire, like their great grandfather, is to finger the pence and carry the bag. But let such hireling murderous hypocrites take care that they don't feel the force of a halter in this world, and an aggravated damnation in the next."

Under the third head he shows "how pity should be expressed on this mournful occasion." 1. We should mourn over those who are destitute of a faithful ministry, and sympathize with them. 2. We should pray for them, and especially pray the Lord of the harvest, that he would send forth faithful labourers into his harvest. 3. We should join our endeavours to our prayers. "The most likely method to stock the church with a faithful ministry, in the present state of things, the public academies being so much corrupted and abused generally, is to encourage private schools or seminaries of learning, which are under the care of skilful and experienced Christians, into which those only should be admitted, who, upon a strict examination have, in the judgment of charity, the plain evidences of experimental religion."

His first inference from this subject is, "If it be so, that the case of those who have no other and no better than pharisee-teachers is to be pitied, then what a scroll and scene of mourning, lamentation, and woe is opened, because of the swarms of locusts, the crowds of pharisees, that have as covetously as cruelly crept into the ministry, in this adulterous generation! who as nearly resemble the character given of the old pharisees, in the doctrinal part of this discourse, as one crow's egg does another. It is true some of the modern pharisees have learned to prate a little more orthodoxly about the new birth, than their predecessor Nicodemus, who are, in the meantime, as great strangers to the feeling experience of it as he. They are blind who see not this to be the case of the body of the clergy of this generation."

2. "From what has been said, we may learn that such who are contented under a dead ministry, have not in them the temper of that Saviour they profess. It is an awful sign, that they are as blind as moles, and as dead as stones, without any spiritual taste and relish. And alas! is not this the case of multitudes? If they can get one that has the name of a minister, with a band and a black coat or gown, to carry on a sabbath-day among them, although never so coldly and unsuccessfully, if he is free from gross crimes in practice, and takes care to keep at a due distance from their consciences, and is never troubled by his unsuccessfulness, O! think the poor fools, that is a fine man, indeed, our minister is a prudent charitable man, he is not always harping upon terror, nor sounding damnation in our ears, like some rash-headed ministers."

3. Such as enjoy a faithful ministry should glorify God on that account, and walk worthy of so distinguished a privilege.

4. "If the ministry of natural men be as it has been described, then it is both lawful and expedient to go from them to hear godly persons; yea, it is so far from being sinful to do this, that one who lives under a pious minister of lesser gifts, after having honestly endeavoured to get benefit by his ministry, and yet gets little or none, but doth find real benefit, and more benefit elsewhere, I say, he may lawfully go, and that frequently, where he gets most benefit to his precious soul, after regular application to the pastor where

he lives, for his consent, and proposing the reasons thereof; when this is done in the spirit of love and meekness, without contempt of any, as also without rash anger, or vain curiosity." He then argues at length the propriety of people leaving their pastors, first, when the pastor is pious, but of inferior gifts; and, secondly, when he is unconverted. As to the former case, he says, it is matter of instinct to seek the greater good in preference to the less; we are commanded to covet earnestly the best gifts; there is diversity of gifts among ministers, and God ordinarily blesses the best gifts to the greater edification of the people; as people have a right to the gifts of all God's ministers, they may use them as they have opportunity; Christ did not reprove John's disciples for coming to hear himself, not only on week-days, but on the Sabbath; to bind men to a particular minister against their inclination is carnal with a witness, it is a cruel oppression of tender consciences, and an infringement of Christian liberty; if the great end of hearing can be better attained elsewhere, then, "I see not why we should be under a fatal necessity of hearing our parish minister, perpetually or generally."

With regard to the latter case he is more strenuous. "If it be lawful to withdraw from the ministry of a pious man, in the case aforesaid, how much more from the ministry of a natural man! Surely it is both lawful and expedient, for the reasons offered in the doctrinal part of this discourse; to which let me add a few words more."

The additional considerations which he urges are the following. 1. It is unwise to trust the care of our souls to those who have no care of their own. 2. God does not ordinarily use the ministry of his enemies to turn others to be his friends. God has not given any promise that he will bless the labours of natural men. If he had he would be as good as his word; but I can neither see nor hear of any blessing upon these men's labours, unless it be a rare wonderful instance of chance-medley; whereas the ministry of faithful men blossoms and bears fruit, as the rod of Aaron. 3. We are commanded to turn away from such as have the form of godliness, but deny the power thereof. 4. Our Lord advised his disciples to beware of the leaven of the pharisees, by which he meant their doctrine and hypocrisy, which were both sour enough. 5. He refers to Matt. xv. 12, &c. "Then came his disciples, and said unto him, Knowest thou that the pharisees were offended? And he answered and said, Every plant that my heavenly Father hath not planted, shall be rooted up. Let them alone; they be blind leaders of the blind; and if the blind lead the blind, both shall fall into the ditch."

He next considers the objections to such a course, as, 1. We are commanded to hear those who sit in Moses' seat. This only means that we are bound to obey the lawful commands of the civil magistrates. 2. Such a practice would cause contentions among the people. It may occasion them, but not properly cause them. If we give up every duty that is the occasion of contention and division, we must give up powerful religion altogether. 3. 1 Cor. i. 12, which speaks of Paul and Apollos, is not against the course recommended, for that only speaks of making sects. 4. Such a course would tend to grieve our parish minister, and to break up congregations. "If our parish minister be grieved at our greater good, or prefer his credit before it, then he has good cause to grieve over his own rottenness and hypocrisy. And as for breaking of congregations to pieces, upon account of people's going from place to place to hear the word, with a view to get greater good, that spiritual blindness and deadness which so generally prevail, will put this out of danger. It is but a few that have got any spiritual relish. The most will venture their souls with any formalist, and be well satisfied with the sapless discourses of such dead drones." 5. Paul and Apollos are said to be nothing. True, they were nothing as efficient causes, but they were something as instruments. 6. Finally, it is objected, people do not get more good over their parish line, for they are out of God's way. There are three monstrous ingredients in this objection, a begging the question, rash judging, and limiting of God. It is a mean thing in reasoning to beg the question in debate. Let it be proved that they are out of God's way. It is rash judging to say people do not get good, when we cannot know it to be so; and it is to limit God to confine him to one mode of action.

He concludes by exhorting those who have a faithful ministry, to make a speedy and sincere use of so rare a privilege. He exhorts gracious souls to pity those who have none but pharisee-teachers. He urges "those who live under the ministry of dead men, whether they have the form of religion or not, to repair to the living, where they may be edified; let who will oppose it." He exhorts vacant congregations to be careful in trying those whom they think of calling as pastors. "I beseech you, my brethren, to consider that there is no probability of your getting good by the ministry of pharisees; for they are no shepherds, (no faithful ones,) in Christ's account. They are as good as none; nay, worse than none on some accounts. For take them first and last, they do more harm than good. They strive to keep better men out of the places where they live; nay, when the life of piety comes near their quarters, they rise up in arms against it, as a common enemy that discovers and condemns their craft and hypocrisy. And with what art, rhetoric, and appearances of piety, will they varnish their opposition to Christ's kingdom! As the magicians imitated the wonders of Moses, so do false apostles and deceitful workers, the apostles of Christ."

This sermon had an extensive circulation. Two editions of it were published in Philadelphia, and a third in Boston. Two of the principal grounds of complaint against Mr. Tennent and his friends, were the censorious condemnation of their brethren, and the encouragement they gave the people to separate from their pastors. Though this sermon was by no means the only ground of these complaints, it was one of the most tangible proofs of their justice, and hence was constantly appealed to in the controversies of that day. On this account a knowledge of its contents and character is necessary to a proper understanding of the history of the period now under consideration.

In this discourse Mr. Tennent describes the body of the ministers of that generation as letter-learned pharisees, plastered hypocrites, having the form of godliness but destitute of its power. That this description was intended to apply to his brethren in the Synod, it is believed was never doubted. Considering the circumstances under which it was delivered, and his frequent avowals of similar sentiments respecting them on other occasions, it could hardly have any other application. In the sermon itself he tells the people that the reason why they had seen so few cases of conviction or conversion among them, was, that "the bulk of their spiritual guides were stone blind and stone dead." In answer to the criticism which it occasioned, he says, "When I composed it, I expected it would be judged, by that tribe which it detected, as guilty of *scandalum magnatum*, as worthy of stripes and of bonds. I supposed it would be like rousing a wasp's nest, and I have found it according to my expectations. The opposers of God's work have dipt their tongues and pens in gall, and by their malignant invectives have endeavoured to bury its author in ruins; but peradventure it may have a resurrection to their terror and shame."* Some members of the Synod had placed together in dreadful array the terms of invective contained in this discourse. In reference to which he says, "I have heard people of piety and good sense observe upon this popular paragraph, that the gentlemen who had put it together in its present form, had taken a pretty deal of pains to draw their own pictures."† He denies that the Nottingham sermon had been the cause of contention; "No," says he, "the true cause is graceless ministers opposing it. Methinks it would be more to their credit, prudently to let it alone on their own account, for when they keep muttering, growling, and scolding at it, it does but give people ground to suspect that they are of that unhappy tribe and party themselves, which is therein detected and censured."‡

The Nottingham sermon, though the principal printed example of Mr. Tennent's manner of treating his brethren, is by no means the only one. In most of his controversial writings of this period, he speaks of them as the malignant opposers of true religion, and ascribes their conduct to the most unworthy motives. In a work published in 1743, we find, for example, the following passage. "Give me leave to propose this query to Mr. Thompson and his associates, whether it was because that such as were convinced of sin had generally a less esteem for his ministry, and of some of the

* Examiner Examined, p. 31. † Ibid. p. 79. ‡ Ibid. p. 146.

rest of his party, that he and some, at least, of them have so fiercely opposed the blessed operations of the Holy Ghost in alarming and convincing a secure world of sin, righteousness, and judgment? If so, is it not selfish and sordid with a witness, and a blow at the root of all piety? For my own part I must say, that I humbly conceive that to be the secret of the story of their opposition, the bottom of the mystery, the true spring of their malignant contending against vital godliness. The false and ungenerous methods, as well as long continuance of their opposition to the work of God, under so much advantage of light and evidence in favour of it, together with their dangerous errors* before mentioned, free me from the just imputation of rash judging in thinking as I have expressed." †

Mr. Tennent was so completely the soul of the party to which he belonged, that without him it never would have existed. He is often, therefore, addressed as the party itself, and his writings and declarations are referred to as speaking the language of his associates. Though the most prominent and the most violent, he was not the only one who indulged in these vehement denunciations of his brethren. Mr. Blair, though a much milder man, was scarcely less severe in his judgments; and Mr. Creaghead, Mr. Finley, and others followed in the same course. Such denunciations as we find in the Nottingham sermon and other writings of that day, cannot be excused on the plea of zeal or fidelity. Their only tendency was to exasperate. Other men as faithful as Mr. Tennent, were never guilty either of his censoriousness or violence. We never hear of any complaints against President Dickinson, Mr. Pierson, Mr. Pemberton, and other active friends of the revival. For these gentlemen the highest respect and the kindest feelings were, on all occasions, expressed by those who differed from them in opinion, as to the general character and probable results of the religious excitement which then prevailed. There can be no doubt, there-

* This refers to Mr. Thompson's doctrine on the nature of conviction of sin, which will be stated in the sequel.

† Examiner Examined, p. 78.

fore, that Mr. Tennent's unhappy violence was one of the principal causes of that entire alienation of feeling, which soon resulted in an open rupture. When such denunciations come from men of doubtful character or feeble intellect, they are commonly and safely disregarded. But when they are hurled by such men as Tennent, men of acknowledged piety and commanding power, they can hardly fail to shatter the society among which they fall. Mr. Tennent became fully sensible of the impropriety of this censorious spirit, and laboured hard to correct the evils it had occasioned. It is difficult to believe that the same man could write the Nottingham Sermon and the Irenicum Ecclesiasticum. The former is full of coarse invective; the latter is distinguished for mildness, liberality, and a conciliatory spirit. And what makes the case the more remarkable, the latter excuses, vindicates, and even praises the very men whom the former denounced. In the Irenicum he lays down the canon, that to declare those persons to be graceless, who are "sound in the fundamental truths of religion, and regular in life," is a grievous offence against God and the church. Yet the brethren whom he denounced, he describes in general as letter-learned orthodox, having a fair outside, the form of godliness, and even in some cases, a great appearance of religion. They were, therefore, both sound and regular. There is no doubt, however, that he understood his brethren of the Synod as coming within the scope of his rule; for it is in express reference to them that he lays it down. His object was to convince the people of his own party, that they had no right to regard those brethren as graceless, and on that ground refuse to unite with them.* Mr. Tennent, therefore, being judge, the denunciation of his ministerial brethren was "an evil pregnant with pride, malice, and mischief, though perhaps not perceived or intended; an evil which, under a cloak of misguided zeal for God, Christian liberty, and superior attainments in knowledge and religion, rebelliously opposes the clearest dictates of reason and humanity, and the plainest laws of revealed religion; an evil that, under the pretext of kindness and piety, cruelly rends our neighbour's character, saps the foundation of the

* Irenicum, p. 78.

church's peace, and turns its union, order, and harmony, into the wildest confusion of ungoverned anarchy, schism, prejudice, and hate."*

The alienation of feeling which existed among the members of the Synod, is not to be attributed solely or even principally to the denunciatory spirit of some of the leading preachers of that day. It was in a great measure due to the intrusion into the congregations of settled ministers, the exhortations given to the people to leave their pastors, when believed to be unconverted or contentedly unsuccessful, and the erection of separate meetings. This was of all grounds of complaint against the New Brunswick brethren, the one most frequently urged. There is abundant evidence that the complaint was well founded. The fact that the Synod twice enacted a rule against such intrusions, is evidence that the evil was then felt; and the opposition of the New Brunswick gentlemen to the rule, shows that they "abhorred all confinement in preaching the gospel." Mr. Blair, in the paper read before the Synod in 1740, said to his brethren, "Unless we can see hopeful encouraging appearances of a work of God's converting grace among such ministers, we believe we shall find ourselves obliged in duty to our glorious Lord, to answer the invitations and desires of people groaning under the oppression of a dead unfaithful ministry, by going to preach to them wherever they are."† Mr. Tennent, in his Nottingham sermon, teaches that it is both lawful and expedient for the people to forsake the ministry of unconverted men. This he confirms by various arguments, and defends from various objections, and then exhorts the people to act accordingly, saying, "Let those who live under the ministry of dead men, whether they have the form of religion or not, repair to the living." Nearly one-third of the whole discourse, six pages out of twenty, was devoted to this general subject. The Presbytery of Donegal state that, in consequence of these divisive schemes, "most congregations in the country are reduced to such disorder and confusion, that the preaching of the word is despised and forsaken, the ministers of

* Irenicum, p. 55.

† Quoted at length in Thompson's Government of the Church, p. 46, &c.

the gospel are contemned and evil spoken of, and their public ministrations and private conduct misrepresented and traduced."* At the meeting of the New Brunswick Presbytery, on the second day after the schism, applications were made for supplies from about eighteen places, almost all of which were out of the bounds of the Presbytery, and came for the most part from fragments of old congregations. There is, therefore, no doubt that separations did extensively take place, and that they were fostered by Mr. Tennent and his friends. Indeed Mr. Tennent himself admits this. In his remarks on the Protest, he says, "That there have been some divisions consequent on our preaching in some places, we acknowledge."†

The answers which he gives to the charge of having encouraged the people to forsake their pastors, are not a little remarkable. He sometimes admits it, sometimes denies it, and sometimes evades it. During the revival he not only asserted the doctrine complained of, but was prepared to justify it. Thus in 1741, in answer to the charge of intrusion and separation, he says, "What is proper in ordinary cases may be prejudicial in extraordinaries. When a church is stocked with a sound, faithful, and lively ministry, no doubt those rules respecting ministers keeping within the bounds of their respective charges, until they are invited in an orderly manner to go elsewhere, may be of service. But, on the supposition that a number of ministers are either unsound in doctrine, or unfaithful and contentedly unsuccessful in their work, then is it not lawful to suspend the aforesaid rules for a season?"‡ Again: "No doubt there is a relation between a pastor and his people, but the design of this being to promote their good, we think it unreasonable that it should subsist to the prejudice of that which it was designed to secure. However, in ordinary cases, we think it to be the people's duty to make regular application to their pastors to go where they can get the most benefit. But when ministers conspire to oppose the work and servants of God, in the most flagrant manner, we see no harm in this case, in their using an extraordinary

* Minutes for December, 1740.

† Remarks, &c. p. 8.

‡ Remarks, &c., p. 19.

method."* And elsewhere in still stronger language, he says, when ministers habitually oppose the revival, "I see not how any that fear God can contentedly sit under their ministrations, (if they persist as aforesaid,) without becoming accessary to their crimson guilt."† It was, therefore, at that time his opinion, that when ministers were unconverted, or contentedly unsuccessful, and especially if they opposed the revival, it was the duty of their people to leave them.

When, however, he saw how these principles were operating in New England,‡ where the separatists had begun to break off from the regular pastors, because they did not come up to their standard of zeal and fidelity, and when the Moravians had begun to make inroads upon some of the Presbyterian churches, he in a measure altered his manner of speaking. In April, 1742, he preached several sermons in New York, against the Moravians, which, together with an Appendix, were soon given to the world. In these sermons he condemns many of the opinions and practices of which he had been hitherto considered the advocate. Among other things, he says, "It is an instance of pride to despise and slight ministers or people that are unconverted, or supposed to be so." "The practice of staying at home, rather than going to hear such ministers, sound in principle and regular in practice, as are judged by some to be unconverted, is unscriptural and of dangerous tendency, in my opinion, for it hangs the whole weight of the public worship of God, on the uncertain judgment of men. Though unconverted ministers are not likely to do so much good as others, yet seeing that many of them doubtless preach the same word of God which others do, why may not a sovereign God, who permits them by his

* Remarks on the Protest, p. 29.

† Letter to Franklin, as editor of the Pennsylvania Gazette, and published in that paper, September 2, 1742.

‡ "The passages referred to in the Moravian sermon were occasioned," he says, "by reports of a separating disposition obtaining in New England; I was informed that some were separating from the ministry of such as were sound in principle, regular in life, and approvers of God's work; and that some staid at home, rather than they would hear such, merely because they judged them to be unconverted."—Examiner Examined, p. 90.

providence to come into the ministry, bless his word delivered by them to the good of mankind?" The inconsistency between these sentiments and those elsewhere advocated by Mr. Tennent, did not escape the notice of his opponents, who arrayed the conflicting assertions in parallel columns.*

This attack evidently placed Mr. Tennent in considerable difficulties. The revival and the excitements by which it was attended, had not yet subsided. He was not prepared, therefore, fully and kindly to retract, as he subsequently did, either his censorious condemnation of his brethren, or his divisive principles. He was thus led to endeavour to reconcile and justify both classes of his conflicting statements. One explanation was that, in the sermons against the Moravians, he meant to condemn the practice of separating from ministers who were not only sound and regular, but also "favourers of God's work," i. e. the revival.† But this last qualification is not found in those sermons. He condemns separation from sound and regular pastors, on the assumption of their being unconverted; and to this he exhorted the people in the Nottingham sermon. A second mode of explanation was, that he only intended, in the Nottingham sermon, to teach that the people might apply for a regular dismission from the congregation to which they belonged. As the pastor might leave the people, so the people might leave the pastor in a regular manner.‡ He says he intended to enjoin on the people to make a regular application to the pastor

* This was done by a Boston writer calling himself Philalethes, in a book entitled, The Examiner, or Gilbert against Tennent. Boston, 1743.

The things for which Mr. Tennent particularly censures the Moravians, are, 1. Censoriousness; speaking reproachfully of all the reformed churches. 2. Dividing congregations, and "scattering Christ's poor sheep." 3. Thrusting ignorant novices into the ministry. 4. For their slight and sudden conversions, done in a moment. "What," he asks, "is the Moravian faith, but a sorry mushroom of a night's growth?" 5. For addressing themselves to the affections rather than to the understandings of the people, and endeavouring to gain over the young, the ignorant, and females. "Whom do they imitate in attacking the weaker part of man, viz.: the passions, and the weaker sex first, but the devil, the father of lies and of errors?"

† Examiner Examined, p. 90.

‡ Ibid. p. 26.

and session for leave to go elsewhere, assigning their reasons for so doing. "If these reasons are not accounted valid, and the case be really so, they ought to desist. But if they are wronged they ought to appeal to a higher judicatory; but if the case should so happen, that after every appeal they can make, and the most humble and impartial examination of the affair, they firmly think they are wronged, and conscience-bound in the matter, they ought to judge for themselves and act according to their consciences."* That this interpretation of his sermon is at variance with its language need hardly be remarked. It is no less obviously inconsistent with the other explanation, to wit, that the people ought not to leave their ministers, whether converted or not, provided they favoured the revival; but if they opposed it, it was a great sin to adhere to them. And it is certain the above interpretation was never put upon his sermon, either by his friends or opponents. The separatists did not wait to apply to one judicatory after another, but went off without asking or desiring leave.

Mr. Tennent sometimes goes still further, and denies that he ever encouraged separations. In reference to this charge, he says, "It is false; there is not a word in that (Nottingham) sermon which encourages separate meetings from any ministry, merely because they are unconverted." Having made a similar denial before, his opponents said it was a notorious falsehood, and that the whole country knew that from the pulpit and the press he had encouraged the people to forsake their ministry. This statement, he says, "is a dreadful instance of effronted impiety. O shame! what sort of men are these who not only assert an egregious falsehood, but appeal to the whole country to prove it! To confront their charge, I do appeal to the numerous multitudes, wherever I have preached the gospel of Christ, if what they alleged be not a groundless and crimson calumny, which those enemies of the power of religion do impute to me. It is the necessity of their wretched cause, that urges those unhappy men to take such sinful and scandalous methods, in order to cloak their horrible wickedness in opposing God's work, which has been the real cause of the divisions

* Examiner Examined, pp. 21, 22.

subsisting among us; which they, without foundation, ascribe to me." * This denial is so hearty it is impossible to doubt its sincerity. It is, however, no less impossible to doubt the truth of the charge. His Nottingham sermon not only teaches that it is lawful and expedient to leave the ministry of natural men, but it argues the point, enjoins it as a duty commanded by Scripture, and earnestly exhorts his hearers to the performance of it. The same thing is taught over and over in this very book, which contains the above denial.

The truth is, Mr. Tennent, like other vehement men, often said more than he meant. He acted more from feeling than from principle. When he thought of the people desirous of fervent preaching, sitting under cold and lifeless ministrations, his soul caught fire, and he urged them to leave their sapless preachers, and justified their doing so. But when he saw rash enthusiasts, who thought all persons dead but themselves, scattering the congregations of pious men, he denounced their conduct, and was obliged to lay down a canon which condemned his own course. That canon was, that we have no right to regard or treat as graceless those who are sound in essential doctrines and regular in life. Mr. Tennent and his friends had grievously offended against this rule. They not only had pronounced such men to be unconverted, but had acted on the assumption of their being so, and treated them as unfit for their offices. It may easily be conceived what a state of things would be produced by some half-dozen ministers assuming the prerogative of judging of the hearts of their brethren, denouncing them as unconverted, entering their congregations, exhorting their people to leave them, and every where erecting new congregations. This the New Brunswick brethren did very extensively; and this, more than any thing else, was the cause of the schism. It was in fact schism itself, in its worst form. As might have been expected, this conduct called forth loud complaints of the arrogant assumption of power on the part of a few men, to judge and condemn their brethren; of the injustice of condemning them without a

* Examiner Examined, pp. 88, 89.

trial before a competent tribunal; and of the grievous injuries which were thus inflicted upon them and their churches.

These complaints were sometimes brought before the Presbyteries, though seldom to any good purpose. Thus in 1740 a representation was made to the Presbytery of Donegal in reference to Mr. Blair, for intruding into the congregations of several of their members; and Mr. John Thompson was requested to go to the Presbytery of New Castle, to which Mr. Blair belonged, and call their attention to the case.* The same year Mr. Alison presented a complaint on the same ground against Mr. Alexander Creaghead, which was accompanied with "a supplication from several members of Mr. Creaghead's congregation, complaining of his mal-conduct in several particulars." The Presbytery met at Middle Octarara to examine these charges. Besides the complaint of Mr. Alison of the Presbytery of New Castle, Mr. Creaghead was charged by some of his own congregation, 1. With absenting himself from Presbytery. 2. With imposing new terms of communion on his people at the baptism of their children. 3. With excluding a person from the communion, because he seemed to be opposed to his new methods. 4. With asserting that the ministers of Christ ought not to be confined to any particular charge. The new term of communion here complained of was, no doubt, the adoption of the solemn league and covenant, which it seems he and Mr. John Cross of the Presbytery of New Brunswick, were often in the habit of imposing on their people.† When the Presbytery were about to proceed with this case, they "were interrupted by the people rising into a tumult, and railing at the members in the most scurrilous and opprobrious manner; so that having concluded with prayer, they were obliged to adjourn to another place."

* Minutes of the Presbytery of Donegal, p. 203.

† Thompson's Government of the Church.—"Some of them preach up the national and solemn league and covenants; and give the breach of those covenants as the great and principal cause of the great decay of religion among us. Others of the same party never mention it, that I hear of. Some of them oblige parents to these covenants at the baptism of their children; and others do not. Yea, the same persons sometimes oblige parents to these covenants, and sometimes do not; as for instance Mr. Alexander Creaghead, and Mr. John Cross." p. 43.

The Presbytery in their account of this trial, if trial it can be called, state that when they came to the church, they found Mr. Creaghead preaching on the text, 'Let them alone, they be blind leaders of the blind;' and that his sermon was almost a continued invective against such as he called pharisee preachers, and against the Presbytery in particular, asserting that they were given over to judicial hardness of heart and impenitency. After the sermon Mr. Creaghead invited the congregation, which was very large, to the tent, where they were entertained with the reading of a paper which he called his defence, containing the most slanderous reproaches against the members of the Presbytery, some of whom were mentioned by name. This paper was read by Mr. David Alexander and Mr. Samuel Finley,* and the Presbytery themselves were summoned to attend.

The next day, when the Presbytery were about to inquire into the complaints against Mr. Creaghead, he came in, accompanied by Mr. Alexander and Mr. Finley, and insisted upon again reading his defence. The Presbytery requested him first to allow the charges to be presented. This he refused to do, and insisted that the defence should be read first. Whereupon Messrs. Alexander and Finley ascended the pulpit and read the paper which had been read to the people the day before. In the beginning of this paper Mr. Creaghead utterly declined the authority of the Presbytery, and protested against their proceeding with the case, on the ground that they were all his accusers. In view of the several complaints against Mr. C., and of his contumacy and disorderly conduct, the Presbytery suspended him from the ministry until their next meeting; directing, however, that if he should signify his sorrow for his conduct to any member, that member should notify the moderator, who was to call the Presbytery together to consider his acknowledgment and take off the suspension.†

There were, at this time, in that Presbytery, together with several excellent men, a few members from Ireland, whose conduct brought a reproach upon the whole body, but who were soon sus-

* Mr. Finley was at this time a licentiate of the Presbytery of New Brunswick.

† Minutes of Donegal Presbytery, pp. 205, 6.

pended and discarded by their brethren. The presence of those members, unconvicted, and even unaccused as yet, could afford little justification for the course pursued by Mr. Creaghead, in absenting himself from the Presbytery, disregarding their authority, and especially in reading his calumnious charges against the whole body to a promiscuous and excited audience.*

The Presbytery had a difficulty also with Mr. David Alexander. In October 1740, he was cited to answer a complaint for preaching in a disorderly manner in Mr. Black's congregation, and for absenting himself time after time from the Presbytery, without excuse.† When the Presbytery met in December following, he assigned as the reasons of his absence, bodily weakness, and certain scruples which he had in reference to the conduct of the Presbytery. One of these scruples was, their "opposing the work of God, in seeming to condemn the crying out of people at sermons, and opposing those ministers who seem instrumental in carrying on these things." Another was, their too superficial examination of candidates. For others, it appears, he referred the Presbytery to the paper above-mentioned as Mr. Creaghead's defence. He added, however, that he was still willing to consider himself a member of the Presbytery. To this the Presbytery replied that they would recognize him as a member, provided he "acknowledged his sinful disorder in absenting himself from Presbytery on account of these scruples, without having remonstrated them to the Presbytery; and provided he promised not to absent himself in future, on account of these or any other scruples, in the same manner, without previously intimating them to the Presbytery in a judicial way."‡ With these provisos

* Mr. Tennent, in 1743, speaking of this gentleman, says, "There is one indeed, who I hope is a pious man, Mr. Alexander Creaghead by name, who was formerly in a state of union with us, but having more zeal and positiveness than knowledge and judgment, has schismatically broken communion with us, and adopted the rigid Cameronian scheme. He is indeed tinged with an uncharitable and party spirit, to the great prejudice of real religion in some places, this way. May the Almighty forgive him, and rectify his judgment. His late and present divisive conduct we utterly detest and disclaim."—Examiner Examined, p. 120.

† Minutes of the Presbytery of Donegal, p. 203.

‡ Ibid. p. 207.

he refused to comply, and the other part of the charge against him not being immediately taken up, he left the place. The Presbytery then determined to cite him to attend their next meeting, to answer for his disorderly conduct in endorsing and reading the charges against the Presbytery, contained in Mr. Creaghead's defence, without the consent of the Presbytery, and before a large congregation; and for leaving the Presbytery after having said in a boasting manner, that the real charge against him was preaching in Mr. Black's congregation, which he acknowledged, and would do it again and again. This citation he refused to answer.* He was cited a second time to answer the above charges, and a *fama clamosa* charge of intemperance. In consequence of this second call, he appeared at the meeting held May, 1741, and "by taking the pulpit prevented the moderator, who had prepared to preach." He gave as his reason for not answering the first citation, that the Presbytery had cut him off from being a member; and that he told the person citing him, that he had appealed to the Synod. With regard to the charge of intemperance, he said it arose from what occurred at a funeral, where he acknowledged "he had drunk some more than was necessary."† The Presbytery acquitted him of the charge of intemperance to the extent reported; but on account of his acknowledged indiscretion, and of his disorderly conduct, and reproaching the Presbytery, they said they could not regard him as a member "until we be satisfied as to these pieces of his disregardful conduct towards us, and refusing to submit to the government of Christ's church in our hands. At the same time we cannot but, with deep sorrow of heart, bewail the unhappy, divided, and distracted state of this poor church, through the uncharitable opposition of both ministers and people against one another."‡

These are melancholy scenes to occur in the midst of a great revival of religion. Such, however, was the tumult excited in the public mind, that, in various parts of the country, every thing seemed to get into confusion, and even good men were alienated from each other. A portion of the ministers of the Synod having

* Minutes of the Presbytery of Donegal, p. 212. † Ibid. p. 224.

‡ Ibid. p. 225.

lost confidence in the majority of their brethren, did not hesitate to denounce them as unconverted men, and exhort their people to leave them. The consequence was, that many congregations were broken up, and many more divided. The Synod of 1741, therefore, met under circumstances very unfavourable to peace and union. The majority felt themselves grievously injured, both in character and in their pastoral relations. It is no wonder then that they came together determined, if possible, to put a stop to the prevailing disorders; nor, considering their state of mind, is it surprising that they mistook their remedy and placed themselves in the wrong.

The Synod met in Philadelphia, May 2, 1741. Mr. Pierson, the moderator for the preceding year, being absent, the sessions were opened with a sermon by Mr. Andrews, who was elected moderator, and Mr. Boyd was appointed clerk. The following ministers were in attendance, viz.: From the Presbytery of New Castle, George Gillespie, Robert Cathcart, Charles Tennent, Francis Alison, Alexander Hucheson, and Samuel Blair. From the Presbytery of Philadelphia, Jedediah Andrews, Robert Cross, Daniel Elmer, Francis McHenry, Richard Treat, and William Tennent, Sen'r. From the Presbytery of Lewes, James Martin, and Robert Jamison. From the Presbytery of New Brunswick, Eleazar Wales, Gilbert Tennent, and William Tennent, Jun'r. From the Presbytery of Donegal, John Thompson, Adam Boyd, John Elder, Richard Sanchy, Samuel Cavin, Samuel Thompson, Alexander Creaghead, and David Alexander. All the members of the Presbytery of New York were absent.

The first matter which occasioned difficulty was the case of Mr. Alexander Creaghead. Having been suspended by his own Presbytery, it would appear to be a matter of course, that he should not take his seat as a member of Synod, until that sentence was reversed. He seems, however, to have been enrolled from the first as a regular member. As he had not submitted to a trial before the inferior judicatory, according to ordinary rules of proceeding, he had no right to appeal to a higher. This point, however, appears to have been waived in his favour, and the Synod took up the question of his right to a seat, "and after much discourse upon it, and a paper of Mr. Creaghead being read, the Synod deferred the further consideration of it." In the afternoon the case was resumed, when "Mr. Creaghead presented another paper, which was read, and after debating on that business, the Synod agreed that this and the former paper be perused by the Donegal Presbytery, in order for trial against to-morrow afternoon." The next minute in relation to the subject, states, that "the Presbytery of Donegal, as appointed, began their reply to Mr. Creaghead's papers, in several particulars, but being late it was deferred." The next morning "the above affair continued, and a great deal of discourse maintained upon it, when the Synod deferred the further consideration of it." This was on Saturday the 30th of May; on Monday the 1st of June the schism occurred, and of course the subject was dropt.

It appears there were two points which occupied the attention of the Synod. The one was the difficulty between Mr. Creaghead and his Presbytery, and the other the complaint of Mr. Alison against Mr. Creaghead for intruding into his congregation. As to the former there seems to have been little progress made in adjusting the matter. It was proposed that a committee should be sent down to try the case. Mr. Creaghead insisted, if that were done, the majority of the committee should be of the "New Brunswick party." To this the other side objected, and in their turn opposed the appointment of certain individuals who had been nominated.*

The other point was most disputed, and seems to have brought matters to a crisis. Mr. Alison contended, that as he had regularly tabled charges against Mr. Creaghead before the Presbytery of Donegal, for intruding into his congregation, "to rend and divide it against his mind, the mind of the session, and the declared opinion of the congregation in general;" and as Mr. Creaghead had refused to submit to a trial before the Presbytery, it was his undoubted right to bring the complaint before the Synod and have the matter tried there. He urged this the rather because there was no need of testimony in the case, as "Mr. Creaghead publicly acknowledged the whole fact" complained of; and because an op-

* Refutation of Mr. Tennent's remarks on the Protest, pp. 37, 38.

portunity would thus be offered to the Synod, and especially to the New Brunswick party, to show how far they were willing to condemn this disorderly intrusion into settled congregations, and to make proposals for peace.* Mr. Tennent and his friends resisted the complaint's being entertained "merely because Donegal Presbytery did not enter it on their records as a prime article." It is difficult to see the force of this objection. The complaint did not come to the Synod through the Presbytery of Donegal, but directly from Mr. Alison. The complaint as presented to the Presbytery had proved inoperative, for though the disorder complained of was one of the several grounds on which the Presbytery suspended Mr. Creaghead, yet he not only refused to answer the charge, but had disregarded their sentence. It seems rather unfair that the action of the Presbytery should be considered a nullity as it regarded Mr. Creaghead, and as valid in satisfying Mr. Alison's complaint. He had applied to the Presbytery for redress and had obtained none; for its authority had been denied and its sentence disregarded. When, therefore, in due course he applied to the Synod, he had reason to expect to be heard. Resisting this course on technical grounds was certainly very unfortunate, as an opportunity was thus lost of satisfying the minds of the aggrieved members, that the New Brunswick brethren would not deliberately sanction "the practice of breaking in upon and dissolving pastoral relations in such an unscriptural and anti-presbyterial way." The result of this attempt to bring up the matter in complaint, the majority of the Synod say, "put us out of all hopes of obtaining peace with our brethren upon such terms as are founded on the word of God, and our Presbyterian constitution."

This last effort at accommodation having failed, the Rev. Robert Cross, pastor of the First Presbyterian Church in Philadelphia, rose and read the following PROTESTATION, viz.:

"*Rev. Fathers and Brethren:*

"We, the ministers of Jesus Christ, and members of the Synod of Philadelphia, being wounded and grieved in our very hearts, at

* Refutation of Mr. Tennent's remarks on the Protest, pp. 39, 40; also the Preface to the printed copy of the Protest.

the dreadful divisions, distractions, and convulsions, which all of a sudden have seized this infant church to such a degree that, unless He who is king in Zion, do graciously and seasonably interfere for our relief, she is in no small danger of expiring outright, and that quickly, as to the form, order, and constitution of an organized church, which hath subsisted for above thirty years past, in a very great degree of order and perfect harmony until of late; we say, we being deeply grieved with these things, which lie heavy on our spirits, and being sensible that it is our indispensable duty to do what lies in our power, in a lawful way, according to the light and directions of the inspired oracles, to preserve this swooning church from a total expiration; and after the deliberate and unprejudiced inquiry into the causes of these confusions, which rage so among us, both ministers and people, we evidently seeing, and being fully persuaded in our judgments that, besides our misimprovement of, and unfruitfulness under, gospel light, liberty, and privileges, the great decay of practical godliness in the life and power of it, and many abounding immoralities; we say, besides these our sins, which we judge to be the meritorious cause of our present doleful distractions, the awful judgments we now suffer under; we evidently see that our protesting brethren* and their adherents are the direct and proper cause thereof, by their unwearied, unscriptural, antipresbyterial, uncharitable divisive practices, which they have been pursuing with all the diligence they were capable of, with any probability of success, for above these twelve months past especially; besides too much of the like practices for some years before, though not with such barefaced arrogance and boldness:

"And being fully convinced in our judgments, that it is our duty to bear testimony against these disorderly proceedings, according to our stations, capacity, and trust reposed in us by our exalted Lord, as watchmen on the walls of his Zion, we having endeavoured sincerely to seek counsel and direction from God, who hath promised to give wisdom to those who ask him in faith, yea, hath pro-

* That is, the brethren who protested against the Synod's act respecting the examination of candidates, viz.:, the four Tennents, Mr. Blair, Mr. Wales, Mr. John Cross and Mr. Creaghead.

mised his Holy Spirit to lead his people and servants into all truth; and being clearly convinced in our consciences, that it is a duty we are called upon in this present juncture of affairs, reverend fathers and brethren, we hereby humbly and solemnly protest, in the presence of the great and eternal God and his elect angels, as well as in the presence of all here present, and particularly of you, reverend brethren, in our own names, and in the names of all, both ministers and people, who shall adhere to us, as follows:

"1. We protest that it is the indispensable duty of this Synod to maintain and stand by the principles of doctrine, worship, and government of the church of Christ, as the same are summed up in the Confession of Faith, Catechisms, and Directory composed by the Westminster Assembly, as being agreeable to the word of God, and which this Synod have owned, acknowledged, and adopted, as may appear from our synodical records of the years 1729, 1730, 1736, which we desire to be read publicly.

"2. We protest that no person, minister or elder, should be allowed to sit and vote in this Synod, who hath not received, adopted, or subscribed the said Confessions, Catechisms, and Directory, as our presbyteries respectively do, according to our last explication of the adopting act; or who is either accused or convicted, or may be convicted before this Synod, or any of our presbyteries, of holding any doctrine, or who acts and persists in any practice contrary to any of those doctrines or rules contained in said Directory, or contrary to any of the known rights of presbytery, or orders made and agreed to by this Synod, and which stand yet unrepealed; unless, or until he renounce such doctrine, and being found guilty, acknowledge, confess, and profess his sorrow for such sinful disorder, to the satisfaction of this Synod, or such inferior judicatory as the Synod shall appoint or empower for that purpose.

"3. We protest that our protesting brethren have at present no right to sit and vote as members of this Synod, having forfeited their right of being accounted members of it, for many reasons, a few of which we shall mention afterwards.

"4. We protest, that if, notwithstanding this our protestation, those brethren be allowed to sit and vote in this Synod, without giving suitable satisfaction to the Synod, and particularly to us, who now enter this protestation, and to those who shall adhere to us in it, that whatsoever shall be done, voted, or transacted by them contrary to our judgment, shall be of no force or obligation to us; being done and acted by a judicatory consisting in part of members who have no authority to act with us in ecclesiastical matters.

"5. We protest, that if, notwithstanding this our protestation, and the true intent and meaning of it, those protesting brethren, and such as adhere to them, or support or countenance them in their antipresbyterial practices, shall continue to act as they have done this last year, in that case we, and as many as have clearness to join with us and maintain the rights of this judicatory, shall be accounted in no wise disorderly, but the true Presbyterian church in this province; and they shall be looked upon as guilty of schism, and the breach of the rules of Presbyterian government, which Christ has established in his church, which we are ready at all times to demonstrate to the world.

"Reverend and dear brethren, we beseech you to hear us with patience, while we lay before you as briefly as we can, some of the reasons that move us thus to protest, and more particularly, why we protest against our protesting brethren being allowed to sit as members of this Synod.

"1. Their heterodox and anarchical principles expressed in their Apology,* pages twenty-eight and thirty-nine, where they expressly deny that presbyteries have authority to oblige their dissenting members, or that synods should go any further in judging of appeals or references, &c., than to give their best advice; which is plainly to divest the officers and judicatories of Christ's kingdom of all authority, (and plainly contradicts the thirty-first article of our Confession of Faith, section three, which those brethren pre-

* That is, the Apology of the New Brunswick Presbytery for not obeying the two acts of Synod respecting itinerant preaching, and the examination of candidates, which was presented to the Synod, May, 1739.

tend to adopt,) agreeable to which is the whole superstructure of arguments which they advance and maintain against not only our synodical acts, but also all authority to make any acts or orders which shall bind dissenting members, throughout their whole Apology.

"2. Their protesting against the Synod's act in relation to the examination of candidates, together with their proceeding to license and ordain men to the ministry in opposition to, and in contempt of the said act of Synod.

"3. Their making irregular irruptions upon the congregations, to which they have no immediate relation, without order, concurrence, or allowance of the presbyteries, or ministers to which such congregations belong; thereby sowing the seeds of division among the people, and doing what they can to alienate and fill their minds with unjust prejudices against their lawfully called pastors.

"4. Their principles and practice of rash judging and condemning all who do not fall in with their measures, both ministers and people, as carnal, graceless, and enemies of the work of God, and what not; as appears in Mr. Gilbert Tennent's sermon against unconverted ministers, and his and Mr. Blair's papers of May last, which were read in open Synod; which rash judging has been the constant practice of our protesting brethren and their irregular probationers, for above these twelve months past, in their disorderly itinerations and preaching through our congregations, by which, alas for it! most of our congregations, through weakness and credulity, are so shattered and divided, and shaken in their principles, that few or none of us can say we enjoy the comfort, or have the success among our people, which otherwise we might, and which we enjoyed heretofore.

"5. Their industriously persuading people that the call of God, whereby he calls men to the ministry, does not consist in their being regularly ordained and set apart to the work, according to the instruction and rules of the word; but in some invisible motions and workings of the Spirit, which none can be conscious or sensible of, but the person himself, and with respect to which he is liable to be deceived, or to play the hypocrite. That the gospel preached in truth by unconverted ministers, can be of no saving benefit to souls; and their pointing out such ministers whom they condemn as graceless, by their rash judging spirit, they effectually carry the point with the poor credulous people, who, in imitation of their example, and under their patronising, judge their ministers to be graceless, and forsake their ministry as hurtful rather than profitable.

"6. Their preaching the terrors of the law in such a manner and dialect as has no precedent in the word of God, but rather appears to be borrowed from a worse dialect; and so industriously working on the passions and affections of weak minds as to cause them to cry out in a hideous manner, and to fall down in convulsion-like fits, to the marring of the profiting both of themselves and others, who are so taken up in seeing and hearing these odd symptoms, that they cannot attend to, or hear what the preacher says, and then after all, boasting of these things as the work of God, which we are persuaded do proceed from an inferior or worse cause.

"7. Their, or some of them, preaching and maintaining that all true converts are as certain of their gracious state, as a person can be of what he knows by his outward senses; and are able to give a narrative of the time and manner of their conversion; or else they conclude them to be in a natural or graceless state; and that a gracious person can judge of another's gracious state, otherwise than by his profession and life: that people are under no sacred tie or relation to their own pastors lawfully called, but may leave them when they please, and ought to go where they think they get most good.

"For these and many other reasons, we protest before the eternal God, his holy angels, and you, reverend brethren, and before all here present, that these brethren have no right to be acknowledged as members of this judicatory of Christ, whose principles and practices are so diametrically opposite to our doctrine and principles of government and order, which the great King of the church hath laid down in his word. How absurd and monstrous must that union be, where one part of the members own themselves obliged in conscience to the judicial determinations of the whole, founded on the word of God, or else relinquish membership; and another part declare they are not obliged and will not submit, unless the determinations be according to their minds, and consequently will submit to no rules in making of which they are in the negative. Again, how monstrously absurd is it, that they should so much as desire to join with us, or we with them, as a judicatory made up of authoritative officers of Jesus Christ, while they openly condemn us wholesale, and where they please apply their condemnatory sentences to particular brethren by name, without judicial process, or proving them guilty of heresy or immorality, and at the same time will not hold Christian communion with them. Again, how absurd is the union, while some of the members of the same body, which meets once a year and join as a judicatory of Christ, do all the rest of the year, what they can openly and above-board, to persuade the people and flocks of their brethren to separate from their own pastors as graceless hypocrites, and yet they do not separate from them themselves, but join with them once every year, as members of the same judicatory of Christ, and oftener when presbyteries are mixed. Is it not unreasonable stupid indolence in us to join with such as are avowedly tearing us to pieces like beasts of prey?

"Again, is not the continuance of union with our protesting brethren absurd, when it is so notorious that both their doctrine and practice are so directly contrary to the adopting act, whereby both they and we have adopted the Confession of Faith, Catechisms, and Directory, composed by the Westminster Assembly? Finally, is not continuance of union absurd with those who arrogate to themselves a right and power to palm and obtrude members on our Synod, contrary to the mind and judgment of the body? In sum, a continued union, in our judgment, is most absurd and inconsistent, when it is so notorious that our doctrine and principles of church government, in many points, are not only diverse, but directly opposite. For how can two walk together, except they be agreed?

"Reverend fathers and brethren, these are a part and but a part of our reasons why we protest as above, and which we have only hinted at, but have forborne to enlarge upon them as we might, the matter and substance of them are so well known to you, and to the whole world about us, that we judged this hint sufficient at present, to declare our serious and deliberate judgment in the matter; and as we profess ourselves to be resolvedly against principles and practice both of anarchy and schism, so we hope that God, whom we desire to serve and obey, the Lord Jesus Christ, whose ministers we are, will both direct and enable us to conduct ourselves in these trying times, so as our consciences will not reproach us as long as we live. Let God arise, and let his enemies be scattered; but let the righteous be glad, yea, let them exceedingly rejoice. And may the Spirit of life and comfort revive and comfort this poor swooning and fainting church, quicken her to spiritual life, and restore her to the exercise of true charity, peace, and order.

"Although we can freely and from the bottom of our hearts justify the divine proceedings against us in suffering us to fall into these confusions for our sins, and particularly for the great decay of the life and power of godliness among all ranks, both ministers and people; yet we think it to be our present duty to bear testimony against these prevailing disorders; judging, that to give way to the breaking down the hedge of discipline and government from about Christ's vineyard, is far from being the proper method of causing his tender plants to grow in grace and fruitfulness. As it is our duty in our stations, without delay, to set about a reformation of the evils which have provoked God against ourselves, so we judge the strict observation of his laws of government and order, and not the breaking of them, to be one necessary means and method of this necessary and much to be desired reformation. And we doubt not, but when our God sees us duly humbled and penitent for our sins, he will yet return to us in mercy, cause us to flourish in spiritual life, unity, and order; though perhaps we may not live to see it, yet this testimony that we now bear, may be of some good use to our children yet unborn, when God shall arise and have mercy upon Zion. Signed, Robert Cross, John Thompson, Francis Alison, Robert Cathcart, Richard Sancky, John Elder,

John Craig, Samuel Cavin, Samuel Thompson, Adam Boyd, James Martin, and Robert Jamison, ministers; and Robert Porter, Robert McKnight, William McCullock, John McEwen, Robert Craig, James Kerr, Alexander McKnight, elders."

It is by no means clear how this protest was intended to operate, even by its authors. They state, 1. That those who will not conform to the constitution of the Synod have no right to sit and vote as members. 2. That the New Brunswick, or former protesting brethren, had violated that constitution, both by the avowal of principles inconsistent with it, and by their practice. 3. This being the case they demanded that such brethren should not any longer be recognised as members. It is evident that this cannot be regarded as a regular judicial process. The accused were not even named. They are sometimes designated as the "protesting brethren;" but that phrase would not include either Mr. Treat, or Mr. David Alexander, who were both included in the accusation.* Besides this, the protest not merely presented charges, it declared the persons implicated to be guilty and determined the punishment. It could not, therefore, have been intended as the commencement of a regular process. Perhaps the protestants expected that, after this solemn declaration of their sentiments, the Synod would by a formal vote exclude the accused brethren. And this, according

* Mr. Alexander was one of the most obnoxious members of that party, as has already been seen. And Mr. Treat, though he, as appears from the minutes of Philadelphia, quoted above, strenuously supported the contested acts of the Synod, was considered as one of the "ringleaders." In a letter to President Clap of Yale College, written in 1746, the Synod say, "We excluded from synodical communion the four Tennents, Blair, Creaghead, (who has since turned a rigid Covenanter or Cameronian,) Treat, and Mr. Wales; those, especially the Tennents, Blair, and Treat, being the ringleaders of our divisions, and the destroyers of good learning and gospel order among us." Minutes of Synod, vol. iii. p. 18.

Mr. Tennent says the ministers protested against were William Tennent, Sen'r, Richard Treat, Samuel Blair, Charles Tennent, James (David) Alexander, Alexander Creaghead, William Tennent, Jun'r, Eleazar Wales. John Rowland, Gilbert Tennent.—Remarks on the Protest, p. 33. Of these, however, Mr. Rowland had never been received as a member, Mr. Creaghead was suspended, and Mr. Alexander disowned, before the Synod met.

to Mr. Alison, was actually done. Of such vote, however, there is no record. The minutes merely state, "A protestation was brought in by Mr. Cross, read and signed by several members, which is kept *in retentis.* Upon this it was canvassed by the former protesting brethren, whether they or we were to be looked upon as the Synod. We maintained that they had no right to sit, whether they were the major or minor number. Then they motioned we should examine this point, and that the major number was the Synod. They were found to be the minor party, and upon this they withdrew. After this the Synod proceeded to business."* This counting of the roll Mr. Alison seems to understand as a formal vote. But it was clearly no such thing. There was no motion and no vote, but an irregular mustering of parties; after which the weaker withdrew.

It is probable that the authors of the protest had no fixed plan as to ulterior measures; that they meant merely to bring the controversy to a point, some way or other. They, therefore, made a formal declaration of their complaints, and an avowal of their purpose, that unless the New Brunswick brethren gave them satisfaction, one party or the other must leave the Synod. By what process this separation was to be effected, they left to be determined by circumstances. This seems to be implied in what is said by the authors themselves. "After reading the protest," they say, "the rejected members offered nothing like a pacific overture, or a satisfaction for said grievances, but instead of this we had unchristian reproaches. This brought the affair to that crisis that both could not sit together in one body, but one of them must withdraw," † and the counting the roll was resorted to in order to determine which party was the stronger.

The actual course which matters took was not foreseen nor provided for. As far as can be gathered from the brief and contradictory accounts of this eventful meeting, which are still extant, it appears that the reading of the protest, avowing as it did a fixed determination to have either a redress of grievances, or a separation, produced a great excitement. As soon as the paper was read,

* Minutes of Synod, vol. ii. p. 75. † Refutation of Remarks, &c. p. 134.

it was laid on the table for the signature of the members. This threw the assembly into disorder. The Brunswick brethren considering the signing the protest as of itself the act of rejection, "were loathe to be cast out hastily, without speaking any thing in their own defence; but their efforts to speak were repulsed, the house being confused, one spoke one thing, and another another, and sometimes two or more at once, so that it is hard to tell what was said." * Some cried out that the brethren were "solemnly protesting gross lies before Almighty God;" others, that the "elders were subscribing what they had never heard nor considered." † In the midst of this confusion the moderator left the chair.‡ As soon as it was ascertained that less than a majority of the whole Synod had signed the protest,§ some of the New Brunswick brethren demanded that as the protestors were dissatisfied they should withdraw, and the galleries, (for the church was

* Tennent's Remarks on the Protest, p. 35. † Refutation, &c. p. 134.

‡ At what stage of the business the moderator left the chair is not stated, but it is said that after the New Brunswick brethren had withdrawn, he *resumed* the chair. See Appendix to the printed copy of the Protest, and also p. 145, of the Refutation, &c.

§ Twelve out of twenty-six ministers, and eight out of eighteen elders signed the Protest, so that the signers were to the non signers as twenty to twenty-four. There were nine ministers present protested against; twelve protesting ministers, and five who were between the two parties. It was, I presume, mainly to ascertain which side these gentlemen would take that the roll was counted. They were Messrs. Andrews, Gillespie, Hucheson, Elmer and McHenry. Mr. Andrews decided at once as to the part he would take, and said openly he would not join with the New Brunswick gentlemen, (Refutation, p. 143,) and resumed the chair in the Synod as soon as they had withdrawn. Mr. Gillespie and Mr. Hucheson hesitated, and were at first inclined to join the New Brunswick brethren. The latter did connect himself with the Synod of New York in 1747. It seems, therefore, that in the struggle for the ascendency there was no minister who appeared decidedly for Mr. Tennent's party, unless it was Mr. Hucheson, who met with them the next day. So that the party stood nine, or, (including Mr. Hucheson,) ten, to twelve, or, (including Mr. Andrews,) thirteen; Messrs. Gillespie and McHenry, it is said, did not "appear for them at the time when it was now or never in the point of out voting."—(Refutation, p. 143.) Of Mr. Elmer nothing is said; he was probably absent at this juncture.

crowded,) rang with the call to cast them out;* for this purpose, they, (the Brunswick brethren,) counted the roll to see if they had a majority;† when it appeared that they were the minor party, they withdrew, followed by a great crowd.‡

It is plain from this statement that not even the forms of an ecclesiastical, much less of a judicial proceeding, were observed at this crisis. There was no motion, no vote, not even a presiding officer in the chair. It was a disorderly rupture. A number of the Synod rise and declare they will no longer sit with certain of their brethren, unless they satisfy their complaints.§ The members complained of, answer, You are dissatisfied and are the minority, therefore you must go out; and then a confused rush is made to the roll to see which was the stronger party. Such was the schism of 1741.

It is presumed there can be but one opinion as to this whole proceeding. There were but two courses which those who felt aggrieved by the conduct of Mr. Tennent and his friends could pro-

* Refutation, p. 145.

† This fact is stated substantially in the minute of the Synod quoted above; it is explicitly asserted in the Appendix to the printed copy of the Protest, and repeatedly in the Refutation of Mr. Tennent's Remarks. Mr. Tennent, however, says the thought of casting the protesters out "did not enter into his heart." To this they answered, he must be speaking of himself, "for it is certain that he was present when Mr. Blair and several other members of that party insisted, that since we had protested, it was our part to withdraw, for they were the Synod. And when the roll was counted to cast them out, he was as active as his brethren." The assumption of such a demand having been made, seems necessary to account for the roll being counted. The protesters had said, The New Brunswick gentlemen must satisfy their complaints or leave the Synod; to which it was answered, We are the majority, therefore you must withdraw; and then the roll was appealed to, to decide which party should go.

‡ Refutation, p. 145.

§ "It is evident," say the protesters, "from the whole tenor of the Protest, especially from pages seven and eight, that the protesters were fully determined never more to sit with these brethren, unless they gave them satisfaction in the points complained of; but were determined, with as many as would join with them, to maintain the rights of the Synod, and the Presbyterian church in these parts."—Refutation, &c. p. 133.

perly take. The one was to appeal to reason and the word of God, and rely on those means to correct the evils of which they complained. It is true, this would at that time have been like talking to a whirlwind; still, when the storm was over, truth and reason would have resumed their sway. We have seen, in our day, examples here and there of ministers who have stood a much more vulgar, if not more violent storm of defamation, combined with new doctrines and new measures; their people carried away, their congregations broken up, and yet these same men rising in the confidence and esteem of the church, and ultimately reaping the reward of their faith and patience. This course would have required, at the time of which we speak, more self-command and self-denial than can be expected even of most good men. The grievances complained of were real and weighty. These opposing brethren were seriously injured in their reputation; they were regarded as enemies of practical religion, as formalists, hypocrites, or bigots. Their comfort and usefulness were for the time being destroyed.* If they found themselves unable to submit to these grievances in silence, their second course was regularly to table charges against the New Brunswick Presbytery. There was the less reason for departing from this course as there was every prospect of its being successful. That Presbytery had already been once censured for its irregular conduct, by a vote of the Synod sustained by a great majority. As they continued their irregular course, the proper method was to repeat and increase the censure. As far as can be ascertained, there were not more than nine ministers out of forty, who approved the conduct of Mr. Tennent and his friends.† As to the three great grounds of complaint, disobe-

* Mr. Tennent answers this complaint with a taunt which was unworthy of him. "As to their comfort, we believe them; but respecting their success, we thought it had been the same as formerly; for truly this is the first time that ever we have heard of the success of most of them."—Refutation, &c. p. 23.

† Indeed the four Tennents, Mr. Blair and Mr. Wales, were the only men of any weight of character who belonged to that party. Mr. Creaghead was violent and bigoted, and soon left the church. Mr. Alexander was not only very disorderly, but also, to say the least, very imprudent in his conduct. Mr.

dience to the decisions of Synod, his rash condemnation of his brethren without a trial, and his intrusion into settled congregations, almost all his brethren were against him. This has been abundantly proved in the preceding pages. There is, therefore, no reasonable doubt that on all these points he and his friends would have been condemned. In Scotland, in consequence of the union between the church and the state, it has been found a difficult matter to discipline a Presbytery. In this country such difficulty does not exist. If a Presbytery persist in violating the constitution, it may, in perfect consistency with our principles, be disowned, as was the case with the Cumberland Presbytery; or dissolved, and its members attached to other Presbyteries. But even if there had been no reasonable prospect of success, this would afford no justification of the aggrieved party for taking the law into their own hands. When men live under a constitution, either in church or state, they are bound to abide by it, and to seek redress only in accordance with its provisions. It is obvious that no society, civil or ecclesiastical, can long exist, whose members assume the prerogative of redressing their own grievances. In this country, more than in most others, it is important that the great duty of abiding by the law, should be graven on the hearts of the people.

The course, then, adopted by the protesting brethren, in 1741, is certainly liable to the grave objection, that it was unconstitutional. It was, moreover, inoperative as to the evils it was intended to repress. The invectives under which the authors of the protest had suffered, were only rendered the more severe; and their churches were more than ever open to the intrusion of their rejected brethren. After the schism, those brethren seem to have thrown off all restraint as to that point, and to have established separate congregations wherever the opportunity was afforded. The situation of the protesters was, therefore, in no respect improved by the course which they pursued; on the contrary, it was worse than before. They now suffered the manifold inconveniences of having placed themselves in the wrong. The large and respectable Pres-

Cross was then under a cloud, and was soon suspended by the New Brunswick Presbytery.

bytery of New York, which had hitherto sided with them, after trying for several years to effect a reconciliation, seceded from the Synod and formed a new body. This threw the superiority as to numbers, character, and influence, on the other side, and was a lasting injury to the prosperity and usefulness of the old Synod. From that time, if it did not actually decline, it with difficulty held its ground, while the other rapidly increased.

This unfortunate protest continued an effectual bar to the union of the parties, long after all the original grounds of difference had ceased to exist. The New Brunswick brethren resented the charges contained in the protest; they denied having held the anarchical principles therein imputed to them. Hence no union was ever effected until the protest was disowned as a synodical act.

The day after the rupture in the Synod, that is, on June 2d, 1741, the Presbytery of New Brunswick held a pro re nata meeting in Philadelphia, at which the following ministers were present: Messrs. Gilbert Tennent, William Tennent, Jun., Eleazar Wales, and John Rowland, together with the following correspondents: Messrs. William Tennent, Sen., Samuel Blair, Charles Tennent, David Alexander, Alexander Hucheson, Alexander Creaghead, and Richard Treat. Mr. Gilbert Tennent was chosen moderator, and Mr. John Rowland, clerk. The following minute was then adopted:

"Whereas, the aforementioned New Brunswick Presbytery and correspondents have all along hitherto been in a state of union with the other ministers in these parts of the world of the Presbyterian persuasion, as joint members with them of one united synod; and, whereas the greater part of the other members of said synod with us in synod met, did yesterday, without any just ground, protest against our continuing members with them any longer, and so cast us out of their communion, the Presbytery and correspondents thus turned off and protested against, first came together to consider how they ought to conduct themselves in their present circumstances, for the fulfilling the work committed to them by the Lord Jesus Christ, as ministers and ruling elders in his house, and they do agree to declare that the aforesaid protestation of their brethren against them, is most unjust and sinful; and do moreover agree, that it is their bounden duty to form themselves into distinct presbyteries for carrying on the government of Christ's church, and do accordingly agree and appoint that Mr. William Tennent, Sen., and Richard Treat, be joined to the standing Presbytery of New Brunswick; and that Messrs. Samuel Blair, Alexander Creaghead, David Alexander, and Charles Tennent, be a distinct presbytery, distinguished by the name of the Presbytery of Londonderry.* Mr. George Gillespie, though not present now, having declared to us his willingness and desire of joining with us, is likewise appointed a member of the said Presbytery. Mr. Hucheson having manifested his inclination to join with the Presbytery, but desiring further time for consideration, his desire was granted; and it was likewise ordered, that on his application he should be received as a member thereof.† Appointed that the said Presbytery of Londonderry meet upon the 30th of this June, at Whiteclay Creek, and that Mr. Blair open the Presbytery with a sermon. It is further agreed and appointed that the said Presbyteries of New Brunswick and Londonderry do meet at Philadelphia on the second Wednesday of August next, in the capacity of a synod. Mr. Gilbert Tennent was appointed to open Synod with a sermon."‡

When the Presbytery met in the afternoon, they received applications for supplies from eighteen or twenty different places, many of which were already provided with settled pastors, and almost all of them were under the care of the existing Presbyteries of Philadelphia, New Castle, and Donegal. It was, however, determined to send preachers to them all, as far as it could be done. The schism was thus effectually carried down among the congregations, and rendered permanent.

The next day the Presbytery entered upon their minutes the following record:

"Inasmuch as the ministers who have protested against our being

* Afterwards called the Presbytery of New Castle; so that there were two Presbyteries of New Castle during the schism.

† As mentioned above, both Mr. Gillespie and Mr. Hucheson concluded to remain with the old Synod; the former permanently, the latter until 1747.

‡ Minutes of the Presbytery of New Brunswick, p. 21.

of their communion, do at least insinuate false reflections against us, endeavouring to make people suspect that we are receding from Presbyterian principles, for the satisfaction of such Christian people as may be stumbled at such aspersions, we think it fit, unanimously to declare, that we do adhere as closely and fully to the Westminster Confession of Faith, Catechisms, and Directory, as ever the Synod of Philadelphia did, in any of their public acts or agreements about them.

"Mr. Blair was appointed to draw up an account of the differences in our Synod for some years past, which have at last issued in this separation, against the time of our next meeting, that it may be prepared for the public, if need be. Mr. Gilbert Tennent was appointed to write an answer to the protest made by our brethren, wherein things are most unjustly represented."*

Thus was commenced a schism which it required seventeen years of uninterrupted effort to heal. Though the separation began in 1741, in the manner above narrated, it was not fully consummated until 1745. It is therefore necessary to detail the progress of events in connexion with this subject, until that time.

The Synod met in 1742, and chose Mr. Dickinson moderator, and Mr. Alison clerk. There were present twenty-four clerical members, including seven from the Presbytery of New York.† On motion made by the moderator, it was resolved, "That the Synod should hold a conference with the New Brunswick brethren that they rejected last year, in order to accommodate the difference, and make up the unhappy breach." It was thereupon agreed,

* Minutes of the Presbytery of New Brunswick, p. 24. The work assigned in the above minutes to Mr. Blair, was prepared and published under some such title as "The Declaration of the conjoint Presbyteries of New Brunswick and New Castle." It is referred to in Mr. Blair's answer to Mr. Creaghead's reasons for seceding from the Presbyterian Church, and is largely quoted in the Detector Detected, which was a reply by Messrs. Samuel Finley and Robert Smith, to the charges of two seceder ministers against the Presbytery of New Castle for loose Presbyterianism.

† These New York brethren were Messrs. Dickinson, Ebenezer Pemberton, John Pierson, John Nutman, Simon Horton, Silas Leonard, and Azariah Horton.

"that Messrs. Dickinson, Pemberton, Pierson, Cross, Andrews, Thompson, Cathcart, David Evans, and Alison, meet with those brethren, and try all methods consistent with gospel truth, to prepare the way for healing the said breach."* The next morning, the Synod resolved itself "into an interloquitur of ministers and elders to manage the conference with the rejected brethren, who were allowed, if they see cause, to bring with them the ministers that they ordained, that were never allowed to be members of this Synod, and all their respective elders. After a great deal of time spent to no purpose, the interloquitur found that all attempts for a coalition were vain and fruitless, and therefore it is agreed to adjourn until three o'clock, P. M. Concluded with prayer."

In the afternoon "the Synod entered upon the affair complained of by the ejected members, and the question put for managing the said affair was, Who should be the judges of the case? The ejected members would submit the business to the consideration of none as judges, but such as had not signed the protest last year; and the protesting brethren answered to the point, that they, with the members that had adhered to them after ejecting said members, were the Synod, and acted as such in the rejection; and in so doing they only cast out such members as they judged had rendered themselves unworthy of membership, by openly maintaining and practising things subversive of their constitution, and therefore would not be called to an account by absent members, or by any judicature on earth, but were willing to give the reasons of their conduct to their absent brethren to consider or review it." The Synod had, the next morning, another interloquitur meeting, without coming to any conclusion; and there the matter rested for that year.

The following protest was given in by several members: "To the Reverend Synod now sitting in Philadelphia: we the subscribers, in our own, and in the name of all that shall see meet to join with us, look upon ourselves as obliged in the most public manner to declare our opinion with respect to the division made in our Synod last year by a protest delivered in by several of our members.

* Minutes of the Synod of Philadelphia, vol. ii. p. 76.

"First. We declare against the excluding the Presbytery of New Brunswick and their adherents from the communion of the Synod by a protest, without giving them a previous trial, as an illegal and unprecedented proceeding; contrary to the rules of the gospel, and subversive of our excellent constitution.*

"Secondly. We declare and protest against the conduct of our brethren, the last year's protesters, in refusing to have the legality of their said protest tried by the present Synod.

"Thirdly. We therefore declare and protest, that those members of the New Brunswick Presbytery and their adherents, that were excluded by the last year's protest, are to be owned and esteemed as members of this Synod, till they are excluded by a regular and impartial process against them, according to the methods prescribed in the Scriptures, and practised by the churches of the Presbyterian persuasion.

"Fourthly. We protest against all passages in any pamphlets which have been lately published in these parts, which seem to reflect upon the work of divine power and grace, which has been carrying on, in so wonderful a manner, in many of our congregations; and declare to all the world, that we look upon it to be the indispensable duty of all our ministers to encourage that glorious work, with their most diligent and faithful endeavours. And in like manner we protest and declare against all divisive and irregular methods and practices by which the peace and good order of our churches have been broken in upon.

"This is what our duty to God, and our regard to the peace and prosperity of his church, oblige us to protest and declare; and we desire it may be recorded in the minutes of the Synod *in perpetuam rei memoriam*. Signed, Jonathan Dickinson, John Pierson, Ebenezer Pemberton, Simon Horton, Daniel Elmer, Azariah Horton,

* To this article is appended a contemporaneous note, in the handwriting of Mr. Andrews, but probably made by Mr. Alison, to the following effect: "This is, in the first article, *protestatio contra factum;* for they were excluded by vote of Synod, if they refused to give satisfaction for the points complained of, and upon this they withdrew." It is certainly strange that there is no intimation or record of such a vote on the minutes.

ministers; and Nathaniel Hazard, David Whitehead, Silas Leonard, Timothy Whitehead, elders."*

To this protest, Mr. Alison gave the following answer. "I, the subscriber, do hereby desire that it may be inserted on the Synod's minute book, that I judge it an open infringement of the rights of society, and particularly of our rights as Presbyterians, for absent members to pretend to a right to call the body to account, and judge of the legality of the proceedings in acts, resolutions, and conclusions, made in their absence; though I firmly believe it is the duty of such a body to submit such resolutions and conclusions to a review by the next Synod. And though I look on it as giving up some of our rights, yet it is my earnest desire, and what I insist on, that the merits of the cause for which the last year's Synod rejected the New Brunswick brethren and their adherents, be fairly tried by this present Synod, in order to manifest the justice of the said proceedings. Francis Alison." †

Had a conciliatory spirit prevailed in either of the contending parties, a reconciliation might probably have been effected, under the mediation of these New York brethren. They were in a proper position to act as mediators. They had not been involved in the dispute. They enjoyed the confidence of both parties. While they complained of the irregular mode of exclusion, they recognized the right to exclude, and protested against the disorderly course which the New Brunswick brethren had pursued. It may well be doubted, however, whether the method which these gentlemen adopted on this occasion, was judicious. It seems they demanded that the legality of the protest should be tried, and that this question should be decided by themselves and the few members present, who had neither protested, nor been protested against. Whatever view be taken of the protest, this course seems fairly liable to the objection so warmly urged by Dr. Alison. If the protesters had assumed the attitude of accusers, the New Brunswick brethren been regarded as accused, and the four remaining members of the Synod the judges, by whose decision the rejected members were excluded, it would certainly be incompetent for ab-

* Minutes of Synod, vol. ii. pp. 77, 78. † Ibid. p. 78.

sent members to re-open the case, and give a new trial. The only proper method would have been, for the Synod, as then constituted, to remove the sentence, as in any other case of ecclesiastical censure. No one pretended, however, that the course just stated was the one actually pursued. The New Brunswick brethren were not arraigned and tried; much less were they excluded by the four non-protesting members. Of those four Mr. Andrews was the only one who decidedly took part against them. The others, viz.: Messrs. Gillespie, Hucheson, and McHenry,* all disapproved of the protest, and of the rupture.

The view which Mr. Alison took of the matter was this. He regarded the protest as a solemn demand upon the New Brunswick brethren for satisfaction, which they refused to give. Whereupon the Synod, by a formal vote, cast them out. Had this been the real history of the case, the proper course would have been to move the reconsideration of that vote. This would have brought up the whole merits of the case; which Mr. Alison did not object to, and could not, therefore, have opposed. The history of the session of the 1st June, 1741, shows, however, that this view of the case is no more consistent with the facts than the one before mentioned. There was no motion to exclude, and of course no vote upon such a motion. The counting of the roll, which Mr. Alison seems to have regarded as taking the vote, was not done to decide any motion, nor was it done, to all appearance, while the moderator was in the chair.†

The only proper view of the matter, seems to have been that taken by the New York brethren, viz.: that the rupture was altogether violent and irregular. There was no trial, and no vote.

* Mr. McHenry's disapprobation of the protest is stated by Mr. Tennent in his Remarks, &c. p. 34.

† Mr. Alison himself frequently says, that the roll was counted on the demand of the New Brunswick gentlemen, and with a view to cast the protesters out. If this is so, then it certainly was not a vote to cast the other party out. The decision must have been yea or nay; the protesters go, or the protesters remain. This, of course, would decide nothing directly as to the New Brunswick brethren.

The protest threw the Synod into utter confusion, and the weaker party, as soon as it ascertained itself to be the weaker, left the house. If this is a correct account of the matter, as the withdrawing was not a voluntary secession, nor the exclusion a regular synodical act, it might have been treated as a nullity. The right of the New Brunswick brethren to their seats remained unimpaired; and when they appeared at the next meeting of the Synod, the regular course was, to move that their names be added to the roll. This again would have brought up the merits of the question, and led to a formal decision one way or the other.* Whatever view, therefore, be taken of the proceedings leading to the schism, the demand that the legality of the protest should be tried, and its signers excluded from voting, does not appear to have been a proper method to heal the breach.

The Synod met in 1743, and was opened with a sermon by President Dickinson. There were present twenty-three clerical members, including five from the Presbytery of New York. Mr. David Cowell was chosen moderator, and Mr. Alison clerk. On the sixth day of the sessions, an overture was presented to the Synod from the Presbytery of New York to the following effect. After lamenting the existing division in the church as dishonourable to God, scandalous to religion, injurious to the best interests of the body, and favourable to the spread of dangerous errors and delusions, they proposed, 1. That as the exclusion of the New Brunswick brethren, by a protest, without a distinct vote of the Synod founded on a hearing of their case was irregular, the protest be withdrawn, and those members be allowed to take their seats. 2. As it is of the greatest importance that the education of candidates for the ministry be properly managed, they proposed that all future candidates should submit to the rule of Synod relating to examinations, or else graduate as bachelors of arts in one of the New England colleges. 3. With regard to itinerant preaching,

* Had this course been pursued, it is not improbable that the New Brunswick gentlemen would have been recognized as members. Four of the signers of the protest were absent; and seven New York members, who were absent the year before, were now present. This might have turned the scales.

they proposed that every pulpit should be considered open to all the regular ministers of the church, and that it should be considered unbrotherly for one minister to refuse his pulpit to another, unless for a reason which shall be approved by the Presbytery, Synod, or the commission; and that no divisions of the congregations, separate meetings, or attempts to alienate the hearts of the people from their pastors, should hereafter be allowed, and that every contravention of this article be looked upon as just ground of censure either by the Presbytery or Synod. 4. That if any minister thinks he has any ground of complaint against any of his brethren, either for doctrine, manner of preaching, or conduct, he shall first present his complaints, in a private way, and if this method fail, he shall make regular charges, and bring the matter before the Presbytery, Synod, or commission. 5. That all past differences be buried in oblivion. 6. Considering the absolute necessity of union, they pray that this, or some other plan of union should be at once adopted; but if this could not be done, they propose that a new Synod be formed, and the several members have liberty to join either at pleasure, and that these Synods should send two correspondents each year, the one to the other.*

As the principal grounds of complaint against the ejected members were disregarding the rule of Synod relating to the examination of candidates, intruding into the congregations of settled ministers and causing divisions among their people and the condemnation of their brethren without trial, there is little doubt, that had these proposals been made before the schism they would have been gladly acceded to; as it was, however, strange to say, they were unanimously rejected.† It may serve to account for the

* Minutes of Synod, pp. 81, 82.

† "Some remarks," it is recorded, "upon the above overture were read, and after some consideration, it was put to vote whether this be accepted as a plan of accommodation or not, and it was unanimously voted in the negative." — Minutes, p. 83. There were present at this meeting of the Synod, besides the five brethren from the Presbytery of New York, Messrs. Robert Cathcart, Francis Alison, Robert Jamison, John Thompson, Adam Boyd, Samuel Black, John Elder, Richard Sanckey, Samuel Cavin, Alexander McDowell, Hamilton

decided rejection of propositions apparently so reasonable, if it is remembered that the schism did not put a stop to the evils by which it was occasioned. Mr. Tennent's denunciations of his brethren were at this time more bitter than ever,* and divisions in congregations were now fostered without any restraint. It is, therefore, probable that the Synod thought there was little probability that these proposals, emanating from the New York, and not from the New Brunswick brethren, would be adhered to. They insisted, therefore, that there should be a distinct acknowledgment made by these last-mentioned brethren, that the course they had hitherto pursued was wrong. It must be confessed that it was very unlikely that Mr. Tennent and his friends would have acceded to the terms proposed in the above overture. So far from opening their pulpits to all their brethren, there were some of them, and those very good men too, with whom some of their number would not even commune. And as to the separate meetings which had already been set up in many congregations, Mr. Tennent says, he and his friends must have "bowels of adamant" to refuse to take them under their care. There were, therefore, practical difficulties in the way of a union, which the New York brethren, living most of them in East Jersey, remote from the scene of conflict, could not so well appreciate.

The reasons assigned by the Synod for rejecting the overture above mentioned, are contained in a paper recorded in the minutes for the following year.† On the first article of the overture they remark, that they still think that the exclusion of the New Brunswick brethren by the protestation, is sufficiently justified by the reasons specified therein, which reasons are further strengthened by the conduct of the said brethren ever since; and therefore they say it is altogether inconsistent with duty and a good conscience to withdraw the protest, or to recede from it; and further, that

Bell, John Hindman, Jedediah Andrews, Robert Cross, Daniel Elmer, Francis McHenry, and Samuel Evans. How many of these were actually present, when the above vote was taken, does not appear.

* See the Examiner Examined, published in 1743, passim.

† Minutes of Synod, vol. iii. p. 2.

the only possible expedient in order to a re-union is for the New Brunswick brethren to let the Synod know, under their own hands, how far they can or will comply, to give the Synod satisfaction for the offences complained of, by acknowledging their past misconduct, and by giving satisfactory security against the fears of the like offences for the future.

On the second article they say, that if the New Brunswick brethren would once give satisfaction for their disregarding the rule about the examination of candidates, it is not unlikely that that matter would be adjusted.

On article third they remark that, in their judgment, to open their pulpits to every itinerant preacher, would be the very way to promote divisions; that it would be better to leave the matter to the discretionary agreement of the ministers concerned; and that no preacher should travel abroad for preaching' sake without an order from his own Presbytery, and the concurrence of the Presbytery within the bounds of which he was to preach. As to separate meetings, it was not enough that they should not be encouraged for the future; all proper means should be taken to heal the divisions already occasioned.

To the fourth article they make no objection, except that complaints against ministers ought not, in the first instance, to be brought before the Synod, but the Presbytery.

The fifth article they also approved of, on the supposition that a satisfactory union was affected. As to the formation of a new Synod, they say, that as it would be to perpetuate schism, they could not sanction it by a synodical act; but if, contrary to their judgment and inclination, the New York brethren should determine to form such a body, they hoped "by the grace of God to cultivate a truly Christian and charitable disposition towards them."

When the Synod rejected the New York overture, a paper "was given in by Mr. Jonathan Dickinson, in his own name, and in the names of Messrs. Ebenezer Pemberton, John Pierson, and Aaron Burr, having previously declared that they complained of no unfriendly or unbrotherly treatment from the Synod in relation to themselves, but that their conduct in this affair may be liable to misrepresentations; which said paper is as follows: As I look on myself to be a member of the Synod of Philadelphia, and have a continued right to sit and act in the same as such, so I look upon the New Brunswick Presbytery, and those brethren that adhere to them, and are therefore shut out of Synod on that account, to be as truly members of this Synod as myself, or any others whatsoever, and have a just claim to sit and act with us. I cannot, therefore, at present see my way clear to sit and act as though we were the Synod of Philadelphia, while the New Brunswick Presbytery, and the other members with them, are kept out of the Synod as they now are."*

In place of the overture from New York, the following plan of accommodation was sent to the New Brunswick gentlemen, through the hands of Mr. Aaron Burr: "Forasmuch as we are informed that the New Brunswick brethren are willing and desirous of reconciliation and union with this Synod, and to know on what terms this may be obtained; that the said brethren may be fully persuaded that we have no delight in division for its own sake, but on the contrary, are sincerely desirous of peace and union on reasonable terms, so that on our cordial agreement there be a foundation laid, that, through God's blessing, may prevent the havoc and destruction of the church threatened by our common enemies. Therefore we propose,

"1. That as they desire to be received and treated as members of our Synod, they will submit to the determinations and conclusions of our judicatories, even in those cases wherein they are negatives in giving their votes, and so allow a determination to be by a majority, or else no longer plead a right of membership. And that they renounce their principles delivered in their Apology, especially that whereby they declare that Presbyteries and Synods have no power to make any agreements, or come to any determinations by votes, which shall bind any members who do not give their consent to those conclusions or determinations; for without this recantation they can never be members of this Synod, seeing they put in a claim for arbitrary power to destroy and overturn all our agree-

* Minutes of Synod, vol. ii. p. 83.

ments, and to despise and disregard our censures, as they have already professedly done in licensing and ordaining so many men for the work of the ministry.

"2. If they profess they will use all endeavours to secure a learned ministry, we desire that they will testify this by desisting from licensing or ordaining men for the work of the ministry who have not complied with the Synod's agreement, or the alternative proposed in the last year's conference with these brethren; and that they give up all those persons that they have heretofore licensed or ordained in opposition to our public agreement, to be examined and tried by the Synod, whether they have suitable ministerial qualifications, or that they will not maintain ministerial communion with any of them for the future, who refuse to be examined by the Synod, or who upon examination are found deficient, until they give suitable satisfaction.

"3. That for the future they will desist from either acting or preaching, or sending their missionaries into the bounds of our Presbyteries or fixed pastoral charges, as heretofore. That they will not encourage new separate societies in congregations as hitherto, nor supply with preaching the societies they have made or occasioned among the people under our care, but declare that all such practices are of pernicious tendency and inconsistent with the presbyterian plan.

"4. That they will not publicly nor privately endeavour to diminish the character of any minister as graceless, or unconverted, or unworthy of his office, until he be tried by a proper judicature and censured; and that they claim no right to judge of men's spiritual estate towards God, so as to determine whether they be gracious or graceless, if sound in the faith, and of a gospel life and conversation; and that they condemn all such practices.

"5. That they renounce all such tenets or doctrines that have been advanced in Mr. Tennent's Nottingham sermon, which are contrary to our presbyterian plan, subversive of gospel order, and a floodgate to let in divisions and disorders into the churches; such as an allowance to church members, to guess at the spiritual estate of their pastors, and upon this guess, without further trial, to leave them as graceless and unconverted; the asserting an inward call to the ministry, in opposition and contradiction to the outward call or ordaining to the gospel ministry. All who maintain them, (i. e. the above doctrines,) can be no members of a Presbyterian society or church, because they take all government out of the hands of a Synod or Presbytery, and give it to any person that hath ignorance or impudence enough to bring God's house into confusion.

"6. That they acknowledge that too many of them have been guilty in all these points, and, notwithstanding, whatever zeal and intention to promote a work of grace they might have been influenced by, yet now they are convinced that such practices have had a dreadful tendency to promote and spread the divisions and confusions which perplex and disturb this church.

"7. We propose that if they have any ground of complaint against any of our members, with respect to their doctrines, conversation, or diligence in the ministry, they shall be welcome to table the charge against them in a proper judicatory, whether they comply with these terms or not; and that if they satisfy us in these points, and accept their seats in our Synod, all other grounds of complaint shall be removed, either by public trial, or such other method as they and we in conjunction shall determine. And we declare that if all or any of those brethren accept these terms, or any other, that they and we can devise or agree to, that will lay a foundation to secure these important rights of society, a learned and pious ministry, and to prevent errors and divisions in a way agreeable to God's word, and the Presbyterian constitution, we are heartily willing to receive them. And we desire that they may give us their answer to these heads as soon as they can conveniently."*

To this paper the following answer was returned: "Upon a paper sent to us from the ministers that protested against us, pro-

* Minutes of Synod, vol. ii. pp. 83, 84.—It is stated in the minutes that the above proposals "were sent in an extra-judicial way to the Brunswick brethren; upon reading of which in open Synod, it was agreed, that these proposals were reasonable, in order to open the way toward an accommodation and interview between those brethren and us."

posing certain terms of union; this conjunct meeting of the Presbyteries of New Brunswick and New Castle, does judge that there can be no regular methods of proceeding toward the compassing a stable union between them and us, until their illegal protest be withdrawn, that so they and we may both stand on an equal footing in the regular trial of the differences between us; that their paper contains sundry misrepresentations and unreasonable demands; and that we have several charges against them to be satisfied in before we could come into a settled union with them."*

In 1744, no member of the New York Presbytery appeared in Synod, and no new effort was made to heal the schism. In 1745, Messrs. Dickinson, Pemberton, and Pierson, were present and enrolled as members. On the second day of the sessions, those gentlemen, "in the name of the Presbytery of New York, and by a commission from them, desired the Synod to appoint a committee to try whether an overture could be prepared, removing any grounds of dissatisfaction or difference between them and the Synod." Whereupon it was "ordered that Messrs. Andrews, Cross, Alison, Thompson, Boyd, Gillespie, McDowell, Samuel Evans, and the moderator, (Cathcart,") be that committee. As this committee did not succeed in preparing an overture, the whole Synod was resolved into a committee of conference. After much consultation, Messrs. Thompson, Alison, Steel, and McDowell, were appointed to draw up a plan of union, and report it at the next meeting. The following day this committee accordingly reported their plan. Before it was read, the New York gentlemen were asked, "whom of the New Brunswick brethren they alleged to be members, whether all who are now of that party, or only such of them as enjoyed membership before? And they declared they account only such of them as have been members and had their seats, to be now members, and no others. The overture drawn up by the committee was twice read, and this vote put: Whether it was a proper plan of accommodation to propose? and it was voted proper to propose it, and it is as follows:

"1. The glory of God and the advancement of Christ's king-

* Minutes of Synod, vol. ii. p. 85.

dom, by the persuading souls to embrace the Lord Jesus Christ on gospel terms, and by preserving peace, truth, and good order in the churches, ought to be the grand design of all Christians, and of the ministers of the gospel in particular. But, to our great concern and sorrow, the disorderly intrusions into the pastoral charges of ministers, and surmises that were raised to blacken their characters as carnal and unconverted; the bold violation of our synodical acts and regulations, and the new method of itinerant preaching, where there is a stated gospel ministry, have, in a great measure, marred this noble design, by rending the churches of Christ, and filling the minds of the people with uncharitable thoughts of one another. To check these evils, prevailing by means of some claiming to themselves a privilege, under pretence of extraordinaries, to trample under foot all rights of mankind, to destroy all pastoral relation, and to lay aside, at least for a season, that form of government and discipline that was practised and used in our churches; a number of the Synod of Philadelphia protested against those illegal disorderly practices in 1741; and being wearied out with fruitless attempts to redress these delusive unscriptural methods of proceeding, determined to withdraw from synodical communion, unless those who were guilty of such practices gave proper satisfaction according to gospel rules. The majority of the Synod then present made this protest their act,* and declared that those brethren should either give such satisfaction, or withdraw from membership; on which they chose to withdraw.

"This method of procedure was complained of next year as contrary to the method of proceeding in our churches, by some members that were absent when this separation was made; upon which it was proposed that the whole affair should be reviewed by the Synod then met, and if any thing was found illegal it should be redressed. But these brethren could find clearness to do nothing until those disorderly brethren who withdrew, should again be

* The narrative given above, shows how this statement is to be understood. The protesters and their friends were a majority of the Synod, but the protest was not adopted, nor were the Brunswick brethren excluded by any synodical act.

allowed to take their seats as members, which the majority of the Synod could not comply with. Upon which they entered a declaration against the method of proceeding the year before. At our next Synod they proposed methods for healing the breach between those brethren that withdrew and the Synod; which occasioned the Synod to send them proposals of peace, which they rejected, and still continued their divisive practices of counteracting the Synod's regulations, and crumbling of congregations to pieces, erecting altar against altar, to the great scandal of religion and the ruin of vital piety. Those brethren from the Presbytery of New York, who were dissatisfied at the method by which that party stand excluded, having on this occasion laboured to have their own scruples removed, and at the same time to have peace and unity restored among all that were ever members of the Synod, all the Synod now met heartily concur with them in this noble undertaking, if it can be obtained in such a method as may and will maintain sound doctrine, and preserve the peace and good order of the church.

"In order to accomplish this, these brethren proposed it as an expedient to remove their scruples and heal all our divisions, that every person that is or has been a member, shall now voluntarily subscribe the essential agreements on which our Synod formerly was established, and which are the general approved agreements of our churches. And as we think that a subscription of these articles will be a renouncing disorder and divisive practice, and will, when obtained, lay a foundation for maintaining peace, truth, and good order, which was what was desired in the protest, by which the New Brunswick brethren stand excluded; we therefore, in compliance with request of these brethren, and in order to remove all scruples, propose that all that are now or ever have been members of this Synod, shall subscribe the following fundamental articles and agreements, as their acts, and all who will do so shall be members of this Synod.

"1. That in all prudential acts for the regular management of the affairs of the church of God among us, every member shall either actively concur, or passively submit to and not counteract, such things as are determined by the majority as being founded upon God's word; or if any do declare that they have not freedom of conscience to comply, they shall withdraw, and no more be acknowledged as members of this Synod, unless they afterwards find clearness, and so return and comply.

"2. That if any member suppose he has reason of complaint against any of his brethren for unsound doctrine, irregularities of life, or unfaithfulness in his pastoral office, he shall proceed in a Christian way according to the rules of God's word, and our known methods of discipline, and shall not in public or private, spread his surmises, offences, or scandals, without proceeding as aforesaid, or else be accounted guilty of unchristian conduct, and liable to censure. Accordingly we look upon such practices to be contrary to the gospel, and of pernicious tendency to the church of Christ.

"3. That no member of this Synod shall preach in the congregation of another brother, without judicial appointment, or being invited by his brother to preach for him, and whoever acts contrary shall be deemed guilty of unbrotherly treatment and divisive practice, and be censured accordingly. And the same way no Presbytery shall invade the charge and rights of other Presbyteries; and all erections within the bounds of regulated congregations that have been or shall be set up by such itinerant preaching and divisive practices, shall be deemed contrary to the peace and good order of this church, and consequently shall not be maintained or supported by any member belonging to us.

"4. We agree that none who have not heretofore enjoyed membership in this Synod, shall be admitted hereto without submitting to the manner of admission determined by our former acts, and such as may and shall be provided in that case, and complying with these general articles now agreed upon. And all such as upon proper trial shall be duly qualified with respect to learning, soundness in the faith, and a gospel conversation, shall, upon agreeing to these articles, and submitting to our method of church government, be cordially admitted to synodical communion.

"5. We agree that each member of this Synod shall keep a day of public and solemn fasting, and thereupon confess and bewail the prevailing evils of infidelity, profaneness, the untenderness and barrenness of professors, and the decay of religion in general, and particularly the debates, divisive practices, uncharitable censures, and unbrotherly treatment that have torn and divided the church of Christ in these parts, to the dishonour of God, the hurt of practical piety, the offence and scandal of the weak, and the hardening of the wicked, and the opening the mouths of the profane; and deprecate the divine displeasure, and implore the blessing of God upon this and all other proper means for the advancement of pure and undefiled religion, and the maintaining and propagating the great truths of the gospel, and the peace, unity, and increase of this infant church." *

The New York brethren immediately refused to accede to this plan of union. This result must excite surprise, when it is remembered how nearly identical the terms here offered are with those which those brethren had previously proposed. The plan happily avoided the necessity of concession on either side, by placing both parties on the same ground, and commencing *de novo*, with a renewed subscription of their original principles of agreement. It is difficult to see to which of the above articles exception could have been taken. Certainly not to the first, for that was adopted almost verbatim as one of the fundamental principles of the new Synod. Not to the second, for that was borrowed from the previous proposals made by the New York Presbytery. Not to the former part of the third, for the right of a minister to his own pulpit could hardly be seriously questioned. It is probable that the difficulty was with the latter part of the third article, which required that the new congregations formed by separatists from the older ones should be given up. This was a real difficulty, and embarrassed the negotiations for a union at a much later period. These congregations had now been formed for some years; and the people were doubtless unwilling to return to their old pastors. Under these circumstances the men by whose influence they had been induced to separate, could hardly be expected to give them up. Some years after this, when Mr. Tennent was earnestly de-

* Minutes of Synod, vol. iii. pp. 11, 12.

sirous of a re-union, he found his greatest difficulty with these people, and wrote his Irenicum principally to answer their objections and allay their feelings. Some of them never would come in, but when, after a schism of seventeen years, the two Synods were united, left the church and joined the Scotch Seceders.

Whatever may have been the grounds of objection, the New York brethren immediately rejected the plan above mentioned, and proposed that "it be mutually agreed that they be allowed, with the consent of this body, to erect another Synod, under the name of the Synod of New York." To this proposal the following answer was returned: "The unhappy divisions which have subsisted among us for some years, cannot but deeply affect all that wish the welfare of Zion; and it particularly affects us that some of our brethren of New York do not at present see their way clear to continue in synodical communion with us. And though we judge that they have no just ground to withdraw from us, yet seeing they propose to erect themselves into a Synod at New York, and now desire to do this in the most friendly manner possible, we declare, if they or any of them do so, we shall endeavour to maintain charitable and Christian affections towards them, and show the same upon all occasions, by such correspondence and fellowship as we shall think duty, and consistent with a good conscience." *

The schism was thus consummated, and the Synod of New York met as a separate and independent body, at Elizabethtown, September 19, 1745.

The above narrative will disclose the real causes of the schism. It was not diversity of opinion as to doctrine or discipline, but loss of confidence and alienation of feeling arising from the different views entertained of the revival which then prevailed. The same causes, which at this period divided the churches of New England, rent asunder the Presbyterian Church. Opposition to the revival was the standing charge against the one party, and was the uniform apology for the denunciations, intrusions, separations, and disobedience to the Synod, which formed the grounds of complaint against the other. Was this opposition to the revival an opposi-

* Minutes of Synod, vol. iii. p. 13.

tion to evangelical religion, or merely to extravagance and disorder? On the part of some few individuals, it is to be feared it was the former; characteristically and generally it was the latter. This appears, in the first place, from the fact that the opposition did not commence until the extravagances and disorders made their appearance. This change of sentiment is made matter of reproach by Mr. Tennent. "What is the reason," he asks, "that our protesting brethren were so full in favour of the work of God last year, in their speeches and acknowledgments, and that they make no honourable mention of it in their protest this year? Has a little space of time altered the nature of things?" * The same men also who were most active in their opposition to the revival, under the form which it assumed in Pennsylvania, approved and rejoiced in all they saw of its effects in Virginia.†

In the second place, all the objections urged in any of the writings which had any claim to represent the opinions of the party, were directed against what was really objectionable.‡ In 1740, there was a paper presented to the Presbytery of New Castle, containing complaints against Mr. Whitefield, in the form of queries, and hence called the Querists. It consisted principally of various extracts from Mr. Whitefield's writings, which were deemed objectionable. Its authors, for example, find fault with him for saying that man at his creation was "adorned with all the perfections of

* Remarks on the Protest, p. 21.

† This fact is stated particularly in reference to Mr. Thompson, by Mr. Davies, in his account of the revival in Virginia, republished in Gillies' Collections.

‡ There were some anonymous pamphlets published during this period, which gave great and probably just offence. One is particularly mentioned, entitled "The History of a Wandering Spirit," which Mr. Blair calls a "scurrilous lampoon." It was attributed to Mr. Samuel Evans, who, however, denied being its author; and it was never acknowledged by any individual or party. Mr. Tennent says, on this subject, "Seeing that piece was anonymous, and was never owned by our brethren as a body, it cannot, without manifest injustice, be ascribed to them as such; nor is there any certain or sufficient proof, that ever it was owned or approved of in all its parts, by any one of them, so far as I know."—Irenicum, p. 120.

the Deity;" that the believer "washes away the guilt of sin by the tears of a sincere repentance, joined with faith in the blood of Jesus Christ." They charged him with denying the covenant of grace, and running into antinomianism in his letter against the book called the Whole Duty of Man. They objected to his saying that men were baptized "into the nature of the Father, the nature of the Son, and the nature of the Holy Spirit;" that the believer depends on "the righteousness of Christ imputed to, and *inherent in* him." They were offended with his claiming immediate inspiration in such passages as the following: "There will certainly be a fulfilling of those things which God, by his Spirit, has spoken in my soul," and, "There are many promises to be fulfilled in me." They did not know how to understand his saying, "Now know I that I have received the Holy Ghost at the imposition of hands. For I feel it as much as Elisha did, when Elijah dropped his mantle. Nay others see it also." They objected also to his saying of the Quakers, "I think their notions about walking and being led by the Spirit right and good." *

* Mr. Whitefield soon published a letter in reply to the Querists, in which he frankly retracted, or satisfactorily explained most of the passages above cited.

Mr. Charles Tennent got into trouble by defending some of the expressions which Mr. Whitefield afterwards retracted.

Mr. Blair published a severe reply to the Querists, whose publication he ascribed to Mr. Evans of Pencader. The true reason, he says, of the opposition to Mr. Whitefield was, the work of God had begun to prevail, and this by all means must be put a stop to, and the former quiet be restored, though thousands should perish. Dead, secure formalists, who know nothing of the regenerating operations of the Spirit of God, or of lively heart exercises in religion, are likely to lose their former high reputation in religion, and groundless confidence in the goodness of their own state, which they are not content to part with. Especially when the people are awakened, they cannot be satisfied with the sapless, careless ministers; this goes hard with these PIOUS MINISTERS. (So printed.) Thus the success of the gospel is very unwelcome to many of its professed friends. Moreover, Mr. Whitefield speaks much against unexperienced, blind, and unfaithful ministers, who settle people upon the lees of their natural and fatal security, and hereupon, as if their own consciences secretly told them, they were the men, or that their management

Mr. Thompson specifies the things of which he and his friends complained in the advocates of the revival: 1. Their bold and uncharitable condemnation of their brethren as graceless. 2. Their unwearied industry to possess the people with prejudices against their pastors. 3. Their irregular intrusions into other men's charges. 4. Their teaching that every true Christian is sure of his own conversion, and that no adult can be converted without undergoing legal, ungracious, preparatory convictions. As to the effects of their preaching he objected, 1. To the crying out during worship, to the falling down, and convulsions which were encouraged by them.* 2. To the despairing terrors which flow from unbelief. 3. To the delusions of some of their followers; as that they had seen Christ, or a great light, during their devotions. 4. To the censorious spirit with which they seem to be immediately affected. "It is," he adds, "a downright calumny and slander to allege that we prejudice the people against the work of God, because we sometimes declare our judgment against such particulars as these, which we verily are persuaded are not the work of God either in ministers or people." He admits that "a great many have been stirred up to more serious thoughts about their soul's concerns than ever before, which is a thing truly to be rejoiced in; and many, it is said, are much reformed in several particulars of moral practice, which also is just matter of satisfaction."†

The testimony of Mr. Tennent, as to the nature and extent of the opposition of his brethren to the revival, will, doubtless, be regarded by many as of more weight than their own declarations.

was such, that they would surely come under suspicion, many are exceedingly vexed.—See Consideration of the Querists, pp. 7, 8.

* That opposition to those bodily agitations which attended the revival, was regarded by its friends as a ground of complaint against their brethren, appears from many passages of their writings. Thus, Mr. Blair censures those who he said "lash and reproach in unlimited terms, as the mere effects of irrational frights or delusive joys, all crying out and bodily faintings, when such things may be, and in numbers have been the effects of the rational, spiritual, strong exercises of the soul, from the laws of the union between the soul and the body."—Works, p. 288.

† Government of the Church, pp. 33, 34.

He then testifies distinctly, that the opposition was not to experimental religion, but to the extravagances and disorders which at that period so much prevailed. "I cannot but believe," he says, "that reverend brethren upon both sides of the question, had sincere and good designs in the different parts which they bore in the late controversy. While some were earnestly contending for the credit of the late extraordinary religious appearances, with design that they might spread far and wide; others were strenuously contending for the order and government of Christ's kingdom, lest they should suffer and be quite unhinged in the uncommon situation and ferment that obtained among the churches. But though the things controverted, considered calmly and in a true distinct light, were small, yet the heat of debate about them run very high. This, together with evil surmisings, severe censurings, and rash judgings of each other, encouraged and inflamed by misrepresentations, carried to and from by the unwearied industry of tale-bearers and tattlers, who are generally busy on such occasions, increased mutual prejudices and suspicions to a melancholy crisis, and occasioned the unhappy rupture of the church's union, which has subsisted among us for some years."*

In the body of the work just cited, he still more explicitly denies that the essentials of religion were involved in the controversy. "What is it," he asks, "that is disputed? Is it the necessity of conversion to God, in order to salvation? No; that is freely acknowledged on both sides of the question. Is it the nature of conversion proposed in the Scriptures and in our excellent Confession of Faith agreeable thereto? No; for that is likewise acknowledged by both the contending parties. Is it the marks and signs of conversion mentioned in the Scriptures? No; for these are also confessed by persons of both sides. Is it the reality of those instances of conversion contained in the Bible? No; the divine authority of the sacred Scriptures is equally asserted by both parties in controversy. Is it whether some have been converted in the successive ages of the Christian Church from the apostles' times to the present day; and whether some have not been converted in

* Irenicum, Preface, p. 6.

this age, and in this part of the world, and whether good has not been done, and some effectually changed, to all appearance, during the late revival of religion? No; for these are also acknowledged. What then is it that is controverted? Why our *opinion* respecting the religious experiences of some in the late times, and concerning the number of such. It has been disputed whether those experiences were of a saving kind, and whether the number is so great as is concluded by some. And is our opinion concerning what we cannot certainly know a great matter, think ye? Or, are we infallible in our judgment about these things which are hidden from the view of mortals? If not, why is all this heat and flame about uncertainties?"*

Again: "I must in justice add to what has been offered, that the reverend brethren, who cast us out of synodical communion, do deny the charge of endeavouring to prejudice the people against the power and grace of God in the conversion of sinners, wherever there is any hopeful appearance of it. Mr. John Thompson, in their name, observes on this head as follows: 'It is true, there are some things in our brethren's conduct which we cannot but condemn, and have condemned and spoken against both in private and public; and some things also which are the frequent effects of their preaching on many of their hearers, which we cannot esteem of as highly as both they and their admirers do.' Among which he mentions crying out aloud in the midst of the congregation in the time of public worship, and others falling down half dead, or working like persons in convulsion fits. And in another paragraph, he speaks in the following candid, charitable strain, to the honour of the late revival of religion, and to the honour of the ministers he opposed." Mr. Tennent then quotes from Mr. Thompson the passage cited above,† and several others to the same effect,‡ and

* Irenicum, p. 84.

† Page 222.

‡ Among the passages quoted by Mr. Tennent are the following: "However, we rejoice that the great God, who rules all events to his own glory and the good of his church, doth make the gospel preached by our brethren effectual in many to stir them up to a more serious consideration of their souls' concerns than ever before. I also hope that our gracious Lord will give

adds: "Seeing the Rev. Mr. John Thompson appeared as the apologist of the present Synod of Philadelphia, it may reasonably be presumed that he speaks the mind at least of the majority of that body; and therefore it is evident from the aforesaid passages, that they were far from opposing, (with design,) the late revival of religion; that on the contrary, they expressly acknowledged it, rejoiced in it, and prayed for its increase; yea, in several instances, as humbly as publicly acknowledged their own imperfections in relation to the present debate. Do not the aforesaid passages breathe the candid, humble spirit of true Christianity? Why, therefore, is the string of acknowledgments so much harped upon? Pray, have we done in this as much as our brethren? or are we, forsooth, absolutely perfect and infallible, even in a time of temptation and debate?"* In several other passages he vindicates the Synod from the charge of opposing the revival of religion, properly so called, and shows that their opposition was confined to the extravagances and disorders above specified.†

It is, indeed, hard to believe that this is the same Mr. Tennent, who, a few years before, denounced these same brethren as the enemies of all religion, as men willing to resort to any falsehood or calumny to cloak their "horrible wickedness in opposing God's work." Mr. Thompson was frequently specified by name as an example of the class of unconverted pharisee preachers, and his opposition to the work of God ascribed to the worst motives. What makes this case the more remarkable and the more instructive, is, that the work which Mr. Tennent, in 1749, could see "breathed the candid and humble spirit of true Christianity," was published by Mr. Thompson in 1741, that is, during the very heat of the

us, who are in the ministry, grace to observe and obey his voice by his providence to us, to search and try our ways, and turn again unto the Lord." Again: "I think it not unlikely that God, in his infinite wisdom, hath permitted our brethren, who appear to be so much more zealous than we for carrying on the work of conversion, which they apprehend is wholly neglected by us, as it is indeed too much, to be instruments in the Lord's hands to chastise us for our neglects and shortcomings."

* Irenicum, p. 86.

† Ibid. pp. 120, 121, 122.

debate. It contained then, all the evidence of a Christian spirit that it did seven years afterwards. Yet Mr. Tennent at that time could see nothing good either in it or its author. This, though a striking, is not a solitary illustration of the fact that, during times of religious excitement, the evil as well as the good feelings even of true Christians, are often brought into vigorous exercise. It appears then, as well from the testimony of the men themselves, as from that of their opponents, that the opposition to the revival of which so much complaint was made, was an opposition to the extravagance and disorder which marked its course, and not an opposition to evangelical religion.*

With regard to the importance of learning in the ministers of the gospel, there was no real difference of opinion between the two parties. As the Synod's object in the act about the examination of ministers, was to secure an adequately learned ministry, and as Mr. Tennent opposed that act, he brought himself under the suspicion of slighting the importance of learning. This suspicion was increased by the manner in which he sometimes allowed himself to speak of letter-learned pharisees, "who came out, no doubt, after they had been the usual time at the feet of Gamaliel, and according to the acts, canons, and traditions of the Jewish church;"† by the avowal of his determination to oppose the design of the Synod to establish a public seminary;‡ and the hasty manner in which his Presbytery sometimes passed over the trials of their candidates.

Mr. Tennent's opposition, however, to the Synod's act, requiring a college diploma of candidates for the ministry, did not arise from a disregard of learning, but from want of confidence in the existing colleges.§ The same motive influenced him in his opposition to the plan of the Synod respecting a seminary. It was not to learning, but to a school under the control of the Synod that he objected.

* In further proof of this point, the reader is referred to the Plan of Union, unanimously adopted by both Synods, in 1758, in which the fullest and most explicit testimony is given to the truth and necessity of experimental religion. See the conclusion of the following chapter.

† Nottingham sermon, p. 1.

‡ Minutes of the Synod, vol. iii.

§ This is expressed in his Nottingham sermon, p. 11.

In his sermons against the Moravians, published in 1742, he insisted upon the necessity of learning in the ministers of the gospel, with all his characteristic ardour. "In order to preserve ourselves and our posterity," he says, "from the infection of error, I think it is needful to use, in our proper sphere, all suitable means to obtain a godly, learned, and regular ministry. When ignorant novices are admitted into the ministerial order, they are apt to be puffed up, to the church's great prejudice, as well as their own; and to spread error, when they know it not. To say that these qualifications may be ordinarily attained without human learning, is notoriously enthusiastical and foolish. In short, either human learning is necessary, or there must be inspiration to supply the want thereof." The efforts which he and his friends made to establish the college of New Jersey, show that he fully appreciated the importance of this subject.

There was also an essential agreement between the two parties on points of doctrine. This is proved by the explicit testimony of Mr. Tennent. "Upon the one hand," he says, "the nature and necessity of conversion to God, as represented in the Scriptures, and in our Confession of Faith, according to them, were acknowledged, and only the opinion of some concerning the reality or number of some late instances of conversion, (or respecting both together,) disputed and contradicted; so upon the other hand, the nature and necessity of order and government in the church of Christ, as they are represented in the holy Scriptures, and our Directory, according to them, were also acknowledged, and only some prudential rules and acts, not expressed in the sacred Scriptures, or our Directory, for worship and government, disputed and opposed. The substance of the points in dispute was freely acknowledged by reverend brethren on both sides of the question, viz. the nature and necessity of conversion, as held forth in the Scriptures, and in our Confession of Faith; and the nature and necessity of church discipline, (in all essentials,) as represented in the holy Scriptures, and in our Directory, so that the controversy, in my apprehension, turns entirely upon circumstantials."*

* Irenicum, preface, p. 5.

A more important evidence is to be found in the "Declaration of the conjunct Presbyteries of New Brunswick and New Castle," issued immediately after the schism. Those Presbyteries say: "We think it proper, for the satisfaction of all concerning us, and as a due testimony to the truth of God, to declare and testify to the world our principles and sentiments in religion, according to which we design, through divine grace, ever to conduct ourselves, both as Christians, and as ministers, and as ruling elders.

"And first, as to the doctrines of religion, we believe with our heart, and profess and maintain with our lips, the doctrines summed up and contained in the Confession of Faith, and Larger and Shorter Catechisms, composed by the reverend assembly of divines at Westminster, as the truths of God revealed and contained in the holy Scriptures of the Old and New Testaments; and do receive, acknowledge, and declare the said Confession of Faith and Catechisms to be the confession of our faith; yet so as that no part of the twenty-third chapter of said Confession shall be so construed as to allow civil magistrates, as such, to have any ecclesiastical authority in Synods, or church judicatories, much less the power of a negative voice over them in their ecclesiastical transactions; nor is any part of it to be understood as opposite to the memorable revolution and the settlement of the crown of the three kingdoms in the illustrious house of Hanover." * *Exceptio probat regulam.* The exception here made to certain parts of the twenty-third chapter, proves the adoption of all the rest. This is as strict an adoption of the Confession of Faith as was ever made by any Synod in our church. Besides this decisive declaration, reference might be made to the fact, that during all the protracted negotiations for a union, there was not a word said about doctrinal differences. Each Synod spoke of the other as holding the same system of doctrines.

Though there was this substantial agreement, there were several points, which, while the excitement lasted, were matters of keen dispute. It has already been mentioned that Mr. Tennent had a doctrinal controversy with David Cowell, a New England gentleman, pastor of the church in Trenton. The subject of dispute, it

* See the Detector Detected, p. 125.

will be remembered, was, whether the glory of God or the happiness of the agent, was the ultimate ground of moral obligation. Mr. Tennent, in the paper presented to the Synod in 1740, charged his brethren with holding false doctrine on this subject. With respect to this charge, it may be remarked, 1. That we never hear of it again. It was never renewed, and never became a matter of discussion between the two parties. 2. That the charge, as far as it bore on the members of the Synod at all, bore particularly upon the committee of which President Dickinson was chairman, and of which other gentlemen were members, who are known to have repudiated the doctrine imputed to them. 3. That the Synod, by an unanimous vote, condemned the doctrine that self-love is the ultimate foundation of moral obligation. The Synod, therefore, are clear in this matter. Mr. Cowell is the only member to whom even suspicion can attach in relation to it.

A subject much disputed at this time, was the nature of conviction. Mr. Thompson published a sermon under the title, "The Doctrine of Conviction set in a clear light." Of this sermon Mr. Tennent, in 1743, expressed himself in very severe terms. Speaking of his brethren, he says, "They likewise opposed God's work, by their false and dangerous Moravian doctrine about conviction. Witness Mr. Thompson's detestable and inconsistent performance, entitled, The Doctrine of Conviction set in a clear light; which divers leaders of that schismatical party have expressed their approbation of. Hardly any thing can be invented that has a more direct tendency to destroy the common operations of God's Holy Spirit, and to keep men from Jesus Christ, than what Mr. Thompson has expressed in that performance."* Mr. Samuel Finley wrote an answer to the sermon, in which he condemns it in terms scarcely less severe.† Mr. Thompson's sermon is a long and excellent discourse on 1 Cor. iii. 12, 13: "Now if any man build upon this foundation, gold, silver, precious stones, wood, hay, stubble, &c." in which the author examined several doctrines then pre-

* Examiner Examined, p. 17.

† Examination and Refutation of Mr. Thompson's sermon, entitled, &c. By Samuel Finley, Philadelphia, 1743.

valent. The first of these he thus states: "Before there be so much as a beginning of any saving work of grace, or of the Holy Spirit in the heart of the sinner, there must be an awakening conviction of sin and misery raised in the soul in a way of common operation; which convictions are previously necessary to prepare the heart for saving grace, but are void of saving grace themselves." * Before refuting this doctrine he premises several general observations, which are in substance as follows: 1. That when the Holy Spirit begins a supernatural work in the heart, he does not implant first one grace and then another; but that true grace is one entire radical principle, the seed and root of all particular graces; just as natural life manifests itself in various exercises. 2. Consequently when any one grace is evident in its exercises, all other graces of the Spirit are to be found in the same person, though they may not be so conspicuous. 3. That these different graces are not so distinct as we are apt to imagine, as though they were separate entities, which may exist independently of each other; whereas they differ only in their object and in the manner of their exercise, yet are the same principle of grace putting forth its various actings, according to the variety of occasions and objects. 4. That although we properly form different apprehensions of these several graces, yet as they are radically one, it will be found that no one can be alone in its exercise any more than in its existence.

Having prepared the way by these remarks, he takes up the subject of "preparatory ungracious convictions," with regard to which he concedes, 1. That there are common convictions arising from natural conscience, or a common work of the Spirit, which often fall short of conversion. 2. That such convictions may be followed by true conversion; but when this happens the conversion is not the proper effect of those convictions. 3. That we should distinguish between those convictions which are common and those which are the effect of saving grace. The latter possess the soul with a sense of the vileness, baseness, and hateful nature of sin, as offensive to God; but the former only alarm the soul with the

* Sermon, p. 13

danger of the wrath and curse of God. Gracious conviction is always attended with grief for sin, on account of its own sinfulness, and the person's vileness on account of it, who loathes himself, and reckons himself among the basest and most disgraceful creatures upon God's earth; whereas in common convictions, the hatred conceived against sin is only on account of its pernicious consequences. Saving convictions, again, are always accompanied with love to God, to holiness, and to the saints. Sin becomes a burden to those thus convinced, under which they groan. In common convictions there is no love to holiness for its own sake, but only for its reward. Again, saving conviction, though it may take its rise from some notorious sin, does not stop there, but traces up all actual sin to the fountain head, the indwelling wickedness of the heart and corruption of nature; whereas common convictions are ordinarily confined to actual transgressions. The former continue an ingredient in the believer's exercises through life; the latter, for the most part, are at an end as soon as the person concerned gets hope or comfort from any source. And finally, we should distinguish between convictions, whether saving or common, and the terror which may accompany or follow them. The former consists in our persuasion of our sinful and miserable state; the latter in the uneasy impression arising from the apprehension of danger. The one is proportionate to the light which is let in upon our real character and condition; the other to the apparent avoidableness or unavoidableness of the danger to which we feel ourselves exposed. Hence though the conviction may be strong, the terror may be slight. These fears and terrors are at best but the language of unbelief, and consequently are in their nature a very great sin. To believe that we are in a perishing state by nature, and that we certainly shall perish if we continue in that state, that is unless we repent and believe in the Lord Jesus Christ, that is, cordially accept of him as he is offered in the gospel, and to be suitably affected by these things according to their nature, do certainly belong to those convictions which make up a part of our conversion; but to disbelieve or to doubt whether mercy is in our offer, or that we may be saved on gospel terms, is unbelief, and is contrary to that revelation which sets death and life, the blessing and the curse, before us at the same time."

After this exposition of his views, he shows from scriptural examples, that "these preparatory, ungracious convictions have no foundation as to their necessity, in order to conversion;" and concludes that, "the convictions which are necessary to conversion, are in truth a part of the work itself; or, to speak more distinctly, are nothing else but that very principle of grace implanted in and by conversion, putting forth itself in the exercise of conviction or persuasion of the person's natural, sinful, and miserable state, according to the word, the heart and conscience bearing witness thereunto."

This is a fair exhibition of Mr. Thompson's views of this subject, which were approved, it seems, by the other leaders of his party. This exhibition is here given, that it may be seen for what kind of doctrine the good men of that day denounced each other. Mr. Tennent appeals to this "detestable performance," and to "the false and dangerous Moravian doctrine" which it contained, in proof that the author and those who agreed with him, not only opposed the work of God, but were themselves graceless.* Yet these good men did not really differ in doctrine. Mr. Thompson admitted that there were convictions resulting from the common operations of the Holy Spirit, which sometimes were and sometimes were not followed by true conversion. He only maintained that they were not necessary, and that those which are essential are themselves the results of saving grace. Against this Mr. Tennent had not a word to say. As he was a believer in instantaneous conversions, he could not believe in the absolute necessity of these preparatory convictions; nor could he well maintain that any exercises, not in themselves holy, were indispensable as a preparation for holiness. The only difference between the parties was, that the one laid more stress upon this "preliminary law work" than the other did. Both admitted that it often occurred; and both admitted that it was not indispensable.

* He refers to it for both purposes; compare Examiner Examined, pp. 17 and 87.

Another subject of dispute was, the call to the gospel ministry. Mr. Tennent in his Nottingham sermon had said, that "Natural men have no call of God to the ministerial work, under the gospel dispensation. Is it not a principal part of the ordinary call of God to the ministerial work, to aim at the glory of God, and in subordination thereto, the good of souls, as the chief marks in their undertaking that work? And can any natural man on earth do this? No! No! every skin of them has an evil eye; for no cause can produce effects above its own power. Man may put them into the ministry, through unfaithfulness or mistake; or credit or money may draw them, and the devil may drive them, knowing by long experience what special service they may be to his kingdom in that office; but God sends not such hypocritical varlets."* This and similar declarations were understood to teach, that though a man be regularly, after due trial and examination, ordained to the sacred office; yet if he is unconverted, he has not the call of God, but only that of man, to the ministry. Thus the matter is stated by Mr. Thompson, in the sermon above quoted. With regard to this point, he concedes, 1. That true grace in the person called, is absolutely necessary to the faithful and acceptable discharge of the duties of the ministry. 2. That there is a distinction between the outward call of the word, and the inward call of the Spirit, to grace and salvation. But the call of God to the ministry is an authoritative act by which he authorizes and commands the person called to enter upon the sacred office. 3. God is truly and properly said to do what is done in virtue of any order or institution of his, and, therefore, 4. That when a person is orderly set apart to this work, by those having authority from Christ for that purpose, he is properly said to be called of God to that work, whatever his qualifications may be. "I entreat my readers," he adds, "that they may not misunderstand me, as if I would plead for an unsanctified ministry. God forbid that such a profane, impious thought should ever be harboured in my breast, much more that I should be wicked enough to maintain it by arguments. Undoubtedly it is the indispensable duty of every one who aspires to this sacred

* Nottingham Sermon, p. 5.

office, to pray and labour for true sanctifying grace and all other necessary qualifications, to fit him for the work, and to propose single ends and views to himself in undertaking it. And it is no less the duty of those, whose part it is to call and ordain men to that work, to take care to inquire into the saving grace, as well as the other qualifications in the persons to be ordained; and the neglect of either is a heinous sin, and of a dreadful tendency, as no doubt a graceless ministry is an awful plague and scourge to any people." What he contended for was, 1. That the qualifications for the sacred office, and the call to enter upon it, should not be confounded; for "if the inward gracious qualifications constitute the call of God, then all who have the qualifications are called to the ministry." 2. That the claim of those who were regularly ordained to be regarded as true ministers should not be denied.

To all this Mr. Tennent replied, that his Nottingham sermon was founded on the assumption, that there "is a two-fold call to the ministry, inward and outward. The first consisting principally in, or rather was evidenced by, the pious dispositions and aims of the person; and the other in his regular external separation to the ministerial work."* He adds, "When I said pharisee or unconverted ministers are no shepherds, (no faithful ones,) in Christ's account, it is plainly intimated that I owned them to be ministers, true and lawful ones, in the sight of the church, but not faithful ones in the account of Christ."† In another place he says: "Whether those inward pious dispositions be termed the inward call of God to the gospel ministry; or only qualifications necessary or pre-requisite in the persons whom God calls; it seems to be the same in substance."‡ He denies that he confounded the outward and inward call, or ever "thought that any person by reason of his good dispositions and aims, had commission or authority to exercise the ministerial office."§ He successfully vindicates the propriety of calling these pious desires the evidence of an inward call, by an appeal to the usage of the church. "This," he says, "is the opinion of the whole church of Scotland, as appears from

* Examiner Examined, p. 10.

† Ibid. p. 12.

‡ Remarks on the Protest.

§ Examiner Examined, p. 12.

her Directory, which they and we have adopted as the standard of our proceedings and sentiments respecting the affairs of church government." He then quotes from the ordination service a distinct recognition of the inward call.* He appeals also to the Church of England, which asks every candidate for orders: "Do you trust that you are inwardly moved by the Holy Ghost to take upon you this office and ministration?" There was, therefore, no real difference of opinion on this subject between Mr. Tennent and his opponents. He erred in the violent and sweeping language of his sermon, which seemed to imply that an unconverted minister is no minister at all; and they erred in restricting the word 'call' to an authoritative act giving a right to exercise the office of the ministry.

A third subject of discussion was the doctrine of assurance. Mr. Tennent complained that his brethren had done great harm by teaching, "that persons might have grace and not know it."† He, at times, went to the opposite extreme. Mr. Thompson says, "I myself have heard Mr. Gilbert Tennent, with great vehemency, assert to a great congregation that every truly gracious person, or true convert, is as sensible of the grace of God in himself, or the love of God to him, as a man would be of a wound or stab, or of the blowing of the wind, or to that effect; and he maintained the same doctrine, alleging some Scripture for his support, when in private I challenged him for it, on the same evening."‡ The same complaint is made against the Brunswick brethren in the Protest and elsewhere. This is one of the doctrines examined in Mr. Thompson's sermon quoted above; with regard to which he teaches, 1. That assurance is attainable in this life. 2. That it is the fault of Christians that it is not more generally attained. 3. That it may be lost. He denies, however, that every believer is assured of his gracious state from the moment that he enters upon it. In answer to the common objection, that a man must be conscious of the exercises of his own mind, he says: "It is one thing to be conscious of such and such a thought in my heart, and another

* Examiner Examined, p. 15. † Ibid. p. 19.

‡ Preface to the Sermon on the Nature of Conviction, p. 5.

thing to be sure that such a thought is an exercise of grace." That Mr. Tennent and his friends, notwithstanding casual unguarded statements, really held the common doctrine on this subject, is plain from his remarks on the Protest. He there says: "Assurance is attainable and loseable; some gracious souls attain it in this life, and some do not." This his opponents owned "to be right orthodox, and the substance of what they had been contending for."

Such were the doctrinal matters in dispute between the two parties. Well might Mr. Tennent say, they were in their own nature small, though greatly aggravated by the distemper of the times. There is not one of these points, with regard to which they did not come to a substantial agreement, as soon as an opportunity was offered for a dispassionate comparison of views.

If the parties were thus agreed with respect to doctrines, were they not widely separated in relation to their views of church government? There is a very prevalent, but very erroneous impression in reference to this point. The schism is often represented as the result of a long-continued struggle between the presbyterian and congregational element in the Synod; between the Scotch and Irish members on the one hand, and the New England members on the other. The preceding narrative shows that there is not the least foundation for this representation. It shows that the opposition to the authority of the Synod, in relation to the two acts which were the matter in dispute, was confined, with one doubtful exception, to the Scotch and Irish members. The ejected members, with the same exception, belonged to the same class. The protesting or Brunswick party, as it was called, was, therefore, as completely a Scotch and Irish party as it well could be. The narrative further shows that the New England portion of the Synod took part with the majority on all the ecclesiastical matters in debate, until the anti-presbyterial ejectment of the New Brunswick brethren; and that those of them who subsequently withdrew, left the Synod not on account of the matters in dispute between the contending parties, but because of the violent and unconstitutional manner in which that dispute was ended. And finally, it shows that, so far from the New England brethren being driven off, their secession was regarded with great regret. The Synod said it was a thing they could not hinder, though contrary both to their "judgment and inclination."

If, then, the members who were violently cast out were Congregationalists, it was not through New England influence. It was Irish congregationalism, if congregationalism at all, which caused the schism. Still, the most interesting question is, Were these ejected brethren really anti-presbyterian in their principles? It has been seen that this was one of the prominent charges against them; and it must be confessed that the charge had a very plausible foundation. Those brethren themselves found it very difficult to reconcile some parts of their Apology with the principles they professed. To all appearance they allowed to presbyteries and synods nothing beyond advisory powers, even in judicial cases. This character of the Apology is no doubt, however, as has already been remarked, to be referred to that habit of exaggerated statement so characteristic of Mr. Tennent, and which involved him in so many inconsistencies. This is evident from the fact that it is in contradiction with other declarations of its authors, and with their uniform practice. These are more trustworthy sources of evidence of the opinions of these gentlemen than any controversial paper written in the midst of an ardent struggle, and to justify an extreme proceding. Certain it is, the New Brunswick brethren considered the charge of anti-presbyterianism as unfounded and injurious. They asserted their faithful adherence to the Westminster Directory. They affirmed that they were as strict Presbyterians as their opponents. They gave such an explanation of their Apology as to remove all objections to it; and their uniform practice, first as a Presbytery, and afterwards as a Synod, was, in fact, as thoroughly conformed to Presbyterian rules, as that of the old Synod during any period of its history.* If all these points are clearly established, it must be admitted that the parties were as thoroughly agreed in their principles of church government, as in

* The evidence of the correctness of this latter statement will be found in the following chapter, containing the history of the church during the schism.

their doctrinal opinions, and the schism will be assigned to its true cause, viz. the disorder and alienation consequent on the excitement produced by the revival.

A very few extracts from the writings of the leading men, on either side, will suffice to prove the correctness of the representation just given, and to show the agreement of the two parties. In a passage just quoted from Mr. Tennent, we heard him say, when speaking of the Directory, that, they and we, his opponents and his friends, had adopted it, "as the standard of our proceedings and sentiments respecting the affairs of church government." Was such a declaration ever made by the Independents in Great Britain, or by the Congregationalists in New England? Was it ever made by any honest man who was not a sincere Presbyterian?

A more authoritative profession is to be found in the Declaration of the united Presbyteries of New Brunswick and New Castle, already referred to. In order to vindicate themselves from the charge of anti-presbyterianism, those presbyteries give a somewhat extended summary of the universally recognized principles of Presbyterianism, and conclude thus: "In a word, we heartily agree with the plan of government laid down by the Westminster Assembly in the Directory for church government, as that which is appointed by Jesus Christ, and contained in his word; and so we disown and reject as unscriptural, all other forms and models of church government whatsoever." They further declare, that they "heartily approve of the directions of the Westminster Assembly in their Directory for public worship, as agreeable to the word of God; only we would not be understood to mean as if every particular direction and advice was of necessary obligation upon us. For instance, that we must always begin public worship with prayer; much less that we can now pray for the same afflicted queen of Bohemia, therein mentioned, and such-like circumstantial things, which no understanding man can judge to be necessary, or of constant obligation.

"We likewise agree to the directions of the General Assembly of the Church of Scotland, in their Directory for family worship, excepting we see not why persons of quality should, on that account, be exempted from performing the worship of God themselves, in their own families, more than others; and the meeting of divers families therein disapproved of, is not to be understood of such private societies as may meet statedly, at proper times, for reading and prayer, and mutual edifying conference.

"This is a summary account of our faith and principles, and agreeable to the same we desire and design, through divine grace, ever to conduct ourselves, that we may be faithful as servants in all God's house."* Stronger professions of Presbyterianism were never made, or desired by the opposite party.

The reader will now not be surprised to hear Mr. Tennent assert that the parties did not differ in their ecclesiastical principles. "What order and government were opposed," he asks, "in the late time of contention among us? Was it the necessity of order and government in the church of Christ in general? No. Was it the nature of the government which the Scripture expresses? No. Was it the plan of government which is expressed in our Directory agreeable to the Scriptures? No. What was then the core of the controversy? Why some circumstantials in government; in other words, some rules or acts of discipline formed by the majority, and reckoned prudential and expedient by them, but on the contrary, prejudicial and sinful by the minor party."†

The agreement between the two parties will be more obvious, if we state distinctly the points on which they ultimately came to a full understanding. They both denied to the church all legislative power in matters of religion; that is, all right to make laws to bind the conscience. This power, it may be remembered, was unanimously disclaimed by the Synod in 1729, in the adopting act. It is formally disclaimed in our present constitution, and it has ever been disclaimed by all parties in the church. Mr. Thompson, in his Government of the Church of Christ, written in answer to the Apology of the New Brunswick brethren, says: "The Lord Jesus Christ hath invested his church with authority to make orders, acts, or diatactic rules for the regulating of circumstances of ecclesiastical matters, which are not, nor possibly could be all

* Detector Detected, pp. 127, 128.

† Irenicum, pp. 98, 99.

condescended upon in Scripture, for preventing disorders and confusion, only these rules must conform to and bear a subordination to the general rules of the word. This authority of the church is only declarative, subordinate, and executive; but not legislative, supreme, or dictating. The meaning whereof is this. The Lord Jesus Christ is head and king of his church; his church is his kingdom; his word contains a complete system of doctrines and laws for his church to believe and obey; but he hath also appointed officers and rulers in his kingdom, who are authorized both to teach and to rule according to these laws; and accordingly they have authority to explain these doctrines, and agree about the meaning of Scripture as to doctrinals; and, by consequence, to compose creeds or confessions of faith. They have also authority to interpret or explain the rules and precepts of the word, and to apply these laws or rules to particular cases."* Again: "These rules, acts, or orders of the church cannot, with any propriety of speech, be termed religious laws, because they contain no new matter but what is supposed to be contained in the divine law, or general rule of the word applied to such and such cases."† Again: "We pretend to no authority to make laws or rules, the matter and penalty of which are not comprehended in the word, though not expressed therein. As, for instance, when the Westminster Assembly gave directions to inquire into the character and qualifications of candidates for the ministry, they judged that the rules in the epistles to Timothy and Titus did require them to form and observe those very directions, which they then and there laid down for that very purpose, viz.: to require certificates, and to inquire into their skill in the several parts of learning, &c."‡ Again: "We aver that the power and authority, by which such acts or rules are made, is only a ministerial, subordinate, declarative power or authority, to explain and apply the rules or laws already made by Christ, and contained in his word . . . . which is no legislative power at all. The constitution of the Presbyterian Church, contained in our Westminster Directory, is made up of such rules."§ "We are obliged," he says, "to remind our readers that we claim no legis-

* Government, &c., p. 60. † Ibid. p. 62. ‡ Ibid. p. 68. § Ibid. p. 75.

lative power, but only a ministerial and executive power, viz.: a power or authority as officers in Christ's church to govern it, according to the laws which he hath already given, and consequently to explain and apply those laws to their particular cases, whether by making rules, or judging facts."* And to the same effect: "We own and plead that every true church hath authority to make rules about prudentials and expedients; but we deny that this power is a power of legislation, and say that it is only a declarative and executive power."†

From these extracts it is plain what was disclaimed, and what was affirmed to belong to church judicatories. All power to make new laws on religious matters was disclaimed, but the authority to make rules to carry into effect the general principles contained in the word of God, was asserted. To both these points the other party fully assented. Mr. Blair, one of the signers of the Apology, wrote a vindication of his brethren from the charge of anti-presbyterianism, contained in Mr. Thompson's work. From this vindication it appears, that the power to which the Brunswick gentlemen intended to object, was precisely that which Mr. Thompson disclaimed; and that the power which he asserted to belong to church judicatories, they readily conceded to them. "I proceed," says Mr. Blair, "to show the weakness of his charge, by giving a just view of those passages of the Apology, which he grounds it upon; and to this purpose it will be necessary to see and consider what that strain of authority in church judicatories is, which the brethren who presented that Apology do reject and reason against." This he describes as "a proper legislative or law-making authority; not only an authority to execute the laws of Christ, but properly to make laws of their own, in addition to the laws of Christ; which might also sometimes happen to be contrary to his laws, as it was with some of the constitutions of the Jews."‡ This is exactly the authority which Mr. Thompson dis-

* Government, &c., p. 97. † Ibid. p. 101.

‡ Vindication of the brethren who were unjustly and illegally cast out of the Synod of Philadelphia by a number of the members, from maintaining

claimed. On the other hand, he concedes every thing when he says: "We heartily agree with our Confession of Faith, that 'it belongs unto Synods and councils to set down rules for the better ordering the public worship of God and the government of the church; to receive complaints in case of mal-administration, and authoritatively determine the same; which decrees and determinations, if consonant to the word of God, are to be received with reverence and submission, not only for their agreement with the word, but also for the power whereby they are made, as being an ordinance of God appointed thereunto in his word.'" It is perfectly evident this was all that was ever demanded on the other side, or by any class of Presbyterians. And "all this," says Mr. Blair, "we freely allow; and there is nothing in the Apology, so far as I can discern, that can be produced, according to the fair rules of interpretation, contrary thereto. For, observe again, the point denied is this, viz.: That church judicatories have a lawful power of oppressing the consciences of their members, by imposing any thing upon them upon pain of censure and non-communion, which they judge sinful, and cannot in conscience comply with; when the majority, in the meantime, are not in conscience bound by the authority of God declaring or ordaining that very thing in his word. Such a power as this, is, I think, properly a legislative power in religious matters." * It is plain then that Mr. Blair and Mr. Thompson thus far perfectly agreed. They both disclaimed what they called a legislative power in religious matters, that is, a power to make laws to bind the conscience; and they both asserted the power to decide authoritatively in judicial cases, and to set down rules for the government of the church.

The parties agreed also as to the limits of this latter power. They both held that the decisions and rules of church judicatories were binding on dissentient members, provided those determinations

principles of anarchy in the church, and denying the due scriptural authority of church judicatories; against the charges of the Rev. Mr. John Thompson in his piece entitled, The Government of the Church of Christ; by Samuel Blair.—Works, p. 209.

* Works, p. 213.

were not regarded as sinful. And further, they agreed, that when the conscience of any member forbad compliance with such determinations, his duty was peaceably to withdraw, and not trample on the rules of the body.* Mr. Thompson says on this subject, "No member of a judicatory is abridged or deprived of his privilege hereby. For first, he hath the privilege as a member to debate and reason; again, he is at liberty to give his vote or keep it; and thirdly, he is at liberty to submit and conform to the determination of the judicatory by vote, or not. Where then, I beseech, is the abridgment? And as for penalty, there is no new penalty inflicted, but what is the unavoidable consequence of differing judgments among the members of a judicatory, viz.: Submission to the judgment of the majority, or separation; which, with its following inconveniences is mutual, and affects both parties in proportion." † "The minority of a church judicatory do virtually promise to be determined by the suffrage of the majority, every time they consent to let the matter in debate go to a vote; and, therefore, afterwards to refuse subjection to such determination is to forfeit their promise. They exercise liberty of conscience and private judgment in voting; and they have still liberty of conscience and private judgment of discretion to determine themselves as to their obedience; i. e. if they apprehend, or come to be persuaded that what is concluded is sinful, they are at liberty to refuse obedience, and that without the least hazard of any penalty or censure, besides what is the unavoidable consequence of the difference of judgment in such cases, and of the authority which they themselves have approved by putting themselves under the government of it." ‡ The authors of the Protest take the same ground: "We utterly renounce," say they, "all claim of power to make any scriptureless canons; and claim a bare ministerial authority, to set down rules and directions for the ordering of public worship of God, and the government of his church agreeable to the thirty-first article, part third, of our Confession of Faith. . . . . If we can-

* It is true the New Brunswick brethren did not act on this principle, but they came to acknowledge its justice.

† Government, &c. p. 90.

‡ Ibid. p. 93.

not agree without voting, the majority have a casting vote in all our determinations, as is usual in all judicatories civil and ecclesiastical, so that the minority or dissenting voters, in rules of common concern, must either comply, or forbear to counteract, or separate." *

Mr. Tennent teaches the same doctrine. "No doubt a smaller number," says he, "ought freely to submit to the conclusions of the majority, in matters of government, which they, the majority, judge essential to the well-being of the church. For without this there could be no government at all. Without this the minor party would have power to impose upon the major, in things which they reckon of the last consequence to the good of the society; which is absurd. It is true the major party may be mistaken as well as the minor, and consequently abuse their power, for which there is no help in the present imperfect state of things, but humble remonstrance by reason and argument. Yet considered as a society, the majority have a right to judge for themselves, (upon the plan of private judgment,) what they reckon essential to their constitution, or to the well-being of the church under their care, and consequently to exclude from their society such as do not comply therewith. Moreover in matters which are reckoned circumstantial by the majority, the minor party ought, for peace' sake, to comply, if they be not conscience-bound in the matter; but if so, they cannot; and whether forbearance should not be exercised towards them in this case, as well as in other parallel cases, I leave to others to determine." † "There are two general cases," says Mr. Blair, "wherein we freely grant church judicatories must require and insist upon submission and obedience from all their members, whether they assent or dissent, whether they be negatives or approbatives, or non-liquets in the making of the acts or rules, on pain of such censure as may appear from Scripture to be due to their disobedience, according to the various instances of it, or cases wherein it may be: First, when the judicature does judge, that that very particular which they determine, appoint, or forbid, is itself particularly declared, appointed, or forbidden by God in

* Refutation of Mr. Tennent's Remarks, p. 55.

† Irenicum, p. 99.

Holy Scripture, whether the point be determined in Scripture in so many express words, or by plain consequence, it is the same thing. The other general case, wherein obedience and submission are necessary to be given to church judicatories and required by them is, when in matters of human prudence and expediency they can submit without conscience of sin in so doing. When the majority of a judicature judge a particular thing or rule to be a good prudential expedient in present circumstances, or to answer the design of some general direction or injunction of God's word, though the minority or lesser number judge it not so, yet they are in duty and conscience bound to submit and obey, unless they judge the thing or rule to be contrary to God's word, and so, that it is sinful for them to obey."* Further than this no Presbyterian ever went. Finally, when these brethren came to unite with others in the formation of a new Synod, it was laid down as a fundamental principle: "That in matters of discipline and those things which relate to the peace and good order of our churches, they shall be determined according to the major vote of ministers and elders, with which vote every member shall actively concur or passively acquiesce. But if any member cannot in conscience agree to the determination of the majority, and the Synod think themselves obliged to insist upon it as essentially necessary to the well-being of our churches, in such case, such dissenting member promises peaceably to withdraw from the body, without endeavouring to raise any dispute or contention upon the debated point, or any unjust alienation from them."† In all the protracted negotiations between the two Synods, this article was acquiesced in by both parties, and was adopted in 1758, when the union actually took place.

Notwithstanding, therefore, the ardent debates and mutual criminations on this subject, it appears the two parties were of one mind. They were agreed in disclaiming all legislative power in religious matters. They were agreed in the right of Synods to set down rules for the government of the church. They were agreed

* Vindication, &c. p. 211 and 212.

† Minutes of the Synod of New York, p. 2.

in the binding authority of these rules even over dissentients, except when such dissentients believed them to be sinful. They were agreed that when a member could not obey a given rule with a good conscience, it was his duty peaceably to withdraw. Finally, they were agreed that when a Synod saw that the minority were opposed to any measure, not in judgment only, but in conscience, they ought not to insist upon it, and thus necessitate a schism, unless they believed the measure to be essential to the well-being of the churches. These principles are all so plain and so reasonable, that we need not wonder they commanded the unanimous consent of both parties, or that they have remained the unquestioned principles of our church from that day to this. If in the exasperation of another conflict, when no truth is clearly seen, and no duty properly appreciated, they have again been called in question by heated partisans, they will resume the sway which belongs to truth and reason when the excitement has died away.

It appears from this history that the great schism was not the result of conflicting views, either as to doctrine or church government. It was the result of alienation of feeling produced by the controversies relating to the revival. In these controversies the New Brunswick brethren were certainly the aggressors. In their unrestrained zeal, they denounced brethren, whose Christian character they had no right to question. They disregarded the usual rules of ministerial intercourse, and avowed the principle that in extraordinary times and circumstances such rules ought to be suspended. Acting upon this principle, they divided the great majority of the congregations within the sphere of their operations, and by appealing to the people, succeeded in overwhelming their brethren with popular obloquy. Excited by a sense of injury, and alarmed by the disorders consequent on these new methods, the opposite party had recourse to violent measures for redress, which removed none of the evils under which they suffered, and involved them in a controversy with a large class of their brethren, with whom they had hitherto acted in concert. These facts our fathers have left on record for the instruction of their children; to teach them that in times of excitement the rules of order, instead of being suspended, are of more importance than ever to the well-being of the church; that no pretence of zeal can authorize the violation of the rules of charity and justice; and on the other hand, that it is better to suffer wrong than to have recourse to illegal methods of redress; that violence is no proper remedy for disorder, and that adherence to the constitution is not only the most Christian, but also the most effectual means of resistance against the disturbers of the peace and order of the church.

CHAPTER VI.

HISTORY OF THE CHURCH DURING THE SCHISM, 1741–58.

SYNOD OF PHILADELPHIA. Accessions to the Synod.—Missionary labours of the Synod.—Its efforts in behalf of education.—Establishment of the widows' fund.—The form of government.—Presbyterial acts performed by the Synod. —Its supervisory power.—Decision of casuistical questions.—Addresses to the churches in reference to the low state of religion, and to public calamities.

SYNOD OF NEW YORK. Articles of agreement on which the Synod was founded. Accessions to the Synod.—Its missionary labours.—Its efforts in behalf of education.—Its standard of doctrine.—Its form of government, illustrated by its acts of review and control; the formation of new Presbyteries; the decision of judicial questions; the strict Presbyterianism of its subordinate Presbyteries.—The Synod conformed to the Scottish model, in appointing annually a commission, in investing committees with full synodical power, and in acting as a Presbytery.—History of the negotiations for an union of the two Synods.—The plan of union ultimately adopted in 1758.

THE number of ministers connected with the Synod of Philadelphia, before the schism, was from forty to forty-five. Nine were excluded in 1741, and eleven or twelve withdrew in 1745, when the Synod of New York was formed, leaving in connection with the old Synod from twenty to twenty-three. During the seventeen years that the separation lasted, the number of ministers in the Synod of Philadelphia remained nearly stationary. This was the result of various causes. The portion of the country which fell within the bounds of that Synod was comparatively new, and settled by a heterogeneous population, Irish, Scotch, German, Welsh, and English. These people to a great extent were poor, and much less cultivated than the original settlers of New England. They were also widely scattered and mixed with other denominations, which rendered the formation of churches, and the support of pastors, exceedingly difficult. The number of young men qualified for the ministry furnished by such a population, was of course small, and the supply of preachers from abroad was tardy and precarious.

During this period also, the colonies, especially Pennsylvania and Virginia, were greatly harassed and injured by the French and Indian wars. In a multitude of cases, settlements, instead of increasing, were entirely broken up, and the people murdered or scattered. This disturbed state of the country was of course very unfavourable to the formation of new congregations, and to the increase of those already established. Missionaries sent by the Synod of New York to Virginia, were more than once entirely prevented from fulfilling their appointments, by the dangerous condition of the frontier settlements.*

Another cause of the slow increase of the Synod of Philadelphia, was the decided superiority of the Synod of New York. This superiority was not merely as to numbers, but as to zeal, weight of character, and facility of obtaining a supply of ministers. To this Synod, therefore, was attracted a large proportion of those young men, who, from their geographical position, most naturally belonged to the other. New England too, even at that day, had begun to be the hive of ministers. The Presbyteries of New York and New Brunswick lying contiguous to the sources of supply, naturally received the ministers who entered our church from the eastern provinces.

The Synod of Philadelphia, however, laboured with no little zeal and fidelity to cope with the difficulties with which they were surrounded, and to cultivate successfully the field which God had committed to their care. The following ordinations and receptions of new members were reported to the Synod during the period now

* Minutes of the Synod of New York, p. 107. "The difficulties and dangers of the times," it is said, "rendered it in a great degree impracticable for Messrs. Spencer and Brainard to answer the end of their appointment to the southward, and for that reason said appointments were not fulfilled. There were like reasons for Mr. Clark not fulfilling his appointment to the southern provinces." These appointments were made in 1755.

under review; in 1742, Messrs. Guild and Samuel Evans, by the Presbytery of Philadelphia, and Mr. Alexander McDowell, by the Presbytery of Donegal; in 1744, Timothy Griffiths and John Steele, by the Presbytery of New Castle, who also reported the reception of Mr. James Scougall, an ordained minister from Scotland, and his settlement at Snowhill, Maryland. In 1747, the Presbytery of Donegal reported the ordination of David Thorn, and the Presbytery of New Castle that of John Dick, John Hamilton, and Hector Alison. In 1748, the Rev. David Brown, from Scotland, was received by the Presbytery of New Castle. In 1749, the Presbytery of Donegal reported the ordination of Mr. Tate; and in 1752, that of Mr. Samson Smith; and in 1754, that of Robert McMurdie; the same year the Presbytery of Philadelphia reported the ordination of John Kinkead. In 1757, the Rev. John Miller was received by the Presbytery of New Castle. This gentleman, the father of the Rev. Dr. Miller, of Princeton, was born in Boston, whither his parents had removed from Scotland. Mr. John Miller was settled at Dover, in the State of Delaware, and continued the faithful pastor of that church until his death in 1791. The same year the Rev. Alexander Miller was received by the Synod. Besides these, we find the names of William McKennan, Matthew Wilson, William Donaldson, and John Alison, on the minutes as ministers or preachers. It thus appears that about twenty-two ministers were added to the Synod of Philadelphia during the continuance of the schism. During the same period the death or removal of ten ministers is recorded.* It is not probable that the minutes give a full account either of the accessions or losses, particularly of the latter, as the number upon record in 1758, was not much larger than it was in 1745.

The attention of the Synod was early turned, not only to the wants of the people within their immediate bounds, but to those

* The deaths reported are those of Thomas Evans and James Martin, in 1743, of Mr. Andrews in 1747, of John Dick in 1748, of David Evans and Samuel Cavin in 1751, of John Thompson and Hugh Conn in 1753, of Robert Cathcart and Timothy Griffiths in 1754, and of Mr. Elmer in 1755. The return of Mr. David Brown to Scotland, is mentioned in the minutes for 1749.

also of the emigrants who were rapidly extending themselves through Virginia and North Carolina. In 1742, a supplication was received "from some of the back inhabitants of Virginia," begging the Synod to write to the General Assembly in Scotland, or to its commission, requesting that a minister or probationer might be sent over to them.* Such a letter was accordingly written. The following year the Synod wrote again to the Assembly, "to lay before them the low and melancholy condition of this infant church, both for want of probationers to supply our numerous vacancies, and also for want of suitable encouragement for ministers in new settlements, and to intreat them both to send ministers and probationers, and to allow them some small support out of their fund for some years, in new places; and that they be pleased to enable us in some measure or by some method to erect a seminary or school for educating young men for these ends among ourselves." †

In 1744, "a representation was laid before Synod from many people in North Carolina, showing their desolate condition, and petitioning that we would appoint one of our number to correspond with them."‡ The same year, "the Rev. Mr. Dorsius, pastor of the Reformed Dutch Church in Buck's County, laid a letter before Synod, from the deputies of North and South Holland, wherein they desire of the Synod an account of the high and low Dutch churches in this Province, and also of the churches belonging to the Presbyterian Synod of Philadelphia, and whether the Dutch churches may be joined in communion with said Synod, or if this may not be, that they would form themselves into a regular body and government among themselves. In pursuance of which letter, the Synod agreed that letters be written in the name of the Synod to the deputies of those Synods in Latin, and to the Scotch ministers in Rotterdam, giving them an account of the churches here, and declaring our willingness to join with the Calvinistic Dutch churches here, to assist each other as far as possible in promoting the common interests of religion, and signifying the present great

* Minutes of the Synod of Philadelphia, vol. ii. p. 79. † Ibid. p. 85.

‡ Ibid. vol. iii. p. 4.

want of ministers among the high and low Dutch, with the desire that they may help in educating men for the ministry. And the Synod ordered that Messrs. Andrews, Cross, Evans, and the Moderator, (McHenry,) write the said letters."*

That there were already congregations formed and furnished with ministers in the frontier settlements in Virginia, appears from the following minute made in 1747: "Upon considering the distance of the brethren in the back parts of Virginia, we think it necessary that we should know the state of the churches which are under our care, though at a distance from us; and, therefore, it is ordered that at least one of those brethren shall every year attend us, that we may have the pleasure of knowing the state of Christ's kingdom among them, and that we may keep synodical communion in reality, and not in name only. And ordered that Messrs. McHenry and Sanchey write them a letter, acquainting them with the mind of the Synod in said affair."† These congregations were formed principally under the ministrations of the members of the Presbytery of Donegal. As early as 1738, the Rev. Mr. Anderson, a member of that Presbytery, was sent to the settlements in the vicinity of Staunton. The following year, Mr. John Thompson supplied in the neighbourhood of Winchester and Staunton; and the same year Mr. John Craig received calls from two settlements near Staunton, which he accepted, having been ordained by the Presbytery of Donegal for that purpose. These congregations he called Augusta Church and Tinkling Spring. He continued to labour in these two congregations, (which are two of the oldest congregations in Virginia,) for about fourteen years, when he took his dismission from Tinkling Spring, and continued the remainder of his days pastor of Augusta Church alone; "which church still continues to be numerous and respectable, distinguished in general for their orthodoxy and good order, and enjoying from time to time some spiritual refreshings."‡ About the year 1744, the Rev. Mr. Black, of the Presbytery of Donegal, was settled at Rockfish."§

* Minutes, p. 5. † Ibid. p. 21.

‡ See MS. History of the Presbyterian Church in Virginia and part of North Carolina, prepared by the Lexington Presbytery in 1799. § Ibid.

In 1748, the Synod, in consequence of an application for supplies, "appointed that one minister should be sent in the fall, and another in the spring, to preach in the back parts of Virginia, each eight weeks, and that such members be exempt, until other members of the Synod do the same."* The following year it was ordered, that Mr. Tate go out eight weeks in the fall, and Mr. McHenry as many in the spring."† In 1750, this duty was assigned to Mr. Griffith and Mr. Samuel Thompson; and in 1751, to Mr. Hector Alison and Mr. Samson Smith.‡ In 1752, it was ordered, that Mr. McKennan supply the congregations of North and South Mountain, Timber Grove, North River, and Cedar Creek, and John Hinton's, until October, chiefly, and other vacancies as often as he can; and that Mr. Kinkead shall supply the same from the middle of November till the first of March."§ In 1753, supplications were again received from Virginia and North Carolina, and Mr. McMurdie was sent to preach in the vacant congregations for ten weeks or longer, if needful; and Mr. Donaldson for a similar term. These missionaries were urged to pay special attention to the congregations in North Carolina, between the Yadkin and Catawba rivers. ||

In 1755, the Synod sent Mr. Donaldson to the same settlements for three months in the fall, Mr. Matthew Wilson for three months in the winter, and Mr. McKennan for three months in the spring.¶ In 1756, it was ordered that Mr. John Alison supply the same "vacancies next fall and winter. And it is recommended to him, and to all such who may be sent by us to supply those distant parts, to study in all their public ministrations and private communications, to promote peace and unity among the societies, and to avoid whatever may tend to foment divisions and party spirit, and to treat every minister from the Synod of New York, of like prin-

* Minutes, p. 24. † Ibid. p. 26. ‡ Ibid. p. 30.

§ Ibid. p. 41. Timber Grove is Timber Ridge. North River runs near Lexington, in which the church is now situated. There is still a church on the old site called New Monmouth. North Mountain is six miles west of Staunton. Cedar Creek ten or twelve miles south-west from Winchester.

|| Ibid. p. 44. ¶ Ibid. p. 49.

ciples and peaceful temper, in a brotherly manner, as we desire to promote true religion and not party designs. And the Synod resolved to send a copy of these instructions to the brethren of the Synod of New York, hoping that they will recommend a like conduct to any they send thither. Ordered, that each of our supplies to those distant parts, carry a copy of this minute with them."*

In 1757, it was ordered, "that Mr. Miller supply the following settlements in order in the fall, each one Sabbath day, viz.: Cather's settlement, Osborne's, Morrison's, Jersey's on Yadkin; Buffler's and Baker's settlement. And that Mr. Craig supply the same settlements, each one Sabbath day in the spring; together with Brown's, North and South Mountain, and Calf-pasture settlements, in Virginia; and that they preach to lesser congregations on week days, as often as they can."†

These notices give but an imperfect idea of the missionary labours of the members of this Synod. Each Presbytery was a missionary society, and most of the missions to vacant congregations or destitute settlements were made under their direction, and therefore do not appear upon the minutes of the Synod.

Next to the religious instruction of their own people, and the supply of the new settlements, the duty of providing some adequate means for the education of ministers of the gospel, seems to have pressed most heavily upon the members of the Synod. From an early period, probably as early as 1719 or 1720, the Rev. William Tennent, Sen., had erected a school at Neshaminy, long known as the Log College, where some of the most distinguished and useful ministers of that generation received their education. This was a private institution, and had no immediate connection with the Synod. In 1739, Mr. John Thompson introduced an overture into the Presbytery of Donegal, proposing the establishment of a school under the care of the Synod. This overture was the same year referred to the Synod, and "unanimously approved;" and Messrs. Pemberton, Dickinson, Cross, and Anderson, were nominated, "two of whom, if they can be prevailed upon, to be sent home to Europe to prosecute this affair, with proper directions. And in order to

* Minutes, p. 55. † Ibid. p. 64.

this, it was ordered, that the commission of Synod, with correspondents from every presbytery, meet at Philadelphia, the third Wednesday of August next, and if it be necessary that Mr. Pemberton go to Boston, pursuant to this design, it is ordered, that the Presbytery of New York supply his pulpit during his absence."* When the commission met in accordance with this appointment, it was resolved that application should be made to every presbytery for their concurrence and assistance, and that a letter should be written to the General Assembly in Scotland, soliciting their co-operation. In consequence, however, of the small number of members in attendance, it was thought best to refer the matter to the whole Synod; and the commission accordingly resolved to call an extra meeting of the Synod on the last Wednesday of September, enjoining "on the members present to inform their respective presbyteries of the appointment, and that the moderator send letters to the Presbyteries of New Brunswick and New York, ordering their attendance at the time appointed." It was further ordered, "that a letter be remitted to Dr. Colman, to be communicated to our brethren of Boston, earnestly desiring their concurrence and assistance in this affair."† It appears from the minutes of the following year, 1740, that in consequence of "war breaking out between England and Spain, the calling of the Synod was omitted, and the whole affair laid aside for the time." A letter from Dr. Colman, in reply to the one written to him by the commission, was read before the Synod, wherein, in the name of the associated brethren of Boston, "he assures the Synod of their readiness to concur with the Synod in their laudable proposal of erecting a school or seminary of learning in these parts."‡

Nothing further was done in this business until 1744. From the minutes for that year, it appears that "a committee was held at the Great Valley, November 16, 1743, by a private agreement between the Presbyteries of Philadelphia, New Castle, and Donegal, the minutes of which meeting were laid before the Synod, showing that the said committee considered the necessity of speedy endeavours to educate youth for supplying our vacancies; but as

* Minutes, vol. ii. p. 67. † Ibid. p. 68. ‡ Ibid. p. 73.

the proper method cannot be so well compassed without the Synod, they refer the consideration of the affair to that reverend body; but agree, in the mean time, a school be opened for the education of youth. And this Synod, it is added, now approve of that design, and take the said school under their care, and agree upon the following plan for carrying on the design:

"First, there shall be a school kept open, where all persons who please may send their children, and have them taught gratis, in the languages, philosophy, and divinity.

"Second, in order to carry on this design, it is agreed that every congregation under our care be applied to for yearly contributions, more or less, as they can afford, and as God may incline them to contribute, until Providence open a door for our supporting the school some other way.

"Third, if any thing can be spared, besides what may support a master and tutor, it be applied by the trustees for buying books and other necessaries for the said school, and the benefit of it, as the trustees shall see proper. And Mr. Alison is chosen master of the said school, and has the privilege of choosing an usher under him to assist him; and he, Mr. Alison, is exempted from all public business, save only attending church judicatories, and what concerns his particular pastoral charge. And the Synod agree to allow Mr. Alison £20 per annum, and the usher £15."* The same day the Synod appointed a board of trustees for the school, three of whom were to visit the school every quarter. "These trustees," it is added, "are to inspect into the master's diligence in, and method of teaching; consider and direct what authors are chiefly to be read in the several branches of learning; to examine the scholars from time to time as to their proficiency; to apply the money procured from our people as ordered above; and, in sum, order all affairs relating to said school, as they shall see expedient, and be accountable to the Synod, making report of their proceedings and the state of the school yearly."

This it must be admited was a very liberal plan. A school was thus established for the gratuitous instruction of the youth of all

* Minutes, vol. iii. pp. 4, 5.

denominations, and sustained by the efforts of one of the poorest; and one of the most accomplished scholars at that time in the country, was placed at the head of it. The only record in the minutes for 1745, relating to the school, is the notice of the report of the trustees, and an order to those ministers who had not taken up a collection for its support, to attend to that duty. It appears that, by the order of the commission, Messrs. Andrews and Cross had written a letter to President Clap and the trustees of Yale College, in relation to this enterprise, as notice is taken of his reply. When President Clap's letter was presented to the Synod in 1746, an answer was prepared, which is inserted on the records at length.

It may be inferred from this answer, that the commission had written to make some arrangements for the admission of the students from the synodical school into Yale College, as the president called for information as to the plan of the school and state of the Synod. This information the answer in question purports to give. It states that the Synod had, some years before, endeavoured to establish a school, but were prevented by the troubles of the time, especially by the war with Spain; that in the mean time, in order to secure a learned ministry, they had agreed that those who had not a diploma from some college should obtain a certificate of competent scholarship from the Synod, before being taken on trials by any Presbytery. It then briefly refers to the opposition made to this agreement, and to the controversies arising out of Mr. Whitefield's preaching, and the subsequent schism in the Synod. The letter then gives an account of the school, and adds, that the Synod had agreed "that after the scholars had passed through the course of studies assigned to them, they shall be publicly examined by the trustees and such ministers as the Synod shall see fit to appoint, and if approved, shall receive testimonials of their approbation, and without such testimonials none of the Presbyteries under the care of the Synod shall improve any of the scholars in the ministry." The writers further express their hope of obtaining assistance from England and Ireland, as soon as the difficulties which then existed allowed of their making the necessary application. They profess their purpose to make the course of instruction in their school correspond as nearly as possible with that pursued in the British colleges. They readily agreed that their scholars, in going to Yale, should be examined by the president and fellows, be required to bring recommendations, and that they should enjoy no privileges inconsistent with the good order of the college. It is not easy to understand the object of this letter, unless it be assumed that the statutes of Yale College required a certain number of years' residence before graduation, and that the Synod wished their students to be allowed to enter the higher classes, when found prepared, in order to avoid the expense of a protracted absence from their own homes. In the minutes for the year 1747, there is a notice of another letter from President Clap, and of a reply on the part of the Synod, but the contents of neither are given.

The Synod continued to watch over the school with sedulous attention, as there is almost every year some record relating to it. In 1749, it was found necessary to modify the plan of gratuitous instruction. Mr. Alison's salary was increased to thirty pounds, and he was allowed to receive the usual tuition fee from all students whom the trustees did not exempt from that charge.* In 1751–2, Mr. Alison removed to Philadelphia to take charge of the academy in that city, and when it was erected into a college he was appointed the vice-provost. Mr. Alexander McDowell was appointed his successor in the mastership of the synodical school. The organization of the college in Philadelphia, and the appointment of Mr. Alison, seem in a measure to have removed the necessity for a higher collegiate institution under the immediate care of the Synod. That college, though principally under the control of Episcopalians, was accessible to all denominations, and a large portion of its officers and trustees have ever been Presbyterians.

In 1754, Mr. Matthew Wilson was appointed Mr. McDowell's assistant, and teacher of languages in the school, Mr. McDowell "from a sense of the public good, continuing to teach logic, mathematics, and natural and moral philosophy."† In 1755, a collec-

* Minutes, p. 26.

† Ibid. p. 46.

tion of books was received from Dublin, which were sent "for the benefit of public schools, the use of students, and the encouragement of learning in this infant church, to be disposed of by the Synod in the best manner to answer these good ends." It was then agreed that these books should "be the foundation of a public library under the care of the Synod." The books proper for the school were to be the property of the master, he giving security for their safe keeping and return; the others were committed to the care of the trustees of the fund for ministers' widows, who were to choose a librarian to take charge of the library for the use of members of the Synod, and for the benefit of students of divinity in the college of Philadelphia.* The same year an application was made to the trustees of the German schools for assistance in the support of the synodical school; the Synod engaging "to teach some Dutch children the English tongue, and three or four boys Latin and Greek, if they offer themselves; and Mr. Samson Smith was directed to open the school at Chesnut Level so soon as this favour was received."† These German schools were under the patronage of a general board in London, and of a subordinate board in Philadelphia. It was to the latter that the application of the Synod was, in the first instance, directed. This application was the more reasonable, as the Synod had for eleven years sustained the school by their own exertions, and offered its advantages gratuitously, to the youth of all denominations. The request for assistance, therefore, was granted without much hesitation, as appears from the following extract from the minutes of the board, communicated to the Synod in answer to their petition. "June 14, 1755; met at Mr. Allen's house near Germantown the following trustees, viz.: Messrs. Allen, Peters, Franklin, and Smith. And taking into their consideration the aforesaid petition of the Synod of Philadelphia, were under some difficulty how to act concerning it. On the one hand they thought that to grant the petition in favour of an English Synod might give offence to the Germans, who generally consider this charity as intended for their own particular benefit. The trustees were also of opinion, that it did not

* Minutes, p. 51.

† Ibid. p. 65.

exactly fall under the great design of promoting the English tongue among the Germans. But they considered on the other hand, the pleas urged by the petitioners. They knew it to be a truth, that the Synod of Philadelphia, at a time when ignorance, even among the ministry, was like to overrun the whole province, had begun, and with much difficulty, long supported a public school under Mr. Francis Alison; and that many able ministers, and some of them Dutch, had been educated in the said school. The trustees were also of opinion that it was no small argument in favour of the petitioners, that the mother church of Scotland had contributed so largely to this useful charity, and that if any future application to said church should be necessary, the interest and recommendation of the Synod of Philadelphia might be useful in that respect, as well as in countenancing the several schools in their present infant state, and educating, according to their proposal, some young men for the Dutch ministry gratis. In consideration of all which it was resolved to grant twenty-five pounds currency for one year to assist the said Synod to support their school, on the following terms, viz.: 1. That it shall be under the same common government with the other free schools, and be subject to the visitation of the trustees general or their deputies, appointed upon the recommendation of the Synod. 2. That the master shall teach four Dutch or English scholars gratis, upon the recommendation of the trustees general, to be prepared for the ministry, and ten poor Dutch children in the English tongue gratis, if so many offer. 3. That the deputy trustees, together with the master and any of the clergy, visit the school at least once a quarter, and send down a statement thereof, to be transmitted by the general trustees to the honourable society. Agreed, that this case be transmitted to the honourable society to obtain their directions thereupon." *

The Synod acceded to these terms and appointed deputy trustees to visit the school every quarter. When this matter came before the society in London, they increased the annual contribution to the Synod's school from twenty-five pounds currency to thirty pounds sterling.† It was thus that the Synod laboured diligently

* Minutes, p. 66.

† Ibid. p. 71.

and successfully in promoting the cause of education. At the synodical school under Mr. Alison and Mr. McDowell, some of the most distinguished of the ministers of the next generation were prepared for their work. This school gave rise to the Newark Academy, which has since been chartered as a college.

The connection between these two institutions is fully set forth in the charter granted to the Newark Academy in 1769, by Thomas and Richard Penn. "Whereas the Rev. Messrs. John Thompson, Adam Boyd, Robert Cross, Francis Alison, Alexander McDowell, and some others, about twenty years since, erected a public school in the province of Pennsylvania for the instruction of youth in the learned languages, mathematics, and other branches of useful literature, and to qualify them for admission into colleges and universities; which school they supported with much care and expense, to the great advantage and benefit of the public: And whereas, the said school, so as aforesaid, originally in the province of Pennsylvania, hath been removed and is now kept in the town of Newark, in the county of New Castle; and whereas, &c."

In one of the preceding extracts, mention is made of the trustees of the fund for ministers' widows. As the institution here referred to still exists, and is one in which many of our clergy are interested, it may not be improper to introduce a brief account of its origin. In 1754, "a proposal was introduced by Mr. Alison for laying some plan for the support of ministers' widows," and a committee was appointed for that purpose, who made a report to the Synod, when it was agreed, "in order to complete the plan, and to carry it into full execution, that each Presbytery should choose a minister to represent them, and send by him their several quotas to the fund; and this representation when met, shall put the stock into the hands of appointed trustees, and fix the proper regulation of it."* The plan thus formed was reported to the Synod the following year and finally adopted. It provided that each subscriber might pay two or three pounds annually; that all future members of the Synod, or candidates for the ministry, might join the association; that the subscription of any member might

* Minutes, pp. 46, 47.

be changed from two to three pounds, provided he made up the difference from the beginning; that the annuity payable to the widows or children of deceased members, should be five pounds, or seven pounds ten shillings, according as the subscription had been two or three pounds; that should a member die before he had made five annual payments, one half of the annuity due to his representatives should be deducted until these deductions, together with the payments made, amounted to the sum of five annual subscriptions; that the annuity should be payable to the widow for life, to the children for twelve years; that nothing beyond the annuities was to be paid, until the capital amounted to eight hundred pounds for every twenty members: after that the profits might be divided among the annuitants.* The following year application was made for a charter, which was ultimately obtained and has been the means of perpetuating an institution which has been the source of incalculable benefits to many widows and orphans.

As the principal object of this history is to exhibit the constitution of our church as to doctrine and order, it would here be in place to state whatever might throw any light on either of these points. As far as doctrine, however, is concerned, there was nothing in the action of the Synod of Philadelphia during the schism of any particular interest. There was no controversy on the subject; no acts of discipline for erroneous opinions, and no new measures adopted with a design to uphold the standards of the church. The only exception to this remark is, a resolution adopted immediately after the schism to the following effect, viz.: "That every member of this Synod, whether minister or elder, does sincerely and heartily receive, own, acknowledge, or subscribe the Westminster Confession of Faith, the Larger and Shorter Catechisms, as the confession of his faith, and the Directory, as far as circumstances will allow and admit in this infant church, for the

* The original members of this association were Francis Alison, Adam Boyd, Francis McHenry, Alexander McDowell, John Steel, John Kinkead, William McKennan, John Elder, Samson Smith, Richard Sanchey, Robert McMurdie, Joseph Tate, Hector Alison, Matthew Wilson, William Donaldson, and George Gillespie.

rule of church order. Ordered, that every session do oblige their elders to do the same at their admission. This was readily approved, *nemine contradicente.*" * Hitherto the adoption of the Confession of Faith had been required only of ministers. It was now required of elders, and that with evident propriety. They are entitled, as members of Presbytery, to sit in judgment on the doctrinal knowledge of candidates for ordination, and on the orthodoxy of ministers. This regulation, therefore, still continues a part of the constitution of the church.

As it regards matters of government, the Westminster Directory continued to be the general standard. The Sessions governed the congregations, subject to the review and control of the Presbyteries; the Presbyteries governed their own members, and received appeals and references from the Sessions, subject to the review and control of the Synod; and the Synod received appeals and references from the Presbyteries, and took care that the constitution was everywhere observed. Agreeably, however, to the Scottish and French principle, that a Synod is a larger Presbytery, and may properly perform all Presbyterial acts, when occasion calls for it, we find the Synod during this period as well as before the schism, frequently acting more or less distinctly in a Presbyterial capacity. Thus in 1741, the name of the Rev. Mr. Stevenson was struck from the roll, or he was disowned as a member, without the intervention of a Presbytery, because, as the Synod say, he had "from time to time, for years past, neglected attending on our judicatures, also had omitted his ministry without giving us any reason for his said conduct." † This suspension, however, was only until he should appear before Synod, "and give an account of his proceedings." In 1749, we find Mr. Cross requesting supplies from the Synod for his congregation, "until it please God to restore his health." Supplies were accordingly appointed for several Sabbaths, and Mr. Cross and his congregation allowed "discretionary power to invite any other of the brethren until the commission met in the fall." ‡ In 1754, he was again obliged to seek

* Minutes, vol. ii. p. 75. † Ibid. p. 74. ‡ Ibid. vol. iii. p. 26.

assistance, and it was "ordered that Mr. Cross or Mr. Alison have allowance to write to any minister, to come and preach two Sabbaths at any time during Mr. Cross's sickness." In 1751, the case of the Rev. Samuel Evans was referred to the Synod for advice, but they took it up and issued it by declaring "that Mr. Evans having acted disorderly in dissolving the pastoral relation between himself and his people, having travelled to England again and again, without any certificates by way of recommendation to the churches in that part of the world, and having in other things acted, from time to time, in a manner unsuitable to his character as a minister, we disown him as a member of this Synod until he give us satisfaction by a return to his duty, and amend his life and conduct." *

In 1753, a minister from Ireland, who had been censured by the Presbytery in his own country, applied directly to the Synod to be allowed to preach in their congregations. This application was refused.† Three years afterwards, however, an application was made by a particular congregation for his services, to which the Synod replied, "that they found it necessary to wait until they received an answer from the Synod in Ireland; but resolved, that as he had offered satisfaction to that Synod by our mediation, and had behaved himself so as to be well approved as a minister among us, if either the Synod of Ireland send us no answer, or inform us that they have accepted his submission, we do order Messrs. Black and Craig to receive him a member, and install him; provided they find his conduct in that part of Christ's vineyard such as becomes a gospel minister."‡ This appointment for some reason was not fulfilled, as the following year "a supplication was received from Cook's Creek, and Peeked Mountain, requesting that we would receive Mr. Alexander Miller as a member, and that at his installation he be appointed as their pastor in the Lord. The Synod, it is added, unanimously agreed to receive him as a member, and ordered that Mr. Craig install him sometime before the first of Au-

* Minutes, vol. iii. p. 30. † Ibid. p. 44. ‡ Ibid. p. 59.

gust next."* All this was done without the intervention of a Presbytery.

The way in which the Synod most frequently interfered in the immediate government of the churches, was by the appointment of correspondents to sit with a Presbytery, either with or without their previous consent. Thus, in 1752, a petition, apparently from a church member, was received and referred "to the Presbytery of Donegal, together with Messrs. McDowell, Cathcart, Griffiths, and Steel, as correspondents from the Presbytery of New Castle, to meet at Octarara the second Tuesday in August; and it was ordered, that Mr. Boyd's session give notice to all parties concerned."†

In 1753, the Presbytery of New Castle "applied to the Synod, that whereas Mr. Hector Alison had laid certain grievances before them, and sued for a dismission from his pastoral charge; and as the affair appeared to be of great importance, and required a final decision at their next meeting, they humbly requested that the Synod would join some of the other members out of the other presbyteries with them, to judge of that affair, and that said Presbytery, with said correspondents, be appointed to act as a commission of the Synod, and in that capacity judge that affair. The Synod," it is added, "granted the request, and accordingly appointed Messrs. Boyd, Tate, and Smith, to meet with the Presbytery of New Castle on the first Tuesday of August next, at New London, for that purpose, and further, enjoined the said Presbytery to give timely notice to Mr. Alison's congregation of the design of the said meeting."‡

Some misunderstanding having occurred between the Presbyteries of Philadelphia and New Castle, as to whose duty it was to ordain Mr. Kinkead, neither finding it convenient to attend, the Synod decided, "that, inasmuch as the congregations of the Great Valley and Norrington, properly belong to the Presbytery of Philadelphia, that the said Presbytery should attend the trials and

* Minutes, vol. iii. p. 63. The place of Mr. Miller's settlement was in Rockingham county, twenty-five miles from Staunton.

† Ibid. p. 40. ‡ Ibid. p. 43.

ordination of Mr. Kinkead; and lest a delay might be occasioned by the paucity and distance of the members of the Presbytery of Philadelphia, Mr. Cathcart, (of the Presbytery of New Castle,) was ordered to correspond with the said Presbytery as an assistant."* Upon an application from the Presbytery of New Castle, in 1754, it was "ordered, that Messrs. Boyd and Smith sit with them until the next meeting of the Synod, and be excused from attending Donegal Presbytery further than they think it convenient; and that Mr. Kinkead correspond with them in August next."†

The Synod, in the exercise of its supervisory care over the churches and its own members, frequently insisted upon a more punctual attendance upon its own meetings. In 1746, it is recorded, "that the Synod finding several of their ministers absent, from year to year, and particularly some members of the Presbytery of Donegal, cannot look upon such conduct otherwise than as irregular and of dangerous consequences; and do therefore order that every Presbytery inform their respective members thereof, and that the Synod expects some reasons of such absence, and better attendance hereafter."‡ A similar order, in reference to the distant members in Virginia, was made in 1747; and, in 1748, it was ordered, "that the Presbytery of Donegal write to Virginia, to let the ministers know that we expect one of their members yearly to attend the Synod, that we may know the state of the churches."§ In 1754, "it was observed, that Messrs. Black and Craig have neglected attending on the Synod for some considerable time, and it was ordered that Mr. McDowell write to those brethren, and signify to them that the Synod expects that they either attend or write; and that, in case of failure, the Synod will be obliged to disown them as members." ||

Whenever any infraction of the constitution occurred, the Synod were in the habit of interposing to censure or rectify the irregularity. In 1752, "the Synod having deliberately considered the affair of Mr. Alison's removal to Philadelphia, referred to them by

* Minutes, p. 44. † Ibid. p. 46 ‡ Ibid. p. 14.

§ Ibid. p. 21. || Ibid. p. 63.

the Presbytery of New Castle, judged that the method he used is contrary to the Presbyterian plan; yet, considering that the circumstances which urged him to take the method he used, were very pressing, and that it was indeed almost impracticable for him to apply for the consent of Presbytery or Synod in the ordinary way; and further, being persuaded that Mr. Alison's being employed in such a station in the academy has a favourable aspect in several respects, and a very probable tendency not only to promote the good of the public, but also of the church, as he may be serviceable to the interests thereof in teaching philosophy or divinity, as far as his obligations to the academy permit; we judge his proceedings in the said affair are in a good measure excusable. Withal the Synod advises that, for the future, its members be very cautious, and guard against such proceedings as are contrary to our known and approved methods in such cases."*

It appears from the minutes for 1755, that some sessions had refused to allow the annual collections to be taken up in their churches: whereupon the Synod resolved, "that as it is a synodical appointment, it is inconsistent with our church government to be under the check of a church session. They, indeed, may give or withhold their charity, but may not prevent a minister from proposing it publicly according to our appointment. Ordered, likewise, that every Presbytery take care of the conduct of their members, how they observe this appointment previous to their coming to the Synod, and that they gather the collection from absent members."†

Not unfrequently the Synod was called upon to decide casuistical questions. For example, a young man having promised marriage to a young woman, was desirous to be freed from his engagement; but the young woman, though willing to release him, scrupled the lawfulness of doing so. The question was, therefore, submitted to the Synod, "Whether a single man and woman, having promised marriage to each other, may lawfully agree again to release each other from the promise? and after mature consideration the Synod resolved the case, that it was lawful: *nemine contradicente.*" The

* Minutes, p. 41. † Ibid. p. 49.

young man in question, however, was called before the Synod, and publicly rebuked, in order, as it is said, "to show our detestation of such rash proceedings."*

In 1751, the question came up from the session of the church at Neshaminy, by a reference from the Presbytery of Philadelphia, Whether a young man to whom an illegitimate child had been imputed upon the oath of the mother, but who denied the charge, and in a civil trial had been acquitted by a jury, might be admitted to church privileges? It was decided that he might.

In the Presbytery of Donegal, the marriage of a man with a niece of his former wife was declared null and void, and separation and confession of sin enjoined.† That Presbytery was in the habit of pronouncing divorces, as far as marriage was a religious bond, referring the parties, however, to the civil authorities for the dissolution of the civil contract between them.

The period of which we are now speaking, as already stated, was a season of great uneasiness and distress. In Pennsylvania there was almost a continued controversy between the Assembly and the proprietary government, which operated greatly to the injury of the colony, which was at the same time the theatre of many of the disasters attending the French and Indian wars. To these events repeated allusion is made in the proceedings of the Synod. In 1755, it is recorded, "the Synod having taken into consideration the prevailing iniquity which abounds in our land, and the many tokens of the Divine displeasure we are under, being threatened with a dangerous war, left to manifold divisions and confusions in church and state, and the rain from heaven restrained, to the great damage of the fruits of the earth; do therefore agree, that the 12th day of June be observed as a day of fasting and humiliation through all our bounds, to bewail our sins and the sins of our land, to deprecate the divine displeasure which we deserve, and implore God to remove these tokens of his anger, and save us from the strokes we now feel, fear, and deserve."‡

Again, in 1757, it is said, "the Synod having taken under serious consideration the melancholy state of the British dominions and of

* Minutes, p. 28. † Minutes of Donegal, p. 165. ‡ Minutes, p. 52.

their allies, the danger of the Protestant interest in general, and particularly of the English colonies of America, arising from the formidable combination of antichristian powers in Europe, and the shocking depredations and barbarities of the heathen on our borders, influenced and abetted by the perfidious, restless enemies of our civil and religious liberties; as also the abounding profanity and wickedness of all ranks and degrees of men; the awful contempt cast upon the glorious gospel of Christ, not only by the professed infidelity of its open adversaries, but also by the unbelief, hypocrisy, and uncharitableness, and loose practices of its professed friends; and being deeply sensible of, and affected with, the ungrateful abuse and misimprovement of the many privileges we have enjoyed; our peace, plenty, and liberty having been turned into wantonness, pride, and licentiousness; and being firmly persuaded that for these things God is testifying his displeasure against us, both at home and abroad, by a calamitous war, in which we are involved, while an amazing insensibility generally prevails under the present gloomy appearances of divine Providence, and a want of public spirit and zeal for the common good, do, for these and the like reasons, recommend the twenty-third day of June next to be observed by the people belonging to the Synod, as a day of public humiliation, fasting, and prayer, throughout their bounds, to bewail our aggravated and crying sins, to deprecate the deserved wrath of heaven, and to implore the divine mercy and forgiveness, that the Spirit of grace may be poured out upon us, that as a people we may turn unto the Lord by a sincere repentance; that God would preserve and bless our gracious king, direct his counsels, go forth with his fleets and armies, also with those of his allies, and crown them with success; that he would guard and defend our sea-coasts and frontiers against all the designs of our enemies; that he would preserve to us our invaluable liberties, both civil and religious; that he would yet bless us with fruitful seasons, mercifully heal our divisions, and cause our present confusions happily to terminate in the glorious advancement of the peaceful kingdom of our Lord Jesus Christ. Accordingly, it is ordered, that our ministers represent these things to the people under our care, and excite them to these solemn exercises; and, for that end, suit their sermons and prayers on that day to the important occasion."*

SYNOD OF NEW YORK.

Immediately after the schism in 1741, as stated in a preceding chapter, the brethren excluded from the Synod of Philadelphia, formed themselves into two presbyteries, those of New Brunswick and of Londonderry, afterwards called the Presbytery of New Castle, and resolved to meet annually as a Synod. This they did, though under the designation of "conjunct Presbytery." The name Synod was not assumed until the Presbytery of New York united with these brethren in the formation of the Synod of New York, which met for the first time at Elizabethtown, September 19, 1745. There were twenty-two ministers present at that meeting.† The ministers and elders thus assembled, "considered and agreed upon the following articles as the plan and foundation of their synodical union:

"1. They agree that the Westminster Confession of Faith, with the Larger and Shorter Catechisms, be the public confession of their faith, in such manner as was agreed unto by the Synod of Philadelphia in the year 1729, and to be inserted in the latter end of this book.‡ And they declare their approbation of the Directory of the assembly of divines at Westminster, as the general plan of worship and discipline.

"2. They agree that in matters of discipline, and in those things

* Minutes, p. 67.

† To wit: Messrs. Jonathan Dickinson, John Pierson, Ebenezer Pemberton, Simon Horton, Aaron Burr, Azariah Horton, Timothy Jones, Eliab Byram, and Robert Sturgeon, of the Presbytery of New York; Messrs. Gilbert Tennent, Joseph Lamb, William Tennent, Richard Treat, James McCrea, William Robinson, David Youngs, Charles Beatty, and Charles McKnight, of the Presbytery of New Brunswick; Messrs. Samuel Blair, Samuel Finley, Charles Tennent, and John Blair, of the Presbytery of New Castle.

‡ The act adopting the Confession of Faith, passed in 1729, is accordingly to be found in the Appendix to the synodical minutes, p. 1.

that relate to the peace and good order of our churches, they shall be determined according to the major vote of the ministers and elders; with which vote every member shall actively concur or pacifically acquiesce; but if any member cannot in conscience agree to the determination of the majority, but supposes himself obliged to act contrary thereunto, and the Synod think themselves obliged to insist upon it as essentially necessary to the well-being of our churches, in that case, such dissenting member promises peaceably to withdraw from the body, without endeavouring to raise any dispute or contention upon the debated point, or any unjust alienation of affection from them.

"3. If any member of their body supposes that he has any thing to object against any of his brethren, with respect to error in doctrine, immorality in life, or negligence in his ministry, he shall not, on any account, propagate the scandal, until the person objected against is dealt with according to the rules of the gospel, and the known methods of their discipline.

"4. They agree that all who have a competent degree of ministerial knowledge, are orthodox in their doctrine, regular in their life, and diligent in their endeavours to promote the important designs of vital godliness, and that will submit to their discipline, shall be cheerfully admitted into their communion. And they do also agree, that in order to avoid all divisive methods among their ministers and congregations, and to strengthen the discipline of Christ in the churches in these parts, they will maintain a correspondence with the Synod of Philadelphia, in this their first meeting, by appointing two of their members to meet the said Synod of Philadelphia at their next convention, and to concert with them such measures as may best promote the precious interests of Christ's kingdom in these parts. And that they may, in no respect, encourage any factious, separating practices or principles, they agree that they will not intermeddle with judicially hearing the complaints, or with supplying with ministers or candidates such parties of men as shall separate from any Presbyterian or congregational churches, that are not within their bounds, unless the matters in controversy be submitted to their jurisdiction by both parties."*

* Minutes of the Synod of New York, pp. 2–4.

No one at all acquainted with the history of the schism can fail to remark that these articles were intended to guard against the occurrence of a similar unhappy division. The principal ostensible causes of the rupture, were disregarding the acts of Synod, the public denunciation of ministers in good standing, and the dividing of congregations. As to all these points, Mr. Gilbert Tennent and his immediate friends, had ever been in a small minority. It was their zeal for practical religion, and not their conduct in the matters just specified, which was the ground of sympathy between them and their numerous associates in the formation of a new Synod. There is little doubt that Mr. Tennent assented to these articles as readily as any man; for it was only on the ground of the extraordinary circumstances of the times, that he justified his occasional disregard of the principles which they contain.

This Synod, founded upon the above truly Presbyterian and Christian principles, and embracing so large a portion of the most fervent and able men of the church, rapidly increased in numbers and influence. In 1746, we find the following names of ministers who were not present at the preceding meeting, John Roan, John Bostwick, Thomas Arthur, John Grant, Andrew Hunter, David Brainerd, William Dean, Eleazar Wales.* In 1747, the following new names occur: Jacob Green, Nathaniel Tucker, James Campbell, James Davenport, Daniel Laurence, Samuel Sackett, Timothy Sims, Alexander Hucheson, and Samuel Davies; in 1748, Job Prudden, Thomas Lewis, and Andrew Sterling; in 1749, John Rodgers, Aaron Richards, Caleb Smith, Silas Leonard, Charles McKnight,† and the whole Presbytery of Suffolk, Long Island. That Presbytery applied the preceding year to be taken into communion with Synod, and requested to be permitted to attend by delegates. This the Synod declined, but offered to receive them upon the same terms as they did other Presbyteries. This was

* Mr. Wales was one of the original members of the Presbytery of New Brunswick. It is not to be inferred, therefore, that a minister was received into the Synod, the year his name first happens to appear on the minutes.

† Mr. McKnight's name does not occur on the books of the Synod before 1749, though he was ordained by the Presbytery of New Brunswick in 1744.

acceded to, and Messrs. Ebenezer Prime and James Brown took their seats as members of Synod in 1749. The absent members of the Presbytery of Suffolk, as then constituted, as far as can be gathered from the minutes, were Silvanus White, Samuel Buel, and Naphtali Dagget. In 1750, the new members reported were Timothy Allen, Israel Read, John Brainard, Elihu Spencer, Daniel Thane, and Enos Ayres; in 1751, John Moffat, Chauncey Graham, Samuel Kennedy, Benjamin Chesnut, Alexander Cummings, Jonathan Elmore, John Campbell, John Todd, and Hugh Henry; in 1752, Conrad Wurtz, Robert Smith, and James Finley; in 1753, Evander Morrison, Samuel Harker, Alexander Creaghead, (who, it seems, had left the Seceders and returned to the Presbyterian Church,) Joseph Park, and Robert Henry; in 1754, John Smith, Nehemiah Greenman, Henry Martin, John Maltby, Eliphalet Ball, and John Wright; in 1755, Hugh Knox, John Brown, and John Hoge; in 1756, Nathaniel Whitaker, Benjamin Hait, Benjamin Talmage, Abner Reeves, Moses Tuttle, and John Harris; in 1757, William Ramsay, George Duffield, and Hugh McAdams; in 1758, Abraham Kettletas. The whole number of ministers reported as in connection with the Synod in 1758, the year in which the union with the Synod of Philadelphia took place, was seventy-two.

In the history of this Synod, the first subject to be considered is their missionary labours. In 1745, at their first meeting, the circumstances of Virginia were brought before them, and the opinion unanimously expressed that Mr. Robinson was the proper person to visit that colony. He was accordingly earnestly pressed to go and spend some months there.* Mr. Robinson had already, as mentioned in a previous chapter, preached in Virginia with great acceptance and success in 1743, having been sent thither by the Presbytery of New Brunswick. In 1746, a supplication for a minister was presented to the Synod from Hanover, in Virginia, which was referred to the Presbyteries of New Castle and New Brunswick. Before Mr. Robinson's visit to Virginia, in 1743, besides the numerous Presbyterian emigrants who had settled in what were then the western portions of the colony, there were four or five

* Minutes, p. 4.

families in Hanover, who had separated from the established church, and were accustomed to celebrate public worship among themselves. For this little company Mr. Robinson preached repeatedly during a stay of four days in their neighbourhood. After his departure they made repeated applications for supplies to the Presbytery of New Castle, who sent them several ministers at different times during four years, who stayed with them two or three sabbaths at a time. During this period they were also visited by Messrs. G. and W. Tennent of the Presbytery of New Brunswick. The number of dissenters in and about Hanover had, by this time, so much increased, that in 1747, when Mr. Davies was first sent to them by the Presbytery of New Castle, in compliance with their earnest request, he "found them sufficiently numerous to form one very large congregation or two small ones; and they had built five meeting-houses, three in Hanover, one in Henrico, and one in Louisa county." * They presented a most earnest call before the Presbytery for Mr. Davies to settle among them as their pastor, which he accepted in 1748. The labours of this eminent man "were very successful in every part of the country where he itinerated, much more so than he supposed; for to this day, (1799,) we find many seals of his ministry scattered up and down the country wherever he preached; and there are few congregations in this Presbytery, (Hanover,) that may not acknowledge that he was in a great measure their founder."†

In 1748, the Synod sent Mr. Cumming to Augusta county, and Mr. Hunter to the lower counties in Virginia, to spend four Sabbaths.‡ In 1749, Mr. Davenport was directed to visit Virginia, and in 1750, the Presbytery of New Brunswick was urged to send Mr. Todd, and the Presbytery of New York Messrs. Syms and Greenman to the same field of labour. The Synod also renewed the appointment of Mr. Davenport. In 1751, "the distressing circumstances of Virginia," were again brought before the Synod,

* See letter of Mr. Davies to the Bishop of London, dated, January 10, 1752, printed in the Biblical Repertory and Princeton Review, for April, 1840.

† MS. History.

‡ Minutes, p. 12.

who appointed Mr. Greenman to go there and supply the congregations for some time. The same year Mr. Davies requested, that an account relating to the dissenting interests in Virginia, should be sent to England, and Messrs. Burr and Pemberton were appointed to prepare a representation of the circumstances of the Presbyterian congregations in that colony, to be forwarded to Drs. Doddridge and Avery.*

As the Church of England was early established in Virginia, the Presbyterians were there legally in the position of dissenters. The colonial assembly had passed a law adopting the English toleration act as a law of the colony. It was on this ground, and not on that of its original enactment, that Mr. Davies and other Presbyterians recognized its authority and complied with its provisions. This is distinctly stated in a letter from Mr. Davies to Dr. Avery of London, dated May 21, 1752. "I am fully satisfied," he says, "that, as you intimate, the act of uniformity and other penal laws against non-conformity, are not in force in the colonies; and consequently that the dissenters have no right, nor indeed any need to plead the act of toleration as an exemption from those penal laws. But, sir, our legislature here has passed an act of the same kind with those laws, (though the penalty is less,) requiring all adult persons to attend on the established church. As this act was passed since the revolution, it was necessary that protestant dissenters should be exempted from its operation, and tolerated to worship God in separate assemblies, (though indeed at the time of its enaction, viz.: the fourth of Queen Anne, there was not a dissenting congregation, except a few Quakers, in the colony,) and for this our legislature thought fit to take in the act of parliament made for that end in England, rather than to pass a new one peculiar to this colony. This, sir, you may see in my remonstrance to the governor and council, which I find has been laid before you. Now it is with a view to exempt ourselves from the operation of the above law, made by our legislature, that we plead it not as an English law, for we are persuaded that it does not extend hither by virtue of its original enaction, but as received into the body of the

* Minutes, p. 32.

Virginia laws by our legislature. And though some pretended to scruple, and others denied that the act of toleration is in force here, even in this sense, yet now I think it is generally granted."* A difference of opinion, however, arose as to the meaning of the act. The Episcopalians were naturally desirous to restrict the privileges granted by it within the narrowest limits, and therefore contended that the law did not permit the same congregation to have more than one meeting-house, or the same minister to officiate for more than one congregation. In a letter written from Virginia to the bishop of London, July 27, 1750, it is made a matter of complaint, that "seven meeting-houses, in five different counties, have been licensed by the general court, for Mr. Samuel Davies;" and, the writer adds, "I earnestly entreat the favour of your lordship's opinion, whether in licensing so many houses for one man they have not granted a greater indulgence than either the king's instructions, or the act of toleration, intended." He further complains of Mr. Davies' "holding forth on working days to great numbers of poor people, who generally are his followers. This certainly is inconsistent with the religion of labour, whereby they are obliged to maintain themselves and families; and their neglect of this duty, if not seasonably prevented, may, in process of time, be sensibly felt by the government." In his reply, dated London, December 25, 1750, the bishop says, "As to Davies' case, as far as I can judge, your attorney-general, (Peyton Randolph, Esq.)

* The account of this matter given by the Rev. Dr. Hawks, in his interesting volume on the History of the Protestant Episcopal Church in Virginia, is suited to lead his readers into a mistake. He says, "The officers of the government, who of course adhered to the establishment, strenuously contended that his (Mr. Davies',) proceedings were illegal, inasmuch as the English act of toleration did not extend to Virginia. This position was denied by the dissenters, who claimed equal rights with their brethren at home, and the matter was brought before the courts of the colony." p. 109. This account gives an erroneous impression, because it is defective. It does not state the ground on which Mr. Davies claimed the protection of the English act of toleration. He appealed to it not as an English, but as a Virginia act. It would indeed be a strange sight to see Presbyterians pleading for the extension of the English ecclesiastical laws to the colonies.

is quite in the right, for the act of toleration confines the preacher to a particular place to be certified and entered." It was "intended," he adds, "to permit dissenters to worship in their own way, and to exempt them from penalties, but it was never intended to permit them to set up itinerant preachers to gather congregations where there was none before. They are, by the act of William and Mary, to qualify in the county where they live; and how Davies can be said to live in five different counties, they who granted the license must explain." As Dr. Doddridge was a friend to the bishop of London, Mr. Davies wrote to him an account of his circumstances, requesting him to communicate to the bishop a correct representation of the case. Dr. Doddridge inclosed to the bishop a large part of Mr. Davies' letter, and received an answer, dated May 11, 1751, containing the above extracts from the letter from Virginia, with the bishop's reply, as containing his opinion on the matter in dispute, and adds, "If the act of toleration was desired with no other view than to ease the consciences of those who could not conform, and if it was granted with no other view, how must Mr. Davies' conduct be justified? who, under colour of a toleration to his own conscience, is labouring to disturb the consciences of others, and the peace of a church, acknowledged to be a true church of Christ. He came three hundred miles from home, not to serve people who had scruples, but to a country where the church of England had been established from its first plantation, and where there were not above four or five dissenters not above six years ago. Mr. Davies says, in his letter to you, 'we claim no other liberties than those granted by the act of toleration,' so that the state of the question is admitted, on both sides, to be this, How far the act of toleration will justify Mr. Davies in taking upon himself to be an itinerant preacher, and travelling over many counties, and making converts in a country too, where, till very lately, there was not a dissenter from the church of England?" Dr. Doddridge sent the bishop's letter, with its enclosures, or copies of them, to Mr. Davies, who wrote a long communication to the bishop, in which he corrected his misapprehensions as to matters of fact, and showed the reasonableness of the claims which the Presbyterians had set up. He shows him that, so far from his volunteering to make dissenters where there were none before, when he first came to Virginia, they were sufficiently numerous to form a large congregation, and that he came and settled among them at their own earnest request. If they had still further increased, it was not from a spirit of proselytism on his part, for "I beg leave to declare," he says, "and I defy the world to confute me, that in all the sermons I have preached in Virginia, I have not wasted one minute in exclaiming or reasoning against the peculiarities of the established church, nor so much as assigned the reasons of my own non-conformity." Those, therefore, who had joined the Presbyterian church since his settlement in Virginia, had done so, not because of his efforts to make dissenters, but because of their preference for his doctrines and preaching. And in thus acting they had violated no law. These remarks were made in reference to his own immediate congregation; as to other Presbyterians equally interested in the points in debate, they had been born and educated in the Presbyterian Church, and had emigrated to Virginia, greatly to its advantage, in the confidence of enjoying the free exercise of their religion. And to this latter class the great majority of the Presbyterians within the colony belonged. He further showed, that it was not only reasonable in itself, but perfectly consistent with the law and with usage, for a congregation, too widely scattered to be able conveniently to assemble in one place, to erect several houses of worship for their accommodation. This was done in all the large parishes connected with the established church, and the Presbyterians claimed, under the law, the right of doing the same thing.

It was in the midst of the controversy on this subject, that Mr. Davies applied for the support of the Synod in the manner stated in the minutes for the year 1751. This subject long continued to be a matter of difficulty. In 1753, a representation was again made to the Synod "of the illegal restraints the Protestant dissenters lie under in Virginia, as to their religious liberties;" and a committee was appointed to draw up a representation to be sent to England with Mr. Davies.*

* Minutes, p. 62.

Notwithstanding these obstacles, the Presbyterian Church continued to increase in the southern provinces, and the Synod almost yearly sent one or more of their number to preach the gospel in that portion of our country. In 1754, Messrs. Beatty, Bostwick, Lewis, and Thane, were appointed to go to the south, particularly to North Carolina, for three months.* In 1755, Messrs. Brainard and Spencer were sent to North Carolina, and Mr. Clark to Virginia.† In 1756, Messrs. Duffield, Ramsay, Brainard, and Rodgers, were directed to go to the south before the winter, and Messrs. Whitaker and Hait to spend four months there.‡ These appointments, however, as appears from the minutes for the following year, were not fulfilled. In 1757, the appointment of Mr. Hait was renewed, and the Presbyteries of New Castle and Hanover were directed each to send another missionary. In 1758, the Presbytery of New Brunswick was directed to send a candidate to North Carolina, and the Presbytery of Suffolk was earnestly recommended to send Mr. Brush to the same important vacancies.§ As so large a portion of the duty of supplying the new settlements was devolved upon the presbyteries, the above notices exhibit but a small part of the missionary labours of this Synod.

Our fathers were not altogether inattentive to the religious instruction of the aboriginal inhabitants of the country. In 1751, "the exigencies of the great affair of propagating the gospel among the heathen being represented to the Synod, the Synod, in order to promote so important a design, do enjoin upon all their members to appoint a collection in their several congregations once a year, to be applied for that purpose; and that the money thus collected be sent yearly to the Synod." ‖ In 1752, it was ordered that the proceeds of the collections in behalf of the Indians, be placed in the hands of Mr. Brainard. In 1755, Mr. Gilbert Tennent reported that he had received two hundred pounds sterling, from England, for propagating the gospel among the Indians, which, agreeably to the directions of the donor, were to be placed in the hands of the trustees of the College of New Jersey, and the interest to be em-

* Minutes, p. 72. † Ibid. pp. 79, 81. ‡ Ibid. p. 116.
§ Ibid. p. 135. ‖ Ibid. p. 33.

ployed in supporting a missionary, or schoolmaster, or for the education of a heathen youth in the college, or of a young man of English or Scotch extraction as a teacher among the Indians; the Synod of New York to determine, from time to time, to which of these purposes the money was to be appropriated.*

The Synod was scarcely less zealous for the promotion of learning, than they were in behalf of religion. They had not indeed any public seminary immediately under their direction, but the college at Princeton really owed its existence to their efforts. It appears from the records of the province, "that a charter to incorporate sundry persons to found a college, passed the great seal of the province of New Jersey, tested by J. Hamilton, Esq., President of his Majesty's Council and Commander-in-chief of the Province of New Jersey, the 22d of October, 1746."† As this charter was never recorded, neither its provisions, nor the names of the trustees created by it, are now known. It was not acceptable to those who asked for it, and was therefore surrendered for another obtained in 1748, from George the Second, through the agency of Governor Belcher. It was under the former charter that Mr. Dickinson acted as president of the college until his death in 1747, when he was succeeded by Mr. Burr, who acted in that capacity until 1757. The college, no doubt, owed much of its early prosperity to Governor Belcher, a religious, able, and accomplished man, to whom the trustees often expressed their obligations. On one occasion they addressed him in the following language: "As the College of New Jersey views you in the light of its founder, patron, and benefactor, and the impartial world will esteem it a respect deservedly due to the name of Belcher, permit us to dignify the edifice now erecting at Princeton, with that endeared appellation; and when your excellency is translated to a house not made with hands, eternal in the heavens, let Belcher-Hall proclaim your beneficent acts for the advancement of Christianity and the emolument of the arts and sciences to the latest generations." This honour the Governor

* Minutes, p. 84 and 96.

† See the History of the College of New Jersey, by Dr. Green, appended to his Baccalaureate Discourses.

modestly declined, and proposed the name of Nassau-Hall, in proof "of the honour we retain in this remote part of the globe to the immortal memory of the glorious King William the Third, who was a branch of the illustrious house of Nassau, and who, under God, was the great deliverer of the British nation from those two monstrous furies, popery and slavery."*

Though the college was greatly indebted to Governor Belcher, it was nevertheless the child of the Synod. All the clerical members of the board of the trustees belonged to the Synod, except Mr. David Cowell, who was a member of the Synod of Philadelphia. The funds also which founded and sustained the institution, were collected by the efforts of the same body. In 1751, the trustees requested that the Rev. Mr. Pemberton might be appointed to go to Europe to solicit benefactions for the college, and the Synod accordingly commissioned Messrs. Burr, Treat, William Tennent, and Davies, to proceed at once to New York to arrange the matter with Mr. Pemberton and his congregation. This committee subsequently reported that they had failed in accomplishing the object of their mission.† In 1752, a general collection was appointed in behalf of the college, and it was "ordered that all other collections before appointed, be suspended on that account."‡

In 1753, the trustees of the college petitioned the Synod to send two of their number to Great Britain to solicit benefactions on its behalf. This request led to the appointment of Messrs. Gilbert Tennent and Samuel Davies, who were made the bearers of an address to the General Assembly in Scotland. In this address, the Synod state that the college had already been the means of educating a number of youth then engaged in the service of the church; that after all that could be done in this country, its resources were entirely inadequate, and the trustees were, therefore, constrained through them to appeal to their friends in Europe for aid. The Synod believing the object to be of the utmost importance to the interests of religion and learning in this infant country, proceeded to lay before the Assembly a general representation of the deplorable circumstances of the churches under their

* Dr. Green's History, p. 275. † Minutes, p. 31. ‡ Ibid. p. 46.

care. "There are," it is added, "in the colonies of New York, New Jersey, Pennsylvania, Maryland, Virginia, and Carolina, a great number of congregations formed on the Presbyterian plan, which have put themselves under the synodical care of your petitioners, who conform to the constitution of the Church of Scotland, and have adopted her standards of doctrine, worship, and discipline. There are also large settlements lately planted in various parts, particularly in North and South Carolina, where multitudes are extremely anxious for the ministrations of the gospel, but who are not formed into congregations and regularly organized for want of ministers." These numerous calls the Synod state they are utterly unable to satisfy, and that their only hope of being able to meet these demands is founded on the College of New Jersey, upon which the Presbyterians in the six colonies above mentioned must depend. "Your petitioners, therefore," say the Synod, "most earnestly pray that this very reverend assembly would afford the said college all the countenance and assistance in their power. The young daughter of the Church of Scotland, helpless and exposed in this foreign land, cries to her tender and powerful parent for relief. The cries of ministers oppressed with labours, and of congregations famishing for want of the sincere milk of the word, implore assistance. And were the poor Indian savages sensible of their own case, they would join in the cry and beg for more missionaries to be sent to propagate the religion of Jesus among them."* As Mr. Tennent and Mr. Davies were not the agents of the Synod, they made no report to that body of the success of their mission. That it was, however, by no means inconsiderable, may be inferred not only from the vote of thanks rendered to the General Assembly for their assistance,† but from the address of the trustees to Governor Belcher, in which they said that the contributions obtained from England and Scotland had "amply enabled them to erect a convenient edifice for the accommodation of the students, and to lay a foundation for a fund for the support of the necessary instructers." Of the sums received by Messrs. Tennent and Davies, there were £307 sterling given for the education of

* Minutes, Appendix, pp. 12—18.

† Dr. Green's History, p. 307.

indigent young men for the ministry, the interest only of which was to be used; and the further sum of £50, the principal of which was to be applied to the same purpose. This money was given to the trustees of the college, the Synod having the right to examine and select the young men who were to receive the benefit of it.* The Synod had, at an earlier date, (1751,) recommended "an annual collection for the support of young students whose circumstances rendered them unable to maintain themselves at learning, and for other charitable purposes."†

The facts above detailed sufficiently prove the intimate connection between the Synod and the College of New Jersey, and show that the Synod of New York was not less zealous in the cause of learning, than that of Philadelphia.

It has been proved in an earlier chapter of this work,‡ that the Synod of New York adopted the same standard of doctrine as the Synod of Philadelphia, and that there was no dispute between the two bodies as to that point. With regard to their form of government, it was no less strictly Presbyterian than that of the other Synod. The Directory was as much the constitution of the one body as it was of the other.§ In the address to the General Assembly of the Church of Scotland, just quoted, the Synod declare they had adopted her standards of doctrine, worship, and discipline; a declaration which admits but of one interpretation. In 1751, the following minute was adopted on this subject: "The Synod being informed of certain misrepresentations concerning the constitution, order, and discipline of our churches, industriously spread by some of the members of the Dutch congregations interspersed among, or bordering upon us, with design to prevent occasional or constant communion of their members with our churches; to obviate all such misrepresentations, and to cultivate a good understanding between us and our brethren of the Dutch churches, we do hereby declare and testify our constitution, order, and discipline, to be in harmony with the Established Church of Scotland.

* Minutes, pp. 81, 85. † Ibid. p. 33.

‡ See Chapter III. p. 172, *et seq.*

§ See on the point also, Chapter III., p. 172, and Chapter V., pp. 163, 199.

The Westminster Confessions, Catechisms, and Directory, for public worship and church government, adopted by them, are in like manner received and adopted by us. We declare ourselves united with that church in the same faith, order, and discipline. Its approbation and countenance we have abundant testimonies of. They, as brethren, receive us, and their members we, as opportunity offers, receive as ours. And as the Church of Scotland and the Reformed churches abroad, agreeable to the Geneva platform, hold a ready and free communion with each other, so we desire the same with our brethren of the Dutch and French churches interspersed amongst and bordering upon us."*

Mr. Davies, in his letter to the Bishop of London, says: "If I am prejudiced in favour of any church, my Lord, it is of that established in Scotland; of which I am a member, in the same sense that the Established Church in Virginia is the Church of England."† As all the ministers of the Episcopal Church in this country received, at that day, ordination from the English bishops, and were under the episcopal supervision of the Bishop of London, the above declaration certainly imports a most intimate agreement and fellowship between our church and that of Scotland.

In order, however, to illustrate the true character of this interesting portion of our church, it will be necessary to refer to some of their ecclesiastical acts. The Synod exercised a general supervisory and governing power over the congregations and presbyteries; and for this purpose revised the records of inferior judicatories, and received from them appeals and references. That this examination of the records was a proper judicial inspection, is evident from such minutes as the following: "The New York Presbytery book brought, revised, and approved, except a paragraph on page 149, on which the Synod has not light to determine."‡

The cases of reference of judicial matters to the Synod for decision are very numerous. In 1750, the Presbytery of New Brunswick referred the case of the congregation of Tehicken, or Tinicum. It appears that the people were divided in opinion as to the

* Minutes, p. 33. Appendix, p. 11. † Princeton Review, April, 1840.

‡ Minutes, p. 133.

proper location of their place of worship, and therefore agreed to decide the matter by lot. The disappointed party, however, refused to abide by the decision, on the ground that it had been unfairly obtained. The Synod censured both parties for resorting to the lot; but as, in their judgment, it had been fairly cast, they decided that the recusants had acted very sinfully in refusing to abide by it, and therefore "ordered that a solemn admonition be administered unto them by Mr. Pemberton, in the name of the Synod, which was accordingly done."*

In 1752, a reference was brought in from the Presbytery of New York, relating to the congregation in that city; "and the plea of all parties having been heard," the Synod came to the following conclusions, viz.:

"1. That the building, grounds, &c. conveyed from the General Assembly of the Church of Scotland, to the Presbyterian Society in New York, belong to Presbyterians without distinction of name or nation, who conform to the general plan of the Church of Scotland, as practised by the Synod of New York.

"2. That it is not inconsistent with the Presbyterian plan of government, nor with the institution of our Lord Jesus Christ, that trustees, or a committee chosen by the congregation, should have the disposal and management of the public money raised by the said congregation, to the uses for which it was designed; provided they leave in the hands, and to the management of the deacons, what is collected for the Lord's table, and the poor. And that ministers of the gospel, by virtue of their office, have no right to sit with, and preside over, such trustees or committee.

"3. That it appears to the Synod, that the trustees of said church have faithfully discharged the trust reposed in them, with respect to its temporalities, much to its advantage.

"4. That as to the articles of complaint brought against Mr. Cumming, it appears to the Synod, that he has been necessarily hindered from performing his part in public service, by his low state of health, but they judge it his duty to discharge it according to his call when his health will admit, and when he is disabled,

* Minutes, p. 33.

he should desire Mr. Pemberton to officiate in his room. That his insisting on a right to sit with the trustees in their conventions about the temporal affairs of the congregation, was not a violation of his ordination vows, which respect only the work of the ministry, although they judge he acted imprudently in so doing. That he is to be commended for insisting on persons praying in their families who present their children for baptism; but inasmuch as it appears expedient that the same form of covenanting should be used in the same church, the Synod do therefore recommend it to Mr. Pemberton and Mr. Cumming to consult with the committee hereafter to be mentioned, about a form that they can both agree in.

"5. That the church proceed as soon as may be, to the choice of elders to join with their ministers in the government and discipline of the church, and that the committee hereafter to be appointed, do nominate the persons to be chosen, and determine the number.

"6. That as to the methods taken to introduce a new version of the Psalms in public worship, the Synod judge it to be disorderly and always to be discountenanced, when the parties in matters in debate in a church do carry about private subscriptions.

"7. That as to the introduction of a new version of the Psalms, the Synod hath not light at present to determine, but do empower the committee to recommend Dr. Watts' version, if upon observation of circumstances, they think it proper.

"And the Synod do appoint the Reverend Messrs. Samuel Davies, Samuel Finley, and Charles Beatty, to be a committee to go immediately to New York, and direct and assist the Presbyterian congregation of New York in such affairs as may contribute to their peace and edification."*

* Minutes, p. 43–46. It has already been shown, chap. I. p. 52, that the Presbyterian congregation in New York was a regularly organized church composed principally of Scotch Presbyterians, and constantly called the Scotch church. A very influential portion of its members, however, were of English origin, who differed in their habits and preferences from their Scotch brethren. This gave rise to constant difficulty about Psalmody, the mode of

This committee met, agreeably to appointment, and executed their somewhat extraordinary mission in selecting and nominating two elders, but decided that it was not expedient "judicially to recommend a change in the version of the Psalms, lest the animosities in the congregation should be the more inflamed."*

managing their secular affairs, and the usages of public worship. The pamphlet entitled, "The case of the Scotch Presbyterian Church in the city of New York," referred to in a previous chapter, throws a clear light on the original character of the church, and indirectly upon the Synod with which it was connected. The object of the pamphlet is to give an account of the several attempts made to obtain a charter, and of the opposition of the Episcopalians, by which these efforts were rendered unsuccessful.

The writers claim, "that all protestant denominations in the colonies, are, in the eye of the law, upon a level," and that this was "the necessary consequence of removing to a distant country, where no religious establishment is set up." It was on this assumption the colonies were settled. The granting of charters, therefore, to the Dutch and Episcopalian churches, was a matter of justice and not of favour. "What shall we say then," it is asked, "to the denial of such charters to the dispersions of the church of Scotland?" The first application was made in 1720, in the name of "the minister, elders, and deacons of the Presbyterian church in New York." A committee of council to whom this application was referred, reported in favour of it; "but the board, to gratify the unexpected and illiberal jealousy of the Episcopalians," desisted from all proceedings upon it. "The Presbyterians soon after renewed their application, and the Episcopalians their unreasonable opposition." The petition was, at their suggestion, referred to the authorities in England. Though made in September, 1720, it was not sent home until 1724. The Lords of Trade consulted counsellor West, afterwards Lord Chancellor of Ireland, who gave his opinion in these words: "Upon consideration of the several acts of uniformity that have passed in Great Britain, I am of opinion that they do not extend to New York; and consequently an act of toleration is of no use in that province; and therefore as there is no provincial act of uniformity according to the church of England, I am of opinion that by law such patent of incorporation may be granted as by the petition is desired." Still no charter was granted. "Notwithstanding all opposition, the *Scotch* church flourished under the long and laborious ministry of the Rev. Mr. Pemberton, who settled here in 1727." In 1759, a third application was made, with no better success. A fourth attempt was made in 1766, when it was thought best, "to lay the case of this distant dispersion of the church of Scotland before his majesty." When the matter came up for consideration,

* Minutes, p. 51.

Sometimes the affairs of a congregation were brought before the Synod without the intervention of a presbytery. Thus in 1753, Mr. Pemberton and others of the congregation of New York, made a representation of the painful divisions existing in that church,

"the bishop of London appeared twice before the commissioners of trade and plantation, in opposition to the petition," which was finally rejected. The grounds on which these applications were opposed, gave more just offence than their rejection itself. It was either assumed that the acts of uniformity were in force in this country, or that the question respecting their obligation must be previously determined by the highest authority, "lest such incorporations might be considered as repugnant to the provisions of those statutes." Such was the language of the Governor's council on the subject; who still more plainly indicate their principles by saying in the same document, that "except the charters granted to the church of England, all the instances of such incorporations within this province, (four only in number,) are confined to the Dutch, whose claims to this distinction are, the committee apprehend, grounded on one of the articles of capitulation, on the surrender of the colony in 1664, by which it is declared, that the Dutch here, shall enjoy the liberty of their consciences in divine worship and church discipline." Thus it appears that the Dutch owed their liberty of conscience to an article of capitulation, and that those who could plead no such ground of distinction, were not entitled to such liberty. Presbyterians could not avoid drawing the inference from such declarations, that Episcopalians in this country and in England were desirous of giving full force to the acts of uniformity. On what other ground was the distinction made between the two denominations? Why were charters granted without hesitation or delay to Episcopal churches and refused to Presbyterian ones? Why did the lords of trade say, that it was inexpedient to grant the latter "any further privileges or immunities than they are entitled to by the laws of toleration?" The toleration act presupposed the act of uniformity. If Presbyterians owed their liberty of conscience in the colonies to the former, it was because the latter was in force in the colonies. Thus the men who had fled from the oppression of those acts in their own country, found their authority asserted in the place of their asylum. What rendered this case the harder was, that the Dutch and English Presbyterians in the province of New York were "a great majority of the whole number of its inhabitants." This is asserted in the petition for a charter, made in 1766; and is virtually admitted in the reply to it. Yet the minority had not only acts of incorporation, but public property granted to them to a large amount. "At this very juncture," says the pamphlet, (1773) "the society for propagating the gospel, though restrained from taking real estates at home, are asking for grants of crown lands in America in mort-

and requested the intervention of the Synod. Whereupon William Tennent, Samuel Davies, Aaron Burr, Caleb Smith, David Bostwick, Elihu Spencer, Richard Treat, Charles Beatty, and John Rodgers, were appointed a committee to meet at New York, "with

main, for themselves and the Episcopal churches, to the amount of many hundred thousands of acres. In some instances they have been gratified already, and in one with circumstances too singular to be unnoticed. All the world knows the Episcopal church of the city of New York to be one of the richest ecclesiastical corporations in the king's dominions. They own a very large portion of the very metropolis. Sixty odd acres divided into small lots will produce, when the present leases expire, a revenue fit for a popish abbey. They had first a lease of it from the crown, which was vacated by a law procured in consequence of orders from home. Impatient under this loss, a project was devised to repeal the vacating act, and regrant it in fee, before the repealing act could be known on the other side of the water. My Lord Cornbury risked the royal displeasure, and sacrificed the crown to the church. Queen Anne repealed the repealing, and confirmed the vacating act; but the church was already possessed of the patent. . . . . They have lately added to their wealth a township of no less than 25,000 acres, out of the crown lands in the county of Gloucester, ... applied for by, and granted to Nathaniel Marston and others as private planters; though they took the estate not for themselves, but for the incorporated churches of which they were officers and members. Chargeable with such practices, is not their opposing the naked incorporation of the Scotch churches, (who ask for no estate or lands,) the most matchless effrontery? . . . : What marvel then that the project of erecting Episcopacy in America, excites such general apprehension in the rest of the American churches?" This assumption, therefore, that the English ecclesiastical laws were of force in this country, and that the vast majority of the people were only tolerated, was a real grievance. It was the same assumption, viz.: that America was a part of the realm of Great Britain, and was subject to the acts of parliament even in matters of taxation, that caused the revolution, and formed its justification.

The character of the church in New York is clearly set forth in their several petitions for a charter. They frequently call themselves "a dispersion of the church of Scotland;" and in the petition presented in 1720, prayed to be incorporated for the exercise of their religion "in its true doctrine, discipline, and worship, according to the rules and methods of the established church of North Britain." That presented in 1766, was in the name of "John Rodgers and Joseph Treat, the present ministers of the Presbyterian church of the city of New York, according to the Westminster Confession, Catechisms, and Directory, agreeable to the established church of Scotland," and of the elders, full power and authority to transact such things with respect to said congregation, as they shall judge necessary for the healing of its divisions, and the best interests of religion therein."*

When this committee met, a paper containing a statement of the grievances of which a part of the congregation complained, was laid before them, on which they gave the following judgment:

"1. As to the first article complaining of the neglect of ministerial visits, and examining into the lives and conversation of the people; it appears from the representation made by Mr. Pemberton, that he has made conscience of his duty in these respects, though of late he has, by reason of the divisions subsisting among his people, desisted from it: we therefore earnestly recommend his persisting in that important part of his ministerial labours; and that he be not discouraged by any disagreeable appearances among them.

"2. As to the third article against the session concerning the new version of the Psalms, the committee cannot think it regular

deacons, and trustees. In the copy of the charter which they sent to England to be executed and returned, they requested the king to say: "We have thought fit to favour the pious purposes of our said loving subjects, and to secure to them, their successors, and others joining with them of the same religious persuasion, the free exercise and enjoyment of all their civil and religious rights, and to preserve to them and their successors, the liberty of worshipping God according to their consciences, and the usages of those Presbyterian churches which have adopted and do regulate themselves by, and conform to the Westminster Confession of Faith, Catechisms, and Directory." And again: "We do also for us, our heirs, and successors, ordain and grant that the said ministers, elders, deacons, and trustees, of the Presbyterian church of the city of New York, according to the Westminster Confession of Faith, Catechisms, and Directory, *in communion with the church of Scotland*, and their successors for ever, by these presents, that this our grant shall be firm, good, and effectual, &c. &c." As all this was said by men who had always belonged to the New-side Synod, and as the Westminster Directory related not merely to a single congregation, but to Presbyteries and Synods, it shows very clearly that they thought their system of church government was in harmony with that of the church of Scotland, of which they called themselves a dispersion, and with which they professed to be in communion.

* Minutes, p. 58.

for the ministers and elders to introduce a new version, without the express consent and approbation of the majority of the congregation; yet since Dr. Watts' version is introduced into this church, and is well adapted for Christian worship, and received by many Presbyterian congregations both in America and Great Britain; they cannot but judge it best for the well-being of the congregation, under their present circumstances, that they should be continued.

"3. As to the fourth article, complaining of the neglect of the Westminster Confession, and not recommending of it in baptism, the committee conceive that the vote of the Synod, as to the latter, is sufficient; and Mr. Pemberton's declaring his high approbation of said Confession, and publicly teaching the Westminster Catechisms, ought to be satisfying to all.

"4. As to praying at the burial of the dead, since it is not practised but at the request of those concerned, and all are left at liberty to request it or not, the committee think it no just matter of offence, especially as it is frequently practised by the Presbyterian ministers in this country, and the reasons for which the General Assembly, in the early times of the reformation from popery, prohibited it, are now evidently ceased.

"5. As to singing anthems, &c., though the committee cannot disapprove of them at proper seasons, yet lest it should tend to take off the minds of the people from the important things which they have heard in the house of God, and as it seems matter of conscience to some, the committee judge it advisable to forbear the practice on the Lord's day.

"6. As to the article complaining of injurious and contemptuous treatment, the committee are much grieved to find there has been so much of it on both sides during the unhappy disputes that have subsisted among them, and do earnestly recommend mutual forgiveness, forbearance, and moderation towards one another, as the most likely method to promote peace and unanimity among them."*

This minute throws no little light upon the causes of the diffi-

* Minutes, p. 66.

culties in that congregation. It shows that one portion of the people, with characteristic pertinacity and scrupulousness, were for adhering to "the rules and methods" of that church of which they all professed to be a "dispersion;" while another portion treated these scruples with very little forbearance. The version of the Psalms was changed without the consent of the people, and even anthems were sung after sermon on the Sabbath. They might as well have said mass, and expect the Scotch Presbyterians of that day to join in the service. If they wished to drive the Scotch from "the Scotch church," this was certainly the proper method to do it, but it was not the way to obtain peace. With our imperfect knowledge of the circumstances, it is impossible to judge on which party the blame should principally be laid, but it appears from the above minute, that the rulers of the congregation did not act on the principles so strenuously inculcated by the apostle of the Gentiles: "If thy brother be grieved with thy meat, now walkest thou not charitably. Destroy not him with thy meat, for whom Christ died."

After the committee had rendered the decision above recorded, Messrs. Pemberton and Cumming requested to be dismissed from their pastoral relation to the church. The former assigned as the grounds of his request the divisions among the people, the appearance of dissatisfaction with himself, and the little prospect of his being useful among them; the latter urged particularly the low state of his health. A number of gentlemen, in behalf of others, earnestly remonstrated against the removal of Mr. Pemberton, and the committee decided "he should be allowed a month's trial; and if, upon a faithful endeavour to heal the divisions, and serve the interests of Christ's kingdom among them, he finds all his attempts vain, and still continues his desire of a dismission, they judge it best he should be left at liberty to remove from, or abide with them, as he shall think most consistent with his duty. As to Mr. Cumming, as no reasons have been offered to the committee against his dismission, the committee do judge from what has appeared to them, and for the reasons urged by him, that his pastoral relation to the Presbyterian congregation in New York should be dissolved, and it is dissolved accordingly. It is with pleasure the committee observe that there have been no objections against Mr. Cumming's moral conduct or ministerial labours; they do, therefore, freely recommend him, if God shall please to restore his health, to any Christian congregation where Divine Providence may call him, as a man of eminent ministerial gifts and abilities, and one whom they think in many respects fitted for special service in the church of Christ."*

The affairs of this congregation were again brought before the Synod in 1755, by a reference from the Presbytery of New York concerning the removal of Mr. Bostwick from Jamaica to the church in New York, and settling the order and discipline of that church, which, after much consideration, was referred to a committee to draw up the judgment of the Synod thereon. This judgment was to the following effect: 1. That the Synod were still of the opinion formerly expressed, that the trustees had faithfully performed their duty; but as the congregation were divided in sentiment as to the propriety of having such a board, and had agreed not to elect them again in that form, the Synod approve of that agreement, and judged that if the congregation chose to have a committee to manage their secular affairs, that committee should hereafter be chosen by the ministers, elders, and deacons, with the consent of the people. 2. That as a number of the congregation were much dissatisfied with the constant use of Dr. Watts' Psalms, "the Synod determined that the Scotch version be used equally with the other in the stated public worship on the Lord's day." 3. That previously to the administration of baptism, the minister shall inquire into the doctrinal knowledge and regularity of life of the parents, and exhort them to instruct their children in the doctrines and precepts of Christianity as contained in the Scriptures, and comprised in the Westminster Confession and Catechisms, which he shall recommend unto them. 4. That as complaint had been made of a number assuming the name of the Scotch Presbyterian Society, it shall be deemed irregular and censurable for a part of the congregation to form a party, and to consider themselves a society distinct

* Minutes, pp. 68–70.

from the rest. 5. That as to the removal of Mr. Bostwick, the people of Jamaica not having been heard on that affair, the Synod were not prepared to decide, but appointed a committee to meet at Jamaica and decide the question.* That committee met accordingly, October 29, 1755, but "not having light to come to a full determination of the affair," referred it to the commissioner of the Synod; who, after mature deliberation, decided in favour of his removal.†

The long-continued difficulties in the church in New York, were presented for the last time to the Synod in 1756. A paper was read from several members of the congregation, complaining of the grievances under which they supposed themselves to suffer. The Synod, after severely censuring the disrespectful terms in which that paper was couched, informed the complainants, "that, by adopting the Westminster Confession, we only intended receiving it as a test of orthodoxy in this church; and it is the order of this Synod that all who are licensed to preach the gospel, or to become members of any presbytery within our bounds, shall receive the same as the confession of their faith according to our constituting act, which we see no reason to repeal.

"That as to the singing of Dr. Watts' version of the Psalms, though the conduct of the congregation in adhering to them contrary to synodical appointment, without waiting for an opportunity to obtain a repeal of the said appointment, was not regular, yet as the said Psalms are orthodox, and as no particular version is inspired, and as the using them is earnestly desired by a great majority of the congregation, contrary to the view we had of the case last year, the Synod for the sake of their peace do permit the use of the said version unto them; and determine that this shall be finally decisive in this affair." They then declare that those who refused to pay their pew-rents acted disorderly, and forfeited their pews; that reading in the desk was "a mere indifferency," not contrary to any divine rule, or to the constitution of the church, and therefore not to be altered by authority. As to the other points brought forward in the paper, they had been already decided, to which decisions the Synod adhered.‡

* Minutes, pp. 85–87. † Ibid. pp. 103–107. ‡ Ibid. pp. 112–114.

These examples may be deemed sufficient to illustrate the controlling supervision exercised by the Synod; and it must be admitted that they exhibit a Presbyterianism sufficiently stringent. It was also in the exercise of ordinary synodical jurisdiction, that this body received and formed new Presbyteries. In 1749, the Presbytery of Suffolk, Long Island, was received; in 1751, those members of the Presbytery of New Brunswick who resided in Philadelphia, and in New Jersey to the southward of that city, were formed into a new Presbytery, and called the Presbytery of Abington;* in 1755, "the Synod appointed the Rev. Samuel Davies, John Todd, Alexander Creaghead, Robert Henry, John Wright, and John Brown, to be a Presbytery, under the name of the Presbytery of Hanover, and that their first meeting shall be in Hanover, on the first Wednesday of December next, and that Mr. Davies open the said Presbytery with a sermon; and that any of their members, (i. e. of the Synod,) settling to the southward and westward of Mr. Hoge's congregation, shall have liberty to join the said Presbytery."†

The Synod were sometimes called upon to decide questions either *in thesi*, or with reference to some special case. Thus, in 1752, we find the following record: "Whereas a certain person pretending at Egg Harbour to be a minister regularly ordained among Presbyterians, and under that character baptised some adults and infants, and it appearing to the Synod that his pretences were false, having at that time no license or ordination; it is our opinion that all the gospel ordinances he administered under that false and pretended character, are null and invalid."‡

In 1753, "it being moved to the Synod what they judge necessary as to the form or method to be used in the administration of baptism, the Synod do refer to our excellent Directory in that case. It being further moved, whether a church session hath power to introduce a new version of the Psalms into the congregation to which they belong, without the consent of the majority of the said congregation, it was voted in the negative: *nemine contradicente.*"§

* Minutes, p. 35. † Ibid. p. 80. ‡ Ibid. p. 42. § Ibid. p. 59.

The character of this Synod is sufficiently plain from its own proceedings; but if it were consistent with the object and limits of this history to bring into view the action of the several Presbyteries within its bounds, its thorough Presbyterianism would be still more apparent. The records of the Presbytery of New Brunswick, for example, furnish as fair a specimen of regular Presbyterian government as can be presented by those of any Presbytery, at any period in the history of our church. When first constituted, through the abundance of its zeal, it paid little regard to geographical limits, and would receive congregations, or supply them with preaching, no matter to what Presbytery they properly belonged. After the revival, however, it became remarkably scrupulous on this point; and even as early as 1743, exhibited a very commendable degree of caution in this matter. This is illustrated by its conduct in reference to the church at New Milford, in Connecticut. In the month of April, 1743, at a *pro re nata* meeting of the Presbytery, the following record was made: "The special occasion of the present meeting of the Presbytery is an application made to some of our members, some time past, from a society in Milford, in New England, by their commissioners, desiring the Presbytery to receive them under their care, and also to take Mr. Jacob Johnson, a candidate for the ministry, then preaching to them, under trials, in order to ordination to the gospel ministry among them; and accordingly said members did send to Mr. Jacob Johnson as pieces of trial, that he prepare a sermon on Rom. viii. 14, and an exegesis, in Latin, upon this question: *An regimen ecclesiae presbyteriale sit Scripturae et rationi congruum?* to be delivered to the Presbytery at this time, to sit upon the said occasion. Now the Presbytery being met, pursuant to the aforementioned occasion and appointment, Mr. Jacob Johnson, together with Mr. Benjamin Fenn and Mr. George Clerk, commissioners from the aforesaid society in Milford, appeared and moved the Presbytery to proceed in their affair, as before mentioned. The Presbytery do agree to take the matter under consideration, and in order to proceed in the best and clearest manner they can, resolve to inquire in the first place, whether said society be a regular society capable of being received under their care and direction or not. And after proper inquiry and consideration of the affair, as far and as fully as at present they are able, the Presbytery doth judge, that although they cannot presbyterially judge and determine any thing as touching the original reasons and grounds of their separation from the established congregation of that town, not having sufficient evidence to proceed upon in that matter, nor does the Presbytery think that matter immediately to lie before them, yet inasmuch as the Presbytery find, upon the verbal relation of the aforesaid commissioners, confirmed by several papers containing the narration of their proceedings, that said society is now a separate body of the Presbyterian denomination, constituted agreeably to, and under protection of the laws of that colony, and no objections against the present proceedings of the new-erected society being offered to the Presbytery by the old congregation, though their design was fully known to them, the Presbytery therefore cannot see any just reason to reject the motion and request made to them by the said newly-erected society of Milford, do unanimously agree to take the said society under their care and government, and do the best they can for them towards their settlement with a minister; and so they are prepared to take the trials of Mr. Jacob Johnson, in order to judge of his qualifications for the sacred office of the ministry among them." The Presbytery then proceeded to the examination of Mr. Johnson, and after having made some progress, they determined to stop, and resolved, 1. That the newly-erected Presbyterian Society in Milford is to be deemed a society capable to call and receive a minister for themselves. 2. That the Presbytery are grieved for the breach thereby made in the said town. 3. That it be recommended to the said society to seek a reconciliation with the old society; and that the Presbytery do not proceed to the ordination of Mr. Johnson, until these further steps have been taken. 4. That in case the efforts for a union should fail, the society "be allowed" to call and settle a minister, and in the mean time to have supplies from settled ministers and approved candidates. 5. That the Rev. Mr. Treat visit Milford, and gain further information, and make a report to Presbytery.* In August of the same year, a call was

* Minutes of New Brunswick Presbytery, pp. 45–7.

presented from that congregation for Mr. Treat, but his removal being opposed by commissioners from the congregation of Abington, of which he was the pastor, the Presbytery decided against his acceptance of the call.* The Presbytery, however, directed Mr. Samuel Finley to visit Milford, "with allowance that he preach in other places thereabouts, where Providence may open a door for him."†

At a meeting of the Presbytery in May, 1744, it is stated, "An important affair was brought before Presbytery from the Presbyterian society of Milford, New England, the determining of which being of very great consequence, and the conjunct Presbytery, (i. e. the united Presbyteries of New Brunswick and New Castle,) being now convened, the Presbytery think it not best to proceed in it, but to refer it to the determination of the conjunct Presbytery at their present meeting."‡ What this affair was, or what was done in the matter, does not appear from the records. But in 1747, a call from Milford was presented to the Presbytery for Mr. Job Prudden, and accepted by him; whereupon the Presbytery, after the usual examinations, and the adoption on his part of the Westminster Confession of Faith and Catechisms, proceeded to his ordination.§

This Presbytery was not less circumspect in the reception of new members. In October, 1743, a request was presented from the congregation of Hopewell, for permission to invite the famous Mr. Davenport to preach for them, with a view to his settlement among them. "The Presbytery, in order to get light in the matter, thought it their duty to discourse with Mr. Davenport about several things they had heard of in some parts of his conduct in times past, which they could not approve of, and were pleased to hear Mr. Davenport declare his conviction of, and humiliation foı some things he had been faulty in, although there be others which he cannot as yet see and condemn which the Presbytery do disapprove of. Whereupon the Presbytery cannot see that the way is clear for said people to give Mr. Davenport a call to settle among them;

* Minutes of New Brunswick Presbytery, p. 52.
† Ibid. p. 55.
‡ Ibid. p. 61.
§ Ibid. pp. 93 and 95.

nevertheless that as God has begun to show him his mistakes, he may be pleased to go on in that way, and being willing to use all means to obtain so desirable an end, the Presbytery do permit the said people to improve Mr. Davenport to supply them until the second Wednesday in May next, to see what may be further done in that affair, referring it to the conjunct Presbytery, then to meet at Philadelphia, to approve or disapprove of this our conduct, and to proceed in regard to Mr. Davenport as their way shall be made clear to them."* He was not received as a member of the Presbytery until 1746, when, as the Presbytery state, "having satisfied us of his consent to the doctrines contained in the Westminster Confession of Faith, together with our plan of government, as far as he had inspected into the same," he was admitted. In 1748, he was dismissed to the Presbytery of New York, "to act under their direction," in relation to a call which he had received to Connecticut Farms.† In 1753, he was again received by the Presbytery of New Brunswick from the Presbytery of New Castle, in order to his settlement at Hopewell. A committee was appointed for his installation, who reported that owing "to the manifest negligence of the people, they could not proceed in that affair; whereupon the Presbytery judged the conduct of the said people to be highly abusive both to the Presbytery and Mr. Davenport; but said people haveing made some just reflections on their conduct, and again presenting a call to Mr. Davenport, he, after some consideration, declared his acceptance of said call;" and the Presbytery, "in consideration of the disappointment and damage sustained by the delay of the installation of Mr. Davenport, when first appointed, through the default of the people of Hopewell and Maidenhead, do order that the said people advance Mr. Davenport's salary to seventy pounds per annum two years sooner than was recommended to them by the last Presbytery."‡ His situation does not appear to have been very agreeable, as in 1757, a petition was presented for his removal, the consideration of which was deferred to the next meeting, and he died in the autumn of that year before it was acted upon.

* Minutes of the Presbytery of New Brunswick, p. 58.

† Ibid. p. 101.

‡ Ibid. pp. 114 and 119.

In the above record we have an example not only of the exercise of the usual presbyterial authority over a congregation, but of something beyond it, especially in the order to increase Mr. Davenport's salary. This was a matter in which the Presbytery often interfered. In 1750, they passed a standing rule, that at least once a year they would "inquire of the elders how their respective ministers were supported, and their salaries paid."* If after such inquiry the people were found deficient, the Presbytery censured them, and "ordered them to give information to the next Presbytery" what they had done to secure the payment of the pastor;† or the people were "ordered to make up the deficiency before the next meeting of the Presbytery."‡

The Presbytery also assumed the right of granting or refusing liberty to one or more members of one congregation to join another. Thus, "Mr. Jacob Reader, a member of the congregation of Hopewell, made a request that for the sake of the convenience of his family, the Presbytery would be pleased to dismiss him from the aforesaid congregation, that he may join with Amwell. And the Presbytery, taking into consideration said request, judge it to be reasonable, and grant it."§ At another time a petition from a number of persons "to be discharged from Mr. Davenport, was presented and granted."|| At the present day few members of the church would think of troubling the Presbytery with such requests, and few presbyteries would think of exercising jurisdiction in the case.

This Presbytery moreover exercised the right of deciding how a minister's time should be apportioned between the several branches of his congregation, and whether new places of worship should be erected or not. In 1752, "a petition was presented from Kingwood for liberty to build a meeting-house for their own convenience; and after hearing said affair, and deliberating thereupon, the Presbytery," it is said, "do grant their petition and order that

* Minutes of New Brunswick Presbytery, p. 155.

† Ibid. p. 163. ‡ Ibid. see pp. 200, 203, 204, 251, &c. &c.

§ Ibid. vol. ii. p. 5. || Ibid. vol. ii. p. 15.

henceforth that half of Mr. Lewis' time which has been hitherto spent in the Western Branch be equally divided between Bethlehem and Kingwood, and that each part pay in proportion to their time."* In those days the villages of Kingston and Princeton, three miles apart, formed one parish, and the people of Princeton wished to have a separate place of worship, and a certain portion of the pastor's time, but their requests were repeatedly disallowed.† In 1755, a motion was again "made in behalf of Princeton for supplies, and for liberty to build a meeting-house there," and the Presbytery, it is said, "do grant liberty to the people of the said town to build a meeting-house."‡

The control exercised by the Presbytery over its own members was no less strict. An example has already been given of the Presbytery's deciding what portion of a minister's time should be given to each of the several congregations under his care. We find too that licentiates, if they wished to officiate out of the bounds of the Presbytery to which they belonged, obtained special permission for that purpose. Thus in 1755, the Presbytery gave "Mr. Hait free liberty to officiate within the bounds of the New Castle Presbytery as much of the time before next commencement, as he inclines to improve for that purpose." This permission was granted in consequence, it is stated, "of an earnest request from our Reverend brethren of the New Castle Presbytery, that we would assist them with respect to the vast number of vacant congregations under their care in Pennsylvania, Maryland, and Virginia, besides fourteen congregations in North Carolina, who have applied to them for gospel ministers, whose circumstances are peculiarly distressing and dangerous; in which letter is also a particular request that Mr. Benjamin Hait may be allowed to join them, or at least to help them this summer."§ It is, therefore, a great mistake to suppose that these Presbyteries were distinguished for a loose form of ecclesiastical government. They carried out the principles of Presbyterianism much further than is now common among us.

* Minutes of New Brunswick Presbytery, p. 200.

† Ibid. pp. 180 and 192. ‡ Ibid. pp. 233 and 236. § Ibid. p. 233.

The character of the Synod of New York may be still further illustrated by a reference to the fact that they conformed to the Scottish usage, as thoroughly as the old Synod of Philadelphia. In the first place, after the manner of the church in Scotland, they had a commission, which sat during the intervals of Synod, clothed with full synodical powers. This commission was appointed regularly every year.*

In the second place they frequently appointed committees with plenary powers to decide particular cases. Thus in 1750, when the German church at Rockaway applied to be taken under the care of the Synod, Messrs. Pierson, Burr, Arthur, Smith, and Spencer, were appointed a committee to visit the place, ascertain the facts, and decide upon the application.† In 1753, the committee sent to New York, received the request of the ministers to be dismissed from their pastoral charge; and decided against the immediate removal of Mr. Pemberton, but dissolved the connection between Mr. Cumming and that congregation.‡ In 1755, a committee was appointed with authority to dismiss Mr. Bostwick from Jamaica, with a view to his removal to New York: they referred the matter to the commission by whom the transfer was effected.§ In the Presbyteries this method of acting by committees was still more frequently resorted to. Men were licensed, ordained, and dismissed by committees specially appointed for the purpose.|| It was not competent, however, for these committees to assume presbyterial powers except for the special purpose of their appointment. Hence in 1750, when application was made to the committee appointed to license Mr. Todd, to make arrangements for the ordination of Mr. Campbell, it was decided "that being only a committee they cannot proceed to the ordination of Mr. C. or make any appointment therefor."¶

In the third place, the Synod frequently acted in a presbyterial capacity. The most common occasion for the exercise of such

* Minutes of Synod of New York, pp. 5, 8, 16, 32, 76, 100, 121, 130.

† Ibid. p. 25.

‡ Ibid. pp. 66–70.

§ Ibid. pp. 103–105.

|| See Minutes of New Brunswick Presbytery, pp. 59, 62, 86, 93, 130, 148, &c. &c.

¶ Ibid. p. 146.

powers was the appointment of supplies for vacant congregations. This was done by the Synod not merely in its character of a missionary society, but in that of a large Presbytery, having the oversight over all the churches, and the direction of all its members. Thus in 1753, they appointed Mr. Blair, Mr. Bay, Mr. Henry, Mr. Finley, and Mr. Rodgers, to supply Mr. Davies' congregation during his absence, and then appointed supplies for the congregations of those ministers. In like manner Mr. Treat, Mr. William Tennent, Mr. Beatty, Mr. Burr, Mr. Pemberton, and Mr. Cumming, were directed to preach, each four sabbaths for Mr. Gilbert Tennent's congregation.* In 1754, an application being received from Hanover for further supplies, the Synod sent Mr. Greenman to them, and directed Mr. Clark, a candidate under the care of the Presbytery of New York, to preach for Mr. Greenman during his absence. In 1756, the committee of Synod sent to Jamaica to decide on Mr. Bostwick's removal, though they did not dismiss him, directed him to preach most of the winter in New York, and then appointed supplies for his congregation. And the commission did the same thing, when they decided on his final removal to New York. It was a common practice, when the Synod sent any of their members on a distant mission, for them to take upon themselves the duty of making provision for their congregations. And even when there was no special reason for it, applications were made directly to the Synod. Thus in 1757, a commissioner from Newark requested supplies for that congregation, and the Synod appointed Mr. Treat to preach for them for three sabbaths, and as much more as he could.† Sometimes one Presbytery was directed to supply the congregations within the bounds of another. Thus "in order to supply the congregations," it is said, "of those ministers who are gone to the southward, the Synod appoint the Presbyteries of New Brunswick and Abington to supply within the bounds of New York Presbytery, each four sabbaths; and the Presbytery of Suffolk to supply either New York or Jamaica, as need shall be, each member two sabbaths."‡

Even calls for ministers, and applications from congregations to

* Minutes, p. 59. † Ibid. p. 127. ‡ Ibid. p. 89.

be taken under the care of the Synod, were at times directed immediately to them and not to a Presbytery. In 1748, "a call was brought into Synod from Falling Spring and New Providence, for Mr. Byram, the acceptance of which he declined."* The German congregation of Rockaway applied immediately to the Synod to be taken into connection with our church, and they entertained the application.† The whole action of the Synod, in reference to the congregation in New York, was presbyterial rather than synodical. A committee of the Synod selected and nominated elders; received and decided complaints against the pastors, one of whom, at his own request, they dismissed conditionally, and the other definitively. The Synod, or its commission, moreover decided what version of the Psalms should be used, and transferred Mr. Bostwick from one church to another. Some of these cases were indeed brought up, by reference from the Presbytery; but in most of them the Synod exercised original jurisdiction.

It appears, then, from this review, that the Synod of New York was a strictly Presbyterian body. They not only declared the Church of Scotland to be their mother church, and claimed to be united with her "in the same faith, order, and discipline," having adopted her standards both of doctrine and government, but in all their measures and modes of action they adhered to the Presbyterian system. There was not only the regular exercise of sessional, presbyterial, and synodical supervision, but the control exercised over ministers and churches was more direct and extended than that to which we are accustomed. And further, in the regular appointment of a commission, in the frequent use of committees with full powers, and in the exercise of presbyterial functions, this Synod conformed to the usages of the Church of Scotland, more nearly than our church has ever done since the formation of our present constitution.

This Synod was no less distinguished for its zeal for sound learning and evangelical religion. It embraced a very large proportion of the best educated, as well as of the most fervent and pious ministers of the church. The field which they had to cultivate was so

* Minutes, p. 11. † Ibid. p. 25.

extensive, and was so rapidly filling with inhabitants, that it required the most laborious exertion to keep it even tolerably supplied. The members of the Synod were therefore obliged to make long and frequent journeys, and to give themselves up to their work with a devotion which would now be deemed extraordinary. Perhaps there is no ecclesiastical body to which our church and country are more indebted than to this Synod of New York.

It only remains to give an account of the negotiations which led to the union of the two Synods. The first overtures were made by the Synod of New York in 1749, when it was carried, "by a great majority of votes," that the following proposals should be sent to the Synod of Philadelphia, viz.:

"The Synod of New York are deeply sensible of the many unhappy consequences that flow from our present divided state; and have, with pleasure, observed a spirit of moderation increasing between many members of both Synods. This opens a door of hope, that if we were united in one body, we might be able to carry on the designs of religion in future peace and agreement, to our mutual satisfaction. And though we retain the same sentiments of the work of God which we formerly did, yet we esteem mutual forbearance our duty, since we all profess the same Confession of Faith and Directory for worship. We would, therefore, humbly propose to our brethren of the Synod of Philadelphia, that all our former differences be buried in perpetual oblivion; and that, for the time to come, both Synods be united in one, and that henceforth there be no contentions among us, but to carry towards each other in the most peaceable and brotherly manner, which we are persuaded will be for the honour of our Master, the credit of our profession, and the edification of the churches committed to our care. Accordingly we appoint the Rev. Messrs. John Pierson, Gilbert Tennent, Ebenezer Pemberton, and Aaron Burr, to be our delegates to wait upon the Synod of Philadelphia with these proposals; and if the Synod of Philadelphia see meet to join with us in this design, and will please to appoint a commission to meet for that purpose, we appoint the Rev. Messrs. John Pierson, Ebenezer Pemberton, Aaron Burr, Gilbert and William Tennent, Richard

Treat, Samuel and John Blair, John Roan, Samuel Finley, Ebenezer Prime, David Bostwick, and James Brown, (whom we appoint a commission of the Synod for the ensuing year,) to meet with the commission of the Synod of Philadelphia, at such time and place as they shall choose, to determine the affair of the union agreeably to the preliminary articles determined upon by this Synod. And it is agreed that any other of our members, who shall please to meet with the commission, shall have liberty of voting and acting in said affair equally with the members of said commission. Which articles proposed as a general plan of union, are as follows, viz.:

"1. To preserve the common peace, we would propose that all names of distinction, which have been made use of in the late times, be for ever abolished.

"2. That every member assent unto and adopt the Confession of Faith and Directory, according to the plan formerly agreed to by the Synod of Philadelphia, in the years ———.

"3. That every member promise that, after any question has been determined by the major vote, he will actively concur, or passively submit to the judgment of the body. But if his conscience permit him to do neither of these, that then he shall be obliged peaceably to withdraw from our synodical communion, without any attempt to make a schism or division among us. Yet this is not intended to extend to any cases but those which the Synod judge essential in matters of doctrine or discipline.

"4. That all our respective congregations and vacancies be acknowledged as congregations belonging to the Synod, but continue under the care of the same presbyteries as now they are, until a favourable opportunity presents for an advantageous alteration.

"5. That we all agree to esteem and treat it as a censurable evil to accuse any of our members of error in doctrine, or immorality in conversation, any otherwise than by private reproof, till the accusation has been brought before a regular judicature, and issued according to the known rules of our discipline."*

* Minutes, pp. 15–17.

The Synod of Philadelphia having acceded to the proposal for a conference, the commissioners of the two Synods met at Trenton, October 5, 1749. From the minutes of this meeting, it appears that "the commissioners of the Synod of New York, considering the protest of the Synod of Philadelphia, whereby they excluded from their communion the Presbytery of New Brunswick and their adherents, as one principal bar to an union, waiving all other matters, immediately insisted that said protest should, by some authentic and formal act of the Synod of Philadelphia, be made null and void. The debates on this head rose very high, and there appearing no prospect of accommodation, the commissioners of both Synods came unanimously into this conclusion, viz.: that whereas certain difficulties arose in the conversation of the commissioners of both Synods, they came finally unanimously into this agreement, that both Synods at their next sessions do more fully prepare proposals for an accommodation, and interchange said proposals; and that, in the mean time, there be a mutual endeavour to cultivate a spirit of candour and friendship. At the same time, these principal things were especially recommended to the consideration of their respective Synods: 1. The protest. 2. That paragraph about essentials. 3. Of Presbyteries."*

From the report of the commissioners made to the Synod of Philadelphia, relating to this meeting, it appears that "the delegates from the Synod of New York agreed to the following concessions and amendments in the aforementioned proposals, which, according to the references in them, are as follows: 1. 'Though great and good men have been of different opinions, (about the revival.') 2. 'Always reserving a liberty for such dissenting member to lay his grievances before Synod in a peaceable manner. N. B. What remains of the sentence to be erased.' (This amendment relates to article three, in the New York proposals.) 3. That there be no intrusions into the bounds of Presbyteries or pastoral charges, against the inclination of the Presbyteries or pastors. 4. That all candidates for the work of the sacred ministry either be examined and approved by the Synod or its commission, previous to their

* See Minutes of the Synod of New York, p. 21.

admission upon trials by any of our Presbyteries, or else that they be obliged to obtain a college diploma, or a certificate from the president or trustees of the college, that they have been examined and found qualified. Mr. Gilbert Tennent only objected against the synodical examination."*

The Synod of New York received, in May, 1750, the report of their commissioners, of the failure of the conference at Trenton, and deferred further action on the subject until their meeting in the autumn. Proposals were then prepared which differed but little from those at first offered. The first article provides for the adoption of the Confession and Directory. The second relates to the decisions of the Synod, and is nearly in the same words as the former article relating to the same subject. The third is against rash judging. The fourth provides, "that no candidate shall be taken upon trials by any Presbytery without a degree, or certificate from the president and a sufficient number of tutors or trustees of some college, testifying to the sufficiency of his learning, except in cases extraordinary, in which the Presbyteries shall be accountable to the Synod for their conduct." The fifth was, "that it shall be treated as irregular for any minister or candidate to preach, or perform other ministerial offices in the congregations of other ministers belonging to our body, contrary to their minds. On the other hand, it shall be esteemed unbrotherly for any minister to refuse his consent, without weighty reasons, when amicably desired." The sixth provides for the Presbyteries and congregations remaining as they then were. The seventh requires "that the protestation made in the Synod of Philadelphia, in the year 1741, be declared henceforth void and of none effect; and that the proposed union shall not be understood to imply an agreement or consent to said protestation on the part of this Synod." And finally, "forasmuch as this Synod doth believe, as they have before declared, that a glorious work of God's Spirit was carried on in the late religious appearances; though we doubt not but there were several follies and extravagancies of people, and artifices of Satan intermixed therewith; it would be pleasing and desirable for us,

* Minutes of the Synod of Philadelphia, vol. iii. p. 34.

and what we hope for, that both Synods may come so far to agree in their sentiments about it, as to give their joint testimony thereto."*

To these proposals the Synod of Philadelphia replied, 1. That it was unreasonable to make the declaration that the protest of 1741 was void, a term of communion, since the Synod of Philadelphia had declared that they would act towards their brethren of New York as though that protest had never been made. If any thing more was intended by declaring it void, they were not prepared for it, as they believed it had been made on sufficient and justifiable grounds. 2. They objected to the Presbyteries remaining as they then were, as they considered it essential to the peace of the church that the distinction between old and new-side Presbyteries should be done away. 3. They objected to making a testimony to the revival a term of communion, as the commissioners from New York had admitted that great and good men differed on that subject; and as the Synod itself acknowledged that it was mixed with extravagancies, and artifices of Satan. Before such a testimony could be given, it must be known what was regarded as genuine, and what as spurious. 4. They agreed that all the members of the Synod of New York should be members of the united Synod, but they thought that where ministers had unjustly intruded into their congregations, and rendered them too feeble to support their pastors, something should be done to rectify the evil.

For a further exposition of their views, they refer the Synod of New York to the proposals sent to them after the Trenton conference, but before the reception of those above stated from New York. They particularly refer the Synod of New York to the article respecting the decision of affairs by majority of votes. "We apprehend," they say, "it is strictly Presbyterian and reasonable, and are not convinced the alteration in that article proposed by you, about what is essential and what is not, is necessary;†

* Minutes of the Synod of New York, pp. 27, 28.

† As the commissioners from New York at the Trenton conference agreed to erase that part of the article which made the distinction referred to, its being introduced anew by the Synod of New York, is called "an alteration."

nay, we apprehend that such an alteration as stated by you has a bad aspect, and opens a door for an unjustifiable latitude in principles and practices." They express their satisfaction at the proposal that candidates should bring a college certificate; and, as that answered every purpose, they withdrew their alternative about synodical examination.*

The proposals sent from the Synod of Philadelphia to that of New York, before the reception of those to which the above objections refer, were substantially as follows: 1. That all names of distinction be abolished. 2. That the Confession of Faith and Directory be adopted "according to the plan agreed on in our Synod, and that no acts be made but concerning matters which appear plain duty, or concerning opinions that we believe relate to the great truths of religion, and that all public and fundamental agreements of this Synod stand safe." 3. Makes the usual provision for conscientious dissentients. 4. Against rash judging. 5. Relates to intrusions and reception of candidates. On these three points the two Synods were already agreed. 6. It was proposed that Presbyteries should be made up of the ministers who lived contiguous to one another; but if any minister was dissatisfied, he might join what Presbytery he pleased. 7. With regard to the divided congregations, or new erections, as they were called, it was proposed that where each party was able to support a minister, both should continue; where neither was thus able, efforts should be made to unite them; and "where new erections have been made to the prejudice of the former standing congregations, and said erections supplied with ministers, said ministers be removed, and all proper methods be taken to heal the breach."

These proposals were received by the Synod of New York in 1751, who made to them the following objections. 1. "Though the Synod make no acts but concerning matters of plain duty or opinions relating to the great truths of religion; yet as every thing that appears plain duty and truth unto the body, may appear at the same time not to be essential; so we judge that no member or members should be obliged to withdraw from our communion upon

* See Minutes of Synod of Philadelphia, vol. iii. pp. 36–39.

his or their not being able actively to concur or passively submit, unless the matter be judged essential in doctrine and discipline." 2. They objected of course to the public acts of the Synod of Philadelphia, made since the schism, being binding on the united body. 3. They thought it would not be for peace or edification in any measure to coerce the union of divided congregations. 4. As they had a college, there was no need of the alternative plan, of synodical examination of candidates.*

The letter from the Philadelphia Synod, above mentioned, containing strictures on the New York proposals, was not received by the Synod of New York until 1752, when on account of the pressure of other business, they returned a very short reply, in which they say: "We shall endeavour to give it a calm and deliberate consideration, and hope we shall return you such an answer as shall give you convincing evidence that we entertain the most affectionate desires of peace and union upon such a bottom as may contribute to the peace and comfort of all our churches."† This answer they gave at their next meeting in 1753. They justify their insisting on the protest being declared void, on the ground that if it was a judicial act, it must stand in full force and virtue, unless it be repealed by an equal act; and that their uniting with them without its repeal would be an implicit approbation of it. They insisted that Presbyteries and congregations should remain as they were, as it would produce but a jarring concord to force people together faster than they have clearness to go. As to the joint testimony to the revival previously proposed, it was not designed as a term of communion, but a desirable thing; as they hoped that upon friendly conference the difference on that subject would not be found to be as great as it had seemed. That no dissenting member should be obliged to withdraw from their communion, unless the matter be judged by the body essential in doctrine and discipline, they say, appeared to them to be strictly Christian and scriptural, as well as Presbyterian, and not liable to the objection

* Minutes of Synod of New York, p. 35.

† Ibid. p. 43.

of unjustifiable latitude, as the Synod had the power of judging what is essential and what is not.*

This latter point does not appear to have been again adverted to, or to have given any further trouble. Neither Synod was disposed to make "every truth or duty" a term of communion; and each had made the adoption of the Westminster Confession of Faith a condition of admission into the sacred office. The article in question indeed did not relate to the admission of members, but to their exclusion; and is therefore analogous to those provisions of our present constitution which declare that, in case of process against a minister, "errors should be carefully considered, whether they strike at the vitals of religion, and are industriously spread, or whether they arise from the weakness of the human understanding, and are not likely to do much injury;" and which direct, "That a minister under process for heresy or schism should be treated with Christian and brotherly tenderness. Frequent conferences ought to be held with him, and proper admonitions administered. For some more dangerous errors, however, suspension may become necessary."†

It has already been proved‡ that this Synod did not make adherence to the mere essential doctrines of the gospel the condition of ministerial communion. This is indeed evident from the form of expression adopted in the article itself, which speaks of what is essential "in doctrine or discipline." The discipline intended is the discipline adopted by the Synod, and the doctrine intended is the system of doctrine which they had adopted. This interpretation is expressly asserted to be the meaning of this language by the members of the Synod themselves;§ and it is the only one at all consistent with the official declarations of the body, that they had adopted the Westminster Confession of Faith "as the test of orthodoxy" among them,‖ and that they had the same standard of doctrine as the church of Scotland. At the very time that these

* Minutes of Synod of New York, p. 55, &c.

† Book of Discipline, chap. V. §§ 13, 14.

‡ Chap. III. p. 173, &c.

§ See chap. III. p. 169.

‖ Chap. VI. p. 255.

negotiations were going on, the Synod of New York had the Rev. Mr. Harker under process for teaching doctrines which had an Arminian tendency,* and for which, after the union of the two Synods, he was suspended. "That therefore," says Mr. John Blair, "is an essential error in the Synod's sense, which is of such malignity as to subvert or greatly to injure the system of doctrine and mode of worship and government contained in the Westminster Confession of Faith and Directory."†

In 1754, a letter was sent from the Synod of Philadelphia to that of New York, which is not on record, containing a request for a renewed conference. A committee was consequently appointed to attend the Synod of Philadelphia at their next meeting.‡ The result of this conference was, that the Philadelphia brethren proposed that all previous differences should be dropped, and the two Synods should unite "as two contiguous bodies of Christians agreed in principle, as though they had never been concerned with one another before, nor had any differences." The New York brethren, however, were not satisfied with this proposal, but insisted that "the protestation made in 1741, should be withdrawn." When this result was communicated to the Synod of Philadelphia, they said they saw not what they could propose further. As to the protest, they had frequently declared they would act in case of an union as though it never had been made; that as every member

* Minutes of Synod of New York, p. 136. "A reference was brought into Synod from the New Brunswick Presbytery, respecting Mr. Samuel Harker, one of their members, as having imbibed and vented certain erroneous doctrines. The Synod, after serious consideration had, do agree, that inasmuch as Mr. Harker is absent, they cannot proceed to a regular determination of said affair; and do therefore appoint Messrs. Gilbert Tennent, Richard Treat, Samuel Finley, and John Blair, to deal with him, as they shall have opportunity, in such manner as shall appear to them best adapted for his conviction, and refer the further determination to the next Synod, if there shall be need. And in the meantime the Synod does recommend it to the Presbytery of New Brunswick to take such measures as they shall judge best to prevent the spread and hurtful influence of those errors."

† The Synod of New York and Philadelphia vindicated, p. 11.

‡ Minutes of Synod of New York, p. 71.

had a right to protest, the judicature could neither forbid it, nor annul or withdraw such protest when made; it was solely in the power of the protesters. As some members of the Synod of New York felt aggrieved by the protest, so some of their members felt themselves greatly injured by the conduct of some of the New York brethren, and unless mutual concessions were made, an union was out of the question.*

As this year the Synod of New York met in the autumn, this minute came before them the same year, viz.: 1755; and they replied to it by saying, that they were fully sensible that peace and union were of the utmost importance in the church of Christ, and that their being dissatisfied with the mere general proposal to drop all former differences, and to unite on scriptural and reasonable terms, and their insisting on particulars, arose simply from the desire to render the union effectual. They admitted that their demand to have the protest annulled, could have no propriety but on the assumption that the Synod of Philadelphia had approved and adopted it; and consequently if they would say "that in their synodical capacity they do not adopt it," all difficulty would be removed on that score. "As the protest," they add, "appears to be a principal obstruction to the union of the two Synods," they proposed, that in case the Synod of Philadelphia admitted it not to be officially their act, the two Synods should unite on the terms previously proposed, and immediately "proceed to hear and determine the differences between the protesters and those protested against, if needful."†

In 1756, the Synod of Philadelphia replied, "We desire to unite on the same terms on which the ministers of the two Synods were united, when one body; and we are glad to join with the Synod of New York in any expedient to cut off all debates about the protestation made in 1741. We allow the protesters the right of private judgment; and you will allow we can neither disannul nor withdraw their protestation; but in our synodical capacity, at your desire, we declare and do assure you, that we neither adopted nor

* Minutes of Philadelphia Synod, p. 52.

† Minutes of Synod of New York, pp. 91–95.

do adopt said protestation as a term of ministerial communion. It was never mentioned to any of our members as a term of communion, more than any of the other protestations delivered into our Synod on occasion of those differences. We only adopt and desire to adhere to our standards, as we agreed formerly when one body; we adopt no other."

The above declaration respecting the protest is historically correct. It was not a synodical act, but the act of certain members in their individual capacity. It was never officially adopted or sanctioned by a vote of the Synod; though it was often spoken of with approbation.

The Synod appointed their commission to meet such committee as the Synod of New York might name, to prepare the terms of union.* This latter Synod accordingly, in September, 1756, appointed a committee to meet the commission of the Synod of Philadelphia in 1757.

When this joint committee met, "the commissioners of the Philadelphia Synod declared for themselves, and doubted not but their Synod would also readily declare that they do not look upon the protest as the act of their body nor adopt it as such." And as there was an agreement on all other points formerly proposed as necessary to an union, it was agreed to propose to their respective Synods to have their next meeting at the same time and place. This proposal was acceded to on both sides, and the commissions of the two Synods were directed to meet in Philadelphia the Monday before the day appointed for the meeting of the Synods, in order "to prepare matters for their happy union."† The two Synods accordingly met in Philadelphia in 1758. The commissions reported the plan of union, which was unanimously adopted by each Synod, who agreed to meet as one body at four o'clock, May 29, 1758. The plan of union, was then read over in joint meeting and unanimously approved, and is as follows:

"The Synods of New York and Philadelphia, taking into serious consideration the present divided state of the Presbyterian church

* Minutes of Synod of Philadelphia, p. 58.

† Minutes of Synod of New York, p. 125.

in this land, and being deeply sensible that the division of the church tends to weaken its interests, to dishonour religion, and consequently its glorious author; to render government and discipline ineffectual, and, finally, to dissolve its very frame; and, being desirous to pursue such measures as may most tend to the glory of God, and the establishment and edification of his people, do judge it to be our indispensable duty to study the things that make for peace, and to endeavour the healing of that breach which has for some time existed among us, that so its hurtful consequences may not extend to posterity, that all occasion of reproach upon our society may be removed, and that we may carry on the great designs of religion to better advantage than we can do in a divided state. And since both Synods continue to profess the same principles of faith, and adhere to the same form of worship, government, and discipline, there is the greater reason to endeavour to compromise the differences which were agitated many years ago, with too great warmth and animosity, and unite in one body.

"For which end, and that no jealousies or grounds of alienation may remain, and also to prevent future breaches of like nature, we agree to unite in one body, under the name of the Synod of New York and Philadelphia, on the following plan:

"1. Both Synods having always approved and received the Westminster Confession of Faith, the Larger and Shorter Catechisms, as an orthodox and excellent system of Christian doctrine, founded on the word of God, we do still receive the same as the profession of our faith, and also adhere to the plan of worship, government, and discipline, contained in the Westminster Directory, strictly enjoining it on all our members, and probationers for the ministry, that they preach and teach according to the form of sound words in said Confession and Catechisms, and avoid and oppose all errors contrary thereto.

"That when any matter is determined by a major vote, every member shall either actively concur with, or passively submit to such determination; or, if his conscience permit him to do neither, he shall, after sufficient liberty modestly to reason and remonstrate, peaceably withdraw from our communion, without attempting to make any schism; provided always, that this shall be understood to extend only to such determinations as the body shall judge indispensable in doctrine, or Presbyterian government.

"3. That any member or members, for the exoneration of his or their conscience before God, have a right to protest against any act or procedure, of our highest judicature, because there is no further appeal to another for redress; and to require that such protestation be recorded in their minutes. And as such a protest is a solemn appeal from the bar of the judicature, no member is liable to prosecution on account of his protesting. Provided always, that it shall be considered irregular and unlawful to enter any protest against any member or members; to protest facts or accusations instead of proving them, unless a fair trial be refused, even by the highest judicature. And it is agreed, that such protestations are only to be entered against the public acts, judgments, or determinations, of the judicature with which the protester's conscience is offended.

"4. As the protestation entered in the Synod of Philadelphia, Anno Domini, 1741, has been apprehended to have been approved and received by an act of the Synod, and on that account was judged a sufficient obstacle to an union, the said Synod declare that they never judicially adopted the said protestation, nor do account it a synodical act; but that it is to be considered as the act of those only who subscribed it; and therefore cannot, in its nature, be a valid objection to the union of the two Synods, especially considering that a very great majority of both Synods have become members since the said protestation was entered.

"5. That it shall be esteemed and treated as a censurable evil to accuse any member of heterodoxy, insufficiency, or immorality, in a calumniating manner, or otherwise than by private brotherly admonition, or by a regular process, according to our known rules of judicial trial in cases of scandal. And it shall be considered in the same view if any Presbytery appoint supplies within the bounds of another Presbytery without their concurrence; or if any member officiate in another's congregation without asking and obtaining his consent, or the session's in case the minister be absent. Yet it shall be esteemed unbrotherly for any one, in ordinary circumstances, to refuse his consent to a regular member when it is requested.

"6. That no Presbytery shall license or ordain to the work of the ministry any candidate, until he give them competent satisfaction as to his learning, and experimental acquaintance with religion, skill in divinity and cases of conscience, and declare his acceptance of the Westminster Confession and Catechisms as the confession of his faith, and promise subjection to the Presbyterian plan of government in the Westminster Directory.

"7. The Synods declare it is their earnest desire that a complete union may be obtained as soon as possible, and agree that the united Synods shall model the several Presbyteries as shall appear to them most expedient. Provided, nevertheless, that Presbyteries where an alteration does not appear to be for edification, continue in their present form. As to divided congregations, it is agreed that such as have settled ministers on both sides be allowed to continue as they are; that where those of one side have a settled minister, the other, being vacant, may join with the settled minister, if a majority choose to do so; that where both sides are vacant, they may be at liberty to unite together.

"8. As the late religious appearances occasioned much speculation and debate, the members of the Synod of New York, in order to prevent any misapprehensions, declare their adherence to their former sentiments, in favour of them, that a blessed work of God's Holy Spirit, in the conversion of numbers was then carried on; and for the satisfaction of all concerned, this united Synod agree in declaring, that as all mankind are naturally dead in trespasses and sins, an entire change of heart and life is necessary to make them meet for the service and enjoyment of God; that such a change can be only effected by the powerful operations of the Divine Spirit; that when sinners are made sensible of their lost condition and absolute inability to recover themselves, are enlightened in the knowledge of Christ, and convinced of his ability and willingness to save; and, upon gospel encouragements, do choose him for their Saviour; and renouncing their own righteousness in point of merit, depend upon his imputed righteousness for justification before God; and on his wisdom and strength for guidance and support; when upon these apprehensions and exercises their souls are comforted, notwithstanding their past guilt, and rejoice in God, through Jesus Christ; when they hate and bewail their sins of heart and life, delight in the laws of God without exception, reverently and diligently attend his ordinances, become humble and self-denied, and make it the business of their life to please and glorify God and to do good to their fellow-men—this is to be acknowledged as a gracious work of God, even though it should be attended with unusual bodily commotions, or some more exceptionable circumstances, by means of infirmity, temptations, or remaining corruptions. And wherever religious appearances are attended with the good effects above mentioned, we desire to rejoice in and to thank God for them.

"But, on the other hand, when persons seeming to be under a religious concern, imagine that they have visions of the human nature of Jesus Christ, or hear voices, or see external lights, or have faintings and convulsion-like fits, and on the account of these, judge themselves to be truly converted, though they have not the scriptural characters of a work of God above described, we believe such persons to be under a dangerous delusion; and we testify our utter abhorrence of such a delusion, wherever it attends any religious appearances in any church or time.

"Now, as both Synods are agreed in their sentiments concerning the nature of a work of grace, and declare their desire and purpose to promote it, different judgments respecting particular matters of facts ought not to prevent their union; especially as many of the present members have entered into the ministry, since the time of the aforesaid religious appearances.

"Upon the whole, as the design of our union is the advancement of the Mediator's kingdom, and as the wise and faithful discharge of the ministerial functions is the principal appointed means for that glorious end; we judge that this is a proper occasion to manifest our sincere intention unitedly to exert ourselves to fulfil the ministry we have received of the Lord Jesus. Accordingly we unanimously declare our serious and fixed resolution, by divine aid, to take heed to ourselves that our hearts be upright, our discourse edifying, and our lives exemplary for purity and godliness; to take heed to our doctrine that it be not only orthodox, but evangelical and spiritual, tending to awaken the secure to a suitable concern for their salvation, and to instruct and encourage sincere Christians; thus commending ourselves to every man's conscience in the sight of God; to cultivate peace and harmony among ourselves, and to strengthen each other's hands in promoting the knowledge of divine truth, and in diffusing the savour of piety among our people.

"Finally, we earnestly recommend it to all under our care, that instead of indulging a contentious disposition, they would love each other with a pure heart fervently, as brethren who profess subjection to the same Lord, adhere to the same faith, worship, and government, and entertain the same hope of glory. And we desire that they would improve the present union for their mutual edification, combine to strengthen the common interests of religion, and go hand in hand in the path of life; which we pray the God of all grace would please to effect, for Christ's sake. AMEN."

This noble declaration is for our church what the declaration of independence is for our country. It is a promulgation of first principles; a setting forth of our faith, order, and religion, as an answer to those who question us. It is the foundation of our ecclesiastical compact, the bond of our union. Those who adhere to the principles here laid down, are entitled to a standing in our church; those who desert them, desert not merely the faith but the religion of our fathers, and have no right to their name or their heritage. It is with grateful exultation we read that this declaration was unanimously adopted, that every member of the united Synod set his hand to this testimony in behalf of truth, order, and evangelical religion. If our church will faithfully bear up this standard, then shall she look forth as the morning; then shall she arise and shine, and the glory of the Lord shall be seen upon her.

CHAPTER VII.

SYNOD OF NEW YORK AND PHILADELPHIA.

1758–88.

Preliminary statements. — General review of the acts of the Synod. — I. Its missionary operations.—II. Its efforts in behalf of education.—III. Its standard of doctrine. — IV. Its discipline. —Its exercise of ordinary powers in the formation of new Presbyteries; in establishing general rules and deciding questions of conscience; in the general supervision of the Church; in the decision of appeals and references.—V. Its exercise of extraordinary powers, in acting by a commission; in the exercise of presbyterial powers; in investing committees with synodical authority.—VI. The Synod's intercourse with other churches. — VII. Its conduct in reference to the revolutionary war.—VIII. Formation of the new constitution.—IX. State of the Church during the existence of this Synod.

THE number of ministers in connection with our church at the time of the union of the two Synods, was not far from one hundred. Among these were some of the most distinguished men who have ever adorned our annals. The two Tennents, Richard Treat, Francis Alison, Alexander McDowell, John Pierson, David Bostwick, Samuel Davies, Samuel Finley, John Roan, Matthew Wilson, John Miller, John Blair, Elihu Spencer, George Duffield, Robert Smith, John Rodgers, and others equally prominent, either for learning or piety, were then in the vigour of their days. To these were added in succeeding years, men no less distinguished for talents or usefulness. In 1759, Mr. John Ewing took his seat as a member of Synod. This gentleman was Pastor of the First Presbyterian Church in Philadelphia, and Provost of the University of Pennsylvania. "In all the branches of science usually taught in seminaries of learning, more particularly in mathematics, astronomy, and every branch of natural philosophy; in the Latin, Greek, and Hebrew languages; and in logic, metaphysics, and moral philosophy, he was probably one of the most accurate and profound scholars which this country can boast of having reared."* In 1760, we find the names of James Latta, Alexander McWhorter, and William Kirkpatrick. The first mentioned is the ancestor of the family which has furnished so many ministers to our church. The second was long the excellent pastor of the church in Newark, New Jersey; and the third, a member of the Presbytery of New Brunswick, was distinguished for his piety and usefulness. In 1761, John Strain became a member of the Synod, and is still remembered as one of the most eloquent and impressive ministers our church has ever produced. In 1763, we find the name of James Waddell, who was to the Virginia church, in point of eloquence, what Patrick Henry was to the Virginia bar. In 1765, the Presbytery of Hanover reported the ordination of David Rice, a man of distinguished usefulness in the southern church. In 1766, the names of Robert Cooper and Samuel Blair were reported. The former was a prominent and pious member of the Presbytery of Donegal, and the latter, a son of the Rev. Samuel Blair, so distinguished for his piety and usefulness at an earlier period of our history. At the age of twenty-eight or thirty years, he was elected president of Princeton College, though he declined the appointment, and soon sank into a state of health which made the residue of his life a protracted disease.† In 1769, John McCreary and Joseph Smith were added to the roll. Both of these were distinguished men. The latter, pre-eminent for piety and energy, was one of the fathers of our church in Western Pennsylvania. The same year the Rev. Dr. Witherspoon, who had already obtained in Scotland, a high reputation as the able advocate of evangelical doctrine, was received as a member of the Synod, and entered upon that course of active usefulness in the service of his adopted church and country, which has rendered his name so conspicuous in our civil and ecclesiastical history. The same year Dr. Sproat was received from the Association of New Haven county, Connecticut, having been called to take charge of the Second Presbyterian

* Dr. Miller's Retrospect, vol. ii. p. 372.

† Dr. Green's Sermons and History of New Jersey College, p. 396.

church in Philadelphia. In 1771, the name of John Woodhull, so long the faithful pastor of the church in Freehold, New Jersey, first occurs on the records. This enumeration would become tedious if further continued. It may, therefore, be briefly stated, that the names of Robert Davidson in 1774, of James Power and John McMillan, apostles of the West, and of John McKnight in 1777, of Thaddeus Dodd and James Armstrong in 1778, of Samuel Stanhope Smith in 1779, of James Hall in 1782, of Moses Hoge in 1786, occur for the first time on the minutes.* To the preceding list there are doubtless many names which ought to be added, whose omission is to be attributed to the writer's limited means of information. In 1787, the Rev. Dr. Nesbit, the learned president of Dickinson college, was received as a member of Synod; and in the same year the venerable Dr. Green first took his seat in our highest judicatory, in whose counsels for a long succession of years he has been so eminently influential. The whole number of accessions to the Synod during this period of thirty years, was considerably more than two hundred. The deaths and removals reported to the Synod were about one hundred; in many cases, however, the decease of members is not recorded in the synodical minutes.

The Synod was soon called to weep over the graves of some of its most distinguished members. In 1760, the death of "that pious, zealous saint of God,"† the Rev. George Gillespie, is recorded. He died at an advanced age, having been received by the Presbytery of Philadelphia, as a licentiate of the Presbytery of Glasgow, in 1712. In 1761, the Synod heard of the decease of the eloquent, devoted, and accomplished Davies, at the early age of thirty-six. "Heu quam exiguum vitae curriculum! Corpore fuit eximio; gestu liberali, placido, augusto. Ingenii nitore, morum integritate, munificentia, facilitate inter paucos illustris. Rei

* Several of these ministers were, no doubt, ordained some years before their names appear upon the records of the Synod. During the war the attendance of the members, and even the reports of the distant Presbyteries, were greatly interrupted.

† This language is used in reference to Mr. Gillespie by Dr. Francis Alison, in his sermon delivered before the Synod in 1758.

literariae peritus; theologus promptus, perspicax. In rostris, per eloquium blandum, mellitum, vehemens simul, et perstringens, nulli secundus. Scriptor ornatus, sublimis, disertus. Praesertim vero pietate, ardente in Deum zelo et religione spectandus."* In 1766, Davies was followed to the grave by Dr. Samuel Finley, his scarcely less distinguished successor in the presidency of Princeton College. The preceding year the Synod were informed that the Rev. Gilbert Tennent had closed his long, laborious, and eminently successful ministry. In 1768, the death of the Rev. Adam Boyd was reported. He was ordained by the Presbytery of New Castle, in 1724, and was an indefatigable and faithful pastor of the church of Octarara, and of two neighbouring congregations.† From this time the older members of the Synod disappear in rapid succession. In 1771, there were seven deaths reported, including that of the excellent Mr. Pierson; in 1772, four, including that of Mr. John Blair; in 1776, Mr. John Roan; in 1777, Mr. William Tennent; in 1779, Dr. Richard Treat, of Abington; in 1780, Dr. Francis Alison; so that but few of the original members of this Synod were now remaining.

The following history of this Synod, from the design of this

* The inscription on the tomb of Davies.

† In the minutes of the Presbytery of New Castle it is stated, that Mr. Thomas Creaghead, and Mr. Adam Boyd, "late from New England," were, received by the Presbytery. This led the writer to suppose that Mr. Boyd was probably of New England origin. He has learned, however, from one of his descendants, the Rev. Mr. Boyd Cross, of Baltimore, that he was from the county of Antrim, in Ireland, and the son-in-law of the Rev. Thomas Creaghead, who was originally from Scotland. Mr. Creaghead was educated as a physician, but subsequently studied divinity and went to Ireland, whence he removed with his family to this country. "He collected, organized, and built up seven of the Presbyterian churches of Lancaster county, Pennsylvania, besides securing the building of their houses of worship. He used whenever a new preacher from Ireland or Scotland came over through his influence, or one who seemed qualified for his work, to give him the congregation which he had collected, and go to some other part and collect another." Two of his sons became ministers, one of whom was settled near White Clay Creek, in Delaware, and the other in Lancaster county. The Rev. Matthew Wilson, father of the late Dr. J. P. Wilson, married his grand-daughter.

work, and from the nature of the materials at the command of the writer, must be in a great measure purely ecclesiastical. That is, it must be in a good degree confined to a classification of the acts of the Synod, with a view to exhibit its character as an ecclesiastical body. Such a classification, though it may not be without its use, cannot be expected to possess the interest which belongs to the history of revivals, or of polemical discussions.

MISSIONARY OPERATIONS OF THE SYNOD.

With a field so extensive as that embraced within the bounds of the Synod of New York and Philadelphia, and which was rapidly filling up with inhabitants, the burden of missionary labour which devolved upon that body was very heavy. In 1759, Messrs. Kirkpatrick, McWhorter, Latta, and Lewis, were sent to Virginia, to act under the direction of the Presbytery of Hanover.* Mr. John Brainerd, then the pastor of the church of Newark, applied to the Synod for advice, whether he should leave his pastoral charge and devote himself anew to the service of the Indians. The Synod unanimously advised him to remove, and promised him the interest of the Indian fund in the hands of the trustees of the college of New Jersey, which was at the disposal of the Synod. Messrs. McKnight, Beatty, and Latta, also were directed to visit the Indians in the course of the summer. In 1760, Messrs. Duffield and Mills were sent to Virginia; and a general collection for the support of the Indian mission was ordered to be taken up. With the view of explaining the necessity for this collection, the Synod state that in consequence of the application of certain pious ministers, the society in Scotland for propagating Christian knowledge had made an annual grant, which was appropriated, first to David Brainerd, and afterwards to his brother John; who had continued to labour among the Indians for seven or eight years. In consequence of the war he had relinquished his mission and settled in Newark; but when the province of New Jersey, having reserved four thousand acres of land for the Indians, requested him, by its

* Minutes of New York and Philadelphia, p. 18.

governor, to resume his mission, he had upon the advice of the Synod, given up his comfortable settlement and recommenced his missionary labours. His support, and that of the Indian school, therefore, now rested on the Synod, who called on all the churches to make a collection and to send the proceeds to Mr. Jonathan Sergeant, near Princeton. President Davies was also directed to write to the society in Scotland, and request them to renew their grant.*

In 1761, an overture was made by Mr. Kirkpatrick, to send a missionary to the Oneida Indians, the importance of which the Synod acknowledged; but as no one could then be found to undertake the service, and as the necessary funds were not at command, the overture was declined. The Synod renewed their promises to support Mr. Brainerd, and ordered a new collection for that purpose. Numerous applications were, the same year, presented for missionaries to North Carolina.†

In 1762, a new order was made respecting the Indian mission; the money to be paid to the Rev. Mr. Ewing, in Philadelphia, or to Mr. Jonathan Sergeant, Princeton.‡ Messrs. Enoch Green and William Tennent, jun'r, were directed to serve each six months under the direction of the Presbytery of Hanover.§

In 1763, a new general collection was ordered for the Indian mission, and thirty pounds appropriated to the support of the schoolmaster. Mr. Occam, the missionary among the Oneida Indians, in the service of the British society, was taken under the care of the Synod, and sixty-five pounds appropriated to his use.‖ The same year a request was presented from the corporation of the Widows' Fund, that some missionaries might be sent to the frontier settlements, to ascertain where new congregations were forming, and what could be done to promote the spread of the gospel among them, and the neighbouring Indians. The board, which held in trust a fund received from the general assembly in Scotland, for propagating the gospel in this country, offered to pay the necessary expenses of the proposed mission. In consequence of this appli-

* Minutes, p. 29. † Ibid. pp. 50 and 52. ‡ Ibid. p. 62.
§ Ibid. p. 71. ‖ Ibid. p. 80.

cation, the Synod appointed Messrs. Beatty and Brainerd to go to the west, and to report to the board the result of their researches.* Mr. Green was appointed to act as a missionary within the bounds of the Presbyteries of Lewes and New Castle, and Mr. William Tennent and Jacob Ker within those of Hanover.† A committee was also appointed to confer with the corporation of the Widows' Fund, with regard to a plan for missionary operations.‡

It appears from the minutes for 1764, that the mission of Messrs. Beatty and Brainerd to the frontiers, was frustrated by the breaking out of the Indian war.§ A new collection was ordered for the support of Mr. Brainerd, and the interest of the fund in the hands of the trustees of New Jersey college was appropriated to his use.|| The same year the Synod, considering the state of many congregations in the south, particularly in North Carolina, and the great importance of having those congregations properly organized, appointed the Rev. Elihu Spencer, and Alexander McWhorter, as their missionaries for that purpose; that they might form societies, help them to adjust their bounds, ordain elders, administer sealing ordinances, instruct the people in discipline, and finally direct them in their conduct, particularly in what manner they should proceed to obtain the stated ministry. They were further directed to assure the people that the Synod had their interests much at heart, and would send them candidates and supplies to the utmost of their power.¶ This was just such a mission as that on which Timothy and Titus were sent, that they might "set in order the things that were wanting, and ordain elders in every city." It would have been perfectly consistent with our system had Messrs. Spencer and McWhorter been authorized to ordain preaching as well as ruling presbyters, had there been any probability of finding suitable candidates for the sacred office.

In 1765, Messrs. Nathan Ker, George Duffield, William Ramsay, David Caldwell, James Latta, and Robert McMurdie, were appointed to labour each six months in North Carolina.** A collection was again ordered for the Indian mission.††

* Minutes, p. 83. † Ibid. p. 88. ‡ Ibid. p. 94. § Ibid. p. 101.
|| Ibid. p. 103. ¶ Ibid. p. 108. ** Ibid. p. 120. †† Ibid. p. 127.

In 1766, it was ordered that every member of the Synod should take subscriptions, or make collections, in his congregation, and in the neighbouring vacancies, to raise a fund for the propagation of the gospel among the destitute.* It was also resolved to sustain the school under Mr. Brainerd. The Synod appointed Messrs. Lewis, Caldwell Chesnut, and Bay, to perform missionary duty at the south, and authorized Mr. C. T. Smith to itinerate in the same quarter.† Messrs. Beatty and Duffield were appointed missionaries to the frontiers, and directed to report to the corporation of the Widows' Fund.‡

In 1767, a report was made of the result of the collections of the preceding year, for sending the gospel to the poor, when it was found that only £112 had been received. The Synod expressed their great sorrow that so many of their members had paid so little regard to the authority of Synod enjoining a liberality for so pious and important a purpose. The Presbytery of New York brought in an overture on the subject of missions, which was amended and adopted. This overture provided that there should be an annual collection taken up in every congregation; that every Presbytery should appoint a treasurer to receive and transmit the moneys thus obtained; that the Synod should appoint a general treasurer to whom all these presbyterial collections should be sent; and that every year a full account of all receipts and disbursements should be printed and sent down among the churches. Mr. Richard Treat was appointed the synodical treasurer under this plan. Thirty pounds were appropriated to the support of Mr. Brainerd's school, and twenty as an addition to his salary.§ A committee appointed to confer with the corporation of the Widows' Fund, reported, "that, agreeably to an act of the General Assembly of the church of Scotland, passed in the year ——, the money raised by collections in the several congregations of that church shall be disposed of by the charitable corporation, in conjunction with a committee of the united Synod of New York and Philadelphia, for the support and relief of such ministers as are, or shall hereafter be called to preach the everlasting gospel among the benighted Indians, or

* Minutes, p. 146. † Ibid. p. 147. ‡ Ibid. p. 148. § Ibid. p. 163, 5.

to such congregations as cannot afford them maintenance." The committee added, they had not been able to ascertain the sum which was at the joint disposal of the corporation and the Synod; another committee was, therefore, appointed to ascertain the sum, and to assist in its appropriation.* A petition was presented from eight congregations in North Carolina, that Mr. Spencer, Lewis, McWhorter, or James Caldwell, might be sent to settle among them, offering to contribute a hundred and sixty pounds to the support of either of them. These gentlemen, however, all declined the invitation. Petitions for supplies were at the same time received from twenty-one places in Virginia, North and South Carolina, and Georgia.† The Synod appointed Messrs. Bay, Potter, Alexander, McCreary, James Latta, jun'r, Anderson, and Jackson, to visit those congregations, and spend at least six months each in their service. Messrs. Beatty and Duffield reported that they visited the frontiers, agreeably to the directions of the last Synod, and found a great number of people exceedingly desirous of being formed into congregations, and ready to do all that they could to support the gospel, though they were in very distressing circumstances, in consequence of the calamities of the late war. They also visited the Indians upon the Muskingum, a hundred and thirty miles beyond Fort Pitt, whom they found anxious to receive religious instruction. The Synod appointed Messrs. Brainerd and Cooper to visit the frontiers, and to spend three months among the Indians above-mentioned.‡ The same year Dr. Rodgers was sent on a mission of six weeks to Albany and the neighbouring places.

In 1768, Messrs. Brainerd and Cooper reported, that in consequence of the discouraging accounts brought by the Indian interpreter, they had not performed the mission assigned them by the last Synod. The usual appropriations were made for Mr. Brainerd's mission; a committee consisting of Dr. Alison, Messrs. Reed, Treat, Ewing, W. Tennent, Rodgers, Brainerd, McWhorter, Caldwell, Dr. Williamson, Charles Thomson, and the moderator, John Blair, was appointed to meet at Elizabethtown, to prepare a general plan for propagating the gospel among the Indians.§ The com-

* Minutes, p. 167. † Ibid. p. 171. ‡ Ibid. p. 173. § Ibid. p. 179.

mittee appointed to confer with the corporation of the Widows' Fund, respecting the money in their hands received from Scotland, and subject to the disposition of the Synod, reported that they proposed several questions to the Board, and had received the following answer. "That it is the sense of this Board, that though a corporate body may not, in the management of its affairs, legally associate with others not in membership, yet in regard to the limitation of the General Assembly of the church of Scotland, we judge it our duty to consult with the committee, and mutually to propose and agree with one another in the uses to which the money is to be applied; provided always, that if the Synod do not appoint a committee, or if that committee do not attend upon the corporation, it shall not be hindered to proceed to business;" and "that the interest of seven hundred pounds sterling is to be disposed of yearly for the time to come, if there be occasion for it, with the advice and consent of the Synod."* These answers were not deemed satisfactory, as they did not state what sum had been received from the General Assembly, nor what use the Board had made of it since it came into their hands. Objection was also taken to the claim of the Board of a right to dispose of the money without the concurrence of the Synod, in case of a failure in the appointment of a committee. The Synod, therefore, appointed another committee to endeavour to get this matter cleared up. Renewed supplications for supplies were presented from the frontiers of Pennsylvania, from Virginia, North and South Carolina; and the Synod appointed Messrs. Bay, Tate, Anderson, Jackson, and McCreary, for missionary service in these several places.†

In 1769, the usual appropriations were made for Mr. Brainerd. Messrs. John Harris, John Clark, Jeremiah Halsey, James Latta, Jonathan Elmore, Thomas Lewis, Josiah Lewis, H. J. Balch and James Anderson, were appointed as missionaries to the south. Dr. Alison, Messrs. Treat, Ewing, and Sproat, were appointed a committee to examine the credentials and to grant certificates to any licentiates or ministers from New England, who might offer themselves as missionaries to the southern provinces. The Synod engaged to pay

* Minutes, p. 181.

† Ibid. pp. 186, 188.

their missionaries at the rate of thirty shillings for every sabbath they preached. The Presbytery of New York was directed to supply the poor vacancies on the frontiers of New Jersey and New York ten sabbaths; and the Presbytery of Donegal those in Pennsylvania ten sabbaths.*

In 1770, numerous applications for supplies were presented from Virginia and Carolina, and Messrs. Lewis, Roe, Close, and McCreary, were appointed to labour in those provinces. Mr. Patrick Alison was sent to Virginia, and Mr. Nathan Niles, a licentiate from Massachusetts, was directed to labour during the summer on the western frontiers of New York, New Jersey, and Pennsylvania, and to spend the winter in Carolina. The Synod agreed to grant the Presbyteries of New York and Donegal each fifteen pounds towards the payment of supplies for the frontiers.†

In 1771, the usual appropriations were made for the support of Mr. Brainerd's mission. Messrs. James Finley, Samson Smith, Schenck, Alexander Miller, Eliphalet Ball, Elam Potter, Joseph Potter, and John McCreary, were appointed as missionaries to the south and west. Fifteen pounds were again appropriated to each of the Presbyteries of New York and Donegal for supplies. The committee of conference with the corporation of the widows' fund, reported that they had made a settlement with the Board, which the Synod subsequently sanctioned. The corporation agreed to pay the Synod annually thirty pounds, to be appropriated to the aid of poor ministers, or to the erection of churches, or the payment of missionaries within the Provinces of Pennsylvania, New Jersey, and Maryland. In consideration of this annual sum, the Synod agreed to acquiesce in and approve of such application of the money entrusted by the Scotch church for the use of the widows' fund, and all such other pious uses as have hitherto been made of it by the corporation. The Synod agreed never to break in upon the capital whence the said thirty pounds were to arise by way of interest; but, if found necessary, the Board were to have the right to use the capital in whole or in part. This, however, was not to be done unless the annuities due from the corporation could not

* Minutes, pp. 204, 205. † Ibid. pp. 213, 215, 226.

otherwise be paid. The Synod was to receive the interest of the remaining portion of the fund at the rate of five per centum, should the corporation at any time find it necessary to use a part of the capital. It was finally agreed that this arrangement should put an end to all debates between the Synod and the Board in reference to this matter.* It does not appear that the Synod ever succeeded in finding out the sum originally received from Scotland; or the uses to which it had hitherto been applied. In this minute the Board say they considered the fund as equal to six hundred pounds, which, as nothing is said to the contrary, probably means pounds currency; whereas three years before the sum was seven hundred pounds sterling. It is evident the corporation considered themselves as having the legal disposal of the money, and as the Synod acquiesced in their measures, it is to be presumed that this was acknowledged on their part. The funds of the corporation were so much injured by the depreciation of money during the revolutionary war, that in 1782 the Synod agreed to remit this fund to them to be applied to the ends of their institution.†

In 1772, a new general collection was ordered; and it was directed that the moneys thus raised should be appropriated for the support of missionaries, the purchase and distribution of useful books, and the promotion of the gospel among the Indians. A committee was appointed in New York and Philadelphia, to procure books and distribute them to the several Presbyteries. The books to be purchased were Bibles, Westminster Confession of Faith, Vincent's Catechism, Doddridge's Rise and Progress of Religion, Alleine's Alarm, A Compassionate Address to the Christian World, Watts' Divine Songs, and the Assembly's Catechism. A pastoral letter was addressed to the churches, urging the importance of the ends to be answered by the proposed collection upon their attention. Missionary appointments were, as usual, made for the south and west.‡

In 1773, it was reported that Mr. Brainerd's school was discontinued the preceding year for want of a teacher; and forty-three pounds were appropriated towards his support. Twenty pounds

* Minutes, p. 147. † Ibid. p. 383. ‡ Ibid. pp. 255, 257, 261.

were assigned to each of the committees in Philadelphia and New York for the purchase of books; and the Presbytery of New York were allowed to appropriate fifty pounds of the money collected within their bounds towards rebuilding the Presbyterian Church in the Island of Saba. The Presbytery of New Castle were appointed to send certain missionaries to the south, whose credentials were to be signed by the moderator of the Synod.*

In 1774, the usual appropriations were made for Mr. Brainerd. Dr. Rodgers, Mr. McWhorter, and Mr. Caldwell, were appointed to visit the northern part of New York, for the purpose of preaching and organizing congregations. Urgent applications for supplies were received from Pennsylvania, Virginia, and North Carolina. A representation was also presented to the Synod from the Rev. Dr. Ezra Stiles and the Rev. Samuel Hopkins, respecting a mission to Africa,† which brought up the subject of slavery. A committee was appointed to prepare an overture on these subjects and report to the Synod. The first part of the report of this committee was adopted as follows: "The Synod is very happy to have an opportunity to express their readiness to concur with and assist in a mission to the African tribes, and especially where so many circumstances concur, as in the present case, to intimate that it is the will of God, and to encourage us to hope for success. We assure the gentlemen aforesaid, we are ready to do all that is proper for us in our station for their encouragement and assistance." The part of the report which related to slavery was deferred to the next meeting of the Synod. As nothing is said of the African mission after this, it is presumed that the war, which commenced the following year, prevented the plan's being carried into effect. Seven missionaries were sent to the south and west, and the several Presbyteries were urged to render what further assistance they could.‡

* Minutes, pp. 277, 288.

† For a full account of the scheme of Dr. Hopkins and Dr. Stiles, to send missionaries to Africa, and the reasons of its ultimate failure, see Princeton Review and Biblical Repertory, for April, 1840.

‡ Minutes, pp. 295, 297, 305, 307.

In 1775, Messrs. Brooks, Debow, Keith, Hunter, and Phithian, were appointed as missionaries to the south and west; and Messrs. Lewis and Ker to Albany, Charlotte, and Tryon counties, in the Province of New York. Mr. Miller was directed to supply every fifth Sabbath until the next Synod, in the vacancies in the neighbourhood of Schenectady.*

In 1776, Messrs. McGill, White, and Carmichael, were appointed missionaries to the western part of Pennsylvania, and the Presbyteries of New Castle and Philadelphia were urged to send missionaries to the south. Nothing is said of the mission under Mr. Brainerd for several years, except the annual order that he should be paid the interest of the three hundred pounds belonging to the Synod in the hands of the trustees of the College of New Jersey.†

In 1777, a society of Highland Scots at Southerland, presented a petition to the Synod requesting a supply of books, and that the Rev. Mr. McFarquhar might be appointed to preach and administer gospel ordinances among them. And the Synod ordered a collection of books to be made for them, and appointed Mr. McFarquhar to supply them for some time.‡

In 1778, there was a very thinly attended meeting of the Synod at Bedminster, Somerset County, New Jersey. The minutes contain no record in relation to missions.

In 1779, Dr. Witherspoon, the treasurer of the Synod, reported that he had received the legacy left by the Rev. Diodati Johnson of Connecticut, for the aid of missions to the southern colonies.§ From a subsequent minute, it appears that the money received was two hundred and eighty-seven pounds and a fraction.|| A member of the Presbytery of Hanover, requested that "some missionaries might be sent to the State of Virginia to preach the gospel, and especially that a few ministers of genius, prudence, and address, might spend some considerable time in attempting to form the people into regular congregations under the discipline and govern-

* Minutes, pp. 331, 332. † Ibid. p. 337, 338, 339. ‡ Ibid. p. 350.

§ Ibid. p. 360, compare p. 295. || Ibid. p. 377.

ment of the Presbyterian Church, and to settle among them, and undertake the education of youth; representing, there appears at present, in many parts of that state, a very favourable disposition towards religion in general, and towards the Presbyterian Church in particular; that it is greatly for the interest of the church to pay particular attention to the southern and western parts of this continent; that congregations which may be formed there will be permanent and fixed, whereas the continual migration of the inhabitants in our interior congregations diminishes their importance and threatens their dissolution; that it is not desirable nor to be expected that that extensive country should continue long without some form of religion; that this Synod has now an opportunity of promoting the interests of religion extensively, which in a few years may be utterly lost by the prevalence and preoccupancy of many ignorant and irregular sectaries." The Synod, in consequence of this representation, earnestly recommended it to all their Presbyteries to turn their attention to this subject as peculiarly interesting and important.*

During the years 1780, '81, and '82, the Synod was able to do but little in the service of missions. In 1783, it was ordered that every member of the Synod "shall use his utmost influence in the congregation under his inspection, and in the vacancies contiguous to it, to raise contributions for the purchase of Bibles for distribution among the poor, and that Drs. Ewing and Sproat, and Mr. Duffield, be a committee to receive such contributions, to purchase Bibles, and to send them to the several members of the Synod, who, in conjunction with their respective sessions, shall distribute them."† This subject was afterwards repeatedly urged upon the attention of the churches.‡

ACTION OF THE SYNOD IN REFERENCE TO EDUCATION AND LEARNING.

With regard to education, the influence of the Synod was constantly and beneficially exerted by insisting on proper literary

* Minutes, p. 362. † Ibid. p. 398. ‡ Ibid. pp. 405, 414.

qualifications in the candidates for the ministry, by patronizing schools and colleges, and by making provision for the education of the poor. The literary institutions in which the Synod were particularly interested, were the academy at Newark, Delaware, and the college of New Jersey. The trustees of the former were almost all members of the Synod, on whose application for a general collection in aid of the institution, it was agreed to countenance the measure and to recommend the academy to the charity of all the churches.* In 1773, the Rev. Dr. Ewing and Dr. Hugh Williamson, a man distinguished for his scientific attainments, and an elder in the Presbyterian church, visited England to solicit benefactions in behalf of this academy. Though it owed its origin to the Synod of Philadelphia, and though at the time of its incorporation in 1769, all its clerical, and, it is believed, most of its lay trustees were Presbyterians,† it has of late years passed into the hands of the Episcopalians, and is now known as Newark College. With the college at Princeton, the connection of the Synod was far more intimate, and the efforts made for its support were frequent and strenuous.

For some time after the union, the arrangement which had been made between the Synod of Philadelphia and the trustees in London, for the support of German schools, was continued, and a committee annually appointed to dispose of the appropriation received from that source.‡

In 1760, a proposition was made for the appointment and support of a professor of divinity, which the Synod recommended to the consideration of the Presbyteries, that some plan might be devised for the accomplishment of the object.§ The following year, though the Synod agreed "to promote this good purpose, yet from

* Minutes, p. 243.

† The original trustees were, Hon. William Allen, Rev. Dr. Francis Alison, Rev. Alexander McDowell, Rev. John Ewing, Rev. William McKennen, Rev. Patrick Alison, Rev. Matthew Wilson, Dr. Hugh Williamson, Mr. Charles Thompson, Andrew Allen, Esq., Thomas McKean, Esq., Mr. John Mease, and Thomas Evans, Esq.

‡ Minutes, pp. 21, 31.

§ Ibid. p. 36.

the pressure of other calls, and the want of funds, they were obliged to defer it." Deeply sensible, however, "that the church suffered greatly for want of an opportunity to instruct students in the knowledge of divinity, it was agreed that every student, after he has been admitted to his first degree in college, shall read carefully, on this subject, at least one year, under the care of some minister of approved character for his skill in theology, and under his direction shall discuss difficult questions in divinity, study the sacred Scriptures, form sermons, lectures, and such other useful exercises as may be directed in the course of his studies. And it is enjoined likewise, that every preacher for the first year after his licensure, shall show all his sermons to some minister in our Presbyteries, on whose friendship and candour he depends, written fairly, to have them corrected and amended. And as they are but young preachers, we are persuaded that no better method can be taken in present circumstances to improve them in Christian knowledge, and render them eminently useful in their station. It is also enjoined that they preach as often as they can before stated ministers, that they may correct their gestures, pronunciation, delivery, and the like. And it is further enjoined, that all our ministers and probationers forbear reading their sermons from the pulpit, if they can conveniently."*

In 1768, in consequence of a request from the trustees of the college of New Jersey, that the Synod would aid in the support of a professor of divinity in that institution, a general collection was ordered for that purpose, and fifty pounds were appropriated towards the salary of the Rev. John Blair, who had been elected to that office.† The wants of the college at this time were so pressing, that in the following year the Synod appointed a committee in every part of the church, for the purpose of raising funds for its support. In consequence of this application, the Presbytery of New Brunswick addressed a memorial to the churches under their care, setting forth the condition and claims of the college. They state that its permanent funds, though once considerable, had been reduced by necessary expenditures to £1300, and must be still further reduced, as the officers could not be supported by the fees

* Minutes, p. 48.

† Ibid. p. 186.

for tuition, without making those fees so high as seriously to interfere with the usefulness of the institution. It was urged that the college had peculiar claims on our church. Even in 1767, there were not fewer than eighty of her sons ministers of the gospel dispersed through the several colonies, since which time there had been considerable addition to the number. "The eyes," it is said, "of by far the greater number of our vacant churches are turned to that college for a supply of ministers; especially the churches in New Jersey and the southern colonies. That from the principles there taught and received, we have reason to think that useful instruments not only have been, but from time to time will be raised up to propagate the pure evangelical doctrines of the gospel, and to make a stand against such as might be glad to abridge our liberties, and to bring us under the yoke of ecclesiastical power; instruments to plead the cause of liberty and religion, and to make our church respectable."* This effort in behalf of the college was continued for several years, with what result is not fully known, except that it is stated, that the several committees had "been very diligent and successful."†

During the period now under review, viz.: from 1758 to 1789, the college was under the presidency of Mr. Davies, of Dr. Samuel Finley, and of Dr. Witherspoon. Mr. Davies entered upon the duties of his office July 26, 1759, and died February 4, 1761, so that he was president little more than eighteen months. Short as was his administration, his talents, and his devotion to his duties, rendered it eminently serviceable to the institution. His successor, Dr. Samuel Finley, entered on his duties as president, July, 1761, and died July 16, 1766. He was a native of Armagh in Ireland, but removed to this country in 1734, in the nineteenth year of his age. He was licensed by the New Brunswick Presbytery in 1740, and preached with great success, especially in Pennsylvania and in the lower counties of New Jersey. In 1744, he settled at Not-

* Minutes of the Presbytery of New Brunswick, p. 310.

† Minutes of Synod, pp. 221, 237.—It appears from the minutes of the Presbytery of Donegal, that in 1772, five hundred and fifty-five pounds had been subscribed within their bounds for the college. p. 61.

tingham in Maryland, where he remained for seventeen years. He there instituted an academy which enjoyed a wide and deserved reputation. "He was justly famed as a scholar, and eminently qualified as a teacher." Dr. John Woodhull, who was one of his pupils, speaks of him as being always solemn and instructive, and often fervent in the pulpit, as extensively learned, and as greatly beloved and respected by his students. Under his administration the college was very flourishing, and his own reputation rapidly extending, when he was cut down in the prime of life. About a year after he entered on the presidency, there was an extensive revival of religion in the college, in which fifty of the students, about one half of the whole number then in the institution, were supposed to have become sincerely pious.

Dr. Finley died in July, 1766: the November following, Dr. Witherspoon was unanimously elected president. Before this appointment was known, a number of gentlemen attached to that portion of the church which, before the union of the two Synods, had belonged to the Synod of Philadelphia, waited upon the trustees to propose the establishment of several professorships in the college, upon a plan which should unite the whole church in the support of the institution. The committee of the trustees appointed to confer with these gentlemen reported, that their proposals being based upon the assumption that the president's chair was vacant, their plan had been disconcerted by the appointment of Dr. Witherspoon, and consequently they could not answer for what their constituents would do under these altered circumstances, but that they were nevertheless truly desirous to complete the proposed design. The committee inquired whether, on the supposition of the nomination of two gentlemen for professorships, viz.: Messrs. Blair and McDowell,* on condition that funds should be raised for their support, their constituents would be satisfied." To this the gentlemen replied, that, however desirous they were to accomplish so excellent a design, they could not engage for the future

* "These gentlemen, Mr. Blair of the new-side and Mr. McDowell of the old-side party, were both of high standing in the public estimation, and of unquestionable excellence of character." — Dr. Green.

conduct of their constituents. The board taking into consideration the above report came to the following resolution: "Whereas it is an object of the greatest concern, that union and the strictest harmony among all the friends and patrons of religion and sound literature, might be promoted by every proper method, and that this institution may have every possible advantage of increasing its reputation, and the cause of learning; and as there appears reason to expect great and happy consequences, both to the interests of religion and of this seminary, from putting into execution the general design of the proposals made, they will gladly do every thing in their power to accomplish the said end; and accordingly declare themselves greatly desirous that a sufficiency of moneys by subscription or otherwise, might be obtained to accomplish this noble design; and are cheerfully willing to join in any particular method that can be devised for raising the necessary sums. For though this board would gladly proceed to the election of professors without delay, were their funds sufficient to support such an additional expense, yet they judge it by no means expedient to take that step before they have a certain medium for their support."

The following year this negotiation was renewed. A number of gentlemen again attended the meeting of the board, and a committee was appointed to confer with them. This committee reported that they found them and their constituents still very desirous of concurring with the trustees of the college in the establishment and support of a faculty, and promising to unite their utmost endeavours to raise the necessary funds; that the said gentlemen being asked by the committee, whether the appointment of all or of any of the particular persons to professorships named and recommended in their proposals, was intended as a term of their acceding to and assisting in the establishment proposed, replied, that it was not intended to make the appointment of any particular persons named by their constituents, a term of the proposed union, but that any other gentlemen who might be deemed qualified for their offices, and indiscriminately chosen without regard to party distinctions, would be acceptable to them. The board taking the subject into consideration, were unanimously of the opinion, that the constitution of a faculty, to consist of well-qualified professors, to be chosen without any regard to little party differences, would greatly subserve the interest of religion and learning in this seminary. They, therefore, determined to proceed to such an election; and accordingly the following day chose the Rev. John Blair professor of divinity and moral philosophy; Dr. Hugh Williamson professor of mathematics and natural philosophy; Mr. Jonathan Edwards professor of languages and logic; and, as Dr. Witherspoon, in consequence of the unwillingness of his wife to leave Scotland, had declined the presidency, the Rev. Samuel Blair was chosen president and professor of rhetoric and metaphysics. For the want of funds these appointments were conditional, and, with the exception of that of Mr. John Blair, were not to take effect for a year, and in the meantime, the college was to be conducted by Mr. Blair and three tutors. Before the expiration of the year the difficulty in the way of Dr. Witherspoon's accepting the presidency was removed, and Mr. Samuel Blair, having generously withdrawn his name, Dr. Witherspoon was re-elected, and arrived in this country August, 1768, and was inaugurated as president on the seventeenth of that month.*

The deficiency in the pecuniary resources of the college prevented the above plan being carried into effect. Even Mr. Blair, to relieve the funds of the institution, resigned his office as professor of divinity, and devolved the duties upon Dr. Witherspoon. Under the auspices of the latter, the college soon began to flourish, its course of instruction was enlarged, its students increased, and the funds necessary for its support were supplied. The revolution-

* The above details respecting the college of New Jersey are derived from Dr. Green's history of the college, already repeatedly referred to. It would seem that the clergy of what was called the old-side, in the Synod, took no direct part in the negotiations for the enlargment of the faculty of the college. At least on both occasions the delegation which waited on the trustees was composed of laymen; in 1766, they were Messrs. George Bryan, John Johnson, William Alison, James Mease, and Samuel Purviance; and in 1767, Messrs. George Bryan, William Alison, John Chevalier, John Boyd, and John Wallace.

ary war, however, soon put a stop to this course of improvement. The college was, in a great measure, disbanded, and though a class graduated in each year, the number of annual graduates was often not more than four or five. When peace returned, prosperity returned to the college, and it continued to reward the labours of its pious founders, by contributing largely to the supply of educated ministers to the church. The number of clergymen educated at this college before 1789, was two hundred and twenty-nine.

In 1771, a plan for the education of poor and pious young men for the ministry, was laid before the Synod by the Presbytery of New Castle, which was approved. This plan provided that every vacant congregation receiving supplies, should pay two pounds towards an education fund, every minister one pound, and that voluntary subscriptions from other quarters should be solicited. Every Presbytery was to appoint a treasurer, to examine candidates, to direct their studies, &c. Every beneficiary was to spend one year after licensure in the service of the Presbytery by which he had been educated; and in case he did not enter the ministry, he was to give a bond to refund the money expended in his behalf within five years.* It appears from the minutes for the following year, that the Presbyteries of New York, New Brunswick, and the second of Philadelphia, had fully complied with the above recommendation, and that several others had done so partially.†

In 1775, the question was proposed, whether a Presbytery could, with propriety, take any candidate upon trial unless furnished with a diploma from some college. The Synod the following year answered, that the advantages of a public education rendered it highly expedient that all candidates should finish their academical studies in some public institution, yet as the Presbyteries were the proper judges of the requisite qualifications of their candidates, it was not intended to preclude from admission to trial all who had not enjoyed those advantages.‡

In 1783, at the request of the Presbytery of Philadelphia, the question was considered, whether a person without a liberal educa-

* Minutes, p. 242.

† Ibid. p. 273. See also p. 294.

‡ Ibid. pp. 318, and 342.

tion may be taken on trials, or licensed to preach the gospel? which was answered in the negative.* And in 1785, the same question came up in a different form, viz.: whether, in the present state of the church in America, and the scarcity of ministers to fill our vacancies, the Synod or Presbyteries ought to relax in any degree in the literary qualifications required of intrants into the ministry? and it was carried in the negative by a great majority."† These decisions, considering the circumstances of the case, certainly reflect great credit upon the Synod.

The same year it was proposed that no candidate should be taken on trial until he shall have employed two years at least in the study of divinity, after his having passed the usual course of a liberal education. This proposition, after discussion, was laid over to the following year, and then, "considering," as the Synod say, "the present circumstances of our churches, it was decided in the negative."‡ It was at the same time "enjoined on every Presbytery to subject every candidate on trials for the ministry, to an accurate examination on the discipline of the Presbyterian Church."

The attention of the Synod, however, was not confined to candidates for the ministry, but "considering the education of youth, and their being early instructed in the principles of religion, as one of the most useful means of promoting the influence of religion in our churches, they resolved, that it be enjoined on every Presbytery, in appointing supplies to their vacant congregations, to take order that every vacant congregation within their limits be carefully catechized at least once in every year, in the same manner as is required by the order of our church in congregations supplied with regular pastors; and that the ministers appointed to this duty be required to render an account of their fidelity in this respect.

"Resolved, also, that it be enjoined on all our congregations to pay a special regard to the good education of children, as being intimately connected with the interests of religion and morality; and that, as schools, under a bad master and careless management, are seminaries of vice rather than of virtue, the session, corporation, or committee of every congregation be required to endeavour

* Minutes, p. 396. † Ibid. p. 425. ‡ Ibid. p. 427.

to establish schools in such place or places as shall be most convenient for the people; that they be particularly careful to procure able and virtuous teachers; that they make the erection and care of schools a part of their congregational business, and endeavour to induce the people to support them by contributions, being not only the most effectual, but, in the end, the cheapest way of supporting them; that the Presbyteries appoint particular members, or, if possible, committees, to go into vacant congregations to promote similar institutions; that the corporation, session, or committee of the congregation, visit the school or schools at least once in three months, to inquire into the conduct of the master, and the improvement of the children, and to observe particularly his care to instruct them at least one day in the week, in the principles of religion; that the Presbyteries, in appointing ministers to supply vacant congregations, require it as an indispensable part of their duty, to visit at the same time the schools, and require at the next meeting of the Presbytery, an account of their fidelity in this respect, and of the state of the schools; and that in these schools effectual provision be made for the education of the children of the poor; and that at the visitation of the schools one or two of the most ingenuous and virtuous of the poor children be selected annually, in order to give them a more perfect education, and thereby qualify these ingenuous charity-scholars to become afterwards useful instructers in our charity-schools."*

THE STANDARD OF DOCTRINE IN THE SYNOD.

The standard of doctrine established and maintained during this period was the Westminster Confession of Faith. In the first article of the plan of union, it is said, "both Synods having always approved and received the Westminster Confession of Faith, and the Larger and Shorter Catechisms as an orthodox and excellent system of Christian doctrine, we do still receive the same as the confession of our faith." In all the Presbyteries every licentiate, or new member, was required to adopt this confession. The Synod

* Minutes, pp. 428, 429.

allowed of no departure from this rule. In 1764, the Presbytery of Suffolk were blamed for "neglecting to record their candidates adopting our public standards at licensure, though they inform us," it is added, "that it is matter of constant practice."*

Thus also the Synod itself, in receiving either a new member, or a new Presbytery, insisted on the same condition. In 1765, it is recorded that the Rev. Jonathan Leavitt, "after adopting the Westminster Confession of Faith, as the confession of his faith, and having promised to conform himself to the Westminster Directory for worship and government, was received as a member of the Synod, and was advised to put himself under the care of some one of our Presbyteries."† In 1763, a request was presented from a Presbytery in New York, to the east of the North River, to be incorporated with the Synod; and it was "agreed to grant their request, provided that they agree to adopt our Westminster Confession of Faith and Catechisms, and engage to observe the Directory as a plan of worship, discipline, and government, according to the agreement of this Synod."‡ This Presbytery complied with these stipulations, and was accordingly admitted.§ In answer to a similar application, made in 1770, from the Presbytery of South Carolina, the Synod replied, "the only conditions which we require, are, that all your ministers acknowledge and adopt, as the standard of doctrine, the Westminster Confession of Faith and Catechisms, and the Directory as the plan of your worship and discipline."||

That this adoption of the Confession of Faith was strict and unequivocal, is strongly asserted both by Presbyteries and Synod. In 1768, the Presbytery of New Brunswick having a missionary in Nova Scotia, had occasion to write a letter to a gentleman in that country, in which they say: "We hear that our Synod has been injuriously represented in your parts, as being lax in principle and discipline. But we assure you, sir, the charge is utterly groundless. The Westminster Confession of Faith is received here without equivocation, and in the true and proper sense of the words. The doctrines of grace are truly taught, and discipline is regu-

* Minutes, p. 107. † Ibid. p. 127. ‡ Ibid. p. 91.

§ Ibid. p. 130. || Ibid. p. 223.

larly and faithfully exercised." At the same time they wrote to the Rev. Mr. Murdock, a seceding minister in Nova Scotia, to whom they say: "We assure you, dear sir, the public standards of the Church of Scotland are our standards. We receive the Westminster Confession of Faith in the true grammatical sense of the words, and are strictly Calvinistic. And the Westminster Directory is the model of our worship and government."* These letters were signed by John Blair, as moderator, and William Kirkpatrick, as clerk.

In like manner a committee of the Synod, in their name and with their sanction, declared, in 1786, "the Synod of New York and Philadelphia adopt, according to the known and established meaning of the terms, the Westminster Confession of Faith as the confession of their faith; save that every candidate for the gospel ministry is permitted to except against so much of the twenty-third chapter as gives authority to civil magistrates in matters of religion. The Presbyterian Church in America considers the church of Christ as a spiritual society, entirely distinct from the civil government, and having a right to regulate their own ecclesiastical policy, independently of the interposition of the magistrate. The Synod also receive the Directory for public worship, and the form of church government, recommended by the Westminster Assembly, as in substance agreeable to the institutions of the New Testament. This mode of adoption we use because we believe the general platform of our government to be agreeable to the sacred Scriptures; but we do not believe that God has been pleased to reveal and enjoin every minute circumstance of ecclesiastical government and discipline as not to leave room for orthodox churches of Christ, in these minutiæ, to differ with charity from each other.

"The rules of our discipline, and the form of process in our church judicatures, are contained in Pardovan's, alias Stewart's Collections, in conjunction with the acts of our own Synod, the power of which in matters merely ecclesiastical, we consider as equal to the power of any Synod or General Assembly in the world. Our church judicatures, like those in the church of Scot-

* Minutes of New Brunswick Presbytery, pp. 283 and 286.

land, from which we derive our origin, are Church Sessions, Presbyteries, and Synods, to which it is now in contemplation to add a national and General Assembly."*

That the Synod really maintained as well as professed this standard of doctrine, is evident from the case of the Rev. Samuel Harker, to which reference has already been repeatedly made in this history. That gentleman was a member of the Presbytery of New Brunswick, and by them his case was referred to the Synod, who appointed a committee, of which Mr. Pierson was the chairman, to meet with and endeavour to convince him of his errors. This committee subsequently reported that they were happy to find, from Mr. Harker's explanations, that his views were correct as to some of the points on which he was supposed to be erroneous, but that as to others, he had departed from our standards. The Synod considered this report so encouraging, that they directed him to go to Nottingham and converse with Messrs. Samuel and James Finley, John Blair, Robert and Samson Smith, and on his return, with Messrs. Treat, Tennent, Ewing, and Alison, in Philadelphia, in hopes that his conversion might be completed. These hopes, however, were disappointed. Mr. Harker published a book in which he set forth and defended his peculiar views. When the Synod met in 1762, they committed this book to Messrs. Spencer, Rodgers, Blair, Laurence, McDowell, Wilson, and Robert Smith, with directions to examine it and make a report to the Synod. This report was not presented until the following year, when it appeared that Mr. Harker taught, "1st. That the covenant of grace is in such a sense conditional, that fallen mankind, in their unregenerate state, by the general assistance given to men under the gospel, have a sufficient ability to fulfil the conditions thereof, and so by their own endeavours to insure to themselves regenerating grace and all saving blessings. 2d. That God has bound himself by promise to give them regenerating grace, upon their fulfilling what he, (Mr. Harker,) calls the direct conditions of obtaining it; and upon the whole, makes a certain and infallible connection between their endeavours and the aforesaid blessings. 3d. That God's pre-

* Minutes, p. 443.

science of future events is previous to, and not dependent on his decrees; that his decrees have no influence on his own conduct; and that the foresight of faith is the ground of the decree of election. It is further observed, that he often uses inaccurate, unintelligible, and dangerous forms of expression, which tend to lead people into false notions in several important matters; as that Adam was the federal head of his posterity, in the second covenant as well as the first; that the regenerate are not (?) in a state of probation for heaven, and such like.

"The Synod judged that these principles are of a hurtful and dangerous tendency, giving a false view of the covenant of grace, perverting it into a new-modelled covenant of works, and misrepresenting the doctrine of the divine decrees as held by the best reformed churches; and, in fine, contrary to the word of God, and our approved standards of doctrine." Mr. Harker was then called in and questioned on many particulars, and the Synod after referring to their several unsuccessful attempts to convince him of his errors, say that he appeared "to be rather confirmed and resolute in propagating his opinions among the people, by a variety of methods, to the great scandal of the church, seducing and perplexing the unwary and unstable; and as he has departed from the truth, and opposed this church in some important articles, and misrepresented the church of Scotland, his doctrine and practice have a schismatical tendency. On the whole, though the exclusion of a member be grievous, yet we judge that the said Mr. Samuel Harker cannot consistently be continued a member of this body, and accordingly declare him to be disqualified for preaching or exercising his ministry in any congregation or vacancy under our care; and do hereby order that all be duly warned not to receive his doctrine, nor admit his ministration, until it shall please God to convince him of his mistakes, and bring him to the acknowledgment of the truth, and recover him from the error of his ways."* As the Synod was thus strict in enforcing adherence to our standards, the fact that this is the only case of discipline for erroneous doctrine recorded on their minutes, during the period from 1758 to

* Minutes, pp. 88, 89.

1789, is satisfactory proof of the general orthodoxy of the body. It is probable there never was a period of equal length in the history of our church, in which there was such a general and cordial agreement among our ministers on all doctrinal subjects.

FORM OF GOVERNMENT. — ORDINARY POWERS.

In illustrating the constitution of the Synod, we shall, agreeably to the plan hitherto pursued, arrange its acts under the general heads of ordinary and extraordinary; meaning by ordinary, such as are conformed to our present usages; and by extraordinary, such as differ from them in a greater or less degree.

To the former of these classes belong of course the formation and alteration of Presbyteries. The Synod was called upon immediately after its formation to enter upon this business, in accordance with one of the provisions of the plan of union. It was agreed that the Presbyteries of Suffolk and New York should continue as they were; that Messrs. Cowell and Guild should be annexed to the Presbytery of New Brunswick; that Messrs. Cross, G. Tennent, Alison, Treat, Chesnut, Martin, Beatty, Greenman, Hunter, Ramsay, Lawrence, and Kinkead, should constitute the Presbytery of Philadelphia; that Messrs. Wilson, Miller, Tuttle, and Henry, should be the Presbytery of Lewes; that the first and second Presbyteries of New Castle, and the Presbytery of Donegal, should, for the present, continue as they were; and that Messrs. Creaghead, Black, Craig, Miller, Davies, Todd, Henry, Wright, Brown, and Martain, should be the Presbytery of Hanover.*

The following year Messrs. Robert Smith, John Roan, Samson Smith, and John Hoge, were attached to the Presbytery of Donegal, and the first and second Presbyteries of New Castle were united, with the provision that these changes should not interfere with the liberties of the several congregations within the bounds of those Presbyteries, provided for in the plan of union.†

In 1762, in consequence of a difference of opinion among the

* Minutes, pp. 7 and 8.

† Ibid. p. 15.

members of the Presbytery of Philadelphia, as to the examination of candidates for the ministry on their personal experience in religion, Messrs. Robert Cross, Francis Alison, John Ewing, John Symington, and James Latta, were formed into a Presbytery for one year, to be called the second Presbytery of Philadelphia.* In 1763, the congregations of West Nottingham and Little Britain, together with the Rev. Messrs. Hunt and Strain, with their congregations, were set off from the Presbytery of New Castle to that of Donegal.† The same year the Presbytery of Duchess in New York, was received, as already mentioned. The question whether the second Presbytery of Philadelphia should be continued, was deferred from year to year until 1766, when it was voted to allow it to remain. Against this decision several members dissented for substantially the following reasons. 1. The decision has an obvious appearance of disunion, and has a schismatical tendency, and will be likely to perpetuate party distinctions. 2. As it is the sense of the Synod that it is the duty of Presbyteries to inquire into a candidate's experimental acquaintance with religion, it involves this body in a self-contradiction to erect a Presbytery which expressly refuses it. 3. While nothing is imposed on persons in point of practice, which they in their conscience judge sinful, and they are not restrained from doing their duty, the rights of conscience are not violated, though, they being a minority, a matter in judicature shall be carried against them by vote. Therefore it is vain to urge the rights of conscience in such cases. And for any to signify that they will not be subject, even in such cases, to the regulations of Synod, but if contradicted will violently break off, is to prefer the private rights of individuals to the public rights, and will destroy all governing authority in the body. 4. It is a very bad precedent which may be pleaded by others for the division of Presbyteries, and by this means congregations now united may be divided, and the formation of new societies prevented. These reasons were signed by Messrs. William Tennent, Charles McKnight, John Blair, William Tennent, Jun., Azael Roe, John Carmichael, Robert Smith, Jacob Ker, David Rose, Nathan Ker,

* Minutes, p. 74. † Ibid. p. 93.

and Simon Horton. Before the schism of 1741, the old-side members, so to call them, being the majority of the Synod, were the advocates of its authority, and the new-side members the remonstrants against its exercise. After the union in 1758, the new-side members being the majority, became the advocates of authority, and the old-side members remonstrants. Of the correctness of this statement, the reader will find in the sequel many illustrations. In the present instance we find the Messrs. Tennent, Blair, &c., complaining that the governing authority of the Synod would be destroyed if its regulations might be disobeyed, except in cases in which they were deemed sinful. And as the members of the New Brunswick Presbytery before the schism pleaded conscience for their disobedience to an act of Synod, so the second Presbytery of Philadelphia made a similar plea on the present occasion.

The same difference of opinion which caused this separation of the Presbytery of Philadelphia, produced still greater difficulties in that of Donegal. In 1765, the Synod having maturely considered the situation of affairs in that Presbytery, determined to erect the members living on the west side of the Susquehanna, together with the Rev. Andrew Bay, into a new Presbytery, to be called the Presbytery of Carlisle, and to attach the remaining members to the Presbytery of New Castle.* Against this decision, the Rev. Messrs. Tate, Beard, Elder, Samson Smith, McMurdie, and Steel, members of the Presbytery of Donegal, remonstrated; because it gave them no relief from the grievances of which they complained, and because it was unjust to dispose of a Presbytery without consulting its members, or allowing them to vote. The Synod consented to review the case, but adhered to their decision, saying, that those brethren were so much interested in the matter, that they had no right to a vote in reference to it, though they ought to have been consulted on the subject. The Synod further expressed the hope that they would find their grievances removed in their new connection, and stated that the Presbytery of New Castle was so small, that the members to the east of the Susquehanna ought to be joined to it, and that it should be henceforth called the Presbytery of Lancaster.†

* Minutes, p. 123.

† Ibid. p. 126.

Messrs. McDowell and Ewing entered their dissent from the foregoing decision, because it made the situation of the dissatisfied brethren worse than it was before; because they had unjustly been deprived of a right to vote in the case; because the Presbytery of Donegal had been destroyed without allowing one of its members any voice in the affair; and because this proceeding was inconsistent with the plan of union, which provided that the Presbyteries then subsisting should not be united, except when it was found for edification. The next year, (1766,) Messrs. Tate and Beard presented a petition to have this decision reviewed. The Synod accordingly put it to vote, whether their former judgment should be reversed, and by a great majority decided that it should stand. It was then proposed that the Presbytery of Donegal, as it existed before the last Synod, should be restored, those members excepted who had been set off to the Carlisle Presbytery, and it was decided in the negative. Another expedient was proposed, viz.: that the dissatisfied members of the old Donegal Presbytery should be allowed for one year to join the second Presbytery of Philadelphia. This also was rejected by a great majority. The following protest against these decisions was entered on the minutes: "We are obliged, (though with great grief,) to enter our dissent from, and declare our protest against the conduct and votes of this judicature respecting the late Donegal Presbytery, for such reasons as these, '1. Because our distressed brethren always declared a scruple of conscience as the foundation of their petition and behaviour, viz.: That they could not in conscience submit to the examination of the hearts or experiences of candidates in the way voted by the Synod, as they esteemed it contrary to the word of God, to common sense, and the uniform practice of the Protestant churches; consequently, whether well or ill informed, it was a matter that could not be voted away. 2. Because it appeared very untender and unbrotherly to deny that those members could be conscientious in the affair, when they declared they were so. We cannot judge what matters will affect other men's consciences. 3. Because even the smallest matter, if imposed against the rights of conscience, obliges the injured to leave the communion. To exclude men from exercising the power of ordination, unless they submit to it in a way contrary to their judgment, is such an imposition; and, therefore, the schism, in consequence hereof, is to be attributed to the imposers, and not to those who are obliged to withdraw. 4. Because by the spirit of the plan of union, Presbyteries were not to be joined, unless for edification; but this modelling evidently tends to ruin and destruction. 5. Because the Synod seem to act too arbitrary a part by forcing members into Presbyteries without their consent, and the consent of their congregations. 6. Because these violent and precipitate votes have rent the church of Christ, alas! too much divided already, to the joy of our enemies, the grief and distress of all sincere Christians, and the reproach of the Christian name, when only exchanging a member or two in two Presbyteries might have prevented the breach.'

"These reasons, together with those entered by two members, (Messrs. McDowell and Ewing,) against a judgment of the last Synod respecting the alteration of Presbyteries, prevail with us to enter this our protest, whereby we exonerate our consciences in order to continue in your communion, and declare before God and the world, that we are free from blame in this whole procedure. Matthew Wilson, John Ewing, Patrick Alison, Francis Alison."

In consequence of the above votes, Messrs. Joseph Tate and John Beard brought in the following document: "To the Rev. Synod of New York and Philadelphia: We the subscribers humbly beg leave to show, that we much desire to be in union and friendship with this Rev. body, and would not knowingly be the real authors of any discord in the church of Christ; yet the determinations of the Synod consequent on our petition presented last year, and again to this present meeting, seem so grievous and oppressive to us, and threatening to the credit and interests of religion, that we find ourselves obliged to declare to this Rev. Synod that we cannot submit to them, and we hereby decline all authority and jurisdiction of this body, and that no judgment or determination thereof shall bind us or affect our persons or ministry, until these differences of sentiment be removed by better light, and satisfactory means be found to reconcile and unite us with this Rev. body again; and as we earnestly desire and pray for this, we reserve to ourselves and expect the liberty at any time respectfully to offer such proposals as we may think likely to answer that end; and upon our satisfying the Rev. Synod, or they us, to return to our enjoyment of our privileges with them. And in the mean time we shall endeavour to carry respectfully towards this Rev. Synod, avoiding whatever might unnecessarily inflame unchristian passions, or tend to hinder the influence of our brethren in the gospel, and expect to be mutually treated by our brethren as ministers of Christ." They then briefly assign the reasons for their declining, which are substantially those given in support of the protest above mentioned, except the third, in which they complain that "the proceedings of the Synod in this as well as in many other affairs, appear plainly calculated to bear down one part of this united Synod, and suppress their influence, contrary to the equality and rights of members, and to the nature and whole professed design of our union."*

The next day, Messrs. Richard Treat and Read brought in an overture as a good expedient for the peace of the Synod, and the satisfaction of the brethren complaining, viz.: that the Presbytery of Donegal should be restored to its former state, as before the last Synod, with the members since settled within their bounds. The Synod agreed to this proposal, and also revived the late Presbytery of New Castle, which was to meet according to its last adjournment when under the name of the Presbytery of Lancaster.†

Unhappily this conciliatory measure did not satisfy the discontented portion of the Donegal Presbytery. In 1767, they addressed a letter to the Synod, saying, that they were willing to return to communion with the church, provided the Synod would erect them into a Presbytery by themselves. This request was refused; but in order, it is said, "to remove the uneasiness of our brethren, and to promote harmony and peace, we appoint Messrs. Buel, Rodgers, Horton, Kirkpatrick, Beatty, Blair, and Miller, a committee to bring in an overture relative to their petition." This committee made a report in which they expressed great disapprobation of the conduct of those brethren; and yet, to put an end to the schism,

* Minutes, p. 140.

† Ibid. p. 143.

they proposed that they should be erected into a separate Presbytery, with the proviso, that if any of them should remove out of the bounds of that Presbytery, they should become members of the Presbytery within whose limits they resided. This proposal, however, was rejected by a considerable majority.*

In 1768, the dissatisfied brethren presented the same petition, which was again rejected by a very strong vote. The next day Mr. Tate informed the Synod that though he was not authorized to make the proposal, he had no doubt his brethren would be satisfied, if the Synod would distribute them among the Presbyteries of Donegal, New Castle, and the second Presbytery of Philadelphia. The Synod, though they expressed strong disapprobation of their past conduct, agreed to authorize the Presbytery of Donegal to receive Mr. Samuel Thompson and Mr. Lang, the Presbytery of New Castle to receive Mr. S. Smith and Beard, and the second Presbytery of Philadelphia to receive Messrs. Tate, Elder, Steel, and McMurdie; provided first, that this regulation should not subject any vacancies within the bounds of the Presbytery of Donegal to any other Presbytery, nor should such vacancies, without express permission, apply to any other Presbytery for supplies; and secondly, if any of the said brethren comply with this regulation, they shall previously and expressly withdraw their declining document, entered in 1766, and without such withdrawal they shall not be received as members either of the Synod or of any of the Presbyteries.† These provisos were just and reasonable, but it is well to remark the tone of authority in the Synod which they indicate. The Rev. Mr. Strain protested against the above decision, and Messrs. John Roan, John Slemmons, Robert Cooper, and George Duffield dissented, assigning their reasons. These reasons are such as might be anticipated, viz. that the decision sanctioned the bad temper and irregular conduct of the dissatisfied brethren, set a bad precedent, tended to strengthen the second Presbytery of Philadelphia, which, in the judgment of many members of the Synod ought not to exist at all, &c.‡ It appears from the minutes for the following year, that this plan was carried into effect, and

* Minutes, pp. 157, 159, 166. † Ibid. p. 183. ‡ Ibid. pp. 184, 185.

this second schism was thus healed. This measure was evidently carried through by the members at a distance from the scene of contention, as Mr. Strain and all the dissentients were members of the Presbytery of Donegal.

In 1770, on a petition from certain members of the Presbytery of Hanover, the Rev. Messrs. Hugh McCaden, Henry Patillo, James Criswell, David Caldwell, Joseph Alexander, Hezekiah James Balch, and Hezekiah Balch, were formed into a Presbytery to be called the Presbytery of Orange.*

In 1781, the Rev. Messrs. Joseph Smith, John McMillan, James Power, and Thaddeus Dodd, were constituted the Presbytery of Redstone.† These were the pioneers of western Pennsylvania, and were a noble set of men.

In 1784, the Rev. Joseph Alexander, Francis Cummings, James Edmunds, John Harris, Thomas Reese, and John Simpson, were set off from the Presbytery of Orange, and constituted the Presbytery of South Carolina.‡

In 1785, at the request of Messrs. Samuel Doak, Hezekiah Balch, and Charles Cummings, the Presbytery of Abingdon was formed out of the Presbytery of Hanover, to be bounded by New River on the side next the Presbytery of Hanover, and by the Apalachian mountains on that next the Presbytery of Orange.§

In 1786, an extensive remodelling of the Presbyteries took place preparatory to the division of the Synod, and the adoption of the new constitution. The Presbytery of Abingdon was divided into two parts, the one to consist of the Rev. Charles Cummings, Hezekiah Balch, John Casson, Samuel Doak, and Samuel Houston, to be known as the Presbytery of Abingdon; the other to consist of Rev. David Rice, Thomas Craighead, Adam Rankin, Andrew McClure, and James Crawford, to be known as the Presbytery of Transylvania. The Presbytery of Hanover was divided into two parts, the one consisting of the Rev. Richard Sanchey, John Todd, James Waddell, William Irvine, John B. Smith, James Mitchell, John D. Blair, and Daniel McCalla, to be known as the Presbytery of Hanover; and the other consisting of the Rev. John

* Minutes, p. 224. † Ibid. p. 378. ‡ Ibid. p. 408. § Ibid. p. 423.

Brown, William Graham, Archibald Scott, James McConnel, Edward Crawford, Benjamin Erwin, John Montgomery, William Wilson, Moses Hoge, John McCrie, Samuel Carrick, and Samuel Shannon, to be known as the Presbytery of Lexington. It was also agreed that the Presbytery of Donegal be divided into two, one of which to consist of the Rev. John Slemmons, James Hunt, Stephen Balch, and Isaac Keith, with Dr. Patrick Alison, of the late second Presbytery of Philadelphia, and the Rev. George Luckey, from the Presbytery of New Castle, to be known as the Presbytery of Baltimore; and the other to consist of the Rev. Samuel Thompson, John Hoge, Hugh Magill, Robert Cooper, James Martin, James Lang, John Craighead, John King, Hugh Vance, Thomas McFarren, John McKnight, Dr. Robert Davidson, John Black, Samuel Dougall, John Lynn, David Beard, Samuel Waugh, Joseph Henderson, Matthew Steven, and James Johnston, with the Rev. John Elder, and Robert McMurdie, from the late second Presbytery of Philadelphia, to be known as the Presbytery of Carlisle. The Rev. Colin McFarquhar, late of the Presbytery of Donegal, was annexed to the Presbytery of New Castle. The distinction between the first and second Presbyteries of Philadelphia was abolished.

GENERAL REGULATIONS; AND CASES OF CONSCIENCE.

Under the head of ordinary powers of the Synod is to be referred, not only the authority which it exercised of resolving questions of conscience, and of determining whether a given doctrine was consistent with our standards, but also of laying down rules of discipline. In reference to this latter point, it must be borne in mind that the right which by our present constitution is reserved to the majority of the Presbyteries, of forming constitutional rules, was formerly exercised by the Synod, in which all the Presbyteries met as one body. Of the exercise of this right by the original Synod of Philadelphia, and by each of the two Synods during the schism, many examples have already been given. In the united Synod of New York and Philadelphia, this authority continued to be exercised until the last. The most common method of proceeding, was for some member, or Presbytery, to submit an overture or query, for the decision of the Synod; and the determination either constituted a rule for the guidance of the Presbyteries, or expressed the refusal of the Synod to make the overture into a rule. Thus, in the preceding pages, when speaking of the subject of education, we had occasion to notice that at one time it was determined that all candidates for the ministry should study divinity for at least one year after the completion of their academical course; at another, the proposition that they should be required to study two years, was rejected. Again, the proposal that every candidate should be required to produce a college diploma, before being taken on trial, was rejected; and, on the other hand, the proposition that a liberal education should be dispensed with, was repeatedly discarded.

In 1760, five such 'propositions or queries were submitted to the Synod. The first inquired how many ministers must unite in a request to the moderator of the commission, or of a Presbytery, in order to oblige him to call a meeting of the judicatory. The Synod decided that, in case of emergency, the moderator himself might call the judicatory together; or, on the application of any two members in the case of a Presbytery, or of four or five in the case of the commission, provided that due notice were given to all the members of the occasion, time, and place of the meeting.*

The second related to the choice of a moderator, with regard to which the Synod agreed, that no moderator had a right to preside in any of our Presbyteries, except in virtue of the choice of the members then met; but that Presbyteries might elect the same person for moderator, from time to time, if they thought proper.†

The third was, whether a candidate might apply to what Presbytery he pleased for examination and licensure. The Synod decided that any student had a right, in our present situation, to study with any divine of reputation connected with the Synod, according to a former act; but when he offered himself for examination, he should apply to that Presbytery within whose bounds he had generally resided. For sufficient reasons, however, such student might be remitted from one Presbytery to another, in which

* Minutes, p. 39.

† Ibid. p. 50.

case the latter was not to receive him on a mere certificate of church membership, but should require him to produce testimonials from his former Presbytery, or from several neighbouring ministers, recommending him as a candidate of exemplary piety and holiness of conversation.*

The fourth question was to this effect, whether a minister ordained either abroad, or by some ecclesiastical body in this country, not in connection with our church, should be received by our Presbyteries, on his producing proper testimonials, provided he adopts our Confession, and promises subjection in the Lord? This question was answered twice; first in 1764, and again in 1765. These answers differ very little from each other. The latter is as follows: "It is undoubtedly the right of Presbyteries to converse with any probationer or minister from foreign parts, as far as may be necessary to give them satisfaction, and not receive him implicitly on a certificate, however fair and regular, together with his general profession of adopting the Westminster Confession and Catechisms. But if such probationer or minister shall come from a church or judicature generally suspected, or known to be erroneous, or lax and negligent with respect to the moral conduct or piety of their candidates or members; or if they shall come from any number of ministers, who may convene without any regular constitution, merely for the purpose of licensing or ordaining particular persons; in that case a certificate from such a judicature, and such a general profession of the parties respecting the Confession of Faith, are still less satisfactory, and render it highly necessary for the Presbytery to which such application shall be made, to be more particular and exact in examining the principles of such probationer or minister before they admit him or employ him in their bounds."†

The fifth question was, whether it was regular for our students of divinity to go into New England or elsewhere for licensure, with the intention of returning to officiate within our bounds. To this it was answered: "Though the Synod entertain a high regard for the associated churches of New England, yet we cannot but judge that students who go to them, or to any other than our own Pres-

* Minutes, p. 104. † Ibid. p. 116, compare p. 104.

byteries to obtain license, in order to return and officiate among us, act very irregularly, and are not to be approved or employed by our Presbyteries; as hereby we are deprived of the right of trying and approving the qualifications of our own candidates; yet if any case may happen wherein such a conduct be thought necessary for the greater good of any congregation, it shall be laid before the Presbytery to which that congregation belongs and approved by them."*

In 1762, an overture, or as it was called a case of conscience, was introduced into Synod respecting the examination of candidates for the ministry on the subject of experimental religion, which gave rise to considerable difficulty. This was a subject of dispute between the two parties in the church before the schism, though it was never prominently presented. Both parties professed to agree as to the necessity of experimental religion as a qualification for the sacred office; and as to the duty of the Presbytery to satisfy themselves that every candidate possessed this qualification. Mr. Thompson, in his sermon on conviction of sin, says: "It is the indispensable duty of every one who would aspire to the sacred office, to pray and labour in the greatest earnest for true sanctifying grace, and all other necessary qualifications to fit him for his work; and to propose single ends and views to himself in undertaking it. And it is no less the duty of those, whose part it is to call and ordain men to that work, to take all possible care to inquire into the saving grace as well as other qnalifications in the persons to be ordained; and the neglect of either is a heinous sin, and of a dreadful tendency; no doubt a graceless ministry is an awful plague and scourge to any people."† In answer to the complaint of Mr. G. Tennent and of Mr. Blair, against their brethren for admitting men to the ministry "without questioning them about their Christian experience," he says: "We are directed by the Westminster Assembly to inquire touching the grace of God in the candidate, and if he be of such holiness of life as is requisite in a minister of the gospel," and adds: "I am sure as to the practice of some Presbyteries, that it is not ordinary or habitual in their

* Minutes, p. 105. † Sermon on Convictions, p. 73; printed in 1741.

practice to neglect this part of their work." And in stronger language: "That we allow ourselves to neglect all inquiry about the grace of God in candidates, is a downright slander and falsehood. That in some instances we may be deficient, is readily acknowledged, as well as in many other parts of our work."* And in the sixth article of the plan of union unanimously adopted by both Synods, it was agreed, "That no Presbytery shall license or ordain to the holy ministry any candidate, until he give them competent satisfaction as to his learning and experimental acquaintance with religion." It was not, therefore, either as to the necessity of this experimental acquaintance with religion, or as to the duty of the Presbytery to examine into this point, that the difference of opinion existed. It was as to the proper method of ascertaining whether the candidate possessed this experimental knowledge or not. The one side contended that a profession of faith, a holy life and conversation, and a knowledge of the nature and evidences of experimental religion, and of the criteria between true and false religious exercises, was all that could, with propriety, be demanded. The other insisted on a detail of the exercises of the candidate's own heart, or of his personal experience. To this it was objected, that such a detail was unsatisfactory, inasmuch as it was the mere testimony of the man in his own behalf; and that it was unauthorized. "No man or judicature on earth," says Mr. Thompson, "hath a right to know my spiritual state further than a profession of the faith of the gospel, and owning subjection to its precepts, go. None has a right to know the secret intercourse between me and my God, or between me and my own wicked heart and Satan's temptations. These things are among the religious secrets which I have a right to conceal or to discover, as Christian prudence or discretion shall direct."†

It is one of the anomalies in the ecclesiastical history of this period, that Mr. Tennent, who was so strenuous for the examination of candidates for the ministry, as to their own personal experience, and in whose Presbytery the difficulty on this subject arose and led to its division, and for a time threatened a new schism, was equally stren-

* Government of the Church, pp. 24, 25, 47. † Ibid. pp. 24, 25, 47.

uous in his opposition to Edwards' doctrine, that none but those who gave satisfactory evidence of true piety, ought to be admitted to the Lord's Supper. "The terms of church fellowship," he says, "which God has fixed, are soundness in the main doctrines of religion and a regular life." To support his opinion, he remarks: "The aforesaid terms that Christ has fixed may be certainly known, and therefore they are rational. But some of the novel and superstitious terms which some good men have invented, though with a pious design, are irrational, because they cannot be certainly known, unless it be supposed that churches are infallible in their determinations; a claim which the Protestants, some enthusiasts excepted, have not pretended to, at least in words; but the Bible is a stranger to such terms of communion; I know not one passage in it, that proves converting grace, or the church's judgment of it, to be a term of Christian communion of divine appointment. If any think otherwise, let them prove it, and I will give an attentive ear and readily submit to their instruction and correction. But I humbly conceive they will find it a hard task without producing another Bible."* In another place he says: "Nor does our church pretend to any right or authority of excluding any from the Lord's Supper upon the precarious foundation of their judgment concerning men's inward experiences of a work of invisible grace. No; the compilers of our Confession had more judgment than to advance such an indefensible notion. See the answer to the one hundred and seventy-third question in the Larger Catechism. 'May any who profess faith and desire to come to the Lord's Supper be kept from it? Answer: Such as are found to be ignorant or scandalous, notwithstanding their profession of faith and desire to come to the Lord's Supper, may and ought to be kept from that sacrament by the power which Christ has left in his church, until they receive instruction and manifest reformation.' It is pleasant to see the amiable

* Irenicum Ecclesiasticum, p. 79. To the passage thus quoted, he adds the note, "I cannot find the Christians of the first three centuries made gracious experiences, or the church's judgment about them, terms of communion. They made no inquiries about them as to baptism; and all that were baptized and free from church censure came to the sacrament."

modesty, the necessary caution and good judgment of our church, in declining to assume the bench, and make her uncertain opinion of men's spiritual experiences, the term of their admission either to the initiatory or confirming seal of the new covenant. No; she well understood and remembered that ancient, scriptural, rational, and equitable maxim, *ecclesia non judicat de internis*, that the church has no business to judge of internals, or to make her opinion of men's spiritual experiences, the ground of her judicial proceedings towards them."* This was the doctrine which one portion of the Synod applied to the admission or rejection of candidates for ordination.

The question was brought up in 1761, by an overture to the following effect: "As holiness is a qualification requisite in a gospel minister: Quere, whether it be the duty of a Presbytery, or possible for them to make candidates give a narrative of their personal exercises, and upon this form a judgment of their real spiritual state towards God, as the ground of admitting or rejecting them?"† The consideration of this question was deferred to the following year. It was then agreed that the persons proposing a query had a right to explain it, and to state the precise point which they wished decided. The authors of the overture were accordingly allowed to present the following exposition of their views:

"A case of conscience being proposed to the Synod concerning the means of obtaining competent satisfaction with candidates' experimental acquaintance with religion, and the Synod finding some difficulty in settling precisely the matter to be considered, having ordered some of us who desire the case should be examined, to bring in a distinct statement of the matter, we give the following as our sense of the article in our plan of union, relating to the affair, and of the case of conscience proposed to consideration.

"According to the sixth article of our plan of union, we think and declare that no Presbytery should license or ordain any candidate, until they have competent satisfaction concerning his learning, experimental acquaintance with religion, skill in divinity and cases of conscience; and so profess ourselves against admitting any

* Irenicum, p. 27.

† Minutes, p. 50.

to that sacred office without such satisfaction, as to his learning, obtained by proper trials; but what these must be, the article does not particularly determine.

"And as exemplary holiness is essential to the ministerial character, we declare all appointed warrantable means are to be used to secure a godly ministry, and allow none to be admitted to that important work, but such as make serious profession of their faith in Christ, and obedience to him, and give proper visible evidence of their sincerity herein, by exemplary holiness in every branch of Christian conversation, respecting God, their neighbours, and themselves, so as to adorn the doctrine of our Lord and Saviour; and so competent satisfaction as to their experimental religion should be had, as well as of their learning; though neither does said article in this define the means of obtaining it.

"We also declare that none should be admitted to that sacred work without competent skill in divinity, and in cases of conscience, that they may be apt to teach, to show the true scriptural marks of real converts, how far hypocrites may go, and whereby deceive themselves; what are the usual exercises of persons in the work of conversion, and after godliness; and so capable to feed the flock, direct their spiritual exercises, and speak to their several cases. And we declare against admitting to that sacred trust, or continuing in it, any who are found ignorant, unsound, unholy, or scandalous.

"And we understand the said article to require competent satisfaction in the particulars mentioned, but not at all to define the way or means by which that satisfaction must be sought; and, therefore, as to the means and grounds of this satisfaction, we think that a serious profession of faith in Christ, and obedience to him, attended with credible evidences of sincerity, in the fruits of an habitual godly, sober life, with like profession that the solemn work is not undertaken for filthy lucre, but out of desire to glorify God and promote the salvation of immortal souls, are the scriptural, prescribed, and only means of said competent satisfaction to a judicature, whose judicial sentence must be founded on things known and certain. And we think that men's declarations of their own experience in religion, which is but their own testimony of themselves, is no commanded, warrantable, or useful means that a judicature should require, or in any measure found their judgment upon.

"From all which we conclude, that our brethren and we are agreed in adhering to the said article of our union, and insisting on the satisfaction it requires; agreed in the duty and importance of using all appointed warrantable means for securing a godly ministry; and agreed as to the means of obtaining competent satisfaction as to candidates' experimental acquaintance with religion, and what should satisfy a judicature in this; such as serious profession, godly life, skill to direct Christian exercises and practice, and to speak to doubts and cases of conscience, &c.; excepting that some insist on requiring and using an account of the candidate's personal exercises and experiences in religion, as a means of judicature's satisfaction and ground of their proceedings with him, which we disallow.

"So the case to be resolved seems only, whether a candidate's declaration of his own personal experiences and exercises in religion, given in the way of narrative of these, or in answer to questions put to him concerning them, should be required by a judicature, as one appointed, warrantable and useful means of forming a judgment of his experimental acquaintance with religion, according to which judgment they are to receive or reject him."*

The case having been thus distinctly presented, the Synod resolved itself into a committee of the whole house, and every member was called upon in order to express his views on the subject. This process having been gone through with, the Synod resumed their former character, and answered the question by deciding that a declaration of the candidate's personal experience should be required, as a proper means of forming a judgment of his experimental acquaintance with religion. There were but thirteen voices in the negative and one *non liquet*.†

* Minutes, pp. 64, 65.

† The number of votes in the affirmative is not stated. It appears from the minutes, that there were forty ministers and twenty-three elders present at this meeting of the Synod. If all voted on this occasion, the result was 54 yeas, 13 nays, one *non liquet*.

This decision gave rise to two other questions, 1. Whether the answer just rendered was a compliance with the plain sense of the sixth article of the plan of union, so often referred to, and agreeable to the order in the Westminster Directory, wherein a Presbytery is directed to inquire touching the grace of God in him, i. e. in the candidate. The second question was, Whether the Synod's answer was not a direct and open violation of the sixth article of the plan of union, by which both Synods were allowed to follow their own judgment for obtaining competent satisfaction as to a candidate's learning and experimental acquaintance with religion, "for it was well known to the Synod of New York, that the Presbyteries belonging to the Synod of Philadelphia, did not examine a candidate's experiences." And in the seventh article of the union it was agreed "the Presbyteries might continue to act separately, as they had done; by which agreement they confirmed the method used by the Synod of Philadelphia in the licensing of candidates."

In order to ascertain how the sixth article of the plan of union was understood, the roll was called for each member to express his sentiments. It appeared that the members of the late Synod of New York, that were at the making of the union, in general agreed in understanding the article so as to enjoin such a declaration of experiences; and that the members of the late Synod of Philadelphia, that were at the making of the union, in general agreed in understanding that article so as not to enjoin such declaration. And each declared they so understood it at the time of making the union.

While the Synod were in great perplexity, and unable to accommodate the difficulty, an overture was presented in the name of the Presbytery of New York, "who, fearing a breach in the Synod on this question, chose to be absent, but sent the following proposals to maintain peace and harmony." The substance only of these proposals is entered upon the minutes in the following words :* "1.

* "The clerk of the Synod," it is stated, did not deliver this excellent paper to Dr. Francis Alison, the transcriber, which he thinks proper to observe, and leave room to insert it, if it can be had from the minutes of the Presbytery of New York; but he gives the substance of it from notes on that occasion, and from his own memory."

That where different Presbyteries follow different methods of examining the qualifications of candidates, they shall continue to do so without censuring or blaming one another. 2. That where the members of the same Presbytery differ in their sentiments respecting the examination of candidates' experiences, it shall be determined how they shall act, by the vote of the majority. 3. They shall desire the candidate to declare *in thesi* what he thinks to be the experience of a real convert, and then they may ask him whether he believes that he has experienced this saving change; or, 4. If peace cannot be thus preserved, it is proposed that ministers be joined together in Presbyteries, so that they may peaceably act according to the best of their judgment, and according to the dictates of a good conscience in the discharge of this important part of their ministerial duty."*

The whole subject was referred to Messrs. Treat, Finley, and Blair, with Dr. Alison, Messrs. Ewing, Alexander McDowell, and Azariah Horton, to attempt an amicable accommodation. This committee not being able to agree upon any one overture, reported several, and the Synod, after "solemn prayer to God for his gracious presence and direction," came to the following conclusion: "Whereas some members complain of two determinations of this Synod, the first a resolution of a query concerning the examination of a candidate's experience, in order to his admission or rejection; the other relating to the obvious sense of the sixth article of the plan of union, apprehending that by said determinations, the Synod laid an obligation on them to act according to the sentiments expressed in them: Now to give relief, and full satisfaction, to such brethren, the Synod declare they had no design by those determinations to lay the least obligation or restraint on said members with respect to their conduct, but only to express their own sense of the meaning of that article, and their sentiments of the query; and, hereupon," it is added, "the members declared themselves satisfied, and withdrew their protest."†

The Synod state further, that being "earnestly desirous that all due liberty of conscience be preserved inviolate, and that peace and

* Minutes, p. 69.

† Ibid. p. 73.

harmony be maintained and promoted, they do agree that when any person shall offer himself as a candidate for the ministry to any of our Presbyteries, every member of the Presbytery may use that way which he in conscience looks upon as proper, to obtain a competent satisfaction of the person's experimental acquaintance with religion, and then the Presbytery, as a Presbytery, shall determine whether they will take him on further trials." This agreement, it is stated, did not satisfy a number of the Synod. It was immediately after the conclusion of this affair, that the Synod erected those members of the Presbytery of Philadelphia, who disapproved of this examination into the personal experience of the candidate for the ministry, into a Presbytery by themselves. On this, as on other occasions, the Synod was saved from schism by the moderation of the New York and other distant members. The new-side men of Donegal and Brunswick, as appears from their protests, were unwilling to compromise any of these difficulties.

In 1773, Mr. John Roan introduced the following overture: "Whereas there have been repeated complaints from serious persons, of the degeneracy of the Presbyterian denomination in Great Britain and Ireland, and of their falling off from the great doctrines of the reformation, so that it is very possible there may be Presbyteries the majority of which would not be unwilling to license, ordain, or recommend, ministers unsound in the faith; it seems to be of moment to guard against the admission of strangers into the body, before their principles and character are thoroughly ascertained. Therefore it is overtured that no Presbytery be permitted to receive any stranger under the character of minister or candidate, or to give him appointments in the congregations under our care until the Synod that shall meet after their arrival, that the whole testimonials and credentials offered by such persons be laid before the Synod to be by them considered and judged of, in order to their admission or rejection."* This proposition was adopted by a small majority. It was afterwards agreed that the word *stranger*, in the above overture, "should not be extended to any person from any part of the continent of America."†

* Minutes, p. 279.

† Ibid. p. 284.

Against the adoption of this rule two protests were entered, the one by the second Presbytery of Philadelphia,* and the other by Messrs. Matthew Wilson, James Latta, John King, and James Lang. The reasons assigned for each are nearly the same, and are substantially as follows: 1. It is inconsistent with the rights of Presbyteries, to whom it belongs to ordain and admit ministers. If they err in the exercise of their powers, they are accountable to higher judicatories; but they are not to be deprived of those powers merely because they may err. 2. It rests upon the suspicion that Presbyteries are unfaithful, and are not to be trusted in the matter. 3. It is uncharitable and unjust towards the foreign churches; "as if all the reformed churches solemnly subscribing or assenting to the same Confession of Faith, the same Catechisms, and the same Directory, or plan of discipline and government, were wholly corrupted in faith or practice, notwithstanding their solemn assent and subscription to the form of sound doctrine." 4. It is unfriendly to the ministers who come among us, and tends to lead them to form Presbyteries independent of the Synod. 5. It sets a bad precedent, as on similar plausible pretexts the Synod might take away all the rights of the Presbyteries. 6. It is unnecessary, as we have rules which long experience proves to be sufficient. 7. It tends to produce contention and schism; for if the Synod assumes such unscriptural powers, some of the Presbyteries may be expected to withdraw from a body which they consider tyrannical. 8. Because the explanatory clause added in order to exempt all ministers coming from any part of America, seems to be a mere subterfuge and equivocation. In the agreements made in 1764 and 1765, which had the same object with this new law, the New England churches were expressly mentioned, and in the course of the debates upon this overture they were repeatedly referred to, and nothing was said or even insinuated to intimate that they were to be excluded from its operation. And, therefore, now to say that they were not intended, merely to relieve "a few members of the

* Signed by Francis Alison, John Elder, Joseph Tate, John Ewing, John Simonton, and Patrick Alison.

Synod," or, (as it is said in the other protest,) "some dissenting brethren," does not appear to be candid.*

The above statement shows how completely the tables were now turned. These protests contain nearly the same reasons as those formerly urged by the New Brunswick Presbytery against the act of which Dr. Alison and his friends were the strenuous supporters. And it must be admitted that they stand very much on the same ground. If the Presbyteries in Synod assembled, had a right to agree that they would not ordain any man without a college diploma or synodical certificate; they had a right to agree that foreign ministers and candidates should be subjected to the proposed probation.

In reply to these protests the Synod say, that neither the overture itself, nor the Synod's judgment on it, includes any claim of power inconsistent with the rights of Presbyteries; that the power of licensure and ordination is not so much as named in either, and that it would be difficult for the protesters to prove that the right to admit persons already licensed or ordained, belonged exclusively to the Presbyteries. They deny that the rule in question was founded upon any want of confidence in their own Presbyteries, or upon the supposition that the ministry in Britain and Ireland were wholly corrupt, but only that there was such a degeneracy among them as rendered caution on our part peculiarly necessary, and that no Presbytery could have the same means of information respecting those foreign ministers as the whole Synod had. They further state, as the overture only held up to view the churches of Britain and Ireland, it is most unfair to infer that the explanatory clause annexed to the judgment, "seemed to be a mere subterfuge and equivocation, and calculated to relieve only a few members of the Synod."†

Dr. Rodgers then moved that the operation of the above rule should be suspended until next year. This motion was sub-

* Besides the ministers who signed these protests, Dr. Rodgers, Joseph Montgomery, Alexander McWhorter, John Miller, Alexander McDowell, James Anderson, Thomas Reed, and James Caldwell, dissented from the decision by which Mr. Roan's overture was adopted.

† Minutes, p. 283.

sequently withdrawn, and the following adopted in its stead: "Whereas many brethren are dissatisfied with the act of Synod respecting the non-admission of ministers and candidates from foreign parts, it is proposed that the Presbytery to which any such gentlemen may offer themselves, may be allowed, if they see their way clear, to employ them in their vacancies, but that they be not admitted to full membership until the next Synod, when their testimonials and recommendations shall be laid before the Synod." This proposition being agreed to, the Presbyteries were directed to regulate themselves accordingly.*

The following year, 1774, this act was repealed, and the following adopted, by an unanimous vote, in its stead: "Whereas it is of the utmost importance to the interests of the Redeemer's kingdom, that the greatest care should be observed by church judicatures to maintain orthodoxy in doctrine and purity in practice in all their members, this Synod, in addition to the agreement on this head, of the year 1764, and further explained in 1765, do most earnestly recommend it to all the Presbyteries to be very strict and careful respecting these matters, especially in examining the certificates or testimonials of ministers or probationers who come from foreign churches; and that they be cautious about receiving them, unless the authenticity of their certificates and testimonials be supported by private letters, or other credible or sufficient evidence. And in order the more effectually to preserve this Synod, our Presbyteries and congregations from imposition and abuse, every year when any Presbytery may report that they have received any minister or probationer from foreign churches, that Presbytery shall lay before the Synod the testimonials and all other certificates upon which they received such minister or probationer, for the satisfaction of the Synod, before such foreign ministers or probationers shall be enrolled as members of our body; and if the Synod shall find said testimonials false or insufficient, the whole proceeding had by the Presbytery in the admission, shall be held to be void; and the Presbytery shall not from that time receive and acknowledge him as a member of this body, or in ministerial communion with

* Minutes, p. 287.

us. And, on the other hand, whensoever any gentlemen from abroad shall come duly recommended as above, we will gladly receive them as brethren, and give them every encouragement in our power."* The difference between this and the former rule was, that the one forbad the Presbyteries to receive a foreign minister at all until he had been approved by the Synod; the other allowed them to receive them subject to that approbation. In case, however, the Synod was dissatisfied, no act of the Presbytery was required to dissolve the connection between the new member and the Presbytery or Synod. The whole presbyterial proceeding was set aside as void. It will appear in the sequel that members admitted by the Presbyteries were, at times, thus rejected by the Synod. This latter act, though passed unanimously, seems as much open to the objection of interfering with the rights of Presbyteries as the former.

The propriety of ordaining ministers, *sine titulo*, was early brought under the consideration of the Synod. In 1763, this subject was referred to the several Presbyteries, that their members might be prepared to discuss it at the next meeting. Accordingly, the following year, after the Presbyteries had delivered their sentiments on the subject, and every member had been called upon to speak, the Synod came to the following conclusion: "That in ordinary cases, where churches are properly regulated and organized, it is a practice highly inexpedient, and of dangerous consequences, not to be allowed in our body, except in some special cases, as missions to the Indians, and some distant places that regularly apply for ministers. But as the honour and reputation of the Synod are much interested in the conduct of Presbyteries in such special cases, it is judged that they should previously apply to the Synod, and take their advice therein; unless the cases require such haste as would necessarily prevent the benefit of such mission, if delayed until the next session of Synod; in which cases the Presbyteries shall report to the next Synod the state of the case, and the reasons of their conduct."†

Agreeably to this rule the Presbyteries were in the habit of

* Minutes, p. 299.

† Ibid. p. 103.

applying to the Synod for permission before they proceeded to such ordinations. Thus, in 1766, "Suffolk Presbytery desired leave to ordain two candidates, Mr. Elam Potter and Mr. Isaac Lewis, *sine titulo*, in order to their being sent to the southward, which was granted."* It appears, however, that in this Presbytery there was some diversity of opinion on this subject, as in 1771, a letter was received from the Rev. Mr. Prime, "signifying the difficulty which he and some of his brethren laboured under, on account of an order of Synod respecting the ordination of ministers *sine titulo*, and requesting some relief in that matter." In their answer the Synod say, that it appears that Mr. Prime, and the brethren in whose name he wrote, agreed with the Synod as to the necessity of being satisfied with the piety, learning, prudence, and aptness to teach, of those sent forth to labour in Christ's vineyard; and that they further agreed with the Synod as to the propriety of making trial of candidates by hearing them preach and expound the Scriptures before ordination. The Synod add, that they "are firmly persuaded that our method of licensing them to preach by way of probation for the gospel ministry before ordination, is founded on general directions given by the apostles, that we should lay hands suddenly on no man, but should commit this charge to faithful men who are known to be able to teach others. But as Mr. Prime, and the brethren in whose name he writes, appear to differ from this Synod only in the mode of making these necessary trials before ordination; the Synod, after serious consideration of their request, which they are persuaded is made from a conscientious regard to what they think their duty, have agreed to lay no burden on them, or on those young men whose consciences will not allow them to preach the gospel without ordination; and therefore, though the Synod cannot repeal the act referred to in the above letter respecting the ordaining ministers, *sine titulo*, as they judge it still expedient and useful, yet they allow the Presbytery to ordain those gentlemen referred to by Mr. Prime in his letter, in case they shall be found on trial to be qualified for the work of the ministry, not doubting but they will take due care on this important head."†

* Minutes, p. 147.

† Ibid. pp. 132, 133.

The same year the Presbytery of New Brunswick were directed to ordain Mr. Schenck *sine titulo*, in order to his going on a mission, provided they saw their way clear.* In 1776, the first Presbytery of Philadelphia applied to Synod for their concurrence in the ordination of Mr. Keith *sine titulo*, provided he consented to go as a missionary to Kentucky.† In 1778, the Presbytery of New York reported that they had ordained the Rev. Thaddeus Dodd *sine titulo*, "in consequence of liberty obtained from the Synod for that purpose."‡ In 1781, the Synod "authorized the first Presbytery of Philadelphia to proceed" to a similar ordination.§ In 1781, the Presbytery of New Castle applied for liberty to ordain Mr. Daniel Jones *sine titulo*, which was granted.‖ A similar request was made in 1782, by the Presbytery of Orange; and in 1785, by the Presbytery of New Castle, both of which were granted.¶

Questions connected with the subject of psalmody were repeatedly presented to the Synod. In 1763, a question was introduced in these words: "As sundry members and congregations within the bounds of our Synod judge it most for edification to sing Dr. Watts' imitation of David's Psalms, do the Synod so far approve said imitation as to allow such ministers and congregations the liberty of using it?" The Synod answered, that as many of their body had never particularly examined the book in question, they were not prepared to answer the question; but as it was approved by many members of the Synod, they had no objection to its use until the matter of psalmody be further considered. And it was recommended to the members to examine the subject, and come prepared the next year to give their views upon it.** In 1764, the matter was again postponed; and in 1765, it was referred to Dr. Finley and Mr. McDowell, who made the following report upon it, which was adopted. "The Synod judge it best, in present circumstances, only to declare that they look on the inspired Psalms in Scripture to be proper matter to be sung in divine worship, accord-

* Minutes, p. 238. † Ibid. p. 338. ‡ Ibid. p. 352.
§ Ibid. p. 371. ‖ Ibid. p. 379. ¶ Ibid. pp. 386 and 424.
** Ibid. p. 92.

ing to their original design, and the practice of the Christian churches; yet will not forbid those to use the imitation of them, whose judgment and inclination lead them so to do."*

In 1773, the subject was again brought up by an appeal entered by certain members of the Second Presbyterian church in Philadelphia, from a decision of their Presbytery. After the several parties had been heard, the Synod declared that though the judgment of the Presbytery seemed to be drawn up with great caution and tenderness, they did not think it proper finally to decide upon it at that time, but appointed Dr. Witherspoon, Dr. Rodgers, Mr. Strain, and Mr. McWhorter, a committee to converse with the parties in the congregation who differed about psalmody, and to make a report to the Synod. This committee reported, that the Synod ought not to judge the merits of the appeal, so as to affirm or disapprove the several propositions laid down by the Presbytery; and as there was not time then to consider the several versions of the Psalms in question, and as congregations had been allowed to settle this matter according to their own choice, the Synod ought not to make any order to forbid the practice now begun, but should exhort the different parties to moderation and peace. This report was adopted.†

In 1785, the following overture was presented to the Synod: "Whereas the nearest uniformity that is practicable in the external modes of divine worship is to be desired, and the using different books of psalmody is matter of offence not only to Presbyterians of different denominations, but also to many congregations under our care; it is queried, whether the Synod may not choose out, and order some of their number to take the assistance of all the versions in our power, and compose for us a version more suitable to our circumstances and our taste than any we yet have." The proposition involved in this query having been assented to, the Synod appointed Dr. Patrick Alison, Dr. Davidson, Dr. Ewing, Mr. Blair, and Mr. Ewing, to make the proposed selection.‡ The following year this committee reported progress and was continued; and, in 1787, the Synod adopted the following resolution: "The Synod did allow, and do hereby allow, that Dr. Watts' imitation

* Minutes, p. 118. † Ibid. pp. 287, 289. ‡ Ibid. p. 430.

of David's Psalms, as revised by Mr. Barlow, be used in the churches and families under their care."

Questions of conscience, relating to marriage, gave the Synod no little trouble. At their first meeting they were called upon to decide, whether a man who had married his half-brother's widow, might lawfully live with her as his wife. It was deferred from year to year until 1761. In the mean time another question had arisen, viz. whether a man could lawfully marry the sister of his deceased wife? With regard to this latter case the Synod, in the first instance, adopted the following minute: "Though the majority of the Synod think that the marriage is incestuous, and contrary to the laws of God and the land, and agree that it is sinful, and of dangerous tendency; yet, inasmuch as some learned men are not so clear in this point, it is agreed to resume the consideration hereof the next year."* Accordingly, in 1761, they included the two cases in the following decision: "That, as the Levitical law, enforced by the civil laws of the land, is the only rule whereby we are to judge of marriages, whoever marry within the degrees of consanguinity or affinity forbidden therein, act unlawfully, and have no right to the distinguishing privileges of the church; and as the marriages in question appear to be within the prohibited degrees, they are to be accounted unlawful, and the persons suspended from special communion, while they continue in this relation."†

The Synod, however, did not abide by the above decision. In 1779, the Presbytery of New Castle referred the case of a man who had married the sister of his former wife, with the query, whether he could properly be admitted to church privileges? As the Synod deferred from year to year answering the question, the person interested presented, in 1782, a petition that he might no longer be debarred from the privileges of the church on account of his marriage. And after full and deliberate discussion, the question was put, shall Anthony Duchane and his wife be capable of Christian privileges, their marriage notwithstanding? which was carried in the affirmative by a considerable majority. Against

* Minutes, p. 36. † Ibid. p. 53.

this decision the Rev. James Finley and Robert Cooper protested; and Alexander Millet, John King, John Creaghead, Colin McFarquhar, and James Power dissented.*

The following year remonstrances were sent in from several congregations, requesting the Synod to reverse the above judgment. The Synod accordingly resumed the case, and, "declared their dissatisfaction with all such marriages as are inconsistent with the Levitical law, and that persons marrying within the degrees of consanguinity prohibited in that law ought to suffer the censures of the church; and they further judged, that although the marriage of a man to two sisters successively, viz. to one after the death of the other, may not be a direct violation of the express words of that law, yet as it is contrary to the custom of the protestant churches in general, and an evidence of great untenderness towards many serious and well-disposed Christians, and may, through the prejudices or generally received opinions of the members of our church, be productive of very disagreeable consequences, the persons contracting such marriages are highly censurable, and the practice ought to be disallowed in express terms by the Synod; and we do, therefore, condemn such marriages as imprudent and unseasonable. Yet as some things may be done very imprudently and unseasonably, which when done ought not to be annulled, we are of opinion that it is not necessary for the persons whom this judgment respects to separate from one another; yet they should not be received into the communion of the church, without a solemn admonition at the discretion of the congregation to which they belong. And the Synod publicly recommend it to all their members to abstain from celebrating such marriages, and to discountenance them by all the proper means in their power."† The Rev. James Finley entered his dissent from this judgment, as being substantially the same as that rendered the year before.

In 1760, the case where "a brother's and sister's relicts had married together," was considered, and the Synod decided, "That however inexpedient such a marriage may be, yet as we cannot find

* Minutes, p. 387. † Ibid. p. 397

it prohibited by the Levitical law, it is not to be condemned as incestuous."*

The first Presbytery of Philadelphia in 1770, referred to the Synod for their decision the question, whether a man may lawfully marry his wife's brother's daughter? The question was not answered until 1772, when the following minute was adopted in relation to it. "After mature deliberation, the Synod declare their great dissatisfaction with all such marriages as are inconsistent with the Levitical law, which in cases matrimonial, we understand to be the law of our nation; and that persons intermarrying in these prohibited degrees, are not only punishable by the laws of the country, but ought to suffer the censures of the church. And further judge that though the present case is not a direct violation of the express words of the Levitical law, yet as it is contrary to the custom of protestant nations in general, and an evidence of great untenderness, and so opposite to such precepts of the gospel as require Christians to avoid things of ill report, and all appearance of evil, and what is offensive to the church, that the persons referred to in this instance ought to be rebuked by the church session, and others warned against such offensive conduct. And in case these persons submit to such rebuke, and are in other respects regular professors, that they be not debarred Christian privileges."†

In 1785, the following question was referred to the Synod by the Presbytery of Donegal, viz.: "Whether on full proof of adultery by one party, the Presbytery has a right to declare the marriage so far void, as that the innocent party may marry again without being liable to church censure?" This question was decided in the affirmative by a small majority.‡

In 1786, the Presbytery of Donegal presented as a case of conscience the following question: Whether Christian masters or mistresses ought in duty to have such children baptized as are under their care, though born of parents not in communion with any Christian church? To this it was answered, that the Synod are of opinion that Christian masters and mistresses, whose professions and conduct are such as to give them a right to the ordinance of

* Minutes, pp. 31 and 36. † Ibid. p. 254. ‡ Ibid. p. 421.

baptism for their own children, may and ought to dedicate the children of their household to God in that ordinance, when they have no scruple of conscience to the contrary.

A second question was: Whether Christian slaves having children at the entire direction of unchristian masters, and not having it in their power to instruct them in religion, are bound to have them baptized? and whether a gospel minister in such circumstances ought to baptize them? The Synod answered both questions in the affirmative.

Under this head of general regulations, may be properly introduced a plan, originally proposed by certain elders in Philadelphia, and which, having been sanctioned by the Synod, was repeatedly urged upon the churches and Presbyteries under the name of 'The Plan of the Lay Elders.' It proposed,

"1. That in every congregation a committee be appointed, who shall twice in every year collect the minister's stipend, and lay his receipts before the Presbytery preceding the Synod; and that ministers at the same time give an account of their diligence in visiting and catechizing their people.

"2. The Synod recommends that a glebe, with a convenient house and necessary improvements be provided for every minister.

"3. That the church sessions and committees appointed, take special care of their poor or distressed widows and orphans, and administer all the relief and assistance they can.

"4. The Synod recommends to the church sessions and committees aforesaid, that they endeavour to prevent all unnecessary lawsuits; and if possible, to have all differences of a civil nature decided by arbitration.

"5. The Synod enjoin that exact registers of births, baptisms, marriages, and deaths, be regularly kept in each congregation.

"6. That special care be taken of the principles and character of school-masters, that they teach the Westminster Catechism and psalmody, and that the ministers, church sessions, and aforesaid committees, (where they consistently can,) visit the schools, and see these things be done. And where schools are composed of different denominations, that said committees and sessions invite proper persons of said denominations, to join with them in such visitations.

"7. That as the too great use of spirituous liquors at funerals, in some parts of the country, is risen to such a height as greatly to endanger the morals of many, and is the cause of much scandal, the Synod earnestly enjoin that the several sessions and committees shall take the most effectual methods to correct these mischiefs, and discountenance by their example and influence, all approaches to said practices, and all ostentatious and expensive parade, so inconsistent with such mortifying and distressing occasions."*

This plan was proposed in 1766, and adopted in 1767; and the clerk was directed to send a copy to the moderator of each Presbytery, to be communicated to the people, and the Presbyteries were directed to take all proper means to carry it into execution. And year after year inquiry was made how far the business had been attended to.

To this head also belongs an overture on the subject of slavery, presented to the Synod in 1787. It was in the following words: "The Creator of the world having made of one blood all the children of men, it becomes them as members of the same family to consult and promote each other's happiness. It is more especially the duty of those who maintain the rights of humanity, and teach the obligations of Christianity, to use such means as are in their power to extend the blessings of equal freedom to every part of the human race.

"From a full conviction of these truths, and sensible that the rights of human nature are too well understood to admit of debate; overtured that the Synod of New York and Philadelphia recommend in the warmest terms to every member of their body, and to all the families and churches under their care, to do every thing in their power, consistent with the rights of civil society, to promote the abolition of slavery and the instruction of negroes, whether bond or free."

On this overture the Synod passed the following judgment: "The Synod of New York and Philadelphia do highly approve of

* Minutes, pp. 142 and 164.

the general principles in favour of universal liberty which prevail in America, and the interest which many of the states have taken in promoting the abolition of slavery: yet inasmuch as men introduced from a servile state to a participation of all the privileges of civil society, without a proper education, and without previous habits of industry, may be in many respects dangerous to the community; therefore they earnestly recommend it to all the members belonging to their communion, to give those persons who are at present held in servitude, such good education as to prepare them for the better enjoyment of freedom. And they moreover recommend that masters, whenever they find servants disposed to make a just improvement of the privilege, would give them a peculium, or grant them time and sufficient means of procuring their own liberty at a moderate rate; that thereby they may be brought into society with those habits of industry that may render them useful citizens. And finally they recommend it to all their people to use the most prudent measures consistent with the interests and the state of civil society, in the countries where they live, to procure eventually the final abolition of slavery in America."

GENERAL SUPERVISION.

The Synod exercised a general supervision over their members and Presbyteries, designed to secure adherence to the rules of the church, and the proper discharge of ecclesiastical duties. The nature of this supervision may be inferred from the few following illustrations: — The Rev. Mr. Leonard having absented himself for several years from the meetings of Synod, a letter was written to inform him, that unless he either attended, or gave satisfactory reasons for his absence, he should be disowned as a member.* The Rev. Mr. Bay, having removed from the bounds of the Presbytery of New Castle, to within those of the Presbytery of Dutchess, without transferring his presbyterial relation, the Presbytery of Dutchess were directed to call upon him to procure a regular dismission from the Presbytery of New Castle, and to connect himself with their body.† In 1773, the second Presbytery

* Minutes, pp. 44 and 77. † Ibid. p. 214.

of Philadelphia received the Rev. Hugh Magill, who had been suspended from the ministry in Ireland by the Associate Presbytery of which he was a member. The Synod thinking that the Philadelphia Presbytery had not sufficient evidence of the grounds of his suspension to authorize them to disregard it, or sufficient testimonials in favour of the applicant, reversed the judgment by which he was received, and refused to recognize him as a member. This gentleman afterwards satisfied the Synod of his good character, and was regularly received.* The same year the Presbytery of Donegal reported that they had received the Rev. Messrs. David McCuer and Levi Frisby; but as it appeared that they were in the service of the board of correspondents from the society in Scotland, and appointed to an Indian mission, and had not been dismissed from the ecclesiastical council by which they were ordained in New England, (and which probably ceased to exist as soon as the ordination was effected,) the Synod reversed the judgment of the Presbytery receiving them to full membership, but approved of their taking them under their care while they were labouring occasionally within the bounds of the Presbytery.†

In 1783, the Presbytery of New York reported that they had left the name of the Rev. William Woodhull out of their list of members, because, on account of feeble health, he had relinquished his ministerial duties. The Synod deeming this reason to be insufficient, directed his name to be restored to the roll. A similar case was brought up in 1785. The Presbytery of New Castle reported that as the Rev. Joseph Montgomery, from bodily indisposition, was unable to preach, and had accepted an office under the civil authority, they had struck his name from their roll. The Synod disapproved of the omission of the name, and recommended "to all Presbyteries, when any ministers under their inspection resigned their charge, or discontinued the exercise of their office, while they remain in the same bounds, to pass a regular judgment on the reasons given for such conduct; and to continue their inspection of those who shall not have deserved to be deprived of the ministerial character, though they may be laid aside from immediate usefulness."‡

* Minutes, pp. 271, 318, 338. † Ibid. p. 271. ‡ Ibid. pp. 415, 421.

APPELLATE JURISDICTION.

The Synod, as the highest judicatory in the church, was frequently called upon to decide references, complaints, or appeals from the lower courts. Some of these cases are interesting as matters of history, or instructive on account of the principles which they involve. In 1759, the Presbytery of Philadelphia referred to the Synod the decision of a question relating to a call from the First Presbyterian Church in that city, for the Rev. Harry Munro. The Synod, after due consideration, decided that although some confusion had attended the vote of the congregation in relation to this matter, yet, as the great majority of the people were in favour of the call, the vote ought to be considered so far legal, that the Presbytery be allowed to present it to Mr. Munro. The Synod, however, expressed great disapprobation of the insulting and injurious manner in which they had been treated by some of the persons prosecuting the call, and exhorted the minority of the congregation to acquiesce in the wishes of the majority.* It does not appear that this call was ever prosecuted any further.

In 1763, an appeal was presented by the Second Church in Philadelphia, from a decision of the Presbytery of Donegal, respecting the removal of Mr. Duffield. The Synod finding that the congregations of Carlisle and Big Spring, of which Mr. Duffield was then the pastor, had not had due notice in the case, remitted the affair to the Presbytery; directing them to meet at Carlisle upon a given day, and decide the matter.† As all parties acquiesced in the decision of the Presbytery, the case was not again brought before the Synod. A few years afterwards this same congregation appealed from a decision of the Presbytery of Suffolk, unfavourable to the removal of Mr. Mills from Jamaica to Philadelphia. After hearing all the parties, the Synod affirmed the decision of the Presbytery.‡

In 1765, the people of New Castle and Christiana Bridge appealed from a decision of the Presbytery of New Castle, respecting their call to Mr. Megaw. "All parties being long and pa-

* Minutes, pp. 20, 22. † Ibid. p. 92. ‡ Ibid. for 1767, p. 169.

tiently heard, the Synod," it is said, "on the whole do judge that the said Presbytery have acted a very cautious and Christian part in making such a stand against bigotry and party spirit in those congregations, and striving so long to prevent a breach of a solemn union stipulated between those societies, and therefore cannot but highly disapprove and condemn the indecent language of their appeal, and their bitter insinuations of injustice from that our worthy Presbytery. And as it appears there was at least a very considerable opposition made against presenting said call, the Presbytery might prudently delay it, with a view, if possible, to obtain a greater union in Mr. Megaw, or some other person. However, as more light in the course of the trial has been thrown on the affair than was given by the congregation to the Presbytery, it now appears the call had better be presented to Mr. Megaw; and as the Presbytery assure us that they never intended to meddle with the civil property of their meeting-houses, even in the alternative proposed to those societies, which was only for the sake of peace, we leave them to settle that matter according to their own articles of union, and to determine the qualifications of their own voters; earnestly recommending it to both parties, in the spirit of meekness, to compromise their own differences, to maintain their union inviolable, and to follow the things which make for peace and edification."*

The same year a reference was brought in from the Presbytery of New Castle, requesting their judgment whether the Rev. John Rodgers should be removed from St. George's to New York, in compliance with a call from the latter place. After hearing the commissioners from both congregations, the Synod decided that Mr. Rodgers should remove, and accordingly "declared his pastoral relation to the congregation of St. George's to be dissolved."†

In 1771, the Third Presbyterian church of Philadelphia, in Pine-street, presented a call for the Rev. George Duffield, of Carlisle, to the second Presbytery of Philadelphia, with the request that it might be forwarded to the Presbytery of Donegal, to be placed in Mr. Duffield's hands. The Presbytery, after much consideration,

* Minutes, pp. 120, 121.

† Ibid. p. 118.

refused permission for the prosecution of the call. The principal reasons assigned in their minutes for this judgment, are, that the whole session were opposed to the call, and cautioned the people against proceeding in the business; that the call was never read to the people, nor made out at public meeting, but handed about and signed by the people separately; that in virtue of a compact between the First church in Market-street and the Pine-street church, their ministers were to preach in rotation at the two houses, and in case of a vacancy in either, a new pastor was not to be chosen by the one church without the concurrence of the other, "or at least the vacant church should study to choose a minister who should be generally agreeable to a majority of the members of each house;" yet in the present case the Market-street congregation had not been consulted, and had appeared before the Presbytery and remonstrated against the prosecution of the call. The Presbytery therefore decided that they had no right to set aside the agreement between the two congregations, or to decide the claim of property advanced by the Market-street people in the Pine-street building; and therefore could not allow the call to be forwarded. They, however, earnestly exhorted the two congregations to meet and endeavour to remove the difficulty; and in case this was done, the Presbytery promised to meet as soon as requested, and send the call to the Presbytery to which Mr. Duffield belonged. From this decision the congregation appealed. The Presbytery entered the appeal, only requiring that due notice should be given them whether it was to be prosecuted before the Synod or the commission."* When the case came before the Synod, in 1773, the judgment of the Presbytery was reversed by a great majority, and it was voted that the Third church should be allowed to prosecute their call before the Presbytery of Donegal. From this decision, Messrs. Alexander McDowell, Matthew Wilson, John Miller, and James Latta, dissented, and assigned substantially the following reasons: 1. Because a vote to prosecute a call, without any concurrence of the eldership, and in direct opposition to their solemn caution, and a call made when not half the people were present, is a new mode

* Minutes of the second Presbytery of Philadelphia, pp. 96–104.

of proceeding among us, and a dangerous precedent, and cause of anarchy and confusion. 2. Because the decision affected the interests of the Market-street congregation, and yet their commissioners were not heard in the case. 3. It was, moreover, inconsistent with the solemn compact between the two congregations. This strange judgment of the Synod was founded on the erroneous assumption that the aforesaid compact gave one society a domination over the other; whereas it appears, the ministers were to preach in rotation, and to be chosen by a majority of both congregations. 4. The votes of the Synod in the present case were directly the reverse of those passed in the case of New Castle and Christiana, which was of a similar character, and therefore the judgment appeared partial. 5. The decision was hurried through in a precipitate and unusual manner. 6. The Synod's decision tended to injure the right of property of the Market-street congregation in the Pine-street church, which they began and carried on at a great expense. To these reasons the Synod replied, that though the dissenting brethren had a right to record their reasons in their own words, the Synod had a right to say that they proceeded on a mistaken view of the facts, and have misrepresented the same, particularly as to the dissolving contracts, and deciding questions of property. The commissioners from the First church remonstrated against this decision, and requested to know whether it was final, and whether the call to Mr. Duffield "was to their church in Pine-street, as a minister to officiate in that church." The Synod replied very briefly that they considered their minutes a sufficient answer to both questions, and recommended to the parties, if they had disputes about property, not to go to law, but to submit the matter to arbitration. The session of the church in Pine-street then applied to the Synod for their advice whether they should continne to act as elders in that congregation. The Synod advised them to continue in the exercise of their office, unless their sense of duty prevented "their acting on the decision of the Synod." In that case they might "resign and allow the congregation to choose elders who may have freedom to act according to the determination of the Synod."*

* Minutes, pp. 263, 366, 367.

At the next meeting of the Synod, in 1773, Mr. Duffield introduced a complaint against the second Presbytery of Philadelphia, because "they had, by one of their ministers, obstructed his entrance to a church in this city under their care, to which he had accepted a call; and had also refused to receive him as a member, although he was dismissed from, and recommended by, the Presbytery of Donegal." The minutes of the second Presbytery of Philadelphia,* assigning their reasons for their conduct, were read; and also, "a petition from the incorporated committee, (trustees,) of the Presbyterian churches in Market and Pine streets, setting forth that Mr. Duffield, by the assistance of a part of the congregation in Pine-street, had taken forcible possession of their church in Pine-street, on the 27th day of September last, and praying us to afford them such relief as the nature of the case required from us." The Pine-street congregation also presented their account of the matter, and after all the parties were fully heard, the Synod decided "That Mr. Duffield had just cause of complaint against the judgment of the second Presbytery of Philadelphia, who ought to have admitted him and allowed him a fair trial; therefore we declare him to be minister of Pine-street, or Third Presbyterian congregation in this city, [without installation, or Presbyterial induction?] and order that he be put on the list of the aforesaid Presbytery."† This may have been all right; but it is certainly pretty high Presbyterianism for these new-side brethren. The question whether the Presbytery would obey the order of the Synod to place Mr. Duffield's name on their list of members, was not brought to an issue, as at the joint request of himself and congregation, they were disconnected from the second, and attached to the first Presbytery of Philadelphia.‡

In 1772, the Presbytery of New Castle presented a complaint against the second Presbytery of Philadelphia, for licensing a candidate who was properly under their care, and in regard to whose

* There is a chasm in the records of this Presbytery from 1772 to 1781. That portion of the minutes was never transcribed into the Presbytery book, and the original papers, it is stated, were lost, at the time of Dr. Alison's death, in whose possession they were. The reasons, therefore, offered by the Presbytery to justify their opposition to Mr. Duffield's settlement, cannot now be learned.

† Minutes, p. 285.

‡ Ibid. p. 288.

character they were engaged in making inquiries. Both Presbyteries were fully heard in the case, and the Synod decided that the Presbytery of New Castle should have power to cite the candidate in question, hear all the charges against him, and issue the affair in a regular manner; and that the second Presbytery of Philadelphia be prohibited employing him until a final decision of the case.*

The same year the Presbytery of Donegal made a complaint against the same Philadelphia Presbytery for sending a Mr. Kennedy to preach within their bounds. The Synod decided that this complaint was founded on misapprehension; and directed Mr. Kennedy to put himself under the care of the Donegal Presbytery, until they could hear and decide upon any charges which might be brought against him. After some difficulty on his part, the case was finally brought to trial before that Presbytery, who decided to prohibit his preaching any longer as a candidate, on account of the errors in doctrine, and schismatical and objectionable conduct of which they found him guilty.† Mr. Kennedy subsequently presented to the Synod a complaint against the Presbytery, which was dismissed as frivolous.‡

In 1774, an appeal was presented from a decision of the Presbytery of New Castle, relating to a call for the Rev. Joseph Smith. After an ineffectual attempt to compromise the difficulty, the Synod decided that Mr. Smith should be allowed to accept the call put into his hands by the Presbytery, which call was to be described as from the Second church in Wilmington united with Brandywine; and that he be directed to preach half his time in the city and half in the country, taking care that his days of preaching in town should not interfere with the appointments of the Rev. Mr. McKen-

* Minutes, p. 267.

† Of this trial a long account is given in the minutes of the Presbytery of Donegal for 1773, pp. 93–113. During the trial, Mr. Kennedy withdrew in an insulting manner, and the Presbytery decided, that as his absence was voluntary, it was their duty to proceed with the case and bring it to a decision; which they accordingly did.

‡ Minutes of Synod, p. 330.

nan; and the members of that Presbytery were earnestly exhorted to cultivate peace, and to strengthen each other's hands.*

In 1776, the Rev. Mr. Bay appealed from a decision of the Presbytery of New York, by which the pastoral relation between himself and congregation had been dissolved. The Synod affirmed the decision of the Presbytery, except so far as it interfered with questions of property, which they said ought to be referred to arbitrators.†

In 1782, the Rev. James Finley appealed from a judgment of the Presbytery of New Castle respecting his removal from his congregation. The Synod having heard all the parties, decided "that the pastoral relation between Mr. Finley and his congregation ought to be dissolved, and they do accordingly dissolve it."‡

EXTRAORDINARY POWERS. — 1. THE COMMISSION.

It appears from this review, that all the functions of a Presbyterian Synod were performed by this body as regularly as by any similar judicatory during any period of our history. In this as in all the preceding cases, however, we find this Synod conforming to the usages of the Scottish church, in the use of a commission, in the exercise of Presbyterial powers, and in the appointment of committees with synodical authority. In 1758, when the union took place, it was resolved, "That the commissions appointed before by the two Synods, with the present moderator, be together the commission of this Synod for the present year."§ Such a body continued to be regularly appointed until the formation of our present constitution. In 1774, "it was moved and seconded, whether a commission shall be appointed and their powers defined, or whether the practice should be discontinued?" In answer to this query the Synod adopted the following minute: "Whereas there have arisen doubts in the minds of some members respecting the utility and powers of what is called by us The Commission, the Synod proceeded to take this matter into consideration, and after due

* Minutes, p. 304. † Ibid. p. 341. ‡ Ibid. p. 385. § Ibid. p. 9.

deliberation, in order to remove any scruple upon this head, and prevent all future difficulties in this matter, do determine that the commission shall continue, and meet whensoever called by the moderator, at the request of the first nine in the roll of the commission, or a major part of the first nine ministers, and when met, that it shall be invested with all the powers of the Synod, and sit by their own adjournments from time to time; and let it be also duly attended to, that there can be no appeal from the judgment of the commission, as there can be none from the judgment of the Synod; but there may be a review of their proceedings and judgments by the Synod; and whensoever this is done, those who sat as members of the commission shall be present and assist in forming all such judgments as the Synod may think proper to make upon any such review."*

2. PRESBYTERIAL POWERS EXERCISED BY THE SYNOD.

The examples of the exercise of Presbyterial powers on the part of the Synod are very numerous. Besides acting as a missionary body, the Synod did not hesitate to appoint supplies for particular congregations, whenever occasion demanded it. Thus in 1760, it was "ordered that Mr. Laurence supply Mr. Beatty's pulpit the first and second Sabbaths of June; Mr. Treat the third Sabbath; Mr. Ramsay the fourth and fifth Sabbaths;" and so on for several months. In 1763, Mr. Gilbert Tennent, in consequence of the state of his health, requested the Synod to supply his pulpit during the summer; and the Synod accordingly appointed supplies from all the neighbouring Presbyteries. When the Synod sent any settled minister on any special mission, they either themselves appointed supplies for his pulpit, or directed his Presbytery to do it; and not unfrequently directed one Presbytery to supply within the bounds of another. In 1765, for example, it was "ordered that the Presbytery of Lewistown supply Mr. Ramsay's congregation, (which belonged to the first Presbytery of Philadelphia,) eight Sabbaths; Mr. J. Finley and Mr. McKennan, (of the Presbytery

* Minutes, p. 305.

of New Castle,) each one Sabbath; and the first Presbytery of Philadelphia the rest of the time. Ordered, that the Presbytery of New Brunswick supply Mr. Latta's pulpit, (who belonged to the second Presbytery of Philadelphia,) sixteen Sabbaths, and the second Presbytery of Philadelphia the rest of the time," and so on.*

At present no minister is admitted as a member of Synod except in virtue of his belonging to some Presbytery in connection with the body. Formerly, however, the Synod itself entertained applications for admission, examined, received, and even ordained members. In 1758, application was made to the Synod from a Welsh congregation, praying them to ordain Mr. John Griffith; and the Synod finding that he had regular certificates from Wales, and that several of their members were well acquainted with him as a man of Christian character and experience, agreed, "That the said John Griffith, though he has not the measure of school learning usually required, and which they judge to be ordinarily requisite, be ordained to the work of the ministry; and appointed the Rev. Samuel Davies, Dr. Alison, Mr. Treat, Mr. Hunter, and Mr. Kittletas, to be a Presbytery *pro re nata* to ordain him to-morrow morning at eleven o'clock." This service was accordingly performed, and it was ordered that Mr. Griffith belong to the Presbytery of Philadelphia.†

In 1765, the Rev. Jonathan Leavitt, after adopting the Westminster Confession of Faith, and promising to conform himself to the Westminster Directory, was received by the Synod and advised to put himself under the care of some one of our Presbyteries.‡

In 1777, the Rev. James Wharton of the Associate Presbytery of Pennsylvania, applied to be received as a member; and the Synod having conversed with him, and heard at considerable length his sentiments on the doctrines of the gospel, and terms of Christian and ministerial communion, and having had sufficient testimonials of his moral character, and of his good standing in the ministry in the church of which he has been a member, unani-

* Minutes, p. 128. † Ibid. pp. 8, 10. ‡ Ibid. p. 127.

mously agreed to receive him, and appointed him a member of the Presbytery of Donegal.*

In 1774, the Rev. Samuel Blair, formerly in connection with the Synod, requested to be enrolled as a member; which request was granted, and he accordingly took his seat; and the Synod desired Mr. Blair to connect himself with some Presbytery as soon as convenient.†

The case of the Rev. Mr. Magill also belongs to this head. In 1773, he was received by the second Presbytery of Philadelphia, but the Synod reversed their judgment. In 1775, he presented additional testimonials, and the Synod decided, "that they could not at present receive him as a member," but being anxious to do all they could for his relief, appointed Dr. Rodgers to endeavour to obtain light as to his case from the Associate Presbytery of Monaghan in Ireland, and Dr. Witherspoon from the Associate Synod in Edinburgh. In 1776, the Synod received him as a member of the second Presbytery of Philadelphia, and appointed him to supply for eight months in the western parts of Pennsylvania, under the direction of the Presbytery of Donegal.

In 1785, the Rev. John Hiddleson, from the Presbytery of Belfast, in Ireland, presented his credentials, and requested to be received as a member of Synod. A committee was appointed to examine his credentials, and "to converse with the young gentleman," and to report their opinion of his case. That committee reported that, in their judgment, he "ought not at present to be annexed as a minister to any Presbytery belonging to the Synod; but, if he chooses, he may commit himself to the care of some Presbytery, who shall proceed with him as they may judge best, and make report to the Synod at their next meeting." This report was adopted.‡

In 1786, the testimonials of the Rev. James Thom, of the Presbytery of Dundee, in Scotland, were laid before the Synod and approved. Whereupon he was admitted to join himself to any Presbytery belonging to this body; and, being present, he was invited to sit as a correspondent.§

* Minutes, p. 347. † Ibid. p. 307. ‡ Ibid. pp. 424, 426. § Ibid. p. 438.

In 1787, "the testimonials of Mr. John Young, a probationer from the Presbytery of Irvine, in Scotland, accompanied by corroborating evidential letters, were laid before the Synod and approved, and he had leave to put himself under the care of the Presbytery of New York."

The Synod also acted more or less in a presbyterial capacity, in allowing calls from congregations to be addressed to them for particular ministers. In 1765, a call from Catry's settlement, in North Carolina, for the Rev. Mr. Spencer, was brought into Synod, and presented to him. At the same time, a call from Hopewell and Centre congregations, in the same state, for the Rev. Mr. McWhorter, was introduced; but the Synod apprehending that some other person might more conveniently be sent, did not present it to him.*

In 1766, two calls for Mr. Nathan Ker, were brought before the Synod and given him for his consideration, with the direction to report his answer to the Presbytery of New York. In 1768, a call for Mr. McCreary, a candidate under the care of the Presbytery of New Castle, was brought in and read, and Mr. McCreary's answer requested. As he was not prepared to give an immediate reply, he was directed to give his answer to his Presbytery, who were requested, in case he accepted the call, to ordain him as soon as convenient.† In all these, and in other similar cases, the calls were from distant congregations not under the care of any particular Presbytery.

The Synod at times acted more in a presbyterial than a synodical capacity, when cases of discipline were referred to them. In 1771, the second Presbytery of Philadelphia referred to the consideration of the Synod, the case of a minister who had left his pastoral charge, whose character laboured under serious charges, and who, though twice cited, had refused to appear before the Presbytery, but had requested his name to be struck from their roll. The Synod, instead of instructing the Presbytery how to proceed, themselves took up the case, directed Dr. Rodgers to prepare a citation specifying the charges against the accused, to be signed by the moderator, and appointed a committee to prepare matters, and

* Minutes, pp. 119, 120.

† Ibid. p. 187.

to cite witnesses. The accused was then informed of the time of trial, and given to understand that the citation then served was to be the last, and that the Synod would proceed to hear and issue the case, whether he attended or not. At the time appointed, the accused appeared before the Synod, and made a free confession of the crimes laid to his charge, and declared himself unfeignedly sorry and deeply penitent, for his very offensive conduct. And the Synod, after prayer to God for direction, declared their opinion that the crimes charged fully merited deposition, but in respect of his humble and penitent carriage, it was agreed to suspend him from the exercise of his ministry *sine die;* and they prohibited him, under pain of the highest censures of the church, from exercising the same, or any part thereof, within the bounds of the Synod or elsewhere; and they discharged any inferior judicatory from taking off this suspension, or from receiving any application for that purpose. The Synod, moreover, dissolved his pastoral relation to his congregation, and suspended him from the sealing ordinances of the church, but left it to the second Presbytery of Philadelphia, or any other where he might reside, to restore him to Christian communion, upon his application, when they shall see proper. It was ordered, that he should be publicly rebuked by the moderator from the chair, and that this whole sentence should be read from the pulpit of his late church on the following Lord's day.* In 1772, this gentleman presented a petition to the Synod to be restored to the exercise of his ministry, and the Synod, after mature deliberation, determined to restore him for one year, under the particular care of the Presbytery of New Castle, and the Rev. Mr. McDowell was appointed to give him a solemn admonition with regard to his future conduct. He was accordingly called in, received the admonition, and took his seat as a member of the Synod.† The following year the Presbytery of New Castle reported that they had received him agreeably to the order of the Synod, that he had since laboured in the work of the ministry under their direction, and behaved himself in a becoming and regular manner as far as was known to them. The Synod then agreed to restore

* Minutes, pp. 239, 240.

† Ibid. p. 256.

him fully to his ministry, and exhorted him to the greatest humility, circumspection, and meekness, through the remaining part of his life. And as he had the prospect of labouring principally within the bounds of the first Presbytery of Philadelphia, he was joined to that body.* This whole proceeding shows a style of Presbyterianism to which we have been long unaccustomed. The Synod itself proceeding to the trial in the first instance, passing sentence, forbidding any Presbytery to remove that sentence, themselves first partially, and then fully restoring him to the ministry, and attaching him first to one Presbytery and then to another, suppose the doctrine that the Synod was a larger Presbytery, and included within itself all the powers of the lower judicatories.

COMMITTEES WITH SYNODICAL POWERS.

The appointment of committees with synodical powers, and sending correspondents to sit with a Presbytery to aid them in any difficult business, were modes of action in which this Synod conformed to the early usages of our church, and to those of the church of Scotland, to a greater extent than is now customary. In 1759, a complaint was presented against the first Presbytery of New Castle, but the matter not being ready for trial, the Synod appointed the existing Presbytery of New Castle, and Messrs. Elder, Roan, John Miller, and Steel, a committee of the Synod, to meet at Chesnut Level, and take such notice of the grounds of the complaint as they might judge necessary.† In 1761, an appeal from a judgment of the Presbytery of New York was presented by Mr. Kittletas, and the minutes of the Presbytery, and their reasons in support of their judgment were read, and then the Synod appointed Messrs. William Tennent, Treat, Hunter, Alison, &c. &c. a committee, to meet at Princeton, and determine the whole matter.‡ This committee reported, the following year, that they met agreeably to their appointment, and "took the affair under consideration; and finding Mr. Kittletas was not present, who sent sufficient reasons to excuse his absence, and earnestly requested that we

* Minutes, p. 276. † Ibid. p. 20. ‡ Ibid. p. 53.

would endeavour to remove the difference between him and the Presbytery of New York; it was unanimously resolved, that the committee could not proceed in a judicial way to determine the cause while one of the parties was absent; that it was thought proper to confer with the Presbytery, and to remove all grounds of complaint between him and them if possible. It plainly appeared from what had been acknowledged both by Mr. Kittletas and the Presbytery, that the Presbytery in dealing with him, intended only to bear a testimony, in a moderate manner, against any thing which deserved censure or admonition, even in a brother for whom they had a very high esteem, and that in so doing they did not intend to suspend him, or remove him from their fellowship as a brother, but only to admonish him in a friendly manner, and in this the committee approve their design; and inasmuch as Mr. Kittletas desired our assistance to remove all misunderstanding, that he may live in peace and friendship with the Presbytery, as well as with his other brethren, we have requested the Presbytery to grant this desire, and they have condescended to what we requested, and from henceforth do receive him into good standing with them without any further censure."*

It has been often a matter of dispute among Presbyterians, whether it is proper to proceed with the trial of an accused person in his absence, or to the decision of a case in the absence of one of the parties. Some have maintained that if the accused refused to attend after due citation, or withdrew during the progress of the trial, the proper method was to censure, either by rebuke, suspension, or deposition, as the case might demand, for contumacy, but not to proceed with the trial. This method of proceeding, it has been supposed, sufficiently protects the church, as unworthy members or ministers may be cut off though they refuse to submit to discipline, while it avoids the apparent violation of the principles of justice in trying a man in his absence. The practice of our church on this point does not seem to be uniform. In the case of Mr. Kennedy before the Presbytery of Donegal, referred to above, the Presbytery proceeded with the trial, though he refused,

* Minutes, p. 61.

after a certain time, to attend. And in the case referred to the Synod by the second Presbytery of Philadelphia, notice was sent to the accused that the Synod would proceed with the trial, whether he attended or not. In the above minute, however, we find the committee unanimously resolving that they could not proceed to a judicial hearing of the case before them in the absence of one of the parties. In this latter instance, it is true, the absence was excusable and not contumacious.

In 1762, an appeal was brought in from a decision of the Presbytery of Donegal, and a committee of eleven ministers was appointed to examine into the grounds of the complaint, as contained in the appeal, with full liberty to consider the case, and determine as they should obtain light.* In 1764, a certain John Harris presented an appeal from a judgment of the Presbytery of New Castle, and the Synod appointed Mr. Robert Smith and twelve other ministers to hear and try the merits of the cause, and to issue the whole affair.†

In 1765, an appeal from the judgment of the Presbytery of Donegal, respecting Mr. Roan and Mr. Edmiston, was presented by Mr. Edmiston, together with a reference respecting the same affair, by the Presbytery; and also an appeal from the judgment of the said Presbytery, by Mr. McMurdie. The Synod appointed a committee of thirteen, to meet at Hanover, and to issue and determine these matters.‡ In 1766, an appeal from the decision of the Presbytery of Suffolk was presented, and after hearing the appellant and the Presbytery, it was ordered that Messrs. Rodgers, Tennent, &c. &c. be a committee to meet each with an elder, at Huntingdon, and try and issue the whole affair.§

In 1768, a petition was presented by the Rev. Mr. Sackett, praying the Synod to take into consideration the differences between him and the Presbytery of Dutchess; and also a supplication from the church at Bedford, Westchester county, praying that a committee might be appointed to settle all differences in their congregation. The Synod accordingly appointed a committee of eleven ministers to meet and examine into these difficulties, and to

* Minutes, p. 73. † Ibid. p. 110. ‡ Ibid. p. 113. § Ibid. p. 144.

settle all differences. The following year this committee reported, and the Synod approved of their proceedings, except of so much of their judgment as disconnected Mr. Sackett from the Presbytery of Dutchess, and annexed him to the Presbytery of New York; which was reversed, and Mr. Sackett returned to his former Presbytery.*

In 1773, when the Presbytery of Donegal were directed to proceed with the trial of Mr. Kennedy, they requested that some members of the Synod might be joined with them on the trial; and it was ordered, that Messrs. Robert Smith, Latta, Foster, and Woodhull, be added to them for that purpose.†

In 1786, the Synod having been informed that several disorders had taken place within the bounds of the Presbytery of Abingdon, appointed a committee of six ministers to meet at Salem church with power to cite such persons, subject to the jurisdiction of the Synod, who had been concerned in these disorders, and if unanimous, to give judgment, otherwise to cite all parties to appear before the Synod at their next meeting. Dr. Moses Hoge was the only member of the committee who attended; the excuses of the other members were sustained. The difficulties in question, however, were brought up by a complaint from the Salem church against the Presbytery of Abingdon. One ground of this complaint, viz.: that the Presbytery had licensed a young man who was under suspension, was found upon examination to be unfounded. The Synod appointed a committee to confer with the members of the Presbytery who were at variance with each other, and by this means a reconciliation was effected. The Synod earnestly recommended, *inter alia*, that so far as questions about psalmody were concerned, difference of opinion on the subject should not be made the ground of unchristian censure against either party; though they had allowed the use of Watts's, they were far from disapproving of the old version. The Synod at the same time found great fault with a printed letter addressed to the Rev. Mr. Balch, and ascribed to the Rev. Wm. Graham, and directed the Presbytery of Lexington to cite Mr. Graham before them, and ascertain whether he was

* Minutes, pp. 187, 193.

† Ibid. p. 278.

the author, and to censure or acquit him as they should see cause.

Our judicatories are sometimes so oppressed with judicial business, that it might be well, on some occasions, to resort to this old usage of our church, and appoint committees with plenary powers. Most men would be as willing to have a cause in which they were interested, decided by ten good men as by a hundred. Much time would thus be saved, and many details of evidence kept from coming before a large assembly.

THE SYNOD'S INTERCOURSE WITH OTHER CHURCHES.

A liberal and catholic spirit has been characteristic of our church from the beginning. It has ever been ready to maintain Christian fellowship with all other evangelical denominations. In accordance with this spirit the Synod of New York and Philadelphia, soon after its organization, sought fraternal intercourse with kindred churches both in Europe and America. At its first meeting in 1758, Messrs. Robert Cross, Gilbert Tennent, Francis Alison, and Richard Treat, were appointed a committee to correspond in the name of the Synod with churches of our persuasion in Britain and Ireland, in these colonies and elsewhere.* In the minutes for 1766, the churches mentioned as those with whom this correspondence was to be conducted, were those of Holland, Switzerland, the General Assembly and the Secession Synod in Scotland, the ministers in and about London, the General Synod of Ireland, the ministers of Dublin, New England, and the churches in South Carolina. The references to this correspondence in the records are very frequent; but as the letters written and received are not inserted, the minutes give no information on the subject, beyond the fact that a friendly intercourse with the several bodies above mentioned was maintained, particularly with the Synod of North Holland, the General Assembly in Scotland, and the church of Geneva, from all of which letters were received.†

In 1769, at the request of several seceding ministers, Dr. With-

* Minutes, p. 10.

† Ibid. pp. 231, 236, 240.

erspoon moved in Synod, that a committee be appointed to converse with them, with a view to bring about a union between them and this Synod. A petition was presented at the same time from several inhabitants about Marsh creek, praying that the Synod would use their endeavour to form a union with the Seceders. A committee, of which Dr. Witherspoon was chairman, was accordingly appointed for this purpose. The following year they reported, that by reason of several disappointments they had not been able to meet. In 1771, it is stated that this committee "brought in the minutes of their proceedings, and their conduct was highly approved."* Certain questions had been submitted to the Associate Presbytery, to which answers were reported to the Synod in 1772. For want of time, however, they were not read, but were referred to Dr. Witherspoon and others for consideration;† who the next year reported, that as the Associate brethren had not given any answer to the proposal of the committee of Synod made the year before, they had not thought it proper to make any further reply to those brethren, than that if any thing was to be done further towards a coalition between the Associate Presbytery and the Synod, the proposal must come from the former, which the committee would be ready to receive.‡

This negotiation does not appear to have been resumed until 1785, when the Synod was informed, "that some of the brethren of the Dutch Synod, and one of the members of the Associate Reformed Synod, had expressed a desire of some measures being taken to promote a friendly intercourse between the three Synods, or for laying a plan for some kind of union among them, whereby they might be enabled to unite their interests and combine their efforts for promoting the cause of truth and vital religion; and at the same time giving it as their judgment that such plan was practicable. The Synod," it is added, "were happy in finding such a disposition in the brethren of the above Synods; and cheerfully concur with them in thinking that such a measure is both desirable and practicable, and therefore appoint Dr. Witherspoon, Dr. Jones, Dr. Rodgers, Dr. McWhorter, Dr. Smith, Mr. Duffield, Mr. Alex-

* Minutes, p. 236. † Ibid. p. 268. ‡ Ibid. p. 279.

ander Miller, Mr. Israel Reed, Mr. John Woodhull, and Mr. Nathan Ker, a committee to meet such committees as may be appointed by the Low Dutch Synod now sitting in New York, and by the Associate Synod, to meet in that city next week, at such time and place as may be agreed upon; to confer with the brethren of said Synods, on this important subject; and to concert such measures with them for the accomplishment of these great ends as they shall judge expedient."*

It appears from the minutes of the following year, that the committees of the three Synods met in New York the 5th of October, 1785, and organized themselves as a convention. Their first measure was to appoint two members from each committee to digest the several subjects to be laid before the convention. In this sub-committee the first inquiry was, what the formulas of doctrine and worship are to which each Synod respectively adheres. The answer given by the Dutch members is not recorded; that given by the members from the Synod of New York was quoted on a previous page;† that of the members of the Associate Synod is stated to have been, "in substance, very analogous to that made by the Synod of New York and Philadelphia." It was then resolved, That the formulas and standards mentioned in the respective representations are mutually satisfactory, and lay a sufficient basis for the fraternal correspondence and concord of the several Synods.

"The second inquiry was, whether the corresponding Synods, in order to lay the foundation of entire confidence in each other, were willing to give solemn and mutual assurances of their vigilance and fidelity, in requiring of their ecclesiastical officers, an explicit and unequivocal assent to their present formulas or standards of discipline and faith; and will take such measures as to them respectively shall seem most reasonable and effectual to secure the same fidelity and orthodoxy in all time to come. The answer was unanimously given in the affirmative. Resolved, that the nature of these assurances be left to be determined by the convention.

* Minutes, p. 418.

† See above, p. 307.

"The third inquiry was, whether they will agree mutually to watch over each other's purity in doctrine and discipline; and whether they will agree mutually to receive complaints that may be made by either of the others against particular members of their respective bodies, who may be supposed to be departing from the faith, or from the exactness of their church discipline. Agreed in the affirmative; but that the mode shall be referred to the General Convention.

"The fourth inquiry was, whether they would mutually promise to introduce and maintain the most exact discipline that the circumstances of the country and spirit of the people will bear. Resolved, that this is an article of the utmost importance; and resolved, moreover, that it be recommended to the convention to consider of and adopt proper means for aiding the exercise of discipline by discouraging fugitives from it, out of any of the churches; and especially by not receiving any persons to church membership without sufficient credentials of their good moral character and orderly behaviour from the church to which they now immediately belong, or have lately belonged.

"The fifth inquiry related to grievances or causes of complaint that may have arisen between the ministers or congregations of the respective Synods. Resolved, that they ought to be candidly heard, and the most speedy and effectual measures taken to redress them.

"The sixth and last inquiry, or proposition, respected some mode of establishing a visible intercourse and permanent correspondence between the several Synods. Resolved, that this subject be referred to the consideration of the convention, but that it be recommended to the convention to establish an annual convention of the three Synods by their delegates, which may consist at least of three ministers and three elders from each; and that the general objects of this convention be to strengthen each other's hands in the great work of the gospel ministry; to give and receive mutual information of the state of religion within their respective churches; to consider and adopt the most prudent means to prevent or remedy any causes of dissension that may happen to arise between our respective congregations, agreeably to the instructions that may be given by the respective Synods; and to concert measures for uniting our efforts to defend and promote the principles of the gospel, and oppose the progress of infidelity and error; and to adopt plans for effectually assisting the exercise of discipline in our churches, and encouraging each other in its execution; and for such other purposes as the convention may think proper. Resolved, to recommend that the first meeting of the above convention shall be held the second Tuesday of October, at New York, and afterwards at such time and place as shall be appointed at the preceding convention."

When this sub-committee of six made the above report to the general committee or convention, it was approved and adopted; and the several points referred by the sub-committee to the Convention, were taken up and acted upon. "On the second inquiry it was resolved, that the manner in which the Synods shall give a solemn pledge to each other of the formula of their faith which they have openly professed, and of their strict attachment to the same, shall be by an act of each Synod, wherein an accurate recital of such formula shall be made, with a positive declaration that it is their sincere determination before God, always to abide by the same, for which purpose they honestly pledge themselves to the two other Synods; which declaration and promise shall be signed by the president or moderator of the Synod, and at the first convention to be formed by delegates from the respective Synods, be read and entered upon the records of the convention, and copies of all the declarations be transmitted to each Synod and entered upon their respective records; which records shall remain a perpetual witness against either party that shall ever deviate therefrom. And also that each Synod shall communicate, by their respective delegates, the form of testimonials or credentials given to their candidates, and of those given to ordained ministers; which copies shall also be entered on the records of the respective Synods.

"Resolved, on the third inquiry, that we will mutually watch over each other's purity in doctrine and discipline, and be ready to receive complaints against any of our ministers upon these subjects; and that the mode in which such complaints shall be preferred and prosecuted shall be, either by individuals, who shall prosecute in their own names, *cum periculo;* or by a classis, Presbytery, or Synod of a sister church: in which case it shall be taken up and prosecuted as a *fama clamosa*, by the classis, Presbytery, or Synod to which the offender or offenders may belong; and the whole proceedings shall be transmitted, properly authenticated by the moderator, the president, the scribe, or clerk, to the informing body for their satisfaction.

"On the fourth inquiry, resolved, that in order to aid the exercise of discipline, and discourage fugitives from it, every classis, Presbytery, or Synod, shall officially communicate to its neighbouring Presbytery, classis, or Synod, the name or names of every minister or candidate subject to censure, either of a lesser or higher nature; after which such Presbytery, classis, or Synod, shall be held to view and treat such minister or candidate as lying under ecclesiastical censure to all intents and purposes, as if they belonged to their own body, until such person or persons shall be regularly acquitted, or restored by the judicatory who had inflicted such censure.

"With reference to the fifth inquiry, relating to such grievances as may hereafter arise in congregations under the jurisdiction of the different corresponding Synods, it is determined that such differences shall be referred to the consideration of a future convention. But as it is possible that some contingencies may arise which will render a call of the convention before the stated time of meeting necessary, it is resolved, that a power be lodged in the moderator of the convention, with the consent of one member at least from each Synod, by circular letters to call an extraordinary convention, provided that such call be not more than once in one year.

"The convention thought proper to amend the resolution of their committee, by agreeing to a biennial instead of an annual convention.

"On motion to ascertain and limit the powers of the convention in all time to come, resolved, That those powers shall be merely of counsel and advice, and that it shall on no account possess judiciary or executive authority, and every subject that shall come regularly before the convention, shall, after being properly digested, be referred to the respective Synods, together with the opinion of the convention, and the reasons on which it is founded, for their judicial and ultimate decision.

"Agreed, that the convention shall, when met, set apart a certain portion of their time for social prayer to Almighty God, for his blessing on their counsels and the churches which they represent; and that said convention, whenever circumstances appear to them to require public and general humiliation or thanksgiving, shall recommend to the corresponding Synods to set apart the same day to be observed throughout all their churches."

When this report was laid by the committee before the Synod, that body "approved of their diligence and fidelity in the matter, and agreed to appoint a committee to meet such delegates as may be appointed by the other Synods, on this business, in the city of New York, on the second Tuesday of October next," the day appointed for the convention. The Synod prepared the following instructions for their delegation: "The delegates, on the part of this Synod, are to inform the convention that this body is about to divide itself into four Synods, subordinate to a General Assembly; that they have under consideration a plan of church government and discipline, which it is hoped when completed, will be sufficient to answer every query of the convention upon that head; and that the mutual assurances mentioned in the minutes of the last convention may, as far as they respect this Synod, be made more properly after the intended system is finished than at present. They are to assure the convention of the readiness and desire of this body, in the mean time, to unite in a consistent manner their influence with that of the other Synods, in order to promote the spiritual interests and best good of the whole. And the delegates from this Synod are to enter into a friendly conference with those of the other Synods, and in conjunction with them, concert such measures as shall be best calculated to diffuse harmony and brotherly love through the several churches, and promote the interest of the

Redeemer's kingdom, and to make report of the whole to this Synod at their next meeting. On motion, resolved, that the Rev. Doctors John Witherspoon, John Rodgers, Alexander McWhorter, Mr. Israel Read, Mr. John Woodhull, Mr. Nathan Ker, with the moderator, (Mr. Alexander Miller,) be appointed, and they are hereby appointed, delegates on behalf of this Synod for the purposes above mentioned."

The next year it is simply recorded, "That the committee appointed to meet committees from the Reformed Dutch Synod and the Associate Synod, made report and delivered the minutes of the convention of the committees of the three Synods, which met in New York last fall, which were read." As the convention was to be biennial, no new appointment was made that year; but, in 1788, we find it stated, that Dr. Witherspoon, Dr. Smith, Mr. John Woodhull, Mr. Armstrong, and Mr. Monteith, were appointed delegates on behalf of this Synod to meet in convention with delegates from the Low Dutch Synod and the Associate Reformed Synod, on the first Thursday of next October.

The preceding account throws no little light upon the character of our church at this period. It is evident, not only from the known strictness of the Reformed Dutch and Associate Synods, but also from the character of the professions, pledges, and guaranties, mutually exacted, that thorough orthodoxy and strict fidelity to the standards of doctrine and discipline, were a necessary preliminary to the intercourse thus established; and that the preservation of that orthodoxy was one great object which the union was designed to answer. It must excite some surprise even in the stricter sort of Presbyterians, to see the unanimity and readiness with which the delegates from our Synod acceded to all the demands made upon them, and even consented to place, to a certain extent, the orthodoxy of their own members under the surveillance of the other Synods. This was carrying the matter too far to last long; but it shows a state of feeling in our church which has long since departed. Could an intercourse, such as was here provided for, somewhat modified, have been preserved, it would probably have been of great service to all the corresponding bodies. We might have gained and might have imparted good, and the character of the three Synods been modified and improved by their reciprocal influence; and thus these three great bodies of Presbyterians been brought into a more cordial fellowship with each other, and each elevated to a higher point of ecclesiastical and Christian excellence.

In 1766, an overture was presented to the Synod, proposing that they should "endeavour to obtain some correspondence between the Synod and the consociated churches of Connecticut. A copy of a letter from the Synod to them was also read and approved; and the Rev. Messrs. John Ewing, and Patrick Alison, and the moderator, were desired to present that letter, and confer with our brethren on this affair. And in case it shall seem meet," it is added, "to our Reverend brethren to attend to this our proposal, so far as to appoint commissioners from their body to meet with commissioners from ours: we appoint the Rev. Dr. Alison, and the Rev. Messrs. Timothy Jones, William Tennent, John Rodgers, Elisha Kent, John Smith, John Blair, and Samuel Buel, to meet with them at such time and place as the reverend brethren of Connecticut shall agree."*

In consequence of this overture, a convention of delegates was held at Elizabethtown, in November, 1766, and a plan of union between the Congregational, Consociated, and Presbyterian Churches, was drawn up and reported the next year to the Synod, and when amended was finally adopted by both parties.† This plan was very simple, and provided,

"1. That a general convention be formed of the Congregational, Consociated, and Presbyterian Churches in North America, consisting of delegates from each of their respective bodies, to meet annually, or as often as may be thought necessary, and that the first general convention be held at New Haven the day after their next annual commencement.

"2. That this general convention shall not be invested with, nor shall it at any time hereafter assume any power, dominion, jurisdiction, or authority over the churches or pastors, or any church or

* Minutes, p. 151.

† Ibid. pp. 170, 180.

pastor; nor shall any counsel or advice be asked or given in this general convention, relative to any internal debates subsisting, or that may subsist in any of these bodies thus united; and it is particularly agreed, that the Congregational, Consociated, and Presbyterian Churches, shall subsist entire and independent of each other, notwithstanding this union; retaining their peculiar usages and forms of government; nor shall ever any attempts be made, nor any authority, directly or indirectly be used by this general convention to change or assimilate the same.

"3. That the general design of this convention be to gain information of this united cause and interest; to collect accounts relating thereto; to unite our endeavours and counsels for spreading the gospel, and preserving the religious liberties of our churches; to diffuse harmony, and to keep up a correspondence throughout this united body, and with our friends abroad; to recommend, cultivate, and preserve loyalty towards the king's majesty; and also address the king or the king's ministers with assurances of the unshaken loyalty of the pastors comprehended in this union, and of the churches under their care; and to vindicate them, if unjustly aspersed.

"4. That summary accounts of all the information and transactions in this general convention be, from time to time, duly transmitted to all the Associations, Presbyteries, or any other bodies that shall accede to or be included in this union."*

It was agreed that letters should be written to the ministers of the Congregational and Presbyterian Churches in Massachusetts, New Hampshire, and Rhode Island, and to the reverend brethren of the Reformed Dutch church, inviting them to send delegates to the convention. And accordingly the following year, the Rev. Messrs. Parsons and McGregore of the Presbytery of Boston did attend; but afterwards the convention was almost exclusively composed of delegates from the Synod and the churches of Connecticut.

It will be observed that in this wise plan, there was no attempt to amalgamate two different denominations; to give the one a voice in the government of the other. Every thing of this kind was

* Minutes of the Convention, pp. 4, 5.

carefully provided against. It was an union only in convention, and for objects in which the two churches had a common interest. This convention of delegates continued to be regularly held every year until the revolutionary war. The great and almost the only subject which occupied their attention, was opposition to the establishment of an American Episcopate. In 1768, a letter was written on this subject by the direction of the convention to the committee in London, for managing the civil affairs of the dissenters, setting forth their reasons for believing that such a measure was in contemplation, and their strong objections to its being carried into effect. To this letter an answer was received, in which the committee state, that they were fully aware of the many civil and religious inconveniences which would attend the introduction of diocesan bishops into America, and were determined to do all they could to oppose the measure. They at the same time informed the convention that, from the best authority, they were assured the English government had, at that time, no such design. The correspondence thus commenced was continued, with some interruptions, from year to year; and was conducted principally through Dr. Alison of Philadelphia, Dr. Rodgers of New York, and the Rev. Mr. Whitman of Hartford. With the same general object in view, the convention appointed from time to time committees, to ascertain and report on the religious laws in force in the several colonies; on the acts of oppression to which non-episcopalians in any of the provinces were subject; and on the proportion which the different denominations bore to each other in different parts of the country. In consequence of these appointments, several valuable reports were presented to the convention, which unhappily have not been preserved. In 1774, it is stated that the Rev. Mr. Halsey of New Jersey, "delivered in a valuable detail of the first settlement of North Carolina, and of the ecclesiastical circumstances of the province in its different periods to the present time." Mr. Montgomery reported, that he had made some progress in collecting materials concerning the rise and progress of religious liberty, and in ascertaining the proportion of dissenters to the established church in Maryland; and Mr. Patrick Alison was requested to fix the proportion between these two classes on the western shore of that province. Dr. Rodgers stated that he expected to be ready to report on New York to the next convention. In 1775, a full and accurate account respecting Connecticut, was received from the Rev. Mr. Goodrich; and also an account of the number of Episcopalians and non-episcopalians in that colony; for which he received the thanks of the convention. The troubles of the times soon put a stop to these labours; and the convention never met after that year.

It does not lie within the scope of the present work to enter fully, either into the history or the merits of the controversy respecting an American Episcopate. It will be proper, however, to say enough on the subject to enable the reader to form a judgment of the propriety of the course taken by the Presbyterian church in so decidedly opposing the measure. After several unsuccessful attempts had been made at an earlier period, to induce the English government to send one or more bishops to America, the effort was renewed by a voluntary convention of the Episcopal clergy of New York and New Jersey, who prepared a petition on the subject to be forwarded to Europe, and requested the Rev. Dr. Bradbury Chandler of Elizabethtown, to write and publish an appeal to the public in behalf of the measure. This appeal was published in 1767, and presents the claims of the Episcopal church in this country to the enjoyment of a complete organization with great force and ingenuity. The appeal was answered by Dr. Charles Chauncey of Boston; and the matter soon became a subject of general controversy throughout the country; even the weekly papers were made the vehicles of vehement arguments on both sides.*

According to Dr. Chandler it was proposed, "That the bishops to be sent to America shall have no authority but purely of a spiritual and ecclesiastical nature, such as is derived altogether from

* Many of these pieces are to be found in "A Collection of Tracts from the late Newspapers, containing the American Whig, a Whip for the American Whig, &c.; being controversial articles relating to protestant bishops in the American colonies: New York, 1768, 2 vols.," in the Philadelphia Library.

the church and not from the state. That this authority shall operate only upon the clergy of the church, and not upon the laity or upon dissenters of any denomination. That the bishops shall not interfere with the property or privileges, whether civil or religious, of churchmen or dissenters. That in particular, they shall have no concern with the probate of wills, letters of guardianship and administration, or marriage licenses, nor be judges of any cases relating thereto. But that they shall only exercise the original powers of their office, i. e. ordain and govern the clergy, and administer confirmation to those who shall desire it."* Against a plan so reasonable as this it is difficult to see what objection could be made. As diocesan bishops are an essential part of an Episcopal church, necessary to ordain, confirm, and exercise discipline, it would seem to be a hard case that the numerous churches already formed in this country, should be deprived of this part of their system: that the clergy should be without supervision; and that candidates for orders should be obliged to make a long and expensive voyage to obtain ordination. The fact, therefore, that strenuous and united opposition was made to the introduction of American bishops, needs explanation. As far as the Presbyterian church is concerned, we should be sorry that it should lie under the imputation of having resisted the reasonable wishes of another denomination to the enjoyment of their own ecclesiastical system.

It should be stated then, that there would have been no opposition to the plan as above presented, had there been any reasonable prospect of its being adhered to. Against bishops who should derive their authority "altogether from the church and not from the state," no voice was raised. The convention of the Synod of New York and Philadelphia and the churches of Connecticut, say: "We would by no means have it understood as if we would endeavour to prevent an American bishop, or archbishop, or patriarch, or whatever else they might see fit to send, provided other denominations could be safe from their severity and encroachments."†

* Appeal to the Public, &c. p. 79.

† Letter to the committee in London, dated September, 1771. Minutes of the Convention, p. 39.

And Dr. Chauncey, in his reply to the Appeal, says: "We desire no other liberty than to be left unrestrained in the exercise of our religious principles, in so far as we are good members of society. And we are perfectly willing that Episcopalians should enjoy this liberty to the full. If they think bishops in their appropriated sense, were constituted by Christ or his apostles, we object not a word to their having as many of them as they please, if they will be content to have them with authority altogether derived from Christ. But they both claim and desire a great deal more. They want to be distinguished by having bishops on the footing of a state establishment."* And again, "Dr. Chandler quite mistakes the true ground of our dissatisfaction. It is not simply the exercise of any of their religious principles that would give us any uneasiness; nor yet the exercise of them under as many purely scriptural bishops as they could wish to have; but their having bishops under a state establishment, which would put them upon a different footing from the other denominations, and, without all doubt, sooner or later expose them to many difficulties and grievous hardships."† The same sentiment is expressed by Dr. Mayhew, in his Observations on the charter and conduct of the Society for the propagation of the Gospel in foreign parts; and also by the American Whig.

The opposition, therefore, was not to bishops with purely spiritual authority, but to bishops sent by the state with powers ascertained and determined by act of parliament. The mere fact that this opposition was so general, and that it was as strong, though not as universal, among Episcopalians as among the members of other denominations, is a proof that it did not owe its origin to any ungenerous bigotry. If the Massachusetts legislature opposed it, so did the house of burgesses in Virginia. The former body, in a letter to their agent in London, dated January 12, 1768, say: "The establishment of a Protestant Episcopate in America, is also very zealously contended for; and it is very alarming to a people whose fathers, from the hardships which they suffered under such an establishment, were obliged to fly from their native country into

* Appeal to the Public, answered, p. 180. † Ibid. p. 189.

a wilderness, in order peaceably to enjoy their privileges, civil and religious. Their being threatened with the loss of both at once must throw them into a very disagreeable situation. We hope in God such an establishment will never take place in America, and we desire you would strenuously oppose it."* In Virginia, when a convention was called to consider the propriety of petitioning for a bishop, only twelve out of a hundred ministers in the province attended, and of those twelve four protested against the decision to forward a petition. And soon after the house of burgesses, by an unanimous vote, thanked the protestors "for the wise and well-timed opposition they had made to the pernicious project of a few mistaken clergymen for introducing an American bishop."† If any thing more is necessary to show the character of this opposition, it may be found in the fact, that as soon as this country was separated from England, and thus all fear of the civil power of the bishops removed, all objection to their introduction was withdrawn.

This apprehension of danger to the religious liberty of the country was not a feverish dread of imaginary evils. It was even better founded than the apprehension of danger to our civil liberties from the claim of the British Parliament to a right to tax the country. As the Episcopal Church was established in England, and as those who had the control of the government were members of that church, the Episcopalians in America were naturally led to be constantly looking for state patronage and legal support. They claimed it as a right, that the support and extension of the Episcopal Church in this country should be made a national concern. Even Dr. Chandler, although his work was written to disarm prejudice and allay apprehensions, could not avoid letting this be distinctly seen. "It has been the practice of all Christian nations," he tells us, "to provide for and maintain the national religion, and to render it as respectable as possible in the most distant colonies;" and, "as some religion has ever been thought, by

* See American Whig, vol. i. p. 67.

† Dr. Hawks' Contributions to the Ecclesiastical History of the United States, vol. i. pp. 127–130.

the wisest legislators, to be necessary for the security of civil government, and accordingly has always been interwoven into the constitution of it, so in every nation that religion which is thus distinguished, must be looked upon as, in the opinion of the legislature, the best fitted for this great purpose. Wherever, therefore, the national religion is not made in some degree a national concern, it will commonly be considered as an evidence that those who have the direction of the national affairs do not esteem their religion; or that they are negligent of the duty they owe to God and the public, as guardians of its happiness." He then proceeds to give the reasons why "the Church of England in America appears not hitherto to have been made a national concern;" reasons which, he says, may account for, although not altogether excuse this neglect.* It was this very thing, which Dr. Chandler considered so much a matter of course, that other denominations deprecated and dreaded. They denied the right of the British government thus to distinguish the Episcopal Church, especially in the northern provinces, where its members, even at this period, hardly constituted the thirtieth part of the population. They denied the fairness of its being made a national concern to the detriment and oppression of other denominations. The whole history of the country showed that the authorities in England acted constantly on the plan of giving the Church of England, in this country, all the ascendency that could with safety be secured for it. In those colonies where the thing was possible, that church was established by law; in others, the public were taxed for its support, or national property assigned for its maintenance.

In South Carolina, according to Dr. Ramsay, the Presbyterians were among the first settlers of the country; and, in connection with the Independents, they organized a church in 1690, and in the early part of the eighteenth century a Presbytery was formed agreeably to the principles and practice of the Church of Scotland.† The Episcopalians had no minister until 1701;‡ and, in

* Appeal, pp. 44–47. † History of South Carolina, vol. ii. p. 25.

‡ Humphrey's History of the Society for the Propagation of the Gospel in Foreign Parts, p. 25.

1710, formed less than a half of the population;* though even then several of the French Presbyterian Churches had gone over to them. Yet in 1696, provision was made by law for an Episcopal clergyman, in Charleston, who was to be allowed one hundred and fifty pounds sterling a year, together with a house, glebe, and two servants. As nothing was yet said of an establishment, this law excited little dissatisfaction. Soon after, however, the Church of England was fully established; a salary of one hundred pounds out of the public treasury was allowed to each of its ministers, and all denominations were taxed for building its churches.† In 1703, a law was passed which "required every man who should be chosen a member of the Assembly to take the oaths and subscribe the declaration appointed, to conform to the religion and worship of the Church of England; and to receive the Lord's Supper according to the rites and usages of that church."‡ The proprietors inserted a clause into the constitution of the colony to the following effect: "As the country comes to be sufficiently planted, it shall belong to the Parliament to take care for the building of churches, and the public maintenance of divines to be employed in the exercise of religion according to the Church of England, which being the only true and orthodox, and the national church of all the king's dominions, is so also of Carolina; and, therefore, it alone shall be allowed to receive public maintenance by act of Parliament."§ The result, therefore, in Carolina, of making the Church of England a national concern, was, that other denominations were not only taxed for its support, but were also debarred from a seat in the Legislature.

As Virginia was more of an Episcopal colony from the beginning, there was less ground of complaint for the mere establishment of the English Church. The severity of her ecclesiastical laws, however, admits of no justification. In 1618, it was enacted, "that every person should go to church on Sundays and holydays, or lie neck and heels that night, and be a slave to the colony the follow-

* Letter from South Carolina, dated 1710, quoted above, chap. ii. p. 85.

† Hewitt's History of Carolina, vol. i. p. 140.

‡ Hewitt, vol. i. p. 166.

§ Ibid. vol. i. p. 46, 47.

ing week. For a second offence, he should be a slave for a month; and, for a third, a year and a day."* In 1624, a law requiring strict conformity, as near as might be, in substance and circumstance, to the canons of the Church of England, was passed. And in 1642, it was enacted that no minister should officiate within the province who could not produce a certificate of his ordination by some English bishop, and promise to conform to the orders and constitution of the Church of England; and the governor and council were authorized to compel any one who transgressed this law to depart the country.† Severe laws also were passed against the Quakers, and subsequently against the Baptists. Even the rights guarantied by the Virginia act of toleration, were repeatedly violated in the case of Presbyterians. Before the revolutionary war the Dissenters had increased so much, that it is said the Episcopalians did not constitute more than one-third of the inhabitants of the province.‡ Yet even in those parishes in which there were very few members of the Established Church, the Dissenters were obliged to purchase glebes, build churches, and make provision for the support of the clergy. This was felt to be a great grievance in a new country, and among a poor people. It is prominently presented as an unreasonable burden in the memorial presented to the Legislature by the Presbytery of Hanover, in 1776.§ The con-

* Stith's History, p. 148. † Laws of Virginia, p. 3.

‡ This statement is given by Dr. Hawks, p. 140, who quotes as authorities, 4 Burk. p. 180; 1 Jefferson's Works, p. 31. The Doctor, however, thinks there are circumstances which would seem to render the statement doubtful. All such estimates, in the absence of any regular census, must be more or less uncertain. There is nothing, however, in the above account that needs excite surprise. The number of Episcopalians had long ceased to be increased by new accessions from the mother country. The great influx of settlers was from Pennsylvania, and consisted of German and Scotch-Irish. The Established Church had suffered a great diminution of numbers by the rise of the Presbyterians, even in the eastern counties; and subsequently, a still greater loss by the rise of the Baptists, who at the breaking out of the war were a large and influential party. Other denominations, therefore, had been for years increasing, while the Episcopalians were decreasing.

§ Illustration of the Character and Conduct of the Presbyterian Church in Virginia. By John H. Rice. Richmond, 1816.

duct of some of the New England provinces in reference to the Episcopal Dissenters within their bounds, was very different. They were relieved from all payments in support of the "standing churches," when they were an inconsiderable minority of the population.

The early ecclesiastical history of Maryland is very much of a riddle. From all that appears, however, it may be fairly referred to as affording another example of the church of the minority being, by the force of the authorities in England, made the established religion of the province. Maryland, though originally settled by Roman Catholics, was soon furnished with a population of a very mixed religious character. When the proprietary government was overthrown, in 1651, the first act of the legislature was to pass an intolerant law denying even protection to the Catholics, and granting liberty of conscience and worship to such as professed faith in God by Jesus Christ, provided this liberty was not extended to *popery* and *prelacy*.* At this period, therefore, the Episcopalians must have been in the minority. Five and twenty years later they were still very inconsiderable in numbers. Under the date 1676, Dr. Hawks remarks: "Hitherto our narrative has been silent with respect to the Protestant Episcopal church in Maryland. The reason is obvious, for though there were members of that church living within the province, yet they were not numerous."† Notwithstanding their fewness, they complained that no provision was made by law for the support of their clergy. These complaints were referred by the bishop of London to the committee of plantations, who called Lord Baltimore, (who had before this been restored to his authority,) to account on this subject. His lordship answered that all denominations were upon a level in Maryland, and that it would be difficult, if not impossible, to get the Assembly to make a law, obliging any denomination of Christians to support other ministers than their own.‡ "This answer," says Dr. Hawks, "did not seem to satisfy the committee, for they declared that, in their opinion, there should be some maintenance for the clergy of the church, and that his lordship should propose means for the support of a com-

* Hawks, vol. ii. p. 42. † Ibid. p. 47. ‡ Ibid. p. 51.

petent number." The revolution of 1688, which placed William III. upon the throne of England, led to a similar revolution in Maryland. In 1691, Maryland was made a royal government; and, in 1692, the Church of England was established; the country was divided into thirty parishes, and provision made for building churches, and for the support of the clergy. It can hardly be supposed that such a sudden revolution had occurred in the religious sentiments of the people, that the Episcopalians, who were so few in 1676, had become the majority of the population in 1692. In 1694, the new governor "found but three clergymen on his arrival; and they," it is added, "had been able to remain, only because they were possessed of property to support them; these three had to contend with double their number of priests belonging to the church of Rome. 'There was also a sort of wandering pretenders to preaching, that came from New England and other places, which deluded not only the protestant dissenters from our church, but many churchmen themselves, by their extemporary prayers and preachments, for which they were admired by the people, and got money of them.'"* There can be little doubt, therefore, that the Episcopalians, compared to the Catholics and protestant dissenters, were a minority of the people. Their connection, however, with the government at home gave them an ascendency, and the whole province was taxed for the support of their worship.

However burdensome upon dissenters the laws for the support of the church of England may have been, there was less ground of complaint in reference to those colonies where that church was established by colonial legislation, on the part of those dissenters who entered them after those laws were enacted. They knew what they had to expect, and acted with their eyes open. We must look to those provinces where the Episcopal church was not established, and notice the claims of its members, and the conduct of the authorities of England in relation to it, if we would learn their true spirit and purpose at this period. In the provinces north of Maryland, the Episcopalians, even so late as 1767, '8, when they had greatly increased, principally by the accession of proselytes, did

* Hawks, vol. ii. p. 77.

not constitute the thirtieth of the population.* In New York they were about the twentieth; or, towards the beginning of the century, the twenty-fifth. Notwithstanding this great inferiority in numbers, and notwithstanding these provinces were settled by

* In 1768, there were in Pennsylvania and New Jersey three Episcopal churches which supported themselves, and nineteen missionaries supported by the society in England. In New York there were three churches self-supported, and eleven missionaries; in New England three churches which sustained themselves, and thirty missionaries. Chauncey's answer to Chandler's Appeal, p. 113. Dr. Chauncey concedes that, taking in vacant congregations and scattered families, the number of Episcopalians in the northern provinces might be estimated at equal to one hundred and four congregations. He allows fifty families to each congregation, which he says Episcopalians would admit to be a large allowance, and five members to a family, and thus brings out twenty-six thousand as his estimate of Episcopalians in those provinces, which he adds "is a mere handful compared with more than a million persons, which, without dispute, live within those bounds."

As to the increase of the church principally by proselytes, the fact is frequently mentioned by Humphrey in his History of the Society for the propagation of the Gospel; and Dr. Chandler, in his Appeal Defended, published in 1768, says, "As to Connecticut, of which I can judge from my own observation, the church has increased there most amazingly for twenty or thirty years past. I cannot at present recollect an example, in any age or country, wherein so great a proportion of proselytes has been made to any religion in so short a time, as has been made to the church of England in the western division of that populous colony; unless where the power of miracles or the arm of the magistrate was exerted to produce that effect." p. 217. This agrees with what Edwards says in a letter written in 1750, viz. that the Episcopal church had trebled itself in New England within seven years.

There is a great deal of information from an unexceptionable source, as to the state of the Episcopal church in this country, about the beginning of the last century, contained in the memorials of Governor Dudley, Colonel Morris, and Colonel Heathcote, presented to the Society for the propagation of the Gospel, and quoted by Humphrey, in his history of that society. "In South Carolina there were computed seven thousand souls, besides negroes and Indians, living without any minister of the church of England, and but few dissenting teachers of any kind; above half living regardless of any religion. In North Carolina above five thousand souls without any minister, any religious ministrations used, no public worship celebrated, neither the children baptized, nor the dead buried in any Christian form. Virginia contained about forty thousand souls divided into forty parishes, but wanting near half

other denominations, and with the exception of New York, were either charter or proprietary governments, yet the conduct of the royal governors, the demands of the Episcopal clergy, and the action of the authorities in England, all showed a purpose to gain and secure, as far and as fast as possible, an ascendency for the church of England, and furnished abundant reason for the anxious apprehension of the people for their religious liberty.

The fundamental assumption on which the conduct of the parties above mentioned rested, was that the Episcopal church was the national established church in all the king's dominions, Scotland only, and not the colonies, excepted: that other denominations were merely tolerated, and consequently were entitled to nothing more than the act of toleration allowed them; whereas the church of

the number of clergymen requisite. Maryland contained about twenty-five thousand, divided into twenty-six parishes, but wanting also about half the number of ministers requisite. In Pennsylvania there are about twenty thousand souls, of whom about seven hundred frequent the church, and there are not more than two hundred and fifty communicants. The two Jerseys contain about fifteen thousand, of whom not above six hundred frequent the church, nor have they more than two hundred and fifty communicants. In New York government we have thirty thousand souls at least, of whom about twelve hundred frequent the church, and we have about four hundred and fifty communicants. In Connecticut colony in New England, there are about thirty thousand souls, of whom, when they have a minister among them, about one hundred and fifty frequent the church, and there are thirty-five communicants. In Rhode Island and Narragansett, which is one government, there are about ten thousand souls, of which, about one hundred and fifty frequent the church, and there are thirty communicants. In Boston and Piscataway government, there are about eighty thousand souls, of whom about six hundred frequent the church, and one hundred and twenty the sacrament. In Newfoundland there are five hundred families constantly living in the place, and many thousands of occasional inhabitants, and no sort of public Christian worship used. This is the true though melancholy state of our church in North America; and whosoever sends any other accounts more in her favour, are certainly under mistakes; nor can I take them, (if they do it knowingly,) to be friends to the church; for if the distemper be not rightly known and understood, proper remedies can never be applied:" pp. 41–43. According to this estimate there were one hundred and eighty-five thousand inhabitants in the northern provinces, of whom three thousand four hundred, or less than one in fifty-four, were Episcopalians.

England was entitled to a legal provision, to national support, and the exclusive favour and patronage of the government. This ground was taken more or less openly, on different occasions and by different persons, according to their disposition or discretion; and it was the only ground on which the language of the most cautious could be either justified or explained. At times this position was assumed with perfect plainness. A writer who styles himself a member of the Society for the propagation of the Gospel in foreign parts, undertakes to demonstrate first, that the churches in New England were not, and secondly, that the Episcopal church was, there established. With regard to this second point he says, "Though it is undeniably manifest that the church of England is established by the act of union, (between England and Scotland,) yet it may not be so clear that this establishment actually took place before that time." To show, however, that it took place from the very settlement of the country, he quotes another Episcopal writer who says, "The Christian religion, as by its evidence and intrinsic excellence, it recommended itself to the English government, so it became by law the religion of the English nation; and the church of England likewise became by law their national church; and when any part of the English nation spread abroad into colonies, as they continued part of the nation, the law obliged them equally to the church of England and the Christian religion. And the statutes for the establishment of the service, ordination, and articles of this church, made and confirmed before and at the union of the two kingdoms, settle and establish it alike in the dominions of England, and in the realm itself." This writer then quotes various acts of parliament made in the reigns of Edward VI., Elizabeth, and Charles II., in which repeated use is made of the phrase "his majesty's dominions," as fixing the limits of the established church.* The great reliance, however, of these writers was upon the act of union. In the fifth year of Queen Anne, "It was enacted, that all acts of parliament then in force, for the es-

* A Candid Examination of Dr. Mayhew's observations on the charter and conduct of the Society for the Propagation, &c., by a member of the society. Boston, 1763, p. 34, vol. 417, of Dr. Sprague's Collection.

tablishment and preservation of the church of England, and the doctrine, worship, discipline, and government thereof, should remain and be in full force for ever; and that every king and queen succeeding to the royal government of the kingdom of Great Britain, at his or her coronation, should take and subscribe an oath to maintain and preserve inviolably, the said settlement of the church of England, and the doctrine, worship, discipline, and government thereof, as by law established within the kingdoms of England and Ireland, the dominion of Wales, and the town of Berwick on Tweed, and the territories thereunto belonging."* As the North American colonies were territories belonging to the kingdom of Great Britain, it was confidently inferred that the church of England was established here by this act, if never before.

The Rev. Mr. Wetmore of Connecticut, took the same ground, with equal decision and greater insolence. "Men," he says, "not only consistently with their duty may, but to discharge their duty, must be of the communion of the church of England, if they are members of the nation of England."† In reference to the charge of schism, which had been brought against the Episcopal proselytes in Connecticut, he says, "If the congregations, the forsaking of which is called schism, be themselves founded in schism and unjustifiable separation from the communion of the church of England, or in their present constitution must necessarily be esteemed abettors and approvers of schism, disorders, usurpation, contempt of the chief authority Christ has left in his church, or any such like crimes, then such congregations, whatever they may call themselves, and whatever show they may make, of piety and devotion in their own ways, ought to be esteemed in respect of the mystical body of Christ, only as excrescences or tumours in the body natural, or perhaps as fungosities in an ulcerated tumour, the eating away of which by whatever means tends not to the hurt, but to the sound-

* Candid Examination, p. 37.

† A Vindication of the Professors of the church of England in Connecticut, &c.; by James Wetmore, Rector of the parish of Rye, and Missionary of the Venerable Society, &c. Boston, 1747, p. 6. Dr. Sprague's Collection, vol. 414.

ness and health of the body."* In another place he says, on the assumption that the constitution of the national church is regular and good, "It may surely be urged on every man that is English, that belongs to this nation, and is properly a part of it, in whatever corner of it he may live, that his duty obliges him to be of the communion of the church of England."† And again, "Every one who makes a part of this nation, owes reverence and submission to them, (the bishops,) under Christ, and may esteem our Saviour's words to his disciples applicable to such prelates; 'He that despiseth you despiseth me.'"‡ The awful crime of schism begun in England, he argues, could not be washed away by crossing the ocean, into "a new country dependent on, and a part of the nation of England."§ The doctrine of this whole Tract is, that the church of England is the established church of the nation of England; the colonies are a part of that nation, and therefore are bound not only morally but legally to be of the communion of that church, or to take the benefit of the act of toleration.

This was the doctrine not merely of heated partisans, but of men in high stations and authority. It has already been stated, that the proprietors of South Carolina distinctly assumed this ground. "The Church of England being the only true, and orthodox, and National Church, of all the king's dominions, is so also of Carolina." And they drew from the principle the legitimate inference, when they added, "And therefore it alone shall be allowed to receive pnblic maintenance by grant of Parliament," i. e. the Provincial Parliament.

When Lord Cornbury was made Governor of New York and New Jersey, in 1702, he was instructed and enjoined by the government to take special care that the Book of Common Prayer, as by law established, should be read every Sunday and holyday, and the blessed sacrament administered according to the rites of the Church of England; that churches should be repaired, or built; that a competent maintenance be provided for the clergy, with a house and glebe in each parish, all at the common charge; and he was forbidden to prefer any man to any benefice who had not a

* A Vindication, &c. p. 29. † Ibid. p. 37. ‡ Ibid. p. 38. § Ibid. p. 40.

certificate from the Bishop of London.* These instructions related to colonies in one of which the Episcopalians, at that time, were six hundred to fifteen thousand; and in the other, twelve hundred to thirty thousand. Lord Cornbury acted up to these directions with a zeal which even his most determined friends must have thought indiscreet. Our limits forbid our entering upon details, which is less necessary, as the complaints and apprehensions of the non-episcopal inhabitants of the colonies were not founded on mere specific acts of injustice or oppression, so much as upon the avowed or tacit adoption of the principle, that the English ecclesiastical laws extended to this country. This assumption was openly made when the Rev. Mr. Makemie was imprisoned by the order of Lord Cornbury for preaching in New York. On his trial, he was charged by the attorney-general with contemning the queen's ecclesiastical supremacy; with using other rites and ceremonies than those contained in the Common Prayer Book; with preaching without proper qualification, at an illegal conventicle, all which was declared to be contrary to the English statutes.†

The same principle was assumed in the case of the application of the Presbyterian Church in New York for a charter. Their petition was opposed by the vestry of Trinity Church, on the ground that it could not be granted consistently with the acts of uniformity, nor with the king's coronation oath, by which he was bound to uphold the Church of England, not only in England and Ireland, but in all the territories thereunto belonging. The provincial authorities considered this too grave a question for them to decide, and therefore referred it to the government at home. The Bishop of London appeared repeatedly before the committee of the privy council in opposition to the petition, and it was finally decided that, without expressing an opinion as to these legal questions, it was on grounds of general policy inexpedient to grant the Presbyterians any greater privileges than they were entitled to by the act of toleration. This was virtually a decision of the whole case; for it assumed that act to be in force in New York, which,

* See his instructions in Smith's History of New Jersey, p. 252.

† Smith's History of New York, p. 128.

from its nature was impossible, unless the acts of uniformity, from whose penalties it provided exemption, were also in force. Hence Dr. Chauncey had good reason to say, "That decision was an alarm to all the colonies on the continent, giving them solemn notice what they might expect, should Episcopalians ever come to have the superiority in their influence."* And what does Dr. Chandler say to this case? "How far," he says, "the grant would have interfered with the king's coronation oath, it becomes me not to say; those to whom it was referred were the proper judges; and in their opinion the petition could not consistently be granted. It is the unquestionable duty of his Majesty's most honourable privy council, to advise him against whatever is thought by them to imply a breach of the coronation oath; it is a duty more peculiarly incumbent upon any such bishops as his majesty thinks fit to call up to that high trust. If, therefore, the Bishop of London, upon the above principle, was more active than others in opposing the measure, it was because his station required it. If general policy, in the opinion of the lords of trade, was also against the grant, they were obliged to discountenance it; and the petitioners, I conceive, ought to rest satisfied, especially as it was a mere favour which was requested, and more than was thought to be allowed by the laws of toleration. I have been moreover told, that, besides the reasons assigned, a particular policy with regard to the Presbyterians in New York, concurred to defeat the petition. It was the belief at home, that the Church of England had been treated with peculiar malevolence by some of those very persons whose names were annexed to that petition. It was, therefore, not unnatural to suspect that any additional power put into the hands of such persons, would, as opportunity should offer, be exerted against the church."† This dread of power in the hands of Presbyterians is peculiarly edifying, when it is remembered that the power asked for was the right to hold their church and grave-yard in their own name, instead of being obliged to vest them in the General Assembly of the Church of Scotland. If Episcopalians, who claimed all

* Chauncey's Reply to the Appeal Defended, p. 179.

† The Appeal Defended, by Dr. Chandler, p. 234.

the power and privileges granted by the English laws to the Church of England, might dread such a power as that, surely Presbyterians may be excused for standing a little in awe of them.

We see, from the above extract, that Dr. Chandler yielded a very cordial assent to the decision that the king's coronation oath bound him to consider the acts, by which the Church of England was established, as extending to the colonies; and that he took it for granted the act of toleration was the measure of the liberties and privileges of the non-episcopal churches in America. The coronation oath was founded on the act of union between England and Scotland. At the time of the union, the Scotch stipulated that the united Parliament should have no power to disturb their ecclesiastical constitution; and the English stipulated that each succeeding sovereign should swear to maintain the Church of England as by law established. The object, therefore, of the act in question was to protect the Church of England, and not to establish it where it did not then exist. Such being its design, it will be seen how monstrous was the assumption, that it upset all the charters of the New England colonies; rendered void all the contracts with the proprietary governments; nullified all the colonial laws relating to ecclesiastical matters, and established the Church of England even in Massachusetts and Connecticut, where, at the time of its passage, that church could hardly be said to have had an existence.

As another instance of the latitude of construction given by those in authority, to the English ecclesiastical laws, may be mentioned the letter of the Lords Justices in England to the Lieutenant-Governor of Massachusetts, in 1725. A request had been made to the authorities of that province, by the pastors, to be allowed to hold a Synod. When this request reached the ears of those in power in England, the justices wrote a severe letter to the governor for allowing the matter to be agitated. They say they can find no warrant for holding such a Synod, "but if such Synods might be holden, yet they take it to be clear in point of law, that his majesty's supremacy in ecclesiastical affairs being a branch of the prerogative, does take place in the plantations; and Synods cannot be held, nor is it lawful for the clergy to assemble as in Synods, without authority from his majesty." In case the Synod had actually met before these instructions came to hand, the lieutenant-governor "was to cause their meeting to cease, acquainting them that their assembly is against law and a contempt of his majesty's prerogative, and that they are forbid to meet any more."*

A still stronger illustration is afforded by the history of New Hampshire. When that province was erected into a separate government, in 1679, it was ordered that all protestants should be tolerated, "and that those especially as shall be conformable to the rites of the church of England shall be particularly countenanced and encouraged." In 1684, an order was issued by the governor and council, requiring the ministers to admit all persons of suitable age, and not vicious, to the Lord's Supper, and their children to baptism, and enjoining, in case any one wished either of the sacraments to be administered according to the liturgy, it should be done, in pursuance to the king's command, in the colony of Massachusetts; and any minister who refused obedience to this order was to suffer the penalties of the statutes of uniformity. This declaration was not an idle threat; the Rev. Mr. Moody, of Portsmouth, having refused to administer the Lord's Supper in the form prescribed, was sentenced to six months' imprisonment.† The same instructions given to Lord Cornbury as governor of East and West Jersey, were given to the governor of this province, with the addition that no one from England was to be allowed to act as schoolmaster, who was not furnished with a certificate from the bishop of London, and no other person without the governor's license.

The non-episcopal denominations, therefore, in this country, had abundant cause for alarm. From South Carolina to New Hampshire, they saw the power and influence of the government exerted to give ascendency to the Episcopal church. This object was constantly though cautiously pursued. It was natural that it should be so. The arguments which were adduced to prove that the church of England was entitled to this ascendency, were sufficiently plausible to command the assent of those who were anxious to be con-

* See the whole letter in the Candid Examination, &c. pp. 28–30.

† Belknap's History of New Hampshire, vol. i. p. 206.

vinced. And the motives of policy in behalf of the measure, were sufficiently obvious to make all see that the English government would pursue it as far as it could be done with safety. Here, as in the contest about taxation, it was not the pressure of the particular acts of injury or indignity that produced the dissatisfaction; but the power that was claimed. The assumption was the same in both cases, viz.: that America was part of the nation of England, that the power of the king and parliament was here what it was there. Hence on the one hand, the inference that the British parliament could here levy what taxes they pleased; and on the other, that the king's supremacy in ecclesiastical matters, extended to the colonies; that every Englishman who came to America, did but remove from one part of the nation to another; that he stood in the same relation to the national church in this country, as he had done in England. It is readily admitted that as there were some English statesmen who denied the authority of parliament to tax America, so there were many distinguished men who denied that the ecclesiastical laws of England were in force in this country. But in both cases the interest, and bent, and general course of the government, were against the liberties of the colonies.

Another cause of irritation and uneasiness, was the conduct of the Society for the Propagation of the Gospel in foreign parts. The principal complaints urged against it were, first, that instead of sending missionaries to the heathen, according to the primary object of its institution, it devoted its resources, in a great measure, to the American colonies. The society was successfully vindicated on this point by its various advocates. It was proved that its charter contemplated the colonies as a prominent if not the chief field of its labours. And when we consider the immense extent and crying destitution of this country, we shall be more disposed to wonder and complain that the society did so little, than that it did so much for its relief. A second ground of complaint was more plausible. It was urged that instead of sending their missionaries where they were really needed, they sent them to New England where they were not wanted. At this time there were at least five hundred and fifty educated ministers in New England, and not a town, unless just settled, without a pastor, unless it was in Rhode Island.* That there was ground for this complaint against the Society, is admitted by its ablest and most dignified defender, who says, "In all that I have hitherto said, I am far from intending to affirm that the Society hath not laid out in Massachusetts and Connecticut too large a proportion of the money put into their hands, considering the necessities of the other provinces."† It is not to be wondered at that the people of New England felt irritated by having the numerous missionaries of a powerful Society located among them, where their most ostensible object was not to supply the destitute, but to make proselytes from established congregations. The claims and conduct of these missionaries, in many cases, greatly increased this irritation. They spoke of all the inhabitants of the town in which they lived, as their parishioners; as bound both by the law of God and the state to be in communion with the church of England; as having no authorized ministers or valid ordinances; as belonging to churches which were mere excrescences or fungosities.

It was principally from the missionaries of this Society that the demand for American bishops proceeded. It has already been stated how small a portion of the Virginia clergy concurred in the application.‡ The origin of the plan, therefore, was not likely to recommend it to the public. For all the legitimate purposes of a bishop, such an officer was most needed where Episcopalians were

* Chauncey's Remarks on the Bishop of Llandaff's sermon. Boston, 1767, p. 37; Dr. Sprague's Collection, vol. 418.

† An answer to Dr. Mayhew's Observations on the character and conduct of the Society for the Propagation, &c.; London, 1764, p. 49; Dr. Sprague's Collection, vol. — p. 49. The author of this Tract is said by Dr. Chandler, to have been one of the dignitaries of the church of England; and it contrasts very favourably with some of the controversial pamphlets of the missionaries of the Society.

‡ Dr. Hawks states, that the applications for a resident bishop were made "principally by the *clergy* of the northern provinces." Dr. Hawks italicises the word 'clergy'. He further says, that the convention of New York and New Jersey sent missionaries to the South, to endeavour to secure the co-operation of their southern brethren in the prosecution of this object.

the most numerous. That the request came from the provinces where they were a small minority, could not fail to produce the apprehension, that the bishop's influence was to be used to give that minority still greater ascendency.

If the source whence this application emanated excited apprehension, the grounds on which it was urged did not tend to allay these fears. It is true the plan was exhibited with much plausibility in Dr. Chandler's Appeal. He frequently asserts that the power of the proposed bishop was to be derived altogether from the church and not from the state; that he was not to be received on the ground of a state-establishment. In this he was no doubt sincere; but he and his readers differed widely as to the meaning of the terms here employed. If the bishop was not to receive any power from the state, why was he to be sent by act of Parliament? Dr. Chandler says, that when bishops were first proposed for this country, they were spoken of as suffragans, whose duty it was to discharge offices merely episcopal, according to the direction, and by virtue of a commission from the diocesan. And he gives his readers to understand that such bishops were still desired. Then why did not the Bishop of London consecrate and commission them, without troubling Parliament about the matter? There was no legislative act necessary to authorize the sending of deacons, priests, or commissaries, to this country; why then was such an act required to authorize the sending a suffragan bishop? Dr. Chandler informs us, however, that when the Society for the Propagation of the Gospel first undertook this business, they "began by making all proper representations of the case to the Queen, (Anne;) they proceeded to purchase a house in New Jersey for the residence of a bishop, and after duly preparing the way, obtained an order from the crown for a bill to be drawn and laid before Parliament for establishing an American episcopate." He confirms his representation by the following extract from the published proceedings of the Society: "A representation was humbly offered to her Majesty, importing what number of bishops was expedient to be sent, where they were to be fixed, and what revenues might be thought proper for their support. To which her Majesty was pleased to give a most gracious answer, highly satisfactory to the Society; and a draught of a bill was ordered proper to be offered to Parliament for establishing bishops and bishopricks in America."* Now, whatever Dr. Chandler might think on the subject, this was a plan for introducing bishops on the footing of a state-establishment. They were to be sent by the state; their residence, revenues, and powers were to be ascertained by the state; all, or at least the last, were to be fixed by act of Parliament. No one at all acquainted with the temper of that period, or who knows the power which the authorities in England were accustomed to see in the hands of a bishop, can wonder that not only the non-episcopal clergy, but also Episcopal laymen rose in opposition to this plan; that the House of Burgesses in Virginia unanimously protested against it. If Parliament was to determine the extent of these Episcopal powers, the country had good reason to be assured they would be made as large as was consistent with safety. It was a plan to let Episcopalians say how much power Episcopal bishops should have over other denominations.

Though Dr. Chandler says it was not intended to allow the American bishops to hold ecclesiastical courts, or to interfere with questions relating to wills, marriage, guardianship, &c.; yet he clearly intimates that it would be nothing unreasonable, if important civil powers were to be conferred upon them. "There is not," he says, "the least prospect at present, that bishops in this country will ever acquire any influence or power, but what shall arise from a general opinion of their abilities and integrity, and a conviction of their usefulness; and of this no persons need dread the consequences. But should the government see fit hereafter to invest them with some degree of civil power worthy of their acceptance, which it is impossible to say they will not, although there is no appearance that they ever will; yet as no new powers will be created in favour of bishops, it is inconceivable that any would thereby be injured. All that the happiness and safety of the public require, is, that the legislative and executive power be placed in the hands of such persons as are possessed of the greatest abilities,

* Appeal, pp. 51, 52.

integrity, and prudence; and it is hoped that our bishops will always be thought to deserve this character."* If Episcopalians were afraid to allow Presbyterians an act of incorporation to enable them to hold their church and grave-yard, lest they should use the power against the church, could Presbyterians be expected to regard with indifference legislative or executive power in the hands of an Episcopal bishop, especially when the nature and extent of that power were to be determined by the English government?†

Another ground of apprehension related to the support of these bishops. The country had abundant reason to expect that this burden would, sooner or later, be thrown upon the public. Wherever the government were able to effect the object, they had already thrown the support of the Episcopal clergy upon the commnnity. This had been done in South Carolina, Virginia, and Maryland. To a certain extent it had been done in New York; and the royal governors in other provinces had orders to accomplish the same object as far as possible. With regard to the bishops, Dr. Chandler says, indeed, that there was no intention to tax the country for their support; yet he distinctly recognizes both the right and reasonableness of such a tax. "Should," says he, "a general tax be laid upon the country, and thereby a sum be raised sufficient for the purpose; and even supposing we should have three bishops on the continent, which are the most that have been mentioned, yet I believe such a tax would not amount to more than four pence in a hundred pounds. And this would be no mighty hardship to the country. He that could think much of giving the six thousandth part of his income to any use which the legislature of his country should assign, deserves not to be considered in the light of a good subject or member of society."‡ What mighty hardship to the country was a tax of three pence on a pound of tea? Yet how great a matter that little fire kindled! Dr. Chandler evidently

* Appeal, p. 110.

† Dr. Chandler says, in the Defence of the Appeal, that the above case was only hypothetical. The hypothesis, however, was so put, as to show that he regarded the possession of civil power by American bishops, as no just ground of complaint.

‡ Appeal, p. 107.

assumed two things, which America never would quietly submit to. The one was, that the English Parliament had a right to lay a general tax upon the country; and the other, that they had a right to tax the whole community for the support of the Episcopal Church. Here was the old error, viz.: that America was part of the nation of England, and consequently that the Parliament had the same power here as there; and that the Episcopal Church was the national church in the one country as well as in the other.*

The political motives urged by Dr. Chandler in support of his plea for bishops, were not suited to conciliate special favour to the plan. "Episcopacy and monarchy," he says, "are, in their frame and constitution, best suited to each other. Episcopacy can never thrive in a republican government, nor republican principles in an Episcopal Church." Experience has proved this opinion to be incorrect. The Episcopal Church never flourished in this country so much as since the establishment of the republic. Dr. Chandler goes on to say, that as episcopacy and monarchy "are mutually

* What Dr. Chandler says in the Defence of his Appeal, in reference to the passage cited above, does not remove its objectionable character. He repeats his denial that the imposition of a tax was either probable or intended, and "Further, to show that America had no need to be terrified on that account," he adds, "I considered the matter under the most unfavourable supposition that could be made, namely, that the deficiency in the Episcopal fund should be answered by a tax upon the inhabitants, and declared it as my opinion, that such a tax would be inconsiderable, and amount to no more than four pence in a hundred pounds," p. 249. The objection was not to the amount of the tax, but to a tax at all; and especially to a tax for such a purpose. His language in both passages clearly implies, that he recognized the power to impose such a tax, and that it would be unreasonable to complain of it. This supremacy of the imperial Parliament, England never would give up. Had she been willing to adopt the theory which Franklin urged in vain upon her statesmen, and agreed to make the king and not the Parliament, the bond of union between the countries, allowing every province, important enough to have a legislature, to govern itself as Scotland did before the union; had, in other words, the bonds of union been made so loose as not to be galling, the British monarch might have swayed a peaceful sceptre over near half the world. God has ordered it otherwise, and therefore it is best it should be otherwise.

adapted to each other, so they are mutually introductive of each other. He that prefers monarchy in the state, is more likely to approve of episcopacy in the church than a rigid republican. On the other hand, he that is for parity and a popular government in the church, will more easily be led to approve of a similar form of government in the state, how little soever he may suspect it himself. It is not then to be wondered, if our civil rulers have always considered episcopacy as the surest friend of monarchy; and it may reasonably be expected from those in authority, that they will support and assist the church in America, if from no other motives, yet from a regard to the state, with which it has so friendly and close an alliance."* As there was at this time a rapidly increasing dread of the power of the mother country, the consideration that the introduction of bishops would tend to increase that power, and strengthen the government, was not suited to allay apprehension or to conciliate favour.

This long detail respecting a controversy now almost forgotten, may be excused since it relates to an important chapter in the history not only of our church, but of the country. This controversy had more to do with the revolution than is generally supposed; and a knowledge of the leading facts in the case is necessary to free Presbyterians and other denominations, from the charge of unreasonable and bigoted opposition to a church fully entitled to confidence and affection. Before the revolution the Episcopal Church, from its connection with the English government, and from its claim to be regarded as a branch of a great national establishment, was justly an object of apprehension. And this apprehension was confirmed and deepened by a long series of encroachments on the rights of other denominations. After the revolution, that church ceased to be the Church of England, and became the Protestant Episcopal Church in the United States. Since she has taken her stand on equal terms with sister churches, she is the object of no other feelings than respect and love, wherever she consents to acknowledge that equality.

* Appeal, p. 115.

THE CONDUCT OF THE SYNOD IN REFERENCE TO THE REVOLUTION.

After reading the preceding section, no one need be at a loss to conjecture the part taken by the Synod in relation to the great struggle for the liberties of America. The position in which the Presbyterians and other non-episcopal denominations stood to the English government, naturally placed them in the opposition. The declaration of the English parliament, "That the king's majesty, by and with the advice and consent of the lords spiritual and temporal, and commons of Great Britain, in parliament assembled, had, hath, and of right ought to have full power and authority to make laws and statutes of sufficient force and validity to bind the colonies and people of America, subjects of the crown of Great Britain, in all cases whatsoever;"* was quite as alarming in reference to the religious as to the civil liberties of the people. No one doubted that the English parliament believed an established church desirable, or that the Episcopal Church was, in their opinion, the best and safest form of religion; and no one could doubt, as they claimed the power, they would give that church an effective establishment in every colony sufficiently under their control. In almost every province, all denominations, except the Episcopal, were regarded as merely tolerated in their own country, and were subject to many unjust demands peculiar to themselves. It was impossible that the great majority of the people could be treated as inferiors; could be denied privileges which they considered their due; or that they could see a small minority of their fellow-citizens regarded as standing in an alliance to the state peculiarly friendly and close, and on that account treated with special favour, without being discontented and uneasy. The declaration of independence was for all such, a declaration of religious, as well as of civil liberty. It is not surprising, therefore, that the non-episcopal clergy entered into the conflict with a decision which, in many cases, would render it more easy to prove that they did too much, than that they did too little.

* Gen. Conway's resolutions, passed by the House of Commons, Feb. 1766.

If it was natural that Presbyterians should side with America in that hour of trial, it was no less natural that the Episcopal clergy should side with the mother country. They had no peculiar grievances to complain of, nor any fear for the liberty of their church. On the contrary, it was to England they looked for support, for patronage, for legal provision, for that property and pre-eminence which they thought due to them as a branch of the national church. Besides, many of them were born, and all had been ordained in England, and personally had taken an oath of allegiance. They were bound, therefore, by peculiar ties; ties which, it can well be imagined, good men would find it hard to break. Instead, therefore, of its being a matter of surprise that the majority of the Episcopal clergy took part with England, the wonder is that so many sided with America. Those who did so, did it at a great sacrifice. They contended against their own apparent interests; and were either very enlightened patriots, or very indifferent churchmen. Considering, then, the peculiar circumstances of the Episcopal clergy at that time, so far from being disposed to make it a matter of reproach that they adhered to their allegiance to the mother country, we are disposed to think that, as a general rule, they were those of most moral worth, and most entitled to respect, who took this course. This, however, must not be considered as an injurious reflection on the patriot clergy. While some of them took commissions in the army, others remained faithful at once to religion and their country. The venerable Bishop White, an ornament to the church universal, was for a long time the chaplain of Congress, and acted with deliberation, and well considered principle in the course which he adopted.* The laymen of the Episcopal Church did not feel them-

* In a letter to Bishop Hobart, he says: "I continued, as did all of us, to pray for the king, until Sunday, (inclusively,) before the fourth of July, 1776. Within a short time after, I took the oath of allegiance to the United States, and have since remained faithful to it. My intentions were upright and most seriously weighed; and I hope they were not in contrariety to my duty."

In another place he says: "Owing to the circumstances of many able and worthy ministers cherishing their allegiance to the king of Great Britain, and entertaining conscientious scruples against the use of the liturgy, with the omission of the appointed prayers for him, they ceased to officiate, and the

selves trammeled in the same manner, or to the same extent as the ministers, and hence some of the most prominent and influential of the public leaders of the day belonged to that church.

The part taken by Presbyterians in the contest with the mother country, was, at the time, often made a ground of reproach; and the connection between their efforts for the security of their religious liberty, and opposition to the oppressive measures of Parliament, was then distinctly seen. Mr. Galloway, a prominent advocate of the government, ascribed, in 1774, the revolt and revolution mainly to the action of the Presbyterian clergy and laity as early as 1764, when the proposition for a General Synod emanated from a committee appointed for that purpose in Philadelphia.* This was a great exaggeration and mistake, but it indicates the close connection between the civil and religious part of the controversy. The same writer describes the opponents of the government, as an "united faction of Congregationalists, Presbyterians, and smugglers." Another writer of the same period says: "You will have discovered that I am no friend to Presbyterians, and that I fix all the blame of these extraordinary American proceedings upon them."† He goes on, "Believe, sir, the Presbyterians have been the chief and principal instruments in all these flaming measures; and they always do and ever will act against government, from that restless and turbulent anti-monarchical spirit which has always distinguished them every where when they had, or by any means could assume power, however illegally."

As the conduct of the Presbyterian clergy during the revolutionary war is not a matter of dispute, all that we are called upon to do, is briefly to exhibit the action of the Synod in reference to this subject. One of the first exercises of the power claimed by Parliament to impose taxes on America, was the passage of the

doors of far the greater number of Episcopal churches were closed for years. In this state there was a part of that time in which there was, through the whole extent, but one resident minister of the church in question: he who ecords the fact."—See Address, &c. by William B. Reed. Philadelphia, 1838.

* Reed's Address, p. 51.

† By Presbyterians, this writer means non-episcopalians.

Stamp-Act in 1764. The opposition to this measure was so general and vehement, that the British Government thought proper to repeal the act, though they accompanied the repeal with the strongest declarations of their right to tax the colonies at discretion. In the controversy relating to this subject, the Synod of New York and Philadelphia publicly expressed their sympathy with their fellow-citizens. As soon as the repeal was known in this country, "An overture was made by Dr. Alison, that an address be presented to our sovereign on the joyful occasion of the repeal of the Stamp-Act, and thereby a confirmation of our liberties; and at the same time proposing a copy of an address for examination, which was read and approved," but not recorded.* The Synod also addressed a pastoral letter to the churches, filled with patriotic and pious sentiments. They remind the people, that after God had delivered the country from the horrors of the French and Indian war, instead of rendering to him according to the multitude of his mercies, they had become more wicked than ever. "The Almighty thus provoked, permitted counsels of the most pernicious tendency, both to Great Britain and her colonies. The imposition of unusual taxes, a severe restriction of our trade, and an almost total stagnation of business, threatened us with universal ruin. A long suspense whether we should be deprived of, or restored to a peaceable enjoyment of the inestimable privileges of English liberty, filled every breast with painful anxiety." They express their joy that government had been induced to resort to moderate measures, instead of appealing to force; and call upon the people to bless God, who, notwithstanding their sins, had saved them from the horrors of a civil war. They, finally, earnestly exhort their people not to add to the common stock of guilt, but "to be strict in observing the laws and ordinances of Jesus Christ; to pay a sacred regard to his Sabbaths; to reverence his holy name, and to adorn the doctrine of God our Saviour by good works. "We pray you," say the Synod, "to seek earnestly the saving knowledge of Christ, and the internal power and spirit of religion. Thus may you hope for the continued kindness of a gracious Providence; and

* Minutes, p. 144.

this is the right way to express your gratitude to the Father of mercies for your late glorious deliverance. But persisting to grieve his Holy Spirit by a neglect of vital religion, and a continuance of sin, you have reason to dread that a holy God will punish you yet seven times more for your iniquities."*

In this letter, as in all the public documents issued before the Declaration of Independence, there are strong expressions of loyalty, and of the wish to preserve inviolate the union with the mother country. In the declaration of rights by the Congress held at New York, in October, 1765, it is said: "The members of this Congress, sincerely devoted with the warmest sentiments of affection and duty to his Majesty's person and government, inviolably attached to the present happy establishment of the Protestant succession, &c., &c., esteem it our indispensable duty to make the following declarations of our humble opinion respecting the most essential rights and liberties of the colonists." The first declaration is: "That his Majesty's subjects in these colonies owe the same allegiance to the crown of Great Britain, that is owing from subjects born within the realm, and all due subjection to that august body the Parliament of Great Britain."† And the Congress held at Philadelphia, September, 1774, in their address to the people of Great Britain, say: "You have been told that we are seditious, impatient of government, and desirous of independence. Be assured that these are not facts, but calumnies. Permit us to be as free as yourselves, and we shall ever esteem an union with you to be our greatest glory and our greatest happiness; we shall ever be ready to contribute all in our power to the welfare of the empire; we consider your enemies as our enemies, and your interests as our own."‡ There is every reason to believe that these declarations were as sincere as they were general. The American patriots regarded separation from the mother country as a great evil; and to the last moment cherished the hope that some accommodation might be made, which should secure them the enjoyment of their rights, and avoid the necessity of a violent separation.

* Minutes, p. 151.

† See Pitkin's Political History of the United States, vol. i. p. 446.

‡ Ibid. 481.

As the indications of the coming conflict began to multiply, the Synod endeavoured to prepare their people for the trial. Almost every year they appointed days for special prayer and fasting, and presented "the threatening aspect of public affairs," as one of the most prominent reasons of their observance. In 1775, the record on this subject is to the following effect: "The Synod considering the present alarming state of public affairs, do unanimously judge it their duty to call all the congregations under their care, to solemn fasting, humiliation, and prayer; and for this purpose appoint the last Thursday of June next to be carefully and religiously observed. But as the Continental Congress are now sitting, who may probably appoint a fast for the same purpose, the Synod, from respect to that august body, and for greater harmony with other denominations, and for the greater public order, if the Congress shall appoint a day not above four weeks distant from the said last Thursday of June, order that the congregations belonging to this Synod, do keep the day appointed by Congress in obedience to this resolution; and if they appoint a day more distant, the Synod order both to be observed by all our communion. The Synod also earnestly recommend it to all the congregations under their care, to spend the afternoon of the last Thursday in every month, in public solemn prayer to God, during the continuance of our present troubles."* This recommendation of the observance of a day for prayer every month, was frequently repeated during the war.

In this memorable year also, the Synod addressed a long and excellent letter to the churches. It thus begins: "The Synod of New York and Philadelphia, being met at a time when public affairs wear so threatening an aspect, and when, unless God in his sovereign providence speedily prevent it, all the horrors of a civil war throughout this great continent are to be apprehended, were of opinion that they could not discharge their duty to the numerous congregations under their care, without addressing them at this important crisis. As the firm belief and habitual recollection of the power and presence of the living God, ought at all times to possess the minds of real Christians; so in seasons of public

* Minutes, p. 317.

calamity, when the Lord is known by the judgments which he executeth, it would be an ignorance or indifference highly criminal, not to look up to him with reverence, to implore his mercy by humble and fervent prayer, and if possible, to prevent his vengeance, by timely repentance. We do, therefore, brethren, beseech you, in the most earnest manner, to look beyond the immediate authors, either of your sufferings or fears, and to acknowledge the holiness and justice of the Almighty in the present visitation." The Synod then exhort the people to confession and repentance; reminding them that their prayers should be attended with a sincere purpose and thorough endeavour after personal and family reformation. "If thou prepare thine heart and stretch out thine hand towards him, if iniquity be in thine hands, put it far away, and let not wickedness dwell in thy tabernacles."

They considered it also a proper time to press on all of every rank, seriously to consider the things which belong to their eternal peace, saying, "Hostilities long feared, have now taken place; the sword has been drawn in one province; and the whole continent, with hardly any exception, seem determined to defend their rights by force of arms. If at the same time the British ministry shall continue to enforce their claims by violence, a lasting and bloody contest must be expected. Surely then it becomes those who have taken up arms, and profess a willingness to hazard their lives in the cause of liberty, to be prepared for death, which to many must be certain, and to every one is a possible or probable event.

"We have long seen with concern the circumstances which occasioned, and the gradual increase of this unhappy difference. As ministers of the gospel of peace, we have ardently wished that it might be, and often hoped that it would have been more early accommodated. It is well known to you, otherwise it would be imprudent indeed thus publicly to profess, that we have not been instrumental in inflaming the minds of the people, or urging them to acts of violence and disorder. Perhaps no instance can be given on so interesting a subject, in which political sentiments have been so long and fully kept from the pulpit; and even malice itself has not charged us with labouring from the press. But things have now come to such a state, that as we do not wish to conceal our opinions as men and citizens, so the relation in which we stand to you, seemed to make the present improvement of it to your spiritual benefit, an indispensable duty."

Then follows an exhortation directed principally to young men who might offer themselves as "champions of their country's cause," to cultivate piety, to reverence the name of God, and to trust his providence. "The Lord is with you while ye be with him; and if ye seek him, he will be found of you; but if ye forsake him, he will forsake you."

After this exhortation, the Synod offered special counsels to the churches as to their public and general conduct.

"First: In carrying on this important struggle, let every opportunity be taken to express your attachment and respect to our sovereign King George, and to the revolution principles by which his august family was seated on the British throne. We recommend, indeed, not only allegiance to him from principle and duty, as the first magistrate of the empire, but esteem and reverence for the person of the prince, who has merited well of his subjects on many accounts, and who has probably been misled into his late and present measures by those about him; neither have we any doubt that they themselves have been in a great degree deceived by false representations from interested persons residing in America. It gives us the greatest pleasure to say, from our own certain knowledge of all belonging to our communion, and from the best means of information of far the greatest part of all denominations in this country, that the present opposition to the measures of administration, does not in the least arise from disaffection to the king, or a desire of separation from the parent state. We are happy in being able with truth to affirm, that no part of America would either have approved or permitted such insults as have been offered to the sovereign in Great Britain. We exhort you, therefore, to continue in the same disposition, and not to suffer oppression or injury itself easily to provoke you to any thing which may seem to betray contrary sentiments. Let it ever appear that you only desire the preservation and security of those rights which belong to you as freemen and Britons, and that reconciliation upon these terms is your most ardent desire.

"Secondly, be careful to maintain the union which at present subsists through all the colonies. Nothing can be more manifest than that the success of every measure depends on its being inviolably preserved; and, therefore, we hope you will leave nothing undone which can promote that end. In particular, as the Continental Congress, now sitting at Philadelphia, consists of delegates chosen in the most free and unbiassed manner, by the body of the people, let them not only be treated with respect, and encouraged in their difficult service; not only let your prayers be offered up to God for his direction in their proceedings, but adhere firmly to their resolutions; and let it be seen that they are able to bring out the whole strength of this vast country to carry them into execution. We would also advise for the same purpose, that a spirit of candour, charity, and mutual esteem, be preserved and promoted towards those of different religious denominations. Persons of probity and principle of every profession, should be united together as servants of the same Master; and the experience of our happy concord hitherto in a state of liberty, should engage all to unite in support of the common interest; for there is no example in history in which civil liberty was destroyed, and the rights of conscience preserved entire.

"Thirdly, we do earnestly exhort and beseech the societies under our care to be strict and vigilant in their private government, and to watch over the morals of their several members." This duty is urged at some length, and then the letter proceeds thus:

"Fourthly, we cannot but recommend and urge in the warmest manner, a regard to order and the public peace; and as in many places, during the confusion that prevails, legal proceedings have become difficult, it is hoped that all persons will conscientiously pay their just debts, and to the utmost of their power serve one another, so that the evils inseparable from a civil war, may not be augmented by wantonness and irregularity.

"Fifthly, we think it of importance at this time, to recommend to all of every rank, but especially to those who may be called to action, a spirit of humanity and mercy. Every battle of the warrior is with confused noise and garments rolled in blood. It is impossible to appeal to the sword without being exposed to many scenes of cruelty and slaughter; but it is often observed that civil wars are carried on with a rancour and spirit of revenge much greater than those between independent states. The injuries received or supposed, in civil wars, wound more deeply than those of foreign enemies. It is, therefore, more necessary to guard against this abuse, and recommend that meekness and gentleness of spirit which is the noblest attendant on true valour. That man will fight most bravely who never begins to fight till it is necessary, and who ceases to fight as soon as the necessity is over.

"Lastly, we would recommend to all the societies under our care, not to content themselves with attending devoutly on general fasts, but to continue habitually in the exercise of prayer, and to have frequent occasional voluntary meetings for solemn intercession with God on this impotant trial. Those who are immediately exposed to danger need your sympathy; and we learn from the Scriptures, that fervency and importunity are the very characters of that prayer of the righteous man that availeth much. We conclude with our most earnest prayer, that the God of heaven may bless you in your temporal and spiritual concerns, and that the present unnatural dispute may be speedily terminated by an equitable and lasting settlement on constitutional principles."

The Rev. Mr. Halsey, it is recorded, dissented from that paragraph of the above letter, which contains the declarations of allegiance. This gentleman, it seems, was at least a year in advance, not only of the Synod, but of Congress. This pastoral letter contains a decided and unanimous expression, on the part of the Synod, of the side which it took in the great struggle for the liberties of America. It certainly does them and the church which they represented, great honour. They adhered to the last to the duties which they owed their sovereign; they approved of demanding no new liberties; they required only the secure possession of privileges which they were entitled to consider as their birthright.

A month after the publication of this letter, the Presbyterian clergymen of Philadelphia published an address to the ministers and Presbyterian congregations of the county of ——, in North Carolina. It seems that there were some Presbyterians in that province who hesitated as to the course which they ought to take in the coming conflict. This is the more to be wondered at, as North Carolina was in advance of almost any province on the continent in its opposition to the British authorities. They had already driven away their governor, and set up a government of their own; and on the 20th of May, 1775, was issued the famous Mecklenburgh declaration of independence, more than a year before Congress ventured upon that step. The name of the county is left blank in the title-page of this address. The Philadelphia ministers say to their North Carolina brethren: "It adds greatly to our distress to hear that you are somehow led aside from the cause of liberty and freedom, by men who have given you an unfair representation of the debate between the parent country and her colonies." They make strong professions of loyalty, and appeal to the declarations of Congress on the subject; and add, "We want no new privileges; let us continue connected with them as we were before the Stamp-Act, and we demand no more." They refer also to the pastoral letter of the Synod, which they beg their brethren to read. They then recount the grievances of the country, especially the claim on the part of the British Parliament, of the power "to make laws to bind us in all cases whatsoever. By virtue of this power," it is added, "they have established Popery in Quebec, and the arbitrary laws of France, and why may they not do the same in Pennsylvania or North Carolina?" "What shall we then do," it is asked, "in these days of trouble and distress? We must put our trust in God, who is a present help in the time of trouble; but we must depend on him in the use of means; we must unite, if possible, as one man, to maintain our just rights; not by fire and sword, or by shedding the blood of our fellow-subjects, unless we are driven to it in self-defence, but by strictly observing such resolutions neither to export nor import goods, as may be recommended by our general Congress." Signed, July 10th, by Francis Alison, James Sproat, George Duffield, and Robert Davidson.

The Presbytery of Hanover, in a memorial presented to the Legislature of Virginia in 1776, expressed with earnestness their hearty adoption of their country's cause. "Your memorialists," they say, "are governed by the same sentiments which have inspired the United States of America; and are determined that nothing in our power or influence shall be wanting to give success to their common cause. We would also represent that dissenters from the Church of England, in this country, have ever been desirous to conduct themselves as peaceable members of the civil government, for which reason they have hitherto submitted to several ecclesiastical burdens and restrictions, that are inconsistent with equal liberty. But now, when the many and grievous oppressions of our mother country have laid this continent under the necessity of casting off the yoke of tyranny, and of forming independent governments upon equitable and liberal foundations, we flatter ourselves we shall be freed from all the incumbrances which a spirit of domination, prejudice, or bigotry hath interwoven with our political systems. This we are the more strongly encouraged to expect, by the declaration of rights, so universally applauded for that dignity, firmness, and precision with which it delineates and asserts the privileges of society, and the prerogatives of human nature, and which we embrace as the magna charta of our commonwealth, that can never be violated without endangering the grand superstructure it was destined to sustain."*

As at the beginning, so also at the close of the war, the Synod directed a pastoral letter to their congregations expressing their sentiments in relation to the contest. In the letter written in 1783, they say: "We cannot help congratulating you on the general and almost universal attachment of the Presbyterian body to the cause of liberty and the rights of mankind. This has been visible in their conduct, and has been confessed by the complaints and resentment of the common enemy. Such a circumstance ought not only to afford us satisfaction on the review, as bringing credit tc the body in general, but to increase our gratitude to God for the happy issue of the war. Had it been unsuccessful, we must have

* Presbyterian Church in Virginia, by Dr. J. H. Rice, p. 21.

drunk deeply of the cup of suffering. Our burnt and wasted churches, and our plundered dwellings, in such places as fell under the power of our adversaries, are but an earnest of what we must have suffered, had they finally prevailed.

"The Synod, therefore, request you to render thanks to Almighty God, for all his mercies spiritual and temporal; and in a particular manner for establishing the independence of the United States of America. He is the supreme disposer, and to Him belong the glory, the victory, and the majesty. We are persuaded you will easily recollect many circumstances in the course of the struggle, which point out his special and signal interposition in our favour. Our most remarkable successes have generally been when things had just before worn the most unfavourable aspect; as at Trenton and Saratoga at the beginning, in South Carolina and Virginia towards the end of the war." They specify, among other mercies, the assistance derived from France, and the happy selection "of a commander-in-chief of the armies of the United States, who, in this important and difficult charge, has given universal satisfaction, who was alike acceptable to the citizen and the soldier, to the state in which he was born, and to every other on the continent; and whose character and influence, after so long service, are not only unimpaired but augmented."

In a history designed to exhibit the character of the Presbyterian Church, some notice of the part taken by its members, and especially by its ministers, in an event so important as the revolutionary war, to the religious as well as the civil destiny of our country, could not be omitted. Enough has been said to show that her influence was thrown upon the side of liberty; upon that side which the most scrupulous Christian moralist, unless he denies the lawfulness of war under all circumstances, must pronounce to be the side of justice and of human happiness. We now turn to the more strictly ecclesiastical portion of our narrative.

FORMATION OF THE NEW CONSTITUTION.

The great increase of the church, and the manifold inconveniences consequent on all the ministers being required to attend every year the meetings of the Synod, led in 1786 to the adoption of the resolution: That the Synod would establish out of its own body, three or more Synods; out of which shall be composed a General Assembly, Synod, or Council, agreeably to a system hereafter to be adopted. A committee was accordingly appointed to prepare a plan of division. This committee recommended the formation of four Synods, viz.: First, the Synod of New York and New Jersey to be composed of the Presbyteries of Dutchess, Suffolk, New York and New Brunswick. Second, the Synod of Philadelphia to consist of the Presbyteries of Philadelphia, Lewes, New Castle, Baltimore, and Carlisle. Third, the Synod of Virginia to include the Presbyteries of Redstone, Hanover, Lexington, and Transylvania. Fourth, the Synod of the Carolinas to consist of the Presbyteries of Abingdon, Orange, and South Carolina. The committee further recommended the formation of a General Assembly, to be composed of delegates from the several Presbyteries in the proportion of one minister and one elder for every six members. This report was subsequently adopted, but the proposed division was not to take effect until the formation of the new constitution.

In order to prepare such a constitution, the Synod appointed Drs. Witherspoon, Rodgers, Sproat, Duffield, Alison, and Ewing, Mr. Matthew Wilson and Dr. Smith, ministers, and Isaac Snowden, Robert Taggart, and John Pinkerton, elders, a committee to examine the book of discipline and government, and digest such a system as they should think adapted to the state of the Presbyterian Church in America. As soon as this draught was ready, the committee were directed to have it printed and sent down to the Presbyteries, who were required to report in writing their observations upon it at the next meeting of the Synod. This committee performed the duty assigned them; and in 1787, the Presbyteries were called upon for their observations on the plan which had been submitted to their consideration. The plan was then discussed at much length, section by section, and various amendments adopted. When this process was completed, the form of government thus adopted was printed, and again transmitted to the Presbyteries "for their consideration, and for the consideration of the churches under their care."

The Synod then "took into consideration the last paragraph of the twentieth chapter of the Westminster Confession of Faith; the third paragraph of the twenty-third chapter, and the first paragraph of the thirty-first chapter, and having made some alterations, agreed that the said paragraphs as now altered, be printed for consideration together with the draught of a plan of government and discipline. The Synod also appointed a committee to revise the Westminster Directory for Public Worship, and to have it, when thus revised, printed together with the draught, for consideration. And the Synod agreed, that when the above proposed alterations in the Confession of Faith shall have been finally determined upon by this body, and the Directory shall have been revised as above directed and adopted by the Synod, the said Confession thus altered, and the Directory thus revised and adopted, shall be styled, "The Confession of Faith and Directory for Public Worship of the Presbyterian Church in the United States of America."

It appears that the Synod were not entirely unanimous, at least in the first instance, in reference to these measures. When the proposed plan of government was transmitted to the Presbytery of Suffolk, that body addressed a letter to the Synod, "praying that the union between them and the Synod might be dissolved." The Synod appointed a committee to attend a meeting of that Presbytery, and to enter on a free conversation with them on the nature of their difficulties. At the same time the following letter was sent to the Presbytery in question:

"*Reverend and Dear Brethren:*

"We received a letter from you, dated April 11, 1787, which both surprised and grieved us, by informing us, 'that you think it needful that the union between you and us should be dissolved.' We are surprised that a matter of so much importance as breaking the peace and unity of the church should be so suddenly gone into, without our receiving any information of the matter in respect to any previous things leading to such an event. We declare that we have done nothing, which we know of, that should be so much as a matter of offence to you, much less a ground of withdrawment or separation. We have always supposed that you as brethren with us, believed in the general system of doctrine, discipline, worship, and church government, as the same is contained in the Westminster Confession of Faith, Catechisms and Directory. You inform us 'that your local situation renders it inconvenient to maintain the union.' This is the same that ever it was, when we took sweet counsel together, strengthened each others' hands in the advancement of the cause of our dear Redeemer, stood firm in opposition to the enemies of our religion, and greatly comforted and encouraged one another.

"You say, 'that concurrence with the draught of the form of government and discipline for the Presbyterian Church in North America is impracticable.' That is only a draught or overture for amendment, and we should have rejoiced much to have had your company and aid in pointing out those impracticabilities, and in altering, correcting, and completing the said draught. We apprehend that there are no principles in it different from the Westminster Directory; only the same rendered more explicit in some things, and more conformable to the state and circumstances of the Presbyterian Church in America.

"You likewise add, 'the churches in your limits will not comply therewith.' Perhaps those churches, from some cause unknown to us, may have hastily imbibed groundless prejudices, which by taking some pains with them, and by giving a proper explanation of the matter, might be readily removed. We are fully of opinion that the general principles in the said draught contain the plan of church discipline and government revealed in the New Testament, and are conformable, (allowance being made for the differences in the states of civil society and local circumstances,) to the practices and usages of the best reformed churches.

"Wherefore, dearly beloved brethren, in the bowels of brotherly love, we intreat you to reconsider the resolution expressed in your letter. You well know that it is not a small thing to rend the seamless coat of Christ, or to be disjoined parts of that one body of his church. We are all members one of another. There should be no schism in the body, but we should comfort, encourage, and strengthen one another, by the firmest union in our common Lord. We are Presbyterians, and we firmly believe the Presbyterian system of doctrine, discipline, and church government, to be nearer the word of God than that of any other sect or denomination of Christians. Shall all other sects and parties be united among themselves for their support and increase, and Presbyterians divided and subdivided, so as to be the scorn of some and the prey of others? In order to testify to you the high sense we entertain of the importance of union in the Presbyterian body in America, we have appointed a committee, viz. the Rev. Dr. Rodgers, Dr. McWhorter, Mr. Roe, Mr. John Woodhull, and Mr. Davenport, to wait on you, to converse with you, and to endeavour to remove difficulties.

"Therefore we request the moderator of your Presbytery to call the same together, to meet our committee at Huntingdon on the first Wednesday in September, for these purposes, at which time and place our committee are appointed to attend. That you may, in a spirit of candour and love, reconsider your resolution, and continue in a state of union with us, and that we may, by our united efforts, advance the kingdom of our glorious Redeemer, is the earnest prayer of your affectionate and grieved brethren."

The committee above named, reported the following year to the Synod, that after a full and amicable conference with the Suffolk brethren, the latter withdrew their request for a dismission, as appeared from the following extract from their minutes. "The Presbytery of Suffolk met at Brook Haven, April 8, 1788, according to appointment. Entered upon the consideration of the petition sent to the Rev. Synod of New York and Philadelphia at their last sessions, requesting a dismission from their body: and after deliberating on it, came to the following conclusion, viz.: to withdraw the petition."

It is known also, that the Rev. Matthew Wilson was far from being satisfied with the form of government ultimately adopted. The only intimation of this fact contained in the minutes is a record to the following effect: "A petition from the Rev. Dr.

Matthew Wilson, detained by bodily indisposition, respecting the draught of the form of government, was presented and read. Ordered, that it lie on the table."*

It does not appear that this dissatisfaction extended to any considerable number of the members; at least there is not the slightest

* Dr. Matthew Wilson, though an old-side man, educated under Dr. Alison, was not in theory a Presbyterian, in the ordinary sense of the term. He seems to have held a system of church government peculiar to himself, though very analogous to that since published by Mr. Haldane, in Scotland. In every congregation he supposed there ought to be a Presbytery, composed of the pastor, or bishop, and presbyters; which presbyters were to teach or preach, if occasion called for it. He questioned the propriety of Presbyteries constituted as ours are, and denied the authority of such Presbyteries, and of Synods over churches and ministers. There is extant a printed sheet containing extracts from an overture of his, presented to the Synod in 1774, presenting twenty-one queries, "the reasonings in support of which had been read before the Synod." The following selection from these queries may serve to give an idea of Dr. Wilson's views.

"1. Whether every apostolic and primitive church had not its bishop or pastor, and deacons? The pastor his assistant presbyters, one of whom was the catechist or doctor? The deacons their assistant widows for the sick and poor?"

"4. Whether, besides the preaching of the word, &c. by the bishop or pastor, they had not, in every congregational church, presbyters ordained to preach, when invited, in their own or any other congregation? Acts xi. 19; 1 Pet. iv. 10, 11, &c."

"5. Whether there was not a Presbytery in every church, i. e. congregation, or city, composed of its proper officers at least? Whether bishops or presbyters were not of the same order essentially, having the power of the keys *in foro exteriore et interiore?* Tit. i. 5–7. Phil. i. 1. Acts xx. 17, 19, &c. as contended for by Jerome, Gregory Nazianzen, &c."

"8. Whether Christ, or his apostles, appointed any stated judicatories or vested any controlling authority in any bishop, or Synod, or Assembly, over particular Churches, or Presbyteries, or pastors?"

"15. Whether there be any other judicatures besides Presbyteries in particular congregations, authorized in God's word, as having powers of ordination and discipline, censures, admission and rejection of officers and members of the church?"

"19. Whether the meeting of pastors and lay-elders, one of each from every congregation, can be a scriptural Presbytery? Does not a Presbytery act in a church, and a church consist of persons assembled for worship, rather than mere government? Can there be a true apostolic Presbytery, unless all the

intimation on the minutes of the want of perfect unanimity. It is there recorded, that the "Synod having fully considered the draught of the form of government and discipline, did, on a view of the whole, and hereby do ratify and adopt the same as now altered and amended, as the Constitution of the Presbyterian Church in America, and as the rule of their proceedings by all inferior judicatories belonging to this body. And they order that a correct copy be printed, and the Westminster Confession of Faith, as now altered, be printed in full along with it, as part of the Constitution.

"*Resolved*, That the true intent and meaning of the above ratification by the Synod is, that the Form of Government and Discipline, and the Confession of Faith, as now ratified, are to continue to be our constitution and confession of faith and practice unalterably, unless two-thirds of the Presbyteries, under the care of the General Assembly, shall propose alterations or amendments, and such alterations or amendments shall be agreed to and enacted by the General Assembly."

The Synod having also "revised and corrected the Directory for Worship, did approve and ratify the same, and do hereby appoint

officers at least of the church convene, and give their consent, or the majority of them, in every affair of discipline before them?"

"21. Finally, whether, from Scripture or the primitive Christian churches, those councils met in the name of Christ, for the purpose of promoting union, love, peace, and edification, in the way of mutual communion, and agreeable holy conversation of all the churches together, have any church power at all properly so called; such as has too often been claimed by our Synods, &c. over any churches, their members, officers, Presbyteries, temporalities, as to receiving or rejecting members, making acts, laws, and canons, assuming the power of Presbyteries to admit or reject pastors, modelling Presbyteries, fixing their limits, ordering one church to one, and another to another; preventing young presbyters going to any church or Presbytery which they may choose, and where they are called in providence. I say, whether all these, and a thousand other acts of church power, are not altogether ordinances of men, and as really anti-Christian additions to the apostolic church regimen and order as diocesan Episcopacy itself? 2 Cor. i. 24."

The overture, containing these queries, was presented by Dr. Wilson just after the difficulty in the Synod about the rule respecting foreign ministers, and the settlement of Mr. Duffield in Philadelphia; on both which occasions, Dr. Wilson protested against the action of the Synod in the premises.

the said Directory, as now amended, to be the Directory for the public worship of God in the Presbyterian Church in the United States of America. They also took into consideration the Westminster Larger and Shorter Catechisms, and having made a small amendment of the Larger, did approve, and do hereby approve and ratify the said Catechisms, as now agreed on, as the Catechisms of the Presbyterian Church in the United States. And the Synod order that the said Directory and Catechisms be printed and bound up in the same volume with the Confession of Faith and Form of Government and Discipline, and that the whole be considered as our standard of doctrine, government, discipline, and worship, agreeably to the resolutions of the Synod at its present sessions.

"Ordered, that Dr. Duffield, Mr. Armstrong, and Mr. Green, be a committee to superintend the printing and publishing of the above said Confession of Faith and Catechisms, with the Form of Government and Discipline, and the Directory for the worship of God, as now adopted and ratified by the Synod, as the Constitution of the Presbyterian Church in the United States of America; and that they divide the several parts into chapters and sections properly numbered."

After this work was finally accomplished, it was resolved unanimously, "That this Synod be divided, and it is hereby divided into four Synods, agreeably to an act made and provided for in the sessions of Synod in the year 1786, and this division shall commence on the dissolution of the present Synod.

"*Resolved*, That the first meeting of the General Assembly to be constituted out of the above Synods be held, and it is hereby appointed to be held on the third Thursday of May, one thousand seven hundred and eighty-nine, in the Second Presbyterian Church in the City of Philadelphia, at eleven o'clock, A. M.; and that Dr. Witherspoon, or, in case of his absence, Dr. Rodgers, open the General Assembly with a sermon, and preside until a moderator be chosen."

After appointing the time and place of meeting of the several Synods, the Synod of New York and Philadelphia was dissolved; and the session was concluded with prayer.

Thus closed the career of this venerable Synod, after an existence of thirty years actively and usefully employed. During this period the church had rapidly increased. The Synod had received an accession of about two hundred and thirty new members; it had grown from eight to sixteen Presbyteries, and had under its care above four hundred and twenty congregations.* Of these about forty were in the State of New York, and three hundred and eighty in the Middle and Southern States. Nothing could prove more decisively the origin and general character of the great mass of our church, up to this period. The overwhelming majority of its members were located in those portions of the country which had been settled by Scotch and Irish Presbyterians.

With regard to the Synod it may be remarked that it consisted in the general, of liberally educated men. Of the two hundred and thirty new members, more or less, received after the union in 1758, about one hundred and twenty were graduates of the College of New Jersey, and from twenty to twenty-five graduates of Yale. Of the residue many were educated in Europe, or at the University of Pennsylvania, or at the Newark Academy in Delaware, or at Pequea, or during the latter part of the period under review, at Hampden-Sydney College, or at the Washington Academy in Virginia. It hence appears, that the great body of our ministers, as well as of our people, were born and educated within the bosom of the Presbyterian Church.

* It appears from a printed list of the ministers and congregations, published in 1788, that there were then one hundred and seventy-seven ministers connected with the Synod, and four hundred and nineteen congregations reported, as follows: Suffolk Presbytery, thirteen congregations; Dutchess nine; New York thirty-nine; New Brunswick twenty-six; Philadelphia twenty-two; New Castle twenty-seven; Lewes nineteen; Baltimore twelve; Carlisle fifty-six; Redstone twenty-seven; Lexington twenty-seven; Hanover twenty-one; Orange seventy-one; Abingdon twenty-five; South Carolina forty-five; Transylvania no report. As this Presbytery consisted of five ministers, it had probably ten congregations under its care. As the Presbytery of New York then included the territory now embraced within the limits of the Presbyteries of Newark and Elizabethtown, nineteen or twenty of its congregations were in New Jersey; leaving the number of congregations in the State of New York forty-one or forty-two.

The members of this Synod were, to a remarkable degree, harmonious in their doctrinal views. There is no indication of diversity of opinion on any important subject; there were no doctrinal controversies, and but one instance of the infliction of censure for erroneous opinions. Besides this negative evidence, we have the positive proof to be found in the frequent declarations of the adherence of the Synod to the Westminster Confession, and the unanimous adoption of that formula as a part of the new constitution.*

The strictly Presbyterian character of the Synod is manifest from its records, which may challenge, as to this point, a comparison with those of any similar body. The men who professed to derive their ecclesiastical "origin from the Church of Scotland;" who declared that they "adopted her standards of doctrine, discipline, and worship," and whose ecclesiastical proceedings are so fully in accordance with their professions, cannot be suspected of a want of Presbyterianism.

A much more interesting point is the religious character of the Synod. On this subject little can be learned from the minutes. The impression, however, made by the plan of union adopted in 1758; by the tone and sentiments of the numerous documents having reference to practical subjects; by the frequent appointment of days for special religious observance; by the care taken to promote the religious education of the young, and to maintain a high standard of piety in the ministry; and by the efforts made to extend the blessings of the gospel to the destitute, is that, as a

* In an interesting letter written by the Rev. Dr. King, of Franklin County, at the beginning of the war, there is a strong testimony to the unanimity of the Synod in reference to matters of doctrine. He tells his correspondent, "I think that our Synod will be very cautious, as they have hitherto been, with respect to the admission of ministers from Europe, and especially from such places as are suspected of encouraging Arminianism, &c., and where they are so lax as to the admission of candidates. It is a particular happiness for us as yet, that we have been cautious, and Divine Providence has favoured our endeavours; for I do not know that any minister belonging to our Synod can be reasonably suspected of leaning to any but the Calvinistic scheme." This letter was written in answer to one dated April 13th, 1775.—See Pittsburgh Herald, April 22d, 1836.

body, the Synod of New York and Philadelphia was distinguished for its piety. And this impression is confirmed by the fact, that so large a number of its members are still held in grateful remembrance as devoted servants of God.

As to the state of religion throughout the Church during this period, neither the limits of this work, nor the materials at the command of the writer, admit of its being here fully considered. It is known that, in general, the gospel was faithfully preached, that many new churches were organized, and old congregations were enlarged. It is known, also, that in many parts of the Church there were revivals to a greater or less extent. Under the administration of Dr. Finley, there was, as already mentioned, a revival in the College of New Jersey, during which about fifty of the students became members of the Church. There were frequent seasons of this kind also in Pennsylvania, especially under the ministry of Mr. McMillan, Mr. J. Smith, and Mr. Powers. With regard to Virginia, it is stated, "that from the constitution of the Hanover Presbytery, (1755,) to the removal of Mr. Davies, (1759,) the progress of religion was more rapid than from that time to the division of the Presbytery, (1770.) In the latter of these periods, it appears to have been declining as to the life and power of it, in those places where before it was most flourishing; but it spread to other places, and the Church was extended much further during this period. And though there was no remarkable revival of religion, it was gradually taking root in a few in many places."* The period from the division of the Presbytery until the formation of the General Assembly, was marked by several revivals. That which occurred within the bounds of the Presbytery of Hanover, "was begun and carried on principally under the ministry of the Rev. J. B. Smith, who had charge of the congregations of Cumberland and Briery. The word at this time appeared to have a peculiar effect on the minds of the people. All who attended seemed to feel in some measure; and many were deeply affected, turned from their wicked practices, and earnestly engaged in seeking the favour of God. Some of these impressions soon wore off, but generally they

* MS. History of the Church in Virginia.

continued for some time. A considerable number of those that were awakened obtained a comfortable hope of their acceptance with God, and joined the Church. The manner of the Spirit's operation was similar to what has been known in revivals, very various, yet producing the same effects in essential points. This work seemed to go on for several years, without any abatement of the fervour which appeared at first; but, as might be expected, this at length subsided."* It is further stated, that, "at this time a greater attention to religion than usual prevailed through the whole country."

Nearly at the same time there "was a very considerable revival within the bounds of the Lexington Presbytery. It began, and continued to prevail most, in the congregations of Lexington and New Monmouth, which were under the pastoral care of the Rev. William Graham, but extended more or less into all the congregations within the bounds of the Presbytery. It prevailed considerably in Washington Academy, so that many who were at that place, have since been licensed to preach the gospel of Christ, and are now settled in the congregations of this and the adjoining Presbyteries."†

The effects of the revolutionary war on the state of our Church was extensively and variously disastrous. The young men were called from the seclusion of their homes to the demoralizing atmosphere of a camp; congregations were broken up; churches were burnt, and in more than one instance pastors were murdered; the usual ministerial intercourse and efforts for the dissemination of the gospel were in a great measure suspended, and public morals in various respects deteriorated. From these effects it took the Church a considerable time to recover; but she shared, through the blessing of God, in the returning health and prosperity of the country, and has since grown with the growth, and strengthened with the strength, of our highly favoured nation.

* MS. History of the Church in Virginia.

† MS. History prepared by the Lexington Presbytery.

A LIST

OF THE

MEMBERS OF THE SYNOD OF NEW YORK AND PHILADELPHIA, FROM 1758 TO 1788, INCLUSIVE.

The years as given in the list, indicate the first appearance of the names of the new members on the minutes, which was in many cases some years after their ordination. The letter P. is placed after the names of the graduates of the College at Princeton, New Jersey; Y. after those of the graduates of Yale; and H. after the graduates of Harvard. The word "received," is placed after the names of those who were admitted as ordained ministers from other churches; and the place whence they were received is mentioned, whenever it was stated on the minutes.*

1758.

Presbyteries.	
Philadelphia,	Gilbert Tennent,
"	Charles Beatty,
"	Richard Treat, Y.
"	Henry Martin, P.
"	Robert Cross,
"	Francis Alison,
"	Benjamin Chesnut, P.
"	Andrew Hunter,
"	Nehemiah Greenman, Y.
"	William Ramsey, P.
"	David Laurence,
"	John Kinkead,
"	John Griffiths,
New Castle,	George Gillespie,
"	John Rodgers,
"	Adam Boyd,
"	Samuel Finley,
"	Hector Alison,
New Castle,	Daniel Thane, P.
"	Charles Tennent,
"	William McKennan,
"	Alexander McDowell,
"	James Finley,
"	John Blair,
"	Alexander Hutcheson,
"	Andrew Sterling,
"	Andrew Day,
New York,	David Bostwick,
"	Andrew Kittletas, Y.
"	Aaron Richards, Y.
"	Nathaniel Whitaker P.
"	Caleb Smith,
"	Alexander Cummings,

* It was found very difficult to make out the list of members here given, on account of the great diversity in the orthography of the names as written in the minutes; to the frequent omission of a full record of the absent members, and to various other sources of perplexity.

Presbyteries.	
New York,	John Brainerd, Y.
"	John Pierson, Y.
"	Timothy Jones, Y.
"	Jacob Green, H.
"	Jonathan Elmore, Y.
"	Simon Horton, Y.
"	John Smith,
"	Chauncy Graham, Y.
"	Enos Ayres, P.
"	John Moffat, P.
"	John Darby,
"	Timothy Allen, Y.
"	John Maltby, Y.
"	Hugh Knox, P.
"	Silas Leonard, Y.
Suffolk,	Ebenezer Prime, Y.
"	Benjamin Talmage, Y.
"	Abner Reeves, Y.
"	James Brown, Y.
"	Sylvanus White,
"	Samuel Buel, Y.
"	Samuel Sackett,
"	Eliphalet Ball, Y.
"	Thomas Lewis, Y.
New Brunswick,	William Tennent,
"	Samuel Kennedy, P.
"	Charles McKnight,
"	Benjamin Hait, P.
"	David Cowell, H.
"	John Guild, H.
"	Job Prudden, Y.
"	Israel Read, P.
"	Elihu Spençer, Y.
"	James McCrea,
"	Conradus Wurtz,
"	Samuel Harker,
Donegal,	Joseph Tate,
"	George Duffield, P.
"	John Steel,
"	John Rowan,
"	John Elder,
"	Samson Smith,
"	Robert McMurdie,
"	Samuel Thompson,
"	Robert Smith,
"	John Hoge, P.
Lewes,	Matthew Wilson,
"	John Miller,
"	Hugh Henry, P.
"	Moses Tuttle, Y.
"	John Harris, P.

Presbyteries.	
Hanover,	Samuel Davies,
"	Robert Henry, P.
"	Alexander Creaghead,
"	Samuel Black,
"	John Craig,
"	Alexander Miller,
"	John Wright,
"	John Brown, P.
"	John Martin,
"	Hugh McCadden, P.
"	Richard Sankey,
"	John Todd, P.

1759.

Suffolk,	Moses Baldwin, P.
New York,	Abner Brush, P.
"	Benjamin Woodruff, P.
Hanover,	Henry Patillo,
"	William Richardson.

1760.

New Castle,	John Ewing, P.
Philadelphia,	James Latta,
New Brunswick,	William Kirkpatrick, P.
"	Alexander McWhorter, P.

1761.

New Brunswick,	James Caldwell, P.
"	John Clark, P.
"	James Hunt, P.
"	John Hanna, P.
Philadelphia,	John Simonton,
"	John Beard,
New Castle,	John Strain, P.
"	John Carmichael, P,
Suffolk,	Ezra Reeves, Y.

1762.

New York,	Azel Roe, P.
New Brunswick,	Samuel Parkhurst, P.
"	Joseph Treat, P.

Presbyteries.	
New Brunswick,	William Mills, P.
Lewes,	Joseph Montgomery, P.

1763.

New Brunswick,	William Tennent, jun'r, P.
"	Enoch Green, P.
Hanover,	James Waddel,
Dutchess,	Elisha Kent, Y. in 1729.
"	Solomon Mead, Y.
"	John Peck.

1764.

Suffolk,	Thomas Payne, Y. received.
New Brunswick,	Amos Thompson, P.
"	Jacob Ker, P.
"	Nathan Ker, P.
"	Thomas Smith, P.
Suffolk	Nehemiah Baker, Y. in 1742.

1765.

Suffolk,	Samson Occam, an Indian.
"	Benjamin Goldsmith, Y.
New York,	Francis Peppard, P.
New Brunswick,	James Lyon, P.
"	John Roseborough, P.
"	Jonathan Leavitt, Y. received from New England.
Hanover,	David Rice, P.
Lewes,	Alexander Houston, P.

1766.

Presbyteries.	
Donegal,	John Slemons, P.
"	Robert Cooper, P.
Philadelphia,	John Murray,*
New Castle,	Samuel Blair, P.
Suffolk,	David Rose, Y.
New Brunswick,	David Caldwell, P.
2d Philadelphia,	Patrick Alison,
Dutchess,	Samuel Dunlap,
"	Wheeler Case, P.

1767.

Suffolk,	Elam Potter, Y.
"	John Close, P.
New York,	Jedediah Chapman, Y.

1768.

New Brunswick,	Jeremiah Halsey, P
Donegal,	John Craighead, P.
2d Philadelphia,	James Lang,
Lewes,	Thomas McCrackin, P.
"	John Bacon, P.

1769.

1st Philadelphia,	Alexander Mitchell, P.
"	James Sproat, Y. received from New England.
New Castle,	John McCreary, P.
"	William Foster, P.
"	Joseph Smith, P.
"	Daniel McClealand, received.
New York,	James Tuttle, P.
New Brunswick,	John Witherspoon, received from Scotland.
Hanover,	James Creswell,
"	Charles Cummings,
"	Joseph Alexander, P.
"	Thomas Jackson,
"	Samuel Leake, P.
Lewes,	John Brown.

* Was not received by the Synod.

1770.

Presbyteries.	
1st Philadelphia,	James Boyd, P.
"	James Watt, P.
Donegal,	John King,
New York,	William Woodhull, P.
Donegal,	Hezekiah James Balch, P.
Hanover,	Hezekiah Balch, P.
2d Philadelphia,	Samuel Eakin, P.

1771.

New Castle,	John Woodhull, P.
"	Josiah Lewis, P.
New York,	Alexander Miller, P.
"	Oliver Deeming, Y.
"	Jonathan Murdock, Y.
Donegal,	Joseph Rhea, received from Ireland.

1772.

New Castle,	Thomas Read,
"	James Wilson, P.
"	James Anderson,
Suffolk,	Joshua Hart, P.
New Brunswick,	Alexander McLean,
"	William Schenck, P.
New York,	Amzi Lewis, Y.
New Brunswick,	Jacob Vanartdalen, P.
Donegal,	Hugh Vance, P.
Dutchess,	Benjamin Strong, Y. received from New England.
"	Ichabod Lewis, Y.
"	Samuel Mills, Y.

1773.

Presbyteries.	
Donegal,	William Thom,
"	Robert Hughes, received from Ireland.
Donegal,	*David McClure, received from New England.
"	*Levi Frisbie, Dart. received from New England.

1774.

1st Philadelphia,	William Hollingshead,
New Castle,	Thomas Smyth, P.
Hanover,	William Irwin,
Orange,	James Campbell, received from South Carolina.
"	Thomas Reese, P.
"	John Simpson, P.
"	James Edmonds, received from South Carolina.
2d Philadelphia,	Robert Davidson.

1775.

1st Philadelphia,	Nathaniel Irvin, P.
"	Daniel McCalla, P.
Suffolk,	John Davenport, P.
New York,	Matthias Burnet, P.
"	Joseph Grover, Y.
New Brunswick,	James Gourly, received from Scotland.
Donegal,	Thomas McPherrin, P.
"	Colin McFarquhar, received from Scotland.
Dutchess,	David Close,
"	Blackleech Burnet.

1776.

1st Philadelphia,	Israel Evans, P.
"	William Linn, P.

* Missionaries not received by the Synod.

Presbyteries.	
New Brunswick,	John Debow, P.
Donegal,	Samuel Dougal,
"	John Black, P.
2d Philadelphia,	Hugh McGill, received from Ireland.

1777.

1st Philadelphia,	Robert Keith, P.
New Castle,	James Power, P.
New York,	Ebenezer Bradford, P.
New Brunswick,	John Warford, P.
Donegal,	John McMillan, P.
"	John McKnight, P.
Hanover,	Samuel Stanhope Smith, P.
Lewes,	Ebenezer Brooks.

1778.

New Castle,	James F. Armstrong, P.
New York,	Andrew King, P.
"	Thaddeus Dodd, P.

1779.

1st Philadelphia,	James Grier, P.
"	Andrew Hunter.

1780.

1st Philadelphia,	Isaac Keith, P.
New Castle,	William Smith, P.
New Brunswick,	Philip Stockton,
"	George Faitoute, P.
Hanover,	John Blair Smith, P.
"	Caleb Wallace, P.
"	Samuel Doak, P.
"	Edward Crawford, P.
Hanover,	James McConnell, P.
Lewes,	John Rankin,

Presbyteries.	
Lewes,	Samuel McMasters,
Orange,	Samuel McCorkle, P.
"	Robert Archibald, P.

1781.

New Castle,	Daniel Jones,
New York,	John Joline, P.
Donegal,	David Bard, P.
"	Samuel Waugh, P.
"	John Linn, P.

1782.

Orange,	Thomas H. McCall, P.
"	James Hall, P.
"	Thomas Creaghead, P.
"	James Templeton, P.
"	James McRee, P.
"	John Cosson,
New Castle,	Nathaniel W. Semple, P.
"	John E. Finley, P.
"	James Dunlap, P.
Donegal,	John Henderson, P.
Orange,	Daniel Thatcher,
"	William Hill,
1st Philadelphia,	William Mackey Tennent, P. received from Connecticut.

1783.

Donegal,	Matthew Woods, P.
"	Stephen Balch, P.
Orange,	John Hill,
"	David Barr.

1784.

1st Philadelphia,	Simeon Hyde, Y.
Orange,	Francis Cummings,
"	James Frazier.

1785.

Presbyteries.	
1st Philadelphia,	William McRee, received from Ireland.
New Brunswick,	Joseph Rue, P.
"	Peter Wilson, P.
"	William Boyd, P.
"	Joseph Clark, P.
"	George Luckey, P.
Donegal,	James Johnston,
"	Matthew Stephens, received from Ireland.
New Castle,	James Munro, received from Scotland.

1786.

Presbyteries.	
1st Philadelphia,	John Johnston, received from Ireland.
"	William Pickels, received from England.
New Castle,	John Burton,†
Suffolk,	Joshua Williams, Y.
"	Nathan Woodhull, Y.
New York,	John McDonald,†
"	James Wilson, received from Scotland.
"	James Wilson, jr.†
"	James Glassbrook, received from England.
New Brunswick,	James Muir, received from Bermuda.
Hanover,	William Graham, P.
"	Moses Hoge,
"	Samuel Carrick,
"	John Montgomery, P.
Hanover,	William Wilson,
"	Benjamin Irwin, P.
"	John McCue,
"	Samuel Shannon, P.
"	Andrew McClure,
"	James Mitchell,
"	John D. Blair, P.
"	Samuel Houston,
"	Adam Rankin,
New Castle,	Samuel Barr,‡
Orange,	Jacob Leake.

1787.

South Carolina,	Robert Hall,
"	Robert Finley,
"	Robert Mecklin,
New York,	James Thompson, received from Scotland.
New Brunswick,	Walter Monteith,
Philadelphia,	Ashbel Green, P.
Carlisle,	Charles Nesbit, received from Scotland.

1788.

North Carolina,	Nathan Grier,
Suffolk,	Noah Wetmore, Y. in 1757.
"	Aaron Woolworth, Y. received from New England.
New York,	Samuel Fordham,
New Brunswick,	Ira Condict, P.
"	Asa Dunham,
Carlisle,	Samuel Wilson, P.
"	Hugh Morrison,‡
"	James Snodgrass,
Suffolk,	Thomas Russel.

† Received as licentiates or candidates from Scotland the year before.

‡ Received the year before as a licentiate from Ireland.

END OF PART II.

www.ingramcontent.com/pod-product-compliance
Lightning Source LLC
LaVergne TN
LVHW021149110826
845150LV00005B/1166

* 9 7 8 1 4 2 5 5 4 6 7 6 2 *